"*Preparing Sunday Dinner*, a long overdue book in the Free Church tradition, comprehensively brings together the meaning and practice of worship in all its aspects. While the book is shaped around the metaphor of eating together, it is hardly a recipe book that guarantees dazzling success by following a recipe closely. On the contrary, the reader learns quickly through the authors' collaborative approach that worship is multi-faceted and diverse. It is not mechanically produced fast food, but rather the result of careful attentiveness to the activity of God and thoughtful, deliberate planning through the empowerment of the Spirit. While the issues and politics of worship planning are acknowledged throughout, this book attempts to keep at the forefront the purpose of worship as the place of encounter between God and God's people, as the place of renewal and transformation. This practical book is a must for all those involved in preaching, planning and leading in worship, and for every church library."
—Irma Fast Dueck, Institute for Theology and the Church,
Canadian Mennonite University

"Those who hunger for meaningful worship that reflects spiritual integrity and practical wisdom will savor *Preparing Sunday Dinner*. This feast for the soul offers a comprehensive and compelling array of topics related to worship preparation and presentation. It encourages a collaborative model of worship design that tempts our awareness of important issues related to public worship. Each chapter is flavored with helpful examples and theological insights to deepen our understanding and practice of Christian worship. The authors give particular attention to symbols, rituals and various ways of experiencing worship across congregational contexts. This book will no doubt be especially helpful to students, congregations and church leaders interested in developing collaborative and creative approaches to worship design."
—Dawn Ottoni Wilhelm, Bethany Theological Seminary

PREPARING SUNDAY DINNER

PREPARING SUNDAY DINNER

A COLLABORATIVE APPROACH TO WORSHIP AND PREACHING

BY
JUNE ALLIMAN YODER
MARLENE KROPF ✦ REBECCA SLOUGH

FOREWORD BY
JOHN D. WITVLIET

Herald Press

Scottdale, Pennsylvania
Waterloo, Ontario

Library of Congress Cataloging-in-Publication Data
Yoder, June Alliman.
  Preparing Sunday dinner : a collaborative approach to worship and preaching/
by June Alliman Yoder, Marlene Kropf, Rebecca Slough.
    p. cm.
  Includes bibliographical references and index.
  ISBN 0-8361-9321-0 (pbk. : alk. paper)
  1. Group ministry—Mennonites. I. Kropf, Marlene. II. Slough, Rebecca.
III. Title.
  BX8126.Y63 2006
  264'.097—dc22

                                                    2005029143

PREPARING SUNDAY DINNER
Copyright © 2005 by Herald Press, Scottdale, Pa. 15683
  Published simultaneously in Canada by Herald Press,
  Waterloo, Ont. N2L 6H7. All rights reserved
Library of Congress Catalog Card Number: 2005029143
International Standard Book Number: 0-8361-9321-0
Printed in the United States of America
Book design by Sandra Johnson
Cover by Gwen Stamm

12 11 10 09 08 07 06 05   10 9 8 7 6 5 4 3 2 1

To order or request information, please call
1-800-759-4447 (individuals); 1-800-245-7894 (trade).
Web site: www.heraldpress.com

*This book is dedicated with gratitude and joy
to all our collaborators,
especially our students in Foundations of Worship and Preaching
and our faculty mentors Mary Oyer and Erland Waltner,
who taught and inspired us.*

CONTENTS

FOREWORD

Every week, 100 or so million North Americans attend worship services. In basement apartments and vast cathedrals, in old village churches and sprawling suburban multiplexes, we join with others to pray, sing, listen to scripture and preaching, celebrate the Lord's Supper and—depending on our particular tradition—participate in healing rituals, testimonies, foot washing, and a host of other liturgical activities. Despite widespread skepticism about organized religion, public worship services remain a common religious practice. For most Christians, "going to church" means, simply, attending a worship service. Whether viewed sociologically or theologically, worship matters. It is a topic of central concern for any Christian leader, as it is for Christian congregations and organizations eager to support them.

But for all this, Christian worship is rarely well-practiced. As Annie Dillard quips, "You'd think we'd be able to get it right after 2000 years of practice." Indeed, on any given Sunday, the 100 million of us who wake up planning to go church have very different attitudes and hopes about the church we will attend. Many of us wake up with a sense of duty, but little joy. The worship service we anticipate will be routine. Our congregations are energy-depleting—perhaps from being embroiled in controversy, perhaps from simply being tired. Yet we persist in going to worship because it's the right thing to do, because we always have, and because we hope against hope that, despite it all, we will experience a taste of God's goodness.

Others of us wake up with eagerness and joy, ready to join a healthy congregation with vital worship. Fellowship there will be palpable and the service will be memorable, perhaps because of its exuberance, perhaps because of its contemplative restfulness. The service will give us texts and songs, insights and questions that will stay with us all week, inspiring or convicting us to deeper discipleship. We will be excited and grateful enough about what happens there to talk

9

about it at work or school. And we will find ourselves eager to return the following week.

This book—and the energy that emanates from the collaboration that produced it—aims to help congregations make progress in moving from the first to the second group, to renew worship as an energizing part of Christian living and congregational life. It is a book with warm and thoughtful reflections. But they don't sit on the page. Rather they aim toward the revitalization of congregational life.

As so many congregations have discovered, this renewal happens best when congregations and their leaders are learning communities, when they are organically and continually learning richer ways of living, working, and worshipping together. As I encounter it, this book promotes learning in three important ways.

Learning Pictorially

First, this book helps us learn through metaphor, starting with its central image of worship as Sunday dinner. Dietitians have taught us to live by the maxim "We are what we eat." Our capability for developing muscle tone and warding off diseases is due in part to the nutritional value of the food we eat. The same is true for the soul. What goes into our soul shapes who we are. It sculpts our fundamental identity. It provides resources to build spiritual muscles and to ward off spiritual diseases.

The virtue of this metaphor is not only its aptness, but also its accessibility. The food metaphor can generate a few hundred pages of analysis. At the same time, however, any local congregational leader could write a one-page newsletter article about worship as "soul food" and be reasonably assured that most readers will understand the message. By teaching through metaphor, this book will help local leaders teach and preach more effectively.

Learning Ecumenically

Second, this book appears at a time when worship has regained the attention of readers, teachers, and pastors in many Christian traditions. One of its crucial strengths is that it offers a Mennonite perspective on worship but in a way that is accessible and instructive to many Christian traditions. One problem of the current age is that ecumenical discussions feature a kind "least common denominator" ecumenism in which the particular emphases of each tradition are downplayed. But this book lifts up a Mennonite perspective in ways that can challenge and instruct many without downplaying its Mennonite identity. In doing so, perhaps it can also lead congregations in the Mennonite tradition to cherish in new ways things that otherwise might be taken for granted.

Learning Collaboratively

Finally, this book is significant because of the way that it both reflects and promotes collaborative ministry. The book not only describes the significance of collaborative leadership, but it models it.

This also suggests how it can best be read. Consider reading this book collaboratively, in active conversations with leaders within a congregation or in a peer learning group of representatives from several congregations. From each chapter, generate a list of insights that are widely shared within your group, and also a list of observations or questions that don't lead to easy consensus. Look for ways that you might restate some of the book's main points to address your context. In sum, the best way to honor the efforts that produced this book is not simply to admire it, but to allow it to be a catalyst for local discussion, prayer, and renewal.

John D. Witvliet
Calvin Institute of Christian Worship
Calvin College and Calvin Theological Seminary
Grand Rapids, Michigan

INTRODUCTION

You prepare a table before me. (Ps 23:5)

This book is about collaboration. As a divine-human partnership, worship is the meal that sustains and nourishes the people of God. While this book explores the human side of that partnership in its examination of the wide-ranging and incredibly complex ministries of worship leadership and preaching, the church must never forget that God prepares the table and provides the feast—offering love, grace, healing, and blessing to us not only on Sunday but every day of the week. We worship in response to God's initiative and at God's invitation: "O come, let us worship and bow down, let us kneel before the LORD our Maker!" (Ps 95:6).

How we carry out our side of the partnership in preparing and serving Sunday dinner at God's table is, however, of vital importance. This book considers many dimensions of such collaboration—with God's Spirit first of all, and then with other leaders, our congregations, and the contexts surrounding us. Examining in turn each step of worship and preaching preparation, leadership, and evaluation, this book provides a comprehensive guide for these ministries at the heart of the Christian community. Left to ourselves, we who lead may not feel adequate to the task to which we have been called. Yet God invites us to participate in the miracle of collaboration that offers all we need—and more—to fulfill our call.

A collaborative approach to worship and preaching

The first collaboration in the ministries of worship and preaching is obviously between God and us. Illuminating this remarkable relationship, the Gospel story of Jesus's feeding of the crowd reveals the miraculous nature of our partnership with God.

> Now when Jesus heard this, he withdrew from there in a boat to a deserted place by himself. But when the crowds heard it, they followed him on foot from the towns. When he went ashore, he saw a great crowd; and he had compassion for them and cured their sick. When it

was evening, the disciples came to him and said, "This is a deserted place, and the hour is now late; send the crowds away so that they may go into the villages and buy food for themselves." Jesus said to them, "They need not go away; you give them something to eat." They replied, "We have nothing here but five loaves and two fish." And he said, "Bring them here to me." Then he ordered the crowds to sit down on the grass. Taking the five loaves and the two fish, he looked up to heaven, and blessed and broke the loaves, and gave them to the disciples, and the disciples gave them to the crowds. And all ate and were filled; and they took up what was left over of the broken pieces, twelve baskets full. And those who ate were about five thousand men, besides women and children. (Matt 14:13–21)

Every preacher or worship leader eventually feels like the frustrated disciples. Faced with the weekly challenge of providing food that nourishes God's people, we ask, "What do we have to give?" Our pockets are depleted, empty. But because ministry is about God's resources, not ours, we should listen carefully to Jesus as he proceeds to ask his followers to bring him what they have. Amazingly, when we look again, we realize we do have something—not much, not enough, but something. When our small something is given to Jesus, he multiplies it and feeds the hungry crowd. And afterward there is more left over than we had to start with—a miracle of abundance![1]

The purpose of this book is to encourage leaders to see what we already have in our hands—the promises of our faithful God revealed in scripture, the rich gifts of the church's tradition of worship, and the empowerment of the Spirit in our time. Yet there is even more. Another dimension of collaboration has to do with partnership at the human level—the inadequately explored and astonishing treasure of gifts waiting to be discovered within leadership teams and within our communities of faith.

How we preach and lead worship on Sunday morning vividly reflects our understandings of the church. As Mennonites, we stand in a 500-year tradition of Anabaptists who have valued collaborative approaches to leadership. Recognizing the gifts of all the members of the community, as well as the varying and indispensable gifts of leaders, we cherish the interdependence of the body of Christ. This conviction does not denigrate leadership. Rather, it affirms leadership ministry as essential for equipping the saints for loving, faithful, creative discipleship and service (Eph 4:11–13).

Today many influences endanger our commitments to collaboration at the human level. With busy and demanding schedules, we struggle to find time to plan and prepare together. Sometimes it is difficult for congregational leaders and pastors to work together fruitfully and harmoniously. Varying preferences in worship styles may threaten collaborative planning. In other situations, longstanding power struggles in the congregation make worship a battleground.

But when worship is not a collaborative ministry, the body of Christ suffers. We become deformed without the creative insights, unique biblical and theological perspectives, and diverse life experiences of the members of the body. When leading a congregation's worship becomes the domain of a single individual, it can deteriorate, becoming exclusive, lifeless, dull, stale.

Does it follow that anyone can preach or guide the congregation on Sunday morning? That anything goes in worship? Certainly not! Rather, congregations must discern the gifts the Spirit is giving for such ministries and then support those gifts with training, mentoring, and equipping. Cultivating these gifts involves a continuous process of spiritual formation, refinement of skills, and reflection on the practice of ministry.

Congregations that invest in collaborative leadership discover the way of abundance rather than scarcity. As the Spirit enlivens the community and its leaders, worship is invigorated and the people are transformed and empowered for fruitful ministry in daily life.

The collaborative leadership team, as we envision it, includes at least three people or functions: the leader of worship, the music leader, and the preacher. The preacher is responsible for proclaiming the Word; the music leader or team provides musical leadership for the service, and the worship leader cares for the overall focus, flow, and coherence of the service, giving particular attention to scripture, prayers, and congregational participation. Though the role of worship leader in some settings also includes music leadership, these functions are more often separated in our tradition.[2]

But there is yet another level of collaboration. A third kind of partnership happens when we connect with worship and preaching what we already know about preparing, hosting, and serving Sunday dinner. Because all of us are engaged every day with food—whether we are shopping, cooking, eating, or cleaning up afterward, we already have a vast repertoire of experience with meals. From the time we enter primary school (if not before), we are taught the importance of good nutrition. Eventually we learn to cook. At some point, we decide we want to invite our friends over for a meal, so we learn the rudiments of hosting and serving. And unless we are blessed with domestic help, eventually we have to clean up our messes.

Though it may not at first seem apparent, each of these skills is directly related to preaching and leading worship. Everything we already know about ordinary meals as well as festive meals for special occasions is knowledge that is potentially transferable to the ministries of the church. What this book does through stories, biblical reflection, and instruction is show us what we already have in our hands: a wealth of insights, experiences, and skills for feeding and serving one another. Though God sets the table, we are called to love one another by hosting and serving there.

Ultimately, then, it's mostly about love. Just as the best meals—however humble the fare—are those served with love, so the best worship is planned and led by those who love the family of faith and the world in which they serve. Perceiving the mysterious alchemy of love and food and words, poet Mary Oliver invites us to open ourselves to the ordinary and ongoing miracle of abundance when these elements unite:

> Why wonder about the loaves and the fishes?
> If you say the right words, the wine expands.
> If you say them with love
> and the felt ferocity of that love
> and the felt necessity of that love,
> the fish explodes into many.
> Imagine him, speaking,
> and don't worry about what is reality,
> or what is plain, or what is mysterious.
> If you were there, it was all those things.
> If you can imagine it, it is all those things.
> Eat, drink, be happy.
> Accept the miracle.
> Accept, too, each spoken word
> spoken in love.[3]

A collaborative approach to writing

Of course, this book had to be written collaboratively. Conceived in collaborative teaching, it grew out of the team-teaching assignment of several professors at Associated Mennonite Biblical Seminary in Elkhart, Indiana. In 1991, June Alliman Yoder, Marlene Kropf, and Mary Oyer began teaching Foundations of Worship and Preaching, a course that introduces seminarians to the basic theology and practice of these ministries. Drawing from our individual professional and academic backgrounds, June taught the preaching units of the course, Marlene taught units on worship and ritual leadership, and Mary taught units on music and art. After Mary retired from AMBS in 1998, Rebecca Slough joined the team in 1999 to teach music and worship arts.

The image of Sunday dinner as a metaphor for Sunday morning worship was originally June's idea. In 1998, she spoke on "The State of the Mennonite Pulpit" at Bethel College, Newton, Kansas, as part of the Marpeck Lectures. In that presentation, she compared Mennonite sermons to snacks, junk food, home cooking, leftovers, carryouts, buffet meals, and company dinners. Those present made immediate connections with the image and generated more comparisons, which she explored in subsequent lectures. Later, when the idea of worship as Sunday dinner was expanded to serve as the organizing principle for our course in worship and preaching, this collaborative writing project was born.

The chapters of this book consider many dimensions of the comparison between the tasks of planning and hosting Sunday dinner and the skills and capacities involved in planning and leading Sunday morning worship. The question, "Why eat?" introduces a discussion of why we worship and presents biblical and theological foundations for this essential ministry of the church. What comes next are perspectives and indispensable tools for analyzing the social and cultural aspects of the body that gathers for worship. From there, the chapters dig into basic issues of planning a balanced, nutritious worship menu and designing individual courses in a satisfying sequence. One chapter offers a recipe for developing a sermon, comparing the sermon to the entrée around which other courses of the meal are arrayed. Story is proposed as the main ingredient of worship, with a discussion of the expansive role of the arts as our most important resource for telling God's story. A detailed case study introduces a collaborative planning process and addresses practical questions arising from the multiple layers of collaboration involved in worship planning.

The many facets of the image of hosting are illuminated in a threefold understanding of this role: the worship leader as host of the people's encounter with God, their engagement with one another, and God's vision for the world. Both mundane and profound communication issues in worship and preaching are examined. The requirements of special occasions receive attention. The call to extend the table serves as a metaphor for the relationship between worship and evangelism and reminds us of how worship functions as a foretaste of the eschatological feast of the Lamb. Because both Sunday worship and Sunday dinner can become occasions for quarrels and in-house wrangling, guidance is offered for negotiating those tricky relationships. And since somebody always has to clean up after a meal, the book concludes with sound advice for the tasks that must be completed after worship: evaluations, expressing gratitude, maintaining adequate supplies of resources, and ongoing care of leaders.

Perhaps the most challenging discussion in this book is its careful analysis of the role of symbols in worship. Broadly understood, symbolic language, actions, and objects form the essential infrastructure of worship in the postmodern world. They offer expansive possibilities for communicating the mystery of faith to worshipers who may be inoculated against faith by secularism, who may be stumbling in confusion, or who may be alienated from God. Because they communicate effectively with children and young people as well as adults, symbolic language, actions, and objects have the capacity to touch everyone who gathers for worship. In short, worship leaders must understand them well and use them purposefully if worship is to have meaning in the twenty-first century.

The three authors outlined the book together and divided up the writing tasks. After each chapter was completed, it was read by the other two writers, who added to or amended the material. June Alliman Yoder is the primary author of chapters 3, 5, and 9. Marlene Kropf is the primary author of chapters 1, 7, 8, 11, and 12. Rebecca Slough is the primary author of chapters 2, 4, 6, 13, and 14. All three authors worked collaboratively on chapter 10.

Our friend, colleague, and department chair Daniel Schipani defines practical theology as "the critical and constructive reflection on the life and ministry of the church—with special focus on the process of spiritual formation and transformation—in the light of the realities of our world and the vision and promise of the reign of God." He is fond of reminding us that the unique contribution of practical theology consists of its fourfold pattern, including an empirical dimension (descriptions of actual ministry situations), an interpretive dimension (why we practice ministry as we do), a normative dimension (what practices best express our theology of the church), and the pragmatic-strategic dimension (guidelines for enriching or improving ministry).[4] In writing this book, we have come to appreciate more fully the multifaceted nature of the discipline of practical theology. We hope that pastors, congregational leaders, seminary students, and all who care for the worship life of the church will find here what they need both to understand the ministry of worship and to carry it out more effectively. We imagine this book might be used as a resource for worship committees, who could read and discuss a chapter a month. It could also be used as a textbook for students or as professional reading for pastors. We hope it will serve as a reference work for the ongoing development and training of worship leaders and preachers.

We are grateful for many blessings and gestures of support as we worked together on this project. Leroy and Phyllis Troyer shared their comfortable lakeside cabin in Michigan with us for retreat space in which to write as we began the project. Jerry Lapp hosted us at Red Bridge Retreat, his bed and breakfast establishment in Goshen, Indiana, and served delicious meals as we worked. Associated Mennonite Biblical Seminary, our employer, provided generous support for our writing, through sabbaticals, research units, and teaching and research conversations. Our students read these chapters in earlier drafts and offered many helpful questions and responses. Without the able editorial assistance of Barbara Nelson Gingerich, our three disparate writing styles would never have become integrated. She worked with us cheerfully and competently to prepare these pages for print. Our particular thanks go to our colleagues in the Church and Ministry Department, who encouraged our efforts, listened to our joys and frustrations, and celebrated our achievements.

We are especially grateful that our friendship has survived new tests of collaboration. Though we knew we could teach happily and productively as a team, we quickly became aware that writing together required another level of commitment. Deciding early on that our friendship was more important than the book, we pledged to be as honest, forthright, encouraging, and supportive as possible—and not to sweep any disagreements under the rug. We are grateful to God's Spirit for preserving and even deepening our friendship.

The culmination of our writing project was a meal we planned, cooked, and served collaboratively to our longsuffering, faithful, and supportive spouses: John Yoder, Stanley Kropf, and Joe Miller. We have appreciated their patience and good humor throughout the writing of this book.

May our Lord, who promises to bless whatever we offer—whether it is loaves and fish or chapters in a book—receive our offering and bless it abundantly for the sake of faithful and fruitful worship ministries in the church.

1

WHY EAT?

Taste and see that the Lord is good. (Ps 34:8)

We eat to live. Three times a day, we pause, partake of food, and then, with replenished energy, go about our tasks and activities. Proteins, carbohydrates, fats, minerals, and vitamins become the building blocks of health. Without such refueling, our bodies weaken and die. We cannot live long without the nourishment of food.

But eating is about more than staying alive. It is a deeply satisfying, sensual experience. Our eyes delight in a colorful array of fruit on a platter—plump red strawberries, golden wedges of melon, frosty purple grapes. The fragrance of bread baking or a turkey roasting stimulates our appetite through the sense of smell. The texture contrasts in a meal—creamy asparagus soup; crisp cucumber slices nestled among tender lettuce leaves; chewy mixed-grain dinner rolls; moist, flavorful pork chops; and wedges of dense, rich chocolate cake—satisfy our need for variety. And then, of course, our sense of taste is intrigued by aromatic herbs and spices as well as salty, sweet, or sour dishes. As we eat, we are abundantly satisfied by the rich appeal to our senses.

Yet even more is going on when we eat. We often eat in company with other people. Food provides a reason to gather, to talk, and to enjoy human fellowship. A morning coffee break with scones and jam or a picnic supper of grilled sausages and corn on the cob creates a context for leisurely conversation. As we eat, we tell stories, listen deeply to one another, laugh together, and nurture warm bonds of connection that sustain us until we meet again.

Good food is nearly always part of special occasions—birthdays, graduations, and weddings, or holidays such as Thanksgiving, Christmas, and Easter. At these events, our tables are richly spread. We take more time to prepare the meal. We serve more courses than usual. We give more thought to presentation. We honor tradition by serving well-loved favorites. We spare no effort in setting the most bountiful table we can afford. The significance of the occasion is underlined by the care and attention given to what we eat, and the festivities are enhanced by the abundance of food.

Food is also intimately associated with sacred rituals. Whether it is roast lamb and bitter herbs served at a Passover meal, lentil soup and fig cakes eaten at the end of a day of fasting during Ramadan, or the bread and wine Christians partake of when they gather to observe the Lord's Supper, food for the body also becomes food for the soul. Because our hunger is more than physical, we require spiritual nourishment. For our souls to thrive, we are dependent on the gift of life mediated to us through "the common creatures of bread and wine."[1]

Here we enter the realm of mystery. Although we can define the role of food and nutrients in preserving and sustaining good physical health, we are less able to describe the relationship between spiritual food and spiritual health. Yet we know a profound relationship exists. Without regular nourishment, our souls wither and die. Furthermore, spiritual food is meant to delight us. The psalmist's counsel, "Taste and see that the Lord is good," is an invitation not only to be nourished but to find abundant joy in the food provided by our Lord.

Although Christians are fed in a multitude of ways,[2] the single most significant source of nourishment for the body of Christ is the weekly gathering for worship. When believers meet at the table of worship on Sunday morning, we are fed and sustained by Word, symbol, and song, and we become healthy, robust witnesses of God's grace and power in daily life.

Perhaps no biblical story better illustrates this mysterious alchemy between the table of worship and the lived life of faith than the story of two disillusioned disciples who meet a stranger on the road to Emmaus. As they walk with him, the disciples confess the depth of their perplexity and sorrow, listen as Jesus interprets the scriptures, and reflect on the meaning of God's activity in their world. As evening draws near, the two disciples invite the stranger to join them for a meal.

> So he went in to stay with them. When he was at the table with them, he took bread, blessed and broke it, and gave it to them. Then their eyes were opened, and they recognized him; and he vanished from their sight. They said to each other, "Were not our hearts burning

within us while he was talking to us on the road, while he was opening the scriptures to us?" That same hour they got up and returned to
Jerusalem; and they found the eleven and their companions gathered
together. They were saying, "The Lord has risen indeed, and he has
appeared to Simon!" Then they told what had happened on the road,
and how he had been made known to them in the breaking of the
bread. (Luke 24:29b–35)

The presence and power of the risen Christ is revealed in the ordinary, daily action of gathering at a table to break bread and share a
meal. As the disciples' physical hunger is satisfied, they become more
deeply aware of the hunger of their souls. Then, as Christ blesses and
breaks bread, their eyes are opened. They are able to receive spiritual nourishment—communion with Christ. Renewed and empowered
by that meeting, they become witnesses to God's grace and power in
the world.

In the same way, when Christians gather regularly at the table of
worship, we are formed in our faith; we are transformed by communion with Christ and with one another; and we are energized by
the power of the Spirit to do God's will. Worship becomes our central source of nourishment, the activating energy that makes it possible to live and move as Christ's body in our daily life in the world.

Why worship?

Despite the obvious connection between spiritual food and spiritual
health, fewer and fewer people in the Western world are finding their
way to worship on Sunday morning. During the past half-century,
many churches have seen a precipitous decline in worship attendance.
In some parts of the United States, for example, as few as 20 percent
of people will be found worshipping in churches on Sunday morning.[3]
A recent report from the British Isles is even more discouraging: only
one in seventy Anglicans attends worship on a typical Sunday. Are
people not hungry for God's presence in their lives? Is worship a
quaint custom that has little relevance today? Have we become so
individualistic that we blithely ignore our need for companionship on
the spiritual journey? Or has the church utterly failed to offer worship that satisfies the longings of modern people?

In "Church going," poet Philip Larkin writes about stopping to
visit a church while on a bicycle tour. Unfortunately, he finds little to
engage him.

Once I am sure there's nothing going on
I step inside, letting the door thud shut.
Another church: matting, seats and stone,
And little books; sprawlings of flowers, cut
For Sunday, brownish now; some brass and stuff
Up at the holy end; the small neat organ;
And a tense, musty, unignorable silence,
Brewed God knows how long. Hatless, I take off
My cycle-clips in awkward reverence,
Move forward, run my hand around the font.
From where I stand, the roof looks almost new—
Cleaned or restored? Someone would know, I don't.
Mounting the lectern, I peruse a few
Hectoring large-scale verses, and pronounce
"Here endeth" much more loudly than I'd meant.
The echoes snigger briefly. Back at the door
I sign the book, donate an Irish sixpence,
Reflect the place was not worth stopping for.[4]

Like a bit of bric-a-brac inherited from another time, worship sometimes seems like an odd relic from the past. We recognize the curio; we still remember where it came from or who gave it to us. But if someone put it in a box and stored it in a dark corner of the attic, it might not be missed for a long time, maybe ever.

For an increasing number of people, Christian worship is perceived as a worn-out tradition rather than a living, breathing reality. Given such trends, what happened after the tragedy of September 11 was nothing short of amazing. Within hours, hundreds of thousands of Americans of all ages gathered to pray in public places with lit candles and other religious symbols. We sang hymns and listened to speeches that sounded much like sermons, in gatherings that took on a relevance and urgency rarely seen on Sunday morning.

What was clear is that the religious impulse, and specifically the impulse to worship, still lies close to the surface in the United States. Although one can be justly suspicious of the uncritical patriotism that dominated many of those services, such a dramatic shift from ego-centricity toward some kind of community was a refreshing change. These responses may have fallen short of true worship, but they can at least be viewed as a move beyond the rank individualism that often characterizes our country (the nation-state being the largest reality around which many can imagine gathering).

For most human beings who have ever lived, worship has been as natural as breathing. We in North America and Europe are the odd people out. Our secularism has robbed us of our birthright—a capacity for experiencing and responding to God that gives life ultimate meaning. It should not be surprising, then, that we seek substitutes for this essential human activity.

Some observers say the shopping mall has replaced the church as the place where North Americans gather on weekends. As the church was the center of life in an earlier time, the mall has come to stand at the center of people's lives. In old European cities, the cathedral occupied a prominent place at city center. And even now if you travel in New England, you will often find steepled churches located at the heart of many villages. Today, however, traffic and road patterns converge not on churches but on shopping centers.

Looking at the architecture of the cathedral and the mall yields interesting comparisons. Typically, malls are constructed in cruciform shapes. High, vaulted ceilings suggest transcendent reality. Large colorful banners and seasonal floral displays are prominent features in both the church and the mall. And any decent-sized mall seems to have a fountain—the secular equivalent, perhaps, of the baptismal font.

One might push the analogy even further. At the mall, we are surrounded with music to enhance the liturgy unfolding on all sides. Choirs and bands as well as dancers and acrobats perform in the high holy shopping seasons. Presiding clerk-clerics welcome us, receive our tithes and offerings at the checkout-counter altar, and offer ritual words of blessing as we depart. And might chewy pretzels and slushy fruit drinks be a substitute for the bread and wine of communion?

In what other setting do the rich and poor, the learned and ignorant, the old and young all mingle with each other? The church used to be the social center of people's lives, but today teenagers go to the mall to hang out together, and elderly people are often seen occupying empty benches, waiting for someone or something.

Nearly everyone who has ever gone shopping knows the experience of coming home empty-handed. We wanted something, although we may not have known quite what it was, and we came home with our desire unsatisfied. Is it possible that the desire that compels us to go shopping is really a longing for God?

Reflecting on our culture's attraction to a variety of substitutes for a healthy, committed relationship with God, Eugene Peterson says: "It should be no surprise that a people so badly trained in intimacy and transcendence might not do too well in their quest. Most anything at hand that gives a feeling of closeness—whether genitals or cocaine—will do for intimacy. And most anything exotic that induces a sense of mystery—from mantras to river rafting—will do for transcendence."[5]

In the physical realm, we understand that we must eat to live. In the spiritual realm, the same law applies. To be healthy and whole human beings, we must regularly respond to God's loving invitation to taste and see God's goodness in the midst of worship. What we need in order to answer the question, Why worship? is an understanding of God's intentions for the biblical practice of Sabbath and an awareness of the gifts it offers.

Worship and Sabbath keeping

According to the book of Genesis, when God created and hallowed the seventh day, one day in seven was set aside for rest and celebration of God's wonderful works.[6] Further, this day of rest and celebration served as a continual reminder that God's ultimate intention for all creation is unending worship and celebration. Isaiah 56:6–7 promises, "All who keep the Sabbath, and do not profane it, and hold fast my covenant—these I will bring to my holy mountain, and make them joyful in my house of prayer." In a similar vein, Isaiah 66:22–23 describes the new heaven and the new earth as a place where "from new moon to new moon, and from Sabbath to Sabbath, all flesh shall come to worship before me."

It is worth noting that the image used for eternal worship both by the prophet Isaiah and by John the Revelator is an abundant feast. Isaiah 25:6 promises: "On this mountain the LORD of hosts will make for all people a feast of rich food, a feast of well-aged wines, of rich food filled with marrow, of well-aged wines strained clear." Revelation 19:9 announces the invitation to the messianic banquet: "Blessed are those who are invited to the marriage supper of the Lamb."

Thus the worship of God's people, which begins on earth, continues throughout eternity. Worship is of ultimate significance. It is the purpose for which humanity has been created. It is our eternal destiny. Pausing to worship one day out of seven is God's idea—it is God's gift to humanity to relativize all our work and striving. This day reminds us that God is the beginning and end of history and will surely accomplish all that God desires.

In one sense, what we do on Sunday morning is practice, rehearsal, or training that prepares us for our destiny. For one hour on Sunday morning, we live as though the reign of God has fully come. This hour of celebration, which renews and clarifies our vision of God and God's world, makes it possible for us to be God's people and to live as God's people. More than a meal that merely sustains us for the week to come, our worship in its cumulative effect sustains us for eternity.

But the rise and growth of secularism has endangered the practice of Sabbath keeping in our culture. The days are gone when the civic and commercial worlds supported the Christian practice of Sabbath keeping and the weekly gathering for worship. In part, that shift has emerged in response to a pluralistic culture. Because not everyone is Christian, no single day can be universally regarded as a holy day. But even more significantly, our insatiable appetite for buying and consuming has displaced our primary hunger, which worship alone can satisfy.

The other danger to Sabbath keeping in our culture is our individualism. Rather than make corporate worship a priority, many North Americans believe they can sustain their spirituality on their own. In fact, many people today see little reason to connect their search for God with the church and its practices. Yet the witness of human experience is otherwise. When Pascal said, "One Christian is no Christian," he meant that we cannot grow into Christ-likeness without the support and guidance of a faith community. Just as an infant cannot survive without a family to provide for its physical and emotional needs, so a new Christian needs sisters and brothers, mentors and teachers, friends and companions to ensure growth and health. Community is a constitutive element of Christian faith; without a connection with the body of Christ, we wither and die. And the common worship of the Christian community is the experience that binds us most effectively into one body, making us a people who reflect the light of Christ in the world. Christian community is the surest antidote to the destructive individualism of our time.

In God's dream for creation, worship is meant to be the core of our lives. It is the act that gives meaning to all the rest of our existence. It is the communion that satisfies our deepest longings. It gives us a family with whom to share the journey, and it unleashes creative energy that empowers us to join what God is doing in the world. If our churches are to remain healthy, then corporate worship is the one thing we must do well.

Although the church as an institution shares many tasks with other social institutions, its life of worship is a distinct and unique responsibility. No matter which branch of the Christian tradition we find ourselves in, the centrality of worship is a shared conviction among all believers. Jack Hayford, founder of a Pentecostal megachurch in southern California, identifies worship as a priority for his congregation, coming before evangelism and mission. He understands the church at worship to be an expression of the power of the kingdom of God, though he admits, "It is infinitely easier to cultivate a congregation that will listen to the Word of God than to cultivate a people who will worship God."[7]

At the other end of the worship-style spectrum, Episcopal priest John Westerhoff affirms: "If the church does nothing else for the world than to keep open a house—symbolic of the homeland of the human soul—where persons come together for cultic life, it is doing both persons and the social order the greatest possible service, and nothing can compare with it. As long as the church bids people to come and worship and provides a credible vehicle for worship, it need not question its place, mission, or influence on the world."[8]

Preparing Sunday dinner

If Sunday worship is the meal that nourishes and sustains individual Christians as well as the Christian community, then it is vital that leaders understand how to prepare and serve this meal. If this is the meal that keeps Christians alive, that delights our souls, that creates a context for fellowship and celebration, and that sustains the church's work and witness in the world, then we must cultivate skill in the kitchen as well as capacities for hosting and serving on the part of worship planners, preachers, music leaders, and others involved in worship ministry.

But it is not enough to possess good knowledge of nutrition or even superb hosting abilities. An even deeper understanding is required of worship leaders. We need to be equipped with a sound biblical theology and vision of worship that provide a dependable framework for planning and leading worship faithful to the God who invites it. Without such a biblical framework, even the best worship planners and leaders can go astray. Especially in the free-church worship tradition, in which leaders make a multitude of choices each week, it is remarkably easy to be seduced by what is fashionable at the moment or by one's personal desires or tastes in worship. Leaders can become discouraged by the energy required to keep planning week after week or by negative responses from the congregation. While it is obviously important to pay careful attention to the needs and character of the congregation,[9] worship leaders must have more solid footing than personal or congregational preferences. Only a vision for worship that is grounded in God's revelation in scripture is capable of sustaining God's people for our arduous and demanding journey.

Biblical framework for planning and leading worship

If Sabbath keeping is a biblical foundation for worship, a practice that undergirds the ongoing renewal of God's people, then what guidance does scripture provide for what God desires in worship? What biblical patterns can provide the focus and content of worship? What models can supply its shape and flow? What framework can assure that worship will be a nourishing and life-giving experience week after week?

If a set of clear guidelines for Christian worship could be found in scripture, the task of worship planning and leading might seem easier, but the Bible does not provide one. Apparently the early Christian writers did not consider such documentation important, perhaps because their worship was essentially Jewish and thus did not seem remarkable. Borrowing the worship traditions of the synagogue and temple, the first believers used songs, scriptures, and prayers from their Hebrew background.[10] Only gradually did new and distinctly Christian worship patterns emerge.

What we do find in scripture is something even more useful than a prescription for worship. Rather than offering a worship blueprint for all time, various scriptures describe a set of movements or a flow of actions that constitute worship. Two texts—one from the Old Testament and one from the New Testament—are especially useful for our purposes. One is the story already alluded to, of the Emmaus journey in Luke 24:13–35. The other text is Isaiah 6:1–8, the story of the prophet's vision of God's call. Together these two texts provide a sturdy biblical foundation for worship and preaching and offer a versatile theological framework for the focus and actions of worship. Because what they offer is simple, basic, and universal, this framework does not wear out from regular use but continues to illuminate the ministry of worship leading week in and week out.

In the Luke passage, the immanent God is revealed—the One who comes alongside us, listens to us, engages us personally, and walks with us on our journey. The Isaiah text reveals a transcendent God—the One who is sovereign, wholly other, majestic, and holy. Both images of God are essential in worship; they represent a range of ways we know and experience God in worship. These contrasting images and the essential actions of each narrative will provide the guidance we need for understanding what makes worship nourishing and life giving.

Three essential movements of worship

At its heart, worship is a response to God's love and grace. Because God reaches out to us, we respond by offering our love and praise. Although the shape of our response may vary from time to time, a typical sequence of response actions can be seen in various scriptures. One of these, the story found in Isaiah 6:1–8, presents an unforgettable picture of three essential movements of worship: a transforming encounter with the living God (vv. 1–4), honest engagement with self and community (vv. 5–7), and lively empowerment for faithful response (v. 8).

The following reading for five voices (adapted from the NIV)[11] helps us see this dramatic sequence of actions:

Isaiah 6:1–8

I	*Isaiah*
ABC	*angels*
D	*the Lord*

I In the year that King Uzziah died, I saw the Lord
   seated on a throne,
  high and exalted, and the train of his robe filled the
   temple.
  Above him were seraphs, each with six wings:

A	With two wings they covered their faces,
B	with two they covered their feet,
C	and with two they were flying,
AB	and with two they were flying.
I	And they were calling to one another:
A	Holy,
B	Holy,
C	Holy,
A	Holy, holy, holy is the LORD Almighty;
B	*[as a round, coming in on the word "is" of A]* Holy, holy, holy is the LORD Almighty;
C	*[as a round, coming in on the word "is" of B]* Holy, holy, holy is the Lord Almighty;
ABC	the whole earth is full of God's glory! THE WHOLE EARTH IS FULL OF GOD'S GLORY!
AB	GLORY!
A	Glory!
A	At the sound of their voices the doorposts and thresholds shook and the temple was filled with smoke.
I	"Woe to me!" I cried. "I am ruined! For I am a person of unclean lips, and I live among a people of unclean lips, and my eyes have seen the King, the LORD Almighty."
A	Then one of the seraphs flew to me with a live coal in his hand, which he had taken with tongs from the altar. With it he touched my mouth and said,
C	See, this has touched your lips; your guilt is taken away and your sin atoned for.
I	Then I heard the voice of the Lord saying,
D	Whom shall I send? And who will go for us?
I	And I said, "Here am I. Send me."

First movement: a *transforming encounter* with the living God

The vision recorded in Isaiah 6 discloses a scene in which the prophet's eyes are opened to see the living God. Although God is always present in the world and in our lives and always desires to be in relationship with us, we do not always see or recognize God's presence. In our finitude, we do not always perceive spiritual reality. To have our eyes opened is a gift of grace.

What Isaiah sees, on this particular occasion, is the Holy Sovereign of the universe, a great and mighty God. Of course, this is not the only biblical image of God. Sometimes in worship we become aware of God as intimate friend or tender healer or flowing stream of living water. But in this story, a veil is drawn aside to reveal the glory and holiness of God. Such splendor and majesty inspire a chorus of praise. The angels call, "Holy, holy, holy," a joyful response reverberating in honor of God's glory.

Unlike Isaiah's vision, which takes place before God's throne, the story of the journey to Emmaus (Luke 24:13–35) occurs on an ordinary road. When two disciples are joined by a stranger along the way, they do not recognize the risen Christ; according to verse 16, "Their eyes were kept from recognizing him." Yet as the narrative unfolds, they are drawn more and more deeply into an encounter with Christ, an encounter that leads to worship and which will ultimately transform their vision of reality.

Worship begins with meeting the living God. No other reason for gathering is adequate—not even our well-intentioned desire for Christian fellowship or our need for instruction or encouragement. Unless we encounter God, we have not worshipped.

It is understandable, however, that we may shy away from such an encounter. Hebrews 10:31 reminds us that "it is a fearful thing to fall into the hands of the living God." Whether or not we know it consciously, we understand in our souls that meeting God will transform us. And we do not always look forward to such a conversion. Our response may be to try to domesticate God—to make God more comfortable, more like one of us. In worship we may avoid the full range of biblical images for God, we may restrict what texts we will hear, and we may sanitize our prayers. We may turn worship into a purely horizontal encounter where religious people get together, speak certain words, and go through certain motions—but we will not have worshipped. In reflecting on the absence of this encounter with the living God, Frederick Buechner once remarked that "God is of all missing persons the most missed."[12]

Our fear of meeting God and being transformed in that encounter can cause us to forget that God is the creator, and we are but creatures—loved creatures, to be sure, but nevertheless finite and limited. Yet we must never confuse who we are with who God is. Suggesting that we would do better to recognize this disparity and prepare ourselves in fear and trembling for the divine-human encounter, Annie Dillard says: "If we really knew what we were doing when we come to church on Sunday, we would come—not dressed in our Sunday finery—but wearing crash helmets on our heads."[13]

That God can be intimidating is one side of the experience. The other side, of course, is that the holy and majestic God reaches out to us with infinite mercy and compassion. A whole lifetime of worship is not long enough to plumb the depths of God's love or exhaust the wealth of God's grace.

And so the place to begin in worship is with God—who God is, what God desires, how God works in our lives. When we recognize and appreciate this beginning point, we are ready to consider the second movement of worship.

Second movement: *honest engagement* with self and community

In the second movement of Isaiah's vision, the prophet's eyes are opened to see himself as he is in God's sight. It is only when we see God clearly that an accurate and honest vision of ourselves is possible. In God's bright, hot, shining light, what Isaiah sees is the truth about himself: he is incomplete, unwhole, unholy.

Confession is the only possible response. What Isaiah sees is not only his personal sin but the sin of his people, of his time, of his place. All are unclean in the presence of a holy God.

When Isaiah confesses the truth about his life and names his reality honestly, he discovers that God is already there, eager and ready to offer cleansing and forgiveness. Holding live coals from the altar, a seraph comes immediately to touch Isaiah's lips and declare absolution: Your guilt has departed and your sin is blotted out. Thus worship includes not only a vision of God but a vision of our human condition—honest, transparent engagement with ourselves and with our community—that reestablishes reality and makes authentic relationships possible.

The honest engagement with self and community experienced by the two disciples on the road to Emmaus begins in their despairing reflections on the things that have just happened in Jerusalem. When the stranger asks what they are discussing, they do not hide their pain; rather, they confess their deepest hope that Jesus, who had been crucified, was the promised one who would redeem Israel. As they name the truth, they are drawn so fully into the stranger's responses that they invite him to stay with them and share a meal. As truthful engagement opens a way for authentic communion, they—like Isaiah—find that God is already present, eager to meet them and offer the grace of new life.

Just as we may be inclined to shy away from the truth about who God is, we may also be reluctant to speak the full truth about who we are. And here the image of worship as a rehearsal or practice serves us again. None of us by ourselves has the courage or strength to face the depth of our own wounds or brokenness. The psalmist paints a vivid picture of our condition: "While I kept silence, my body wasted away through my groaning all day long. For day and night your hand was heavy upon me; my strength was dried up as by the heat of summer" (Ps 32:3–4).

In the act of confession, however, in the context of public worship, worshipers do find courage together to name both corporate and personal sin and open themselves to God's grace. We practice being a confessing people, and in so doing, discover the pattern for confession and forgiveness that will bring healing and wholeness in our daily lives. The ancient Christian church spoke of this dynamic principle of Christian formation as *lex orandi, lex credendi*: what we do in worship and prayer becomes the way we believe and live. Worship guides us or tutors us in practices that are essential for ongoing growth toward maturity.

For corporate confession to do its work, however, more is needed than public prayer. Christians need intimate, face-to-face settings in which to reflect honestly on the pattern of sin in our lives and be set free from its bondage. What we discover through the ongoing practice of confession is that a hidden wound or a prevailing sin is often the source of brokenness in our lives. Whether in the safety of a small group, in spiritual friendship, or in spiritual direction, each of us must find a place where we can muster the courage to face our fiercest fears and most abysmal failures. At those times, other people become Christ to us, mediate God's love, and empower us to believe that "forgiveness is the answer to the child's dream of a miracle by which what is broken is made whole again, what is soiled is again made clean. The dream explains why we need to be forgiven, and why we must forgive. In the presence of God, nothing stands between God and us—we are forgiven."[14]

Being who we are, being honestly and completely present in worship, makes possible the second movement in worship. Yet this step is not the end. A life-giving flow of praise, communion, forgiveness, and reconciliation between God and God's people is not all that God has in mind for worship. Worship also has an outcome that extends to a farther horizon.

Third movement: *lively empowerment* for faithful response

After we see the glory of God and the truth of our own humanity (that we are loved and received, just as we are), the third movement of worship begins. With regained clarity of vision, we are prepared to hear the Word of God in fresh, engaging ways, to see God's vision for the world, and to hear God's call to us and our community. Our obedient response to God's call is our life of witness, service, and peacemaking in the world.

As a story-formed community, the people of God gather regularly to remember the story of God's mighty acts and tender compassion. We listen to these stories, pondering their meaning today. We listen to the voice of God, remaining alert to God's call. When the prophet Isaiah listens carefully to the voice of the Lord, he hears a call to join with God's loving, creative, reconciling work in the world. In response to God's persistent call, he offers his whole self—his love, energy, and creativity—to God: "Here am I. Send me."

Honestly present to their own grief and their reality, the two disciples on the road to Emmaus listen carefully to the words of the stranger, life-giving words that kindle a flame of truer understanding in their hearts. As they listen, they are moved to welcome the stranger into their home, an act of trust opening the way for transformation. Across the table from one another, they see the stranger break bread, and in that moment, their eyes are opened, and they recognize the Christ who has accompanied them along the way. They receive the living Word, the living bread that comes down from heaven. But the story doesn't end with illumination. Like Isaiah, who listens and acts, these two are empowered by Christ's presence to become faithful witnesses of what they have seen and heard, sharing the good news of Jesus's resurrection with the other disciples.

Worship is not complete when we have met God and remembered God's story. Worship has consequences, an outcome. It issues forth in a life of witness. Thomas Long suggests,

> The doors of the sanctuary, like those in saloons,
>   ought to be swinging doors.
> What happens in worship ought to flow into the world,
>   and the mission of the church to the world
>   ought to find expression in worship.[15]

Worship that is faithful to a biblical vision engages in a lively flow of traffic between the community gathered in worship and the community scattered in the world of work, family, and neighborhood relationships, as well as in the larger world beyond. The followers of Christ carry the sweet fragrance of Christ's presence into every encounter and action: "For we are the aroma of Christ to God among those who are being saved and among those who are perishing; to the one a fragrance from death to death, to the other a fragrance from life to life" (2 Cor 2:15–16).

The very act of worship expands the presence of God in the world, uniting us with God's larger purposes of redemption and restoration. Old Testament scholar Millard Lind describes this outward dimension of worship as a political act, a declaration of loyalty to the rule of God as experienced in the life of the new community in Christ. Lind concludes that worship must therefore be seen as central to the life of the church, the foundational political structure from which the congregation involves itself in the world.[16]

Just as our vision of God and of ourselves may be flawed or obscured, so our vision of this transforming dimension of worship may be inadequate. Sometimes worship is conducted as though the church exists in isolation and has no life beyond the four walls of the sanctuary. Prayers of petition and intercession may not reflect concerns beyond a narrow circle. Lament for injustice may be mute or nonexistent. Preaching may be unconnected with the desperate lives people lead or with the disconcerting realities of the local community.

Song texts may soothe and comfort but rarely disturb or convict. Rituals may perpetuate tradition and not lead to a transformed future.

On the one hand, worship is an end in itself. It is pure praise, an offering given in response to God's love and grace, with no utilitarian goal. But when true communion occurs, when worshipers meet the living God, such encounters set loose dynamic consequences. Just as a spouse's daily affirmation, "I love and honor you," has consequences for the marriage, so the words and actions of God's people in worship open them to transformation.

Walter Brueggemann describes this transforming role of worship as "world-making": through our words and actions in worship, we create a world of meaning. We construct a vision of reality—a perspective not only about *what is now* but also of *what can be* through the power of the Holy Spirit. In such world-making, we already begin to participate in the new world of God's gracious reign.[17]

A rhythm of formation and transformation

The three movements of worship—encounter, engagement, and empowerment—create a dynamic rhythm that pulses through our lives, forming and transforming us individually and corporately into the image of Christ. Just as we count on our daily food to sustain and empower us for healthy, vigorous living, so we count on the food we receive in worship to form and transform us as spiritual beings. With our vision of God continually expanding, our self-awareness and insight into our community continually drawing us toward forgiveness and reconciliation in Jesus Christ, and our call and capacity to act on God's behalf in the world continually being strengthened and guided by the Spirit, we truly become the people of God in the world—salt and light, trustworthy signs of God's redeeming grace and compelling witnesses to God's saving power.

A simple way of conceptualizing these three movements of worship is to see them as vertical, horizontal, and centrifugal (outwardly flowing) actions. Worship moves us toward the transcendent God, it engages us with one another, and it propels us into the world.

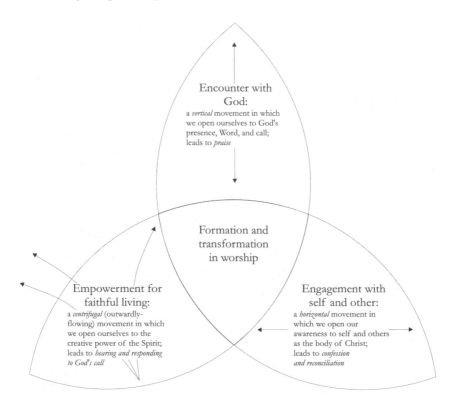

It should be obvious by now that these formative movements of response in worship correspond to three worship actions that typically occur in Christian worship:

1. In response to an encounter with God, we offer praise to God.
2. In response to honest engagement with ourselves and the body of Christ, we confess the truth about our lives and receive God's cleansing and renewing grace through Jesus Christ.
3. In response to the Spirit's empowering presence, we are set free to hear and obey God's Word, loving and serving God in the world.

Praising God, confessing the truth about our lives, and hearing and responding to the Word become, then, the basic framework of actions in worship or the skeleton for weekly worship. If we attend to these three things, we will have engaged in biblical worship. Not a formula to follow or an agenda to cover, these movements in worship become the contours of a relationship. And although these actions may take place in an endless variety of ways,[18] the underlying rhythm of praising, confessing, and hearing/responding that flows through worship is the basic and essential forming and transforming practice for Christians through which the Spirit brings new life.

If we asked cooks what constitutes essential Sunday dinner fare, many North Americans would respond that an entrée, a salad, a vegetable side dish, bread, and dessert should be served. With such rubrics, even a novice cook can be assured of creating and serving an acceptable meal. In the same way, those who plan and lead worship can be assured that by creating space for the three movements described above, they will have included what is essential. In fact, at the conclusion of this discussion, we can offer a working definition of Christian worship as we experience it corporately: *Christian worship is an encounter with the triune God experienced in the midst of community, which transforms and empowers members of Christ's body for loving witness and service in the world.*

Worship as foretaste of the feast to come

Yet worship is more than a Sunday dinner that comes around week after week, served with imagination, commitment, and care. We engage in something more than an ordinary meal when we gather for worship. Paradoxically, worship is both an ordinary Sunday dinner and also a foretaste—an appetizer—of a greater feast to come.

A good appetizer is a small, colorful, tasty morsel designed to whet our appetites. When a tempting array of such morsels is set before guests, a sense of expectancy is created. Though we don't serve hors d'oeuvres for everyday meals, we may pull our appetizer cookbooks from our shelves for special meals. Will it be grilled shrimp with a glaze of ginger, lemon, and tamari? Or perhaps almond-stuffed prunes wrapped in bacon and served with hot mango chutney? Or bruschetta, topped with chopped fresh tomatoes and arugula, drizzled with olive oil? Not a meal itself, the appetizer course nevertheless partakes of the reality to come. As guests sample and savor the appetizers, they delight in a foretaste of the meal or banquet about to be served.

As Sunday morning worship progresses through the ordinary actions of encounter, engagement, and empowerment, we are prepared to see the hidden dynamic that is unfolding. Beneath and beyond the visible actions of weekly worship, our worship functions as a foretaste of eternal worship around the Lamb's throne—a kind of appetizer served and enjoyed before the main course. According to the book of Revelation, the eternal destiny of God's people is to sing and offer glory and praise to God forever. When God's vision for the world has been fulfilled, when all tears have been wiped away and God's presence is known in fullness, then the saints of God will delight in offering eternal praise to the One who has restored and renewed all things.

What Christians do now in worship is a rehearsal for daily life, which shows us how to live in the week to come. Yet our worship is also a rehearsal for eternity. Because we live in hope that all God has promised will indeed come to pass, ordinary Sunday morning worship can also reflect and anticipate that wider horizon of God's ultimate purposes.[19]

When we partake of worship as a satisfying meal for today and also as a foretaste of an abundant feast to come, we will no longer need to ask the question, Why worship? Because worship will be doing its work of connecting us with God, with one another, and with God's world, its role and purpose will be clear.

Just as we eat to live, so we worship to keep our souls alive. Yet Christian worship is about more than survival. Worship is meant to make our souls flourish; it keeps us strong and vibrant and empowers us to be faithful signs of God's reign in the world. Like the anonymous poet who penned these lines, we will sing our praise to Christ who enlivens our worship:

> This fruit doth make my soul to thrive.
> It keeps my dying soul alive,
> which makes my soul in haste to be
> with Jesus Christ the apple tree.[20]

2
WHO'S COMING TO DINNER?

Amazed and astonished, they asked, "Are not all those who are speaking Galileans? And how is it that we hear each other in our own native language? . . . In our own languages we hear them speaking about God's deeds of power." (Acts 2: 7, 8, 11)

My paternal grandmother always brought yeasty rolls to our small extended family dinners. They were heavenly—light, buttery crescents that melted in your mouth. My maternal grandmother, my mother, and my aunt provided vegetables, salads, and desserts, when they were not hosting the meal. The host always supplied the meat—ham, roast beef, or pork. Other responsibilities were assigned according to gender, age, and birth order.

After the host prayed, we passed and passed and passed food. Invariably, we got tired of passing all the bowls and platters: "Can we eat yet?" When the food had all gone around, we ate nearly as quickly as we had passed it. In our family, the word *leisurely* did not apply to eating.

After dessert, the real conversation began. Younger cousins departed, and the rest of us remained at the table. An hour or two passed as we talked amid dirty dessert dishes. Food dried on dinner plates and serving bowls stacked in the kitchen. We discussed church activities and safe religious issues. We shared stories—gossiped—about other members of the family, friends, and co-workers. We learned what topics were safe for discussion and what subjects would upset people. Sometimes we fought about trivial things. Sometimes someone introduced a taboo subject just to enjoy the ensuing fight. We also laughed a lot; Gram would often laugh so hard that she cried.

The fare at our extended family dinners was wonderful but unimaginative. While some experimenting with new vegetable, salad, or dessert recipes was acceptable, we avoided exotic foods at these gatherings. Our conversations were lively but not deep. Our meals

together bred familiarity but not closeness. The intensity of our disagreements bore little relationship to their significance. Nonetheless,
these dinners shaped the ethos of my family in profound ways. They
created space for us to tell stories about ourselves and the communities around us. Some hidden clock seemed to signal that it was time
to negotiate the assignments and location for the next gathering.

Dinners changed as we cousins got older and joined our voices to
the conversation. Then we brought boyfriends, girlfriends, and eventually spouses to the table. These newcomers made us more aware of
our established patterns, and through our participation in their families, we became conscious of other ways of being family. My spouse's
family, for example, does not share my family's expectation that everyone comes together for the holidays. His family gathers at other times,
but always at the family farm. Their mealtime conversations are far
headier than my family's.

We cousins now live in far-flung places across North America,
and our spouses have their own family commitments. These changes,
together with the disability and death of grandparents, mean that our
holiday gatherings are more fragmented. We struggle to find a new
sense of our family.

But at our holiday meals, the host still provides the meat dish and
opens the meal with prayer. Ham, roast beef, and pork continue to
dominate the menu, although turkey sometimes appears now, too.
Aunts and cousins still provide salads and desserts, and too much
food means passing too many bowls and platters. "Can we eat yet?"
re-echoes across the years. Although my grandmother's crescent roll
recipe is available, no one has taken up her art. We still sit around the
table and tell stories amid dirty dishes, unless someone cannot stand
the mess and begins to clean up. My brother's infectious laughter
invites us all to join in. Our sense of family keeps changing around
the meat, vegetables, salads, and desserts of our shared table.

Families build traditions with shared stories, customs, rituals, values, and faith. We create a culture, a history and identity, as we share
experiences around the table. Like families, congregations develop
their own character. Stories, cycles of celebrations, patterns of leadership, potlucks, communion observances, and customs surrounding
births and deaths—all of these are the makings of the complex,
multifaceted, and wondrously rich life of the congregation.

Congregations cultivate ways of sustaining life in the midst of change through shared beliefs, and perhaps more importantly, through shared practices. To understand a congregation's culture takes time, patience, observation, and listening.

Why would we want to understand a congregation's culture?

Congregations are incarnations of Christ's body in the world. Just as God took a big risk in coming to the world as a human being, born into a particular culture[1] and time, God takes a big risk in using local congregations as signs of Christ's presence in the world. Congregations are located in particular cultures and times. With other people in their cultural homes, congregations share languages, patterns of communication, work, social activities, family interests, beliefs, values, and practices. As the body of Christ, they also are at odds with some aspects of the wider society. A congregation's purpose in society is to witness to the reality of God's reign begun in Jesus— a reign that challenges and transforms every society since his time on earth.

Each congregation is a small culture, a subculture within the larger society. If it participates in the life of a denomination, it shares values and beliefs with a network of other congregations. Yet it expresses those beliefs in practices that are peculiar to its character. It participates in the Christian tradition that has been shaped by interpretations of scripture in specific cultural settings over the course of two millennia. Every congregation expands the tradition through its shared practices of faith. Congregations worship in their particular cultural environments and in the unique social circumstances of their local communities.

Worship is an incarnational activity. It arises out of the congregation's shared life as the body of Christ. It witnesses to the sovereignty of God who is present in the church through Jesus. Worship is an encounter and engagement with God, who meets us in our cultural contexts. By the Holy Spirit's power, God's redeeming activity continually breaks into the congregation's life in culturally accessible and relevant ways. At its best, worship connects the truth of God's salvation with the everyday realities of our lives.

Cultures create the means of and patterns for communication. Symbols, images, and words provide ways for human beings to tell one another what they sense, feel, think, and know. We invent ways of communicating so we can do things together. We share ways of interpreting meaning and gaining knowledge. The symbols, images, and words we have available—the languages we create—are conditioned by where we live, who we are, what we do, and whom we encounter. Sociologists call this social knowledge. This knowledge makes it possible for us to be in relationship with one another, to build communities, and to worship in congregations. With the Holy Spirit's help, God uses our knowledge to address us, transform us, redeem us, and sustain us. The congregation's relationship with God is formed through the communication patterns its members share in common.

Who needs to understand the congregation's culture?

Pastors and those with authority for worship leadership must be adept at using the social knowledge of the congregation. We nurture a culture that supports worship authentic to our time, place, and heritage. This undertaking is one of our primary leadership responsibilities. Our task as preachers and worship leaders is to help the Holy Spirit make the vital connection between God's saving activity and the life of the congregation and its members. Effective worship leaders frame the congregation's praises, confessions, and prayers to communicate the social and cultural truth of peoples' lives.

Preachers communicate the Word of God in culturally relevant forms that believers and nonbelievers can understand. We graciously attend to the spiritual needs of each age group and both genders within the congregation. We respect styles of communication used by worshipers from various ethnic, economic, and educational backgrounds. We use illustrations and images that connect with the types of jobs our people hold.

Worship leaders choose words, music, and themes that reflect our members' life experiences. We know the stresses of those who are unemployed, ill, estranged from their families, struggling in school, or despairing of life. We pay such close attention to these dimensions of social knowledge to help the congregation respond to God with integrity as Christ's body.

How can we understand the congregation's culture?

No one can fully know a congregation's culture. It is far too complex and changeable. The congregation's worship leaders and preachers must work collaboratively to pool our knowledge of worshipers' living realities. We start by listening for the Spirit's movement within our congregational life, and we attend to our congregation's unique character. Together the team notices aspects of our common life that have vitality and energy—perhaps the children's program is growing, or a number of new volunteers want to help with community outreach. We observe what appears to be languishing—the budget has a deficit, the congregational singing is uninspired. Rather than jump to congratulations or solutions, leaders pray for wisdom to discern what the Spirit is revealing and whether and how to address these promptings in worship. In many congregations, the pastor and deacons or elders do this listening discernment. There is good reason to include in this process those who lead worship. This involvement reminds worship leaders that we are servants of the congregation, not independent agents of our own creative interests.

Ideally, the group responsible for planning worship should include women and men who span the spectrum of age, education, occupation, and spiritual maturity. The parent of young children will be in touch with their developmental processes and the needs of parents who find little time for personal prayer and Bible study. The factory worker will know about the economic and employment needs of blue-collar families. The middle-school choir director will have a window on styles of music young teens listen to. A long-time member will recall significant stories that shaped the congregation's identity. A youth knows how the social pressures of high school challenge a Christian identity. The pastor knows the family stresses, economic challenges, educational achievements, and ethical dilemmas of many worshipers. Open conversations about our experiences will help worship leaders and preacher in making music, prayer, and scripture choices that speak to the congregation's deepest needs.

Perhaps it is obvious that a significant part of worship planners' work is not planning worship. Our first tasks are to listen and observe with one another what has been happening in the congregation and the community beyond. We discern the meaning of what we see and hear for shaping worship that arises authentically out our shared life. This kind of worship leadership takes time, commitment, and spiritual maturity. Indeed, worship leadership is a spiritual discipline undertaken by leaders who deeply love God and the people of our congregation.

To what in our congregational culture are we attending?

Congregational cultures change, sometimes slowly and other times quickly. This chapter addresses aspects of congregational culture that worship leaders will want to attend to over time. The boxes contain questions that will help focus observations. The broad categories of social connections, interaction styles, and spiritual/theological resources are places to start in this important pastoral discipline.

Social connections

Social networks. Social connections create networks that form personal identity and communities of shared values. These networks regulate access to information and resources, and they shape patterns for exerting authority and power. In many congregations, nuclear and extended families provide the primary social network. Members of extended families have their own ways of passing on information. Often family activities take priority over other social relationships. Friendships are consigned to leftover time not taken up by family demands. One large congregation in western Ohio had only ten adults who were not related to someone in the congregation; these few wanted to form a small group to create a sense of belonging. Sometimes family networks exert significant control over decisions and decision-making processes in congregations.

> ### Social connections
> What are the kinship ties in our congregation?
> Who is married? Single? Divorced? Widowed?
> Where are worshipers from?
> What are the ethnic backgrounds of the worshipers?
> Where do worshipers live? How far are they from the church build-
> ing or meeting place?
> Where do worshipers go to school?
> In what professions and occupations are worshipers employed?
> Where do worshipers work?
> Which worshipers have lived in other parts of the country or in
> other countries?

Most families in North American participate in a variety of social networks beyond those of family and church. Our network of friends in the local community often reflects our values, income, and level of formal education. Co-workers and students, people we spend a lot of time with each day, form another network. We create networks of colleagues who do similar kinds of work, in order to share expertise and information. We participate in networks of community service or business that provide products and resources for our day-to-day living. We may belong to networks of international colleagues, agencies or missions, that connect us with people in other parts of the world.

These networks may at times intersect, producing a circle of friends who relate to each other in many ways. But more and more often, these networks do not overlap. We see church friends only on Sunday morning. Our families may never meet our co-workers. Knowing how people are connected helps preachers and worship leaders determine what words, actions, or music will gather the body together. We need to know that comments about "our church family" mean different things in different congregations.

Visitors and newcomers do not know all the in-house expressions, secrets, codes, abbreviations, and acronyms used by the congregation. New believers may still be learning basic biblical stories and tenets of faith. These worshipers will not share in the knowledge of the congregation's culture. Worship leaders show hospitality and graciousness in keeping in-group talk to a minimum.

Worshipers' ethnic background and gender shape particular ways they experience life and find meaning. A middle-aged Latina woman will likely hear the good news for life differently than a middle-aged white woman. A young African-American man will probably hear the gospel differently still, because society has opened other possibilities and set up obstacles for him that the women may not experience. Because a variety of forms of racism and sexism exist in society and in the church, worship leaders and preachers need to stay close to the lives of people whose ethnic background and gender are different from our own.

With this knowledge of social networks, worship leaders make informed choices about how to help the congregation connect with God. Passing the peace or allowing time to greet other worshipers acknowledges the presence of newcomers, strangers, and outsiders in the congregation. Prayers for needs in the local community—with its various networks of school, services, businesses, and civic groups—

can be focused clearly. These prayers name specific needs and rejoice in particular accomplishments. Mother's and Father's Day recognitions will be tempered by the knowledge that not all worshipers who wish to be parents are parents. Not all worshipers have trouble-free relationships with their mother or father. Parents' identities are constantly changing as they age and their children grow. Stories from other regions of the country and world strengthen worshipers' connections with the global church and may connect with their memories of living somewhere else.

Many pastoral teams and worship leaders operate from a vague intuitive sense of who is worshipping in the congregation. But we lead with greater wisdom and authority if our collective knowledge of who is coming to worship is better informed and more sensitive.

Life stages. Congregations include worshipers across a spectrum of ages. As worship leaders and preachers collaborate, we hold in mind people of each age group, so their interests and needs are addressed in appropriate ways. The needs of one age group are not more important than others' needs, but certain ages have greater numbers than others. Awareness of significant cultural icons, celebrities, or heroes can be sources for illustrations or social commentary. Honoring the interests, stresses, and worries of the various ages can focus themes and shape decisions for how particular worship actions are accomplished.

Elderly worshipers experience many losses as their lives move into the closing years. Often they yearn for familiar hymns and well-known scriptures. A slower pace in worship allows them to follow along; they often associate dignity in language with reverence.

Life stages

What percentage of our worshipers are 0–5 years old? 6–12? 13–18? 19–25? 26–35? 36–50? 50–65? 65–80? over 80?

How many high school students regularly come to worship?

How many families with young children regularly come to worship?

How many middle-aged professionals regularly come to worship?

Who are the empty-nesters?

Who is retired or retiring soon?

How are the elderly connected with the congregation's worship?

Young children are readily engaged by Bible stories narrated in a lively manner. Stories that are told well, without moralizing commentary, give children an opportunity to find their own meanings in biblical accounts.

Youth often seek experimentation in worship, with higher levels of active participation. They grapple with questions of faith and personal identity, freely borrowing from popular culture. They hope to find connections between their experiences in school, leisure activities, and congregational life.

Young adults continue working with life choices around discerning vocation, selecting a career, determining whether to marry, starting a family, and finding an identity as a person of character. The sense of responsibility for their future can seem overwhelming. Societal temptations to overwork, compete ruthlessly, and pursue distorted values are alluring.

Middle-aged adults, many who are in their most productive years, often exercise authority in their families and work environments. The moral issues they face call for deeper levels of integrity, wisdom, and self-giving. Often they need opportunities to confess their errors and to receive assurance of forgiveness in order to make changes needed to live out their Christian ethics.

Worship planning groups that span the age range of the congregation will be in touch with the particular concerns each group feels. Together we can find ways to communicate the gospel to everyone and make room for authentic response by people of all ages in the congregation.

Education. Each of us gains informal and formal education that affects how we seek out, evaluate, and use information. Much of the formal education we receive centers on building skills to analyze problems, reason out viable solutions, and act competently on them. The best environments of formal education nurture capacities to wonder, imagine, and create. These skills and capacities often open possibilities for occupations in which we continue to learn skills for successful employment. The capacities to learn and to continue learning are essential for growth in Christian faith.

Worshipers with less formal education, or whose life experiences have limited their informal education, often prefer stories and clear-cut answers for daily life. They may have no time for metaphoric, symbolic, and abstract language. They may rely more on their ears and prefer oral communication. Worshipers with more formal education are often more comfortable with using written language, considering complex ideas, and living into the tension of conflicting values. They frequently enjoy discussion as a means for discovering truth.[2]

Education

How many children in our congregation are currently in preschool? Elementary school? Middle school?

How many worshipers are in high school?

How many worshipers have attended or are currently enrolled in trade schools? College or university? Graduate school?

What are the primary methods used for teaching children and youth in school? Rote memorization? Question and answer? Critical thinking? Hands-on projects?

What technologies are used in teaching children and youth in school? Books? Films/DVD? Sound recordings? Computer programs? The Internet? Multimedia?

What methods and technologies is our congregation using in educating children, youth, and adults?

What continuing education events are offered by the congregation?

How is our congregation thinking critically about faith matters?

Worship leaders and preachers usually reflect our own educational backgrounds. Sensitive ones respect the range and types of educational experience of the worshipers and communicate effectively across that range. Some adult members of a Mennonite congregation in Ontario did not graduate from high school, and other members have advanced degrees. Yet the pastoral team routinely connects with individual worshipers by drawing from the various kinds of knowledge their worshipers bring and have in common.

Two congregations assigned to a United Methodist pastor have completely different educational backgrounds. In one congregation, most worshipers have completed high school, but few have attended college. The pastor's sermon preparation for this congregation does not stir her imagination much, and she preaches concrete and direct messages. Many of the adult worshipers in the other congregation have college degrees. The sermons they expect leave more spaces for them to consider and imagine the gospel's implications for their lives. Each week, the pastor creates two sermons on the same text for two distinctly different congregational cultures.

Every congregation has worshipers who possess a rich mixture of informal and formal education. Whether we are preparing worship for adults with basic formal education or for children in the process of gaining education, we need to consider what is best communicated orally. What is best written? What experiences do members of the congregation hold in common, regardless of education? What patterns of communication do all share that make worship in the body of Christ possible? The answers to these questions will vary from congregation to congregation. It is the responsibility of the pastoral team and worship planners to notice how the kind and amount of education shapes the congregation's ability to respond to God.

Economic class. The distinctions of economic class control social life in North America far more than we usually acknowledge. Ruby Payne and Bill Ehlig have described the distinct class assumptions and the hidden rules that operate in the poverty, middle, and wealthy economic classes.[3] Schools, businesses, and many churches in the United States operate primary by middle class values.[4] Most megachurches are grounded in middle and wealthy class assumptions. Until recently, many Pentecostal and Holiness congregations operated by poverty class assumptions. Educational achievement and economic power are closely related, but education alone does not prevent a slide into situational poverty.

Economic class

What percentage of our worshipers participate in social networks rooted primarily in the wealthy economic class? Middle class? Poverty class?

How is money gathered, discussed, handled, and distributed in the congregation? By individual worshipers?

What assumptions about money operate in our congregation?

What assumptions about money crop up in conversation?

Have any worshipers lost their homes, filed for bankruptcy, or needed public assistance, because of unemployment, illness, or personal disaster? How did the congregation respond to this need?

Stinginess is most prevalent in the middle class, where possessions and security are valued more highly than the needs of other people. People in the poverty class tend toward generosity, sharing with friends or relatives in greater need, regardless of one's own short-term future needs. For poor people, money is an extension of personality for the sake of relationships and entertainment.[5] The wealthy contribute to significant programs or people to extend their own influence.

A Mennonite congregation in Indiana intentionally bridges the expanse between the lower and middle economic classes. This group is creating a congregational culture that moves between oral and written communication, works with different understandings of the need for planning, and uses a variety of musical styles for congregational singing. They recognize that some of their scripture readers need extra time to prepare for presenting scripture in worship; these people can tell stories more easily than they can read them.

Economic class values shape offering practices. Worshipers in poverty will likely give cash as it is available, often in sums that are disproportionate to their income. Middle class worshipers use cash or checks. The wealthy usually pay by check to meet their pledges.[6] Middle class and wealthy worshipers may not have something for the offering plate each week.

The prevailing sins of each economic class are specific to them. Middle class and wealthy worshipers may need to confess their lack of trust in God's all-sufficient care, their disregard for the needs of people around them, or their abuses of power. Confessions of worshipers in the poverty class may include tendencies toward impulsive violence, especially when they or family members are slighted.

Gender, race/ethnicity, and economic class constitute social locations in North American society. They open possibilities for strong identity and character formation. At the same time, they create particular expressions of deadly vices. There are aspects of our lives that are controlled by powerful social systems external to the congregation. Worship leaders and preachers must address the blessings and vices of our own social locations and deal compassionately with those of other members.

Languages. Distinctions in economic class show up in how worshipers use language registers and communication patterns. A register is a style of language used in specific situations. Formal register in the United States and Canada uses standard English, carefully chosen phrases, clearly articulated thoughts, expansive vocabulary, and a narrow range of voice modulation. We expect to hear formal register at special events and solemn occasions, at times when dignity and authority are required. Prayers such as those in the Episcopal *Book of Common Prayer* are written in formal register. These prayers have a poetic beauty, but they can seem distant and impersonal. Worshipers from middle and wealthy economic classes tend to be comfortable using formal spoken and written registers.

Languages

How many of our worshipers read? At what level do they read? How much do they read?

What do our worshipers read?

Do our worshipers usually communicate verbally or in writing (e-mail, notes, letters, etc.)?

What radio stations do our worshipers listen to? What television stations or programs do they watch?

Most news reporting is in the middle or informal register, because it is designed to appeal to middle class viewers and their values. Reporters use standard English, but they are less concerned with well-formed thoughts, lyrical phrases, and interesting words. Many written and extemporaneous prayers use middle register.

A low language register uses slang, nonstandard English, sentence fragments, limited vocabulary, and phrase repetitions. Often speakers use a wide range of voice modulations and gestures to communicate. This register can be emotionally engaging. Prayers repeating the formula "Lord, we just want to. . . ," an example of low register, often build energy and intensity.

Every profession develops a specialized language. To perform well, computer programmers, surgeons, plumbers, teachers, accountants, and psychologists must be fluent in the language of their field. Sometimes, certain words from these specialized languages become part of informal talk radio, television, and magazines, and they are shared by everyone in touch with popular culture.

Newspapers, magazines, radio broadcasts, television, and the Internet shape language. Worshipers who listen to National Public

Radio or Canadian Broadcasting Corporation programs are socialized into communication and language patterns that differ markedly
from those of worshipers who listen to talk radio. Fox News communicates in a style different from that of public television. *USA
Today* uses an idiom different from that of the *Globe and Mail* or the
New York Times.

Worship leaders and preachers must listen carefully to the language the worshipers in our congregations hear and use. They do well
to fit their words and illustrations with what is widely used. In some
congregations, oral communication—with its multiple phrase repetitions, voice modulations, and rhythmic patterns—will prevail, as in
the Black church. Often these congregations do not trust written worship materials.[7] Other congregations favor formal communication,
with expanding thoughts and refined emotion. They trust the power
of the written word. Worship leaders and preachers can expand and
change the preferred language register of worship in their congregations, but they must be fluent in its dominant language.

Interaction styles

Expressive styles. Worshipers in every culture develop patterns
for expressing deep feeling, passion, and commitment. Then they pass
these patterns on to their children. Congregations express reverence
by kneeling, sitting with bowed heads and closed eyes, or standing
with open arms. African-American and Pentecostal worshipers talk
back to preachers and worship leaders in a call-response pattern.
Some worshipers move to a song's rhythm as they sing. Others find
strength in standing still. Styles of congregational song—gospel

Expressive styles

What body postures do people in our congregation use during
  worship?

What parts of the worship service are most intense? What are
  worshipers doing at those times?

In what ways does the congregation speak during worship?

Does our worship space best serve the hearing aspects of worship?
  Seeing aspects? Bodily movement aspects?

What words describe our congregation when it responds wholeheartedly in worship?

songs, English or German hymns, spirituals, international songs, or Christian contemporary rock—all encourage types of expression that may be uncomfortable when they are first introduced to a group unfamiliar with them.

White worshipers rarely respond to Black preachers with their Amens in the right spots. Many whites are taught not to make noise during the sermon; Blacks teach their children to help the preacher shape the message with their verbal encouragements. These expressive styles emerged from two radically different social contexts and experiences of church.

One aspect of recent worship renewal is acknowledgment of the role all the senses play in experiencing the presence of God. Protestants, with their roots in the Reformation, have created worship cultures that value hearing above the other senses. With a growing number of artists staying in the church, and with the advent of affordable projection equipment, Protestants are cautiously discovering how visual arts can open scripture. Roman Catholic, Orthodox, and Episcopalian cultures of worship have trusted seeing at least as much as hearing. Since Vatican II, Roman Catholics have worked at improving the heard and spoken aspects of worship, as well as setting new standards for visual art in their worship spaces. Pentecostal and charismatic worship cultures, which have always used the whole body, are influencing Protestants and Catholics alike.

Worship leaders and preachers harness the group's expressive patterns, so the congregation's responses are unified. For worship to be authentic, the congregation must respond in ways that are natural to its learned patterns of expression. The range of expressiveness can be expanded, but worship leaders need to work wisely, patiently, and with sensitivity when introducing something new. Repetition is required to get a new gesture or musical style "into the bone," so that it eventually becomes a natural expressive response.

Spiritual types. Some worshipers naturally lean into faith, and their hearts respond to God with a warm love, passionate trust, and great joy. Their minds work to piece together an understanding of faith that their hearts know. Other worshipers lean into faith with their minds. God's reasonable, comprehensible, and persuasive truth convicts them. These people fall into a love of God tempered by knowledge.

Spiritual types

How do worshipers describe services that move them deeply?

How many of these descriptions use words about feelings or emotions?

How many of these descriptions use words about thoughts, insights, or vision?

Do our services tend toward the spontaneous and emotive, with expansive expressions, or toward the thoughtful and reflective, with planned responses?

Which type do the majority of our worshipers value most? Why?

What opportunities and problems does our dominant style currently present?

The passion of heartfelt faith usually burns hotter than a mindful faith, but it can also cool more quickly. When the ardor fades, the certainty of faith often goes with it. The certainty of a mindful faith smolders with persistent commitment, but it may never spark into a blaze of abandon. Mature Christians know that faith, whether it is first of all heartfelt or mindful, is a gift. Yet, both aspects of the gift need to be cultivated.

Congregations tend toward a heartfelt spirituality or a mindful spirituality. But no congregation is entirely one or the other. Heartfelt and mindful worshipers exist in all congregations, though in differing proportions.

Heartfelt worshipers respond best to songs that speak of Jesus as friend, personal Savior, or lover. Gospel songs and many contemporary worship songs, which often express a personal relationship with Jesus or a close encounter with God, help them worship. Spontaneous prayers, personal testimonies, and convicting sermons that elicit a response rejuvenate their souls.

Mindful worshipers respond best to songs that name truths about God's character, salvation in Christ, and the Holy Spirit's nature. Their prayers, sung and spoken, keep some distance between themselves and God. Evocative language in prayers and songs, well-organized and intellectually stimulating sermons, scriptures that are well read, and silence for reflection galvanize their faith.

The excesses of a heartfelt faith can lead to emotionalism that is not focused into disciplined action. The excesses of mindful faith can lead to legalism and rigidity that numb feeling and stunt the capacity to experience God's grace.

Worship leaders and preachers will work out of the heartfelt or mindful side of faith, whichever is our gift. But we need to respect both approaches to faith and keep alive those expressions appropriate to both.

Personality types. Many worshipers in our congregations are extroverts—people whose energies flow outward to engage others.[8] They are stimulating people who seek connections with others to feel alive. Extroverts have needs for sociability and are energized by being around people.[9] They focus outward, constantly driving for contact with others and for new experiences.

In North America, fewer worshipers are introverts—people whose energies are depleted by being with others. They are not anti-social, shy, or backward; they take the energies of social gatherings into themselves and soon feel exhausted. Introverts like space—lots of personal space to withdraw from intense activity and reflect on or unpack what they have experienced.

Personality types

How many worshipers in our congregation are outgoing, thrive in groups, enjoy the energy of personal interactions, and tend to be spontaneously expressive?

How many worshipers in our congregation need to be drawn into activities, hang at the edges of groups, find ways to break off from larger group activities into smaller conversations, and tend to calculate their responses?

Does our worship leadership group consist mostly of extroverts or introverts?

Are our services tilted toward the needs of extroverts or introverts? What would need to change to attend to both personality types?

David Keirsey and Marilyn Bates identify a variety of differences between extroverts and introverts, in their needs and preferences.[10]

Extrovert	Introvert
Sociability	Territoriality
Prefers breadth	Prefers depth
Extensive	Intensive

External focus	Internal focus
Prefers interaction	Prefers concentration
Prefers multiplicity of relationships	Prefers limited relationships
Prefers to expend energy	Prefers to conserve energy
Interested in external happenings	Interested in internal reactions

Congregations create cultures that tend to be more comfortable for either extroverts or introverts, but no congregation is composed exclusively of one type. Many heartfelt worshipers, who are outwardly expressive, tend to be extroverts; the contemporary worship movement appeals to these personalities. A majority of mindful worshipers are introverts drawn to the space created by liturgical forms. It is a mistake to think that extroverts or introverts make better worshipers. Introverts need the expressive energy of extroverts, and extroverts need the internal centeredness that introverts often achieve. Both types are necessary if worshipers are to grow in spiritual maturity.

Worship leaders should attend to the needs of introverted and extroverted worshipers and make choices of music, styles of prayer, and scripture presentations accordingly. Energetic music, rousing sermons, and opportunities to make verbal or physical contact with others helps extroverts worship. Spaces for silence and opportunities to reflect through music come as a great relief for introverts. Worship that is active and busy can tire introverts. Contemplative worship can deaden the spirits of extroverts.

Spiritual/theological resources

Stories. Human experience, including experience with God, occurs within intersecting and often-overlapping systems of relationships. In any social network, actions and people are connected to one another; the behavior or choices of one person affect the actions of others. A computer network, which creates many opportunities for communication, functions as a web of relationships. We tell stories to make sense out of the events of life which explore the ways various characters act and react to conflict and adversity.

Christians tell the biblical stories, particularly the gospel, over and over in worship. Assuming that more than a snippet is read in each service, scripture reading is the primary way we hear the story of God. We also tell stories of Christians who remained faithful in adversity, as well as stories of the church throughout history. Congregational stories continually extend webs of connection, meaning, identity, and possibility, creating shared history and knowledge. We pass on these stories of our efforts to live faithfully in our time and place. Stories—exemplary and infamous—used in sermons and prayers, connect God's steadfast love with the life of the congregation.[11]

Stories

What biblical stories are most important in our congregation?

What stories from the tradition of the Christian church and our denomination shape our congregation's identity?

What stories from our congregation's history (the good and troubling) are important for our children, youth, new believers, and newcomers to know?

Pastors and worship leaders are stewards of the congregation's stories. Knowing these stories helps us shape authentic prayers of praise, thanksgiving, and confession. Knowledge the stories contain is useful when we want to introduce change into congregational patterns. If the organ was a memorial gift from a founding family, then using it less often or selecting congregational songs that do not require its use may require sensitive conversation with the donor family.

Worship leaders should help congregations understand what stories are appropriate for telling in public worship. Sometimes congregational sharing time includes stories that are better told in smaller settings, where troubling content can be dealt with responsibly and pastorally.

Signs, symbols, rituals, and rites.[12] The congregation's celebrations over the year are the context for telling its more important stories. The necessary people, objects, and actions for telling these stories appear: water or oil, bread and cup, Advent candles, seasonal banners, cloths of various hues. Christians share common stories—such as those associated with Holy Week—but denominations and congregations develop their own ways of telling and living those stories.

Signs, symbols, rituals, and rites

What are the primary official celebrations of our congregation? (List all you can.)

What are the unofficial celebrations of our congregation? (List all you can.)

When do these celebrations occur during the year? Why do they occur then?

What are the important words, gestures, objects, and actions that help create a shared congregational identity?

What in these celebrations seems tired or no longer fits the present reality of the congregation's life?

Congregations create unofficial rituals, such as the children's Christmas pageant, Easter sunrise breakfast, recognition of Sunday school teachers, or mission Sunday. Many congregations reserve one Sunday each year as Memorial Sunday or All Saints/All Souls Sunday. The congregation names and remembers those with connections to the congregation who have died during the year. Rituals and rites create patterns that enable the congregation to remember and to create a shared story of faith.[13]

Some congregational search committees focus on a prospective pastoral leader's ability to tell the story of God's saving love. They may place greater emphasis on this person's ability to narrate the biblical story in compelling and engaging ways than on his or her ability to preach doctrine. Pastoral leaders who know God's story "by heart" are often able to weave the stories of the congregation and its members into the ongoing story of God's people.

As stewards of these stories and rituals, worship leaders and pastors plan the best ways to enact them. We expand and adapt the patterns to fit our circumstances. We aid the Holy Spirit in drawing the congregation into the biblical and congregational stories that give rituals and rites purpose.

Congregations often get into ritual ruts. Tradition—"We've always done it this way"—becomes the albatross that stifles inspiration. Pastors and worship leaders need to monitor when tradition is becoming traditionalism. Rituals and stories must communicate to contemporary worshipers and not be cluttered by words, actions, or objects that obscure the intent. No matter how lovely poinsettias or

Easter lilies may be, or how many years they have graced the front of the church, worship leaders must ask how they draw worshipers into Christ's coming, his death, and his resurrection.

Theological accents. Over time, denominations and congregations develop cultures that express certain theological accents. These expressions arise from our experiences of God's presence with us interpreted through scripture. We convey these accents through the stories we tell, the pattern of our rituals, and the ways we create and abandon practices. Every congregation develops its own theological character, and worship is the primary place in which these accents are refined.

Theological accents

What Christian doctrines are of primary importance for our congregation?

What distinctive denominational understandings of these doctrines are important?

Are there particular kinds of theological or spiritual language that are important for our congregation?

Are there any doctrines or theological understandings that worshipers are questioning?

How does the pastoral team handle these theological questions or controversies?

How do these theological understandings guide our worship planning and leadership?

Some examples of theological accents readily noticed in congregational practice include:

- •Addressing God exclusively as father
- •Naming God using other biblical images, including feminine ones
- •Claiming praise as the only form of worship
- •Claiming a variety of actions that constitute worship
- •Drawing from popular culture to connect with "secular" people
- •Rejecting popular culture as a vehicle for worship
- •Valuing tradition
- •Valuing the contemporary
- •Valuing tradition and adapting it to contemporary life
- •Proclaiming the Bible's literal truth

- •Congregational singing in four parts, a cappella
- •Singing with a pipe organ
- •Singing with bands using electronic instruments
- •Proclaiming Jesus's imminent return
- •Proclaiming the presence of the kingdom here and now
- •Accenting personal salvation and evangelistic ministry
- •Accenting peace and social justice
- •Celebrating the Lord's Supper as a memorial
- •Celebrating the Lord's Supper as Eucharist
- •Allowing women to serve as worship leaders
- •Allowing only men to serve as worship leaders

Some congregations take official stands on these and many other theological issues. Others negotiate and refine the accents as the need arises. The pastoral team has primary responsibility for ensuring that the central accents of a congregation's identity remain clear and persuasive. But pastors and worship leaders must guard against the danger of believing that a congregation's particular accents constitute the whole of God's relationship with the church and its people. Congregations tend to interpret the Bible through the limited perspectives created by their favorite accents. Rather than seeing the large tapestry of God's relationship with the church and the world, in which the accents are bright and luminous threads, congregations may believe their threads to be the whole tapestry.

The absolute necessity of leaders working in collaboration

No one can know everything about the body and its members who gather for worship. The answers to the questions posed through this chapter are never finally answered. The people in Christ's body are always changing, facing new challenges, opportunities, and temptations. The task this chapter sets out is overwhelming unless leaders work together. Our leadership group must listen deeply and observe the body in action if we are to communicate effectively with the people of our congregation.

Preachers and worship leaders who collaborate with the Holy Spirit will be able to discern the realities of the worshipers we serve with compassion and joy. The Spirit can guide us to address the congregation's deepest needs. We will know what faces of God will open the congregation's praises or laments. We will know the pain and suffering the body needs to confess to receive God's healing word. We know what biblical stories, what congregational stories, and what distinctives of our denomination will strengthen the body for ministry in the world. We will communicate in ways appropriate to the congregation's social, expressive, and theological experience.

Through this discernment, worship and preaching become the foods that nourish the body of Christ. As eating practices shape the character of a family, so worship leaders use the social and cultural realities embodied in the congregation to form and reform the identity of the family of faith through its encounter and engagement with the living God.

3

PLANNING THE MENU

"One does not live by bread alone, but by every word that comes from the mouth of God." (Matt 4:3)

In our informal society, menu planning is an often-neglected aspect of meal preparation. But whenever people eat a meal, someone somehow has shaped the menu. The hosts who invite a circle of friends to a festive al fresco meal may take their inspiration from Martha Stewart and make elaborate plans for a four-course dinner, but Dagwood Bumstead standing in the light of the open refrigerator door is also doing menu planning. The tired spouse who comes home from work and asks, "What's for supper?" is voicing the hope that someone has planned a menu and begun to prepare supper. The chef who just starts cooking and adds things to the menu as the preparations proceed is doing menu planning in a stream-of-consciousness style. However planning happens, someone plans the meals we eat.

The cook is not always the one who makes the final menu selection. In homes where breakfast is not served, dad may quickly survey the fridge or the cupboard en route to the garage, picking up whatever suits his appetite at the moment. The kids in the minivan are each doing their own meal planning as they select burgers, fries, and soft drinks from the screen beside the drive-thru lane. The chef decides what will be printed on the restaurant menu or what will appear on the serving table, but customers decide what they will eat as they make choices from the menu or the buffet. The cook in the middle-school cafeteria may make meal plans, but what the students in the cafeteria line put on their trays is their real menu.

To call the process by which we decide what to eat or serve *menu planning* may seem too formal. We may remember watching mom pencil her outline for the family's suppers for the coming week, posting them on the refrigerator before making her weekly trip to the grocery store. For many of us, much of the time, the practice of menu planning has become less intentional and more individual than in those days. Still, whenever people are eating meals, someone is in fact shaping their menus.

This glimpse at menu planning also provides a window into the planning that goes into worship and preaching. Selecting what will be included and what will not is part of preparing for each service. Though sometimes services seem to be thrown together with little forethought, someone has made decisions about what will be part of worship. Someone has put together a menu.

Planning the worship and preaching menu

Factors that can be profitably addressed by more intentional and careful planning of worship include nutrition (biblical and theological sustenance), the needs and preferences of those to be served, and the possibilities and limitations the planners confront.

Issues in menu planning	
Nutrition	Issues for the cook
Issues related to the guests	Availability of ingredients
The guests' needs	Time
The guests' tastes	Ability of the cook
	Finances

A balanced biblical and theological diet

The factors that may enter into menu planning are many, but nutrition is arguably the most important. This phase of menu planning speaks to the broader meaning of the word *diet:* all the food that we ingest. The basic question is, does the food we eat meet our nutritional needs? Without good planning, our food consumption can get out of balance. If we eat on the run, grabbing whatever food is readily available without regard to good nutrition, we may compromise our physical health. If we latch onto the latest diet craze because it promises rapid weight loss but not balanced nutrition, we lose sight of the basic biological reason to eat. If our diet is to be healthy—with a good variety of foods and plenty of vegetables and fruit, low in sugar and fat and high in fiber, with adequate but not excessive caloric content—we will need to give meal planning some care and sustained attention.

A key word here is *planning*. Few of us eat all the nutrients our bodies need in one meal. No one food provides everything necessary for good health, so our planning should give thought to the whole day and even the whole week. Balance for good nutrition is a basic reason to shape our diets carefully.

In the same way, biblical and theological nutrition is a fundamental reason for using care in planning worship and preaching. It is easy to slip into tired patterns, singing the same familiar songs, preaching from the same texts, and featuring the same themes. No matter how well these old standards are delivered, the worship diet that lacks variety may lead us to take it in with our minds elsewhere, instead of encouraging us to savor each morsel. A couple of questions may help us assess the quality of our worship diet.

Is the congregation hearing generous portions of scripture from the entire biblical canon over a period of time? It is the task of preachers and worship planners to attend to the diet of biblical texts that is presented to the congregation, to assure that the people present are well fed. We will want to see that generous helpings of scripture are being served. And worship planning also needs to consider the entire biblical canon. To be sure, not every verse of the Bible is an appropriate focus for Sunday worship, but scripture is the most significant source of nutrition for us as spiritual beings, and a rich assortment of biblical texts will best address our congregation's hunger.

Some preachers and worship planners usually gravitate toward Gospel texts, and their congregations seldom hear from the Old Testament or Acts and the Epistles. The importance of the Gospels should not be underestimated; it is the Jesus they tell of whom we follow. But the Hebrew Bible, the sacred text of Israel and Jesus and the early church, should not be overlooked or under-served in our worship.

Not long ago, I was asked to preach from the Ezra-Nehemiah story, and I realized that I had never preached from these books. Preachers need to notice what we never preach and what we preach too often. I do not mean to imply that all Bible passages are equally worthy of attention in the pulpit. Again the food analogy helps us. To be sure, we need more servings of vegetables than of meat in our meals, but if we neglect sources of complete protein in our diet, we will have nutritional deficits.

Is the theological content of our worship substantive, insightful, and sufficiently broad? Effective worship planners step back and consider the big picture. Does our worship attend to all the core convictions of the faith the church confesses? What theological themes are overplayed, and what is seldom heard? Only if the theological diet is thought out carefully and reviewed periodically will the balance over time be complete.

Who among the planners maintains and reviews the records of biblical texts, theological themes, and hymns and songs that have been used in worship in our congregation? A record of past practice is a vital resource. Planners do well to look back at records rather than relying on memory and impressions to remember, for example, what faces of God have been seen in the congregation's worship.[1]

Clearly we cannot experience everything about God in one worship service. But if the theology in our preaching and worship represents only a God of mercy and never a God of judgment—or the reverse—our view of God is incomplete. Has our worship represented Jesus as Son of God, as fully human, as our example, as Savior, Messiah, Lord, and as the Lamb who reigns? What characteristics of the Holy Spirit have been reflected? Does our preaching and worship give attention to the Spirit as source of the church's power, as bestower of gifts and ministries in the church, as the one who is present among us to guide, comfort, convict, and disturb? Does our worship express a full-orbed understanding of salvation? What does our worship reveal about our view of the Christian life? Where is the balance off, and what do we need to attend to, to set it right?

If our congregations are going to be well-nourished by the public worship that we plan, then—just as when we plan our meals we think about calories, about vitamins and minerals, about protein and carbohydrates and fats—worship planners and preachers must think about the biblical and theological scope and balance in our worship.

Congregational issues

Other issues in meal planning include the particular needs of those to be served. The thoughtful host will ask about guests' special dietary needs. Then the menu planning can accommodate food allergies and intolerances, and perhaps even chewing problems of the younger and older guests.

The dietary preferences of the guests need attention as well. It may not be a good idea to cater to our child's every like and dislike, but if we know that certain foods will not be eaten without a battle, we can serve them less frequently than—or in combination with—more favored dishes. As a child, I spent way too much time gazing disconsolately at my bowl of oatmeal, when cream of wheat would have been infinitely preferable and would have entailed little sacrifice in food value or principle!

In the same way that the needs and preferences of dinner guests have a role in shaping what is served for the meal, the needs and preferences of congregations also play a part in shaping their corporate worship.[2] But careful worship planners will note the difference between congregational needs and congregational tastes, as parents do well to distinguish between the nutritional needs and the dietary preferences of the children for whom they prepare meals. This is the sort of distinction that has given rise to the oft-repeated instruction, "Eat your vegetables!"

The particular *needs* of the congregation shape worship planning. According to one of the simplest definitions, preaching occurs when a word from God intersects with human need. This definition assumes that the preacher will keep in mind either specific needs that individuals or the congregation as a whole are facing (such as unemployment, hurricane damage, or catastrophic illness) or more universal needs (such as the need to be loved, the need for forgiveness, or the need for hope). If worship touches on our congregation's needs, people are more likely to enter in and be transformed. Worship that addresses concerns that the congregation does not share is unlikely to draw people in.

Although worship planners need to beware of planning solely with a view to the likes and dislikes of the congregation, we ought to keep these *preferences* in mind. Yes, leaders must provide a complete, theologically and biblically balanced diet. But if we serve a healthy theological menu and people turn away because the parts don't appeal to their palate, what have we accomplished? The process of successfully expanding our worship menu may be akin to that entailed in acquiring an appetite for new tastes and textures.

Wise worship leaders will move the congregation gently, caring for needs and preferences, and introducing unaccustomed flavors in small portions alongside the tried and true. If our congregation enjoys praise songs, we may need some encouragement to enter into the experience of singing laments, but our spiritual health will benefit from the broadened range of expression in worship. A survey has shown that school kids eat lots of burgers and not enough fruit. The U.S. Department of Agriculture has responded by adding fruit to burgers served in the National School Lunch Program; combining blueberry puree with the ground beef lowers the burgers' fat content and adds lots of health-enhancing antioxidants. Sometimes we can accept the invitation to enter into a new experience, even one that moves us beyond what we find comfortable, when something familiar is part of the package.

Leaders may well need discernment to distinguish between needs and desires. Careful planners know the congregation's needs and their preferences, and will patiently plan to meet the needs.

Planners' limits

Not all of the menu-planning concerns are issues of the guests. Many are issues for the cook. And not all of the worship-planning issues are the congregation's problems. Many are limitations that the planners face or create.

The *availability* of particular foods is an issue for cooks. Out-of-season ingredients can be difficult to locate. A large urban area will offer greater access to specialized foods needed for certain ethnic cuisines. A chef in a more rural environment can draw inspiration for meal planning from a stroll through the garden to see what fresh flavors it offers. Is there enough asparagus to serve six? Wouldn't a rhubarb pie bring the meal to a fitting conclusion? The cook who can select items from a well-stocked pantry and a full refrigerator is likely to create more interesting fare than one whose supplies are meager.

Worship planners must also keep in mind the availability of resources. Coming up with a good idea is not the same thing as having the resources to pull it off. Worship planners in one congregation wanted an eight-trumpet fanfare on Easter morning but had only two inexperienced musicians. This committee wanted a drummer to accompany the story of the crossing of the Red Sea, and although they had timpani, they had no one to play them. A large congregation may be able to assemble a small orchestra composed of members of the congregation. Other groups are fortunate to have someone who plays the piano proficiently.

Time also imposes constraints on meal preparation. When meal planning is one task in a busy schedule, the cook must consider the time available and the time needed to prepare the food in question. Not everyone can devote a day to baking Christmas goodies.

Time can also be an issue if it takes more hours to prepare the dish we'd like to serve than there are between now and serving time. If it is too late to shop for groceries, menu planning will happen in the pantry. Something that needs to be marinated overnight cannot be started this afternoon and served this evening. Slow-cooker recipes just take time. The bacteria that produce the distinctive flavor of sourdough bread need several days to do their work. We can bring some dishes to the dinner table but not others, depending in part on when we begin our meal planning.

Time limits also create boundaries for worship planning. If your congregation functions with worship planning volunteers, and if the church's music is led by amateurs with other full-time jobs, their limited time constrains what they can contribute. Drama teams can only rehearse so often in a week's time. We may plan glorious and imaginative services, but then we must discipline ourselves to consider the available time and make the necessary adjustments. Planning well in advance allows worship planners many more options. Collaborative worship planning requires that we see lead-time as the important tool that it is.

The *ability of the cook* is also a factor in meal planning. Beginners usually don't tackle complicated recipes. Gourmet challenges are appropriately the province of the more experienced cook. If I have never baked a cake from scratch, a multilayered concoction such as Schwartzwälder Kirschtorte is probably not the place to start. Cooks can learn to prepare new things, of course, but undertaking a dish that requires a big culinary leap may be ill advised.

In the same way, worship planners need to bear in mind the abilities of the people who are available to lead worship. We cannot perform Handel's *Messiah* without the musical talent to do it. The same applies to preachers. Complex, multi-text sermons should be reserved for the experienced preacher who has mastered the simpler forms. We do not serve our congregations well when we try to do more than we are competent to do. A simple service, prepared well, provides a more meaningful worship experience than a complex service attempted with inadequate resources.

Finances are another issue for the cook. The family food budget dictates aspects of our meal planning. The catch of the day may be too pricey if you live in the Midwest. Making macaroni and cheese or Ramen noodles a staple of one's diet may be a budget-driven choice for the student with little income. Most of us set limits on what we will spend for food. Sometimes a special occasion means modifying those limits. At their wedding, the bride and groom gladly pay more for a few bites of cake than they would expend on the same small piece of cake for lunch at home.

Finances can also be a factor for worship planners. Generally speaking, worship need not be expensive, but some ideas do cost money. The worship budget should have resources for the basics, and good planning can keep the budget on course. Major expenses such as commissioning new banners or refurbishing the organ are projects that with careful planning could be located in two different budget years. Working with the arts requires investment for music, copyright fees, equipment, royalties, fabrics, candles, and costumes.

Obviously, some of the issues we face in worship planning are issues not unlike those we encounter in other areas of our lives. Planning enables us to address these issues well.

Guides for planning the worship menu

A number of resources are available to guide our planning for worship and preaching. In deciding on the guide or guides we will use, we should bear in mind the principles outlined above: we will attend to the fullness of the biblical canon, the breadth and depth of the theological content, the needs and preferences of the congregation, and the resources and limitations of the planners. Being mindful of all these pieces is a tall order, and we ought not leave it to chance, impressions, or intuition.

Outside calendars that influence us

Many calendars shape our lives outside the congregation, and these may also at times have an impact on our worship. They include the Hallmark calendar, the calendar of national holidays, and the school calendar.

The folks at *Hallmark* have a plan for our year. Valentine's Day, Mother's Day, Father's Day, Grandparent's Day, and Halloween are big events in our society, but these "holidays" have been created more to exploit an economic opportunity than to address an authentic human need. Not that I object to honoring mothers and fathers—far from it! But these are not holy days around which our worship should take shape. In the context of our families, acknowledging what our fathers and mothers mean to us is most appropriate. But these celebrations are not appropriate for the focus of our worship. Too much horizontal emphasis endangers the God-focus of worship.

The *nation* has a plan for our year. Our governments establish holidays to honor national heroes and events of historic significance for the country. We may observe Martin Luther King Day, Presidents' Day, Victoria Day, Memorial Day, Independence Day, Labor Day, Columbus Day, Veterans Day or Remembrance Day, and Thanksgiving. Like the Hallmark holidays, these occasions are not faith-based days around which we should organize our worship. Even Thanksgiving, which has many religious overtones, is not a Christian holy day: although giving thanks is an important theme in worship every time our congregations gather, the gratitude desired by the God known to us through scripture is different from the gratitude our nation's leaders call for.

School schedules have effects on our church life. During summer vacation, attendance at worship may drop dramatically, and the Sunday school program may be difficult to sustain. We may schedule the Christmas pageant in the middle of Advent because many families are out of town at Christmas. The return of students to school each fall may be acknowledged in our worship, as is the crop of new graduates each spring, but these rites of passage need to be infused with the opportunity of new beginnings as we bring our whole lives to the faith circle. As worship planners, we must think through how we will respond to these events, and to the attendance fluctuations caused by the school calendar.

Internal guides

Unlike the calendars listed above, some approaches that worship planners draw on are explicitly Christian. These guides to planning may be developed with the congregation, or they may be adopted from outside the congregation.

Internal guides	*External guides*
Bible book studies	Bible book studies
Thematic series	The Christian year
Local plan design	The lectionary
	Denominational calendar

As worship planners, we may decide to shape our own guide for our congregation, after prayerfully considering the group's needs. These particular guides may take a variety of forms, all with potential as well as problems.

Bible book studies. Many congregations are concerned that biblical literacy is declining. We hear such small portions of scripture, often out of canonical context, and the result is that many of us lack a good understanding of the big picture of the Bible. Book studies can enable a congregation to become acquainted with larger portions of scripture. Some groups have even taken on the task of walking through the entire Bible from Genesis to Revelation. This represents a major commitment for preachers and other worship planners, and one that may be difficult for a congregation to sustain. Devoting more than four years to preaching from the book of Acts, as John Calvin did, would probably be too much for most congregations today.

One pastor described his experience with preaching from the Gospel of Luke for an entire year. Except for using the birth narrative during Advent and Christmas, and the passion account during Holy Week, he took the congregation through the Gospel in order. He reported that this approach gave him freedom to preach on some texts that might have been too hot to handle had he singled them out; the fact that these texts were just the next ones that presented themselves allowed him to address some difficult topics.

The only way to really know the Bible is to delve deep. In book studies, the work the preacher does to prepare one sermon helps in preparing the next one as well. This pattern allows time for extra study. Listeners appreciate this depth and are grateful for new ideas and images that emerge. Too often we underestimate the hunger of our listeners.

Thematic series. Many worship services are planned around a thematic focus rather than around a text. (A thematic series is a series of services focused on a topic, while a topical service is one service focused on a topic.) The experience of listeners is often that one sermon in a thematic series helps reinforce the content of the other sermons in the series, and they are more likely to remember more from all the sermons. Like book studies, a thematic series allows preacher and planners to treat a theme or topic in greater depth than a single sermon or service can.

Thematic worship planning can focus on doctrines, theological concepts, or contemporary needs in the congregation. Examples of theological or doctrinal sermon topics include baptism, prayer, grace, sin, and salvation. During the 2004 run of the film *The Passion of the Christ*, worship in many churches focused on atonement. This kind of approach can give more sustained attention to the theology of the church, and it can do so in a way that relates our convictions to popular culture.

A thematic series may also address personal issues. Christian singleness, marriage, and family need the support of biblical preaching, and worship planners can foster careful attention to these concerns through thoughtful planning. Any of a host of ethical concerns in our lives can be a focus for a thematic series. Wealth, generosity, honesty—the list of topics is endless. A series on a theme allows us to go deep and to look at the theme from a variety of perspectives.

A strength of a thematic series is the ability to highlight a need or opportunity in the congregation and address it. A series on the congregation's mission statement can help us understand our part in the mission of the church. What is the work of the congregation? Are we achieving our goals?

The same can be done for a need or opportunity in the community at large. The violence and fear in our communities, our country, and our world need to be addressed, using the insights of the Bible. A prophetic voice can bring a concern for justice to bear on abuses in our families and violence in our communities. Peace and reconciliation are large themes that need our sustained attention.

Depth is an advantage for the thematic series, but thematic preaching also has disadvantages. A topical sermon can easily become a speech on a religious topic without a biblical text, or a sermon that misuses the biblical text. When we begin with an issue and then find scripture texts to support our point of view, we are in a risky position. We are in danger of forcing the text to say things it does not intend to say. Instead of deciding in advance what we want to say and then looking for a passage that we can interpret to support the position we arrived at independently, we treat the text with more integrity if we start by studying it.

Local plan. Some congregations have their own distinct design for planning worship. In one group, on the first Sunday of the month the pastor preached from an issue in the church, on the second Sunday on a doctrine of the church, on the third Sunday on the mission of the church, on the fourth Sunday on an issue of the Christian life. In a month with five Sundays, the pastor decided what he would preach about on the fifth Sunday. All of the sermons were based in scripture, and those who planned sought to balance these four kinds of topics in their worship, month by month.

Some planners combine their own local planning with a guide that is more broadly recognized; they use internal guides for worship during part of the year, while the rest of the time worship is shaped by the Christian year, with its special seasons. For Sundays in ordinary time, one pastor invited worship planners to select from several possible themes the ones they thought the congregation could most profitably focus on. He took the initiative to propose several themes and topics, and the worship committee provided valuable discernment. This collaboration in selecting themes enriches the menu.

When we work with plans devised in our local congregation, keeping good records helps future worship planners know what the worship focus has been. Particularly helpful are notes that give the name of the sermon series, central text, sermon title, hymns and songs, sermon message, and main ideas. Record keeping of this kind always has value, but it is particularly important when we lack the external structure that other plans give.

External guides

External guides are shaped outside the congregation—whether by denominational, national, or international groups—for use in a number of congregations.

Bible book studies. Unlike the internally guided Bible book study, this kind of Bible book study is shaped externally, by the book chosen. The contents and purpose of the selected book or section of the Bible establishes the topics and themes and messages that will be the focus for worship. Ordinary time use of the lectionary provides opportunity for Bible book studies of this kind.

Christian year. The Christian year is the daily bread, the rice and beans, of worship planning. Almost all churches plan worship around key holy days: Christmas, Holy Week, Easter, and Pentecost. These observances are the simplest version of the Christian year.

In fuller form, the Christian year begins with Advent, Christmas, and Epiphany. It continues through the season of Lent into Holy Week, followed by the Easter season, and then by Pentecost, with its celebration of the coming of the Holy Spirit and the birth of the church.

Often the special seasons of the Christian year inspire exceptional activity and creativity on the part of worship committees. They focus energy on splendid worship events and beautiful worship space. Some congregations appoint a special committee to plan worship for each of the Christian year seasons, because it would be too much work for the same people to take responsibility to do the extensive planning expected for all the seasons.

In the excitement that worship planners may feel for the season we are working with, and given all the energy we are investing in planning, we sometimes become possessive about the worship time. Will there be time for the special choirs to sing? Will there be time for the children's drama? Will there be time for a sermon? The importance of preacher and worship planners working together cannot be overemphasized. The amount and quality of communication between the preacher and the rest of the worship-planning group will be evident in the worship services. If planners hope to provide a unified and focused time of worship, we must be talking and listening to everyone involved. Music planners, worship leaders, and preachers are all more effective when we have shared planning with one another and respond with sensitivity to one another's concerns.

Everyone involved in worship planning needs to know who bears ultimate responsibility for the shape of a given worship service. Sometimes that may be the preacher, sometimes it may be the worship leader, and other times it may be the music leader. Working together with clarity about leadership responsibilities is essential. When planners collaborate effectively, the process is a joy, and the good fruits are evident to all. The Spirit can use the gifts each person brings to build up the whole body.

If worship planners are tempted to decide the themes and even determine the content of the sermon before consulting the preacher, we need to remember that sermons that do not come from the preacher's heart and study can be difficult to preach. The result of trying to impose a topic on a preacher may be a sermon that lacks passion, or alternatively, a sermon that has little to do with what the worship committee planned, because the preacher could not go there. A collaborative process that involves give and take between preacher and worship planners will yield the richest fare.[3]

The rest of the Christian year is called *ordinary time,* but not because these Sundays are commonplace or run-of-the-mill. *Ordinary* has the same root as *ordinal,* a number showing relative position in a sequence. These Sundays are ordered by number. In ordinary time, the sermon more often is the centerpiece of the worship, whereas during the special seasons, the sermon often stands in service of the larger worship event. In ordinary time, the preacher needs to bring sermon ideas to worship planning meetings. The services are still planned together, but the preacher has a more prominent role in the early stages of planning.

One of the great gifts of ordinary time is the opportunity for consecutive or series preaching. Ordinary time provides opportunity to work with the Prophets, the Epistles, or other major segments of scripture.

Lectionary. A lectionary is a collection of readings from the scriptures intended to guide worship planning and sermon preparation for the worship of the people of God. These tables of readings were used as early as the fourth century. The early lectionaries usually involved continuous readings, with each Sunday's texts picking up where the previous Sunday's had left off.

This practice of assigning particular readings to each Sunday continued down through the history of the church. Important recent examples are the Roman *Lectionary for Mass* of 1969, the *Common Lectionary* of 1983, and the *Revised Common Lectionary* of 1992. They usually designate an Old Testament passage, a Psalm, a Gospel lesson, and an Epistle reading for each Sunday. If planners include all the lectionary passages in worship every Sunday, over the three-year cycle the congregation will receive significant biblical nutrition.

There are other lectionaries, other cycles of prescribed readings. *The One Year Bible* is a daily lectionary designed so readers read the whole Bible in the course of a year.[4] The Amish also use a lectionary with a one-year cycle; it includes longer passages than one finds in the *Revised Common Lectionary.*

In *Living with the Lectionary: Preaching through the Revised Common Lectionary,* Eugene L. Lowry helpfully outlines assets associated with using the lectionary in worship and preaching.[5] The following assessment draws from his work.

The lectionary calls us to begin with the scripture in our worship and preaching. In this way of planning, the Bible is the focus for our worship. It is not an aid or tool or resource for our worship; it is the source. What we do in gathered worship flows from the scripture. Instead of asking first what the theme of a worship service is, we become accustomed to asking what the central texts are. The Word is focal, and the lectionary helps us keep that focus.

The lectionary assists comprehensive worship planning. One can know what the texts for a particular Sunday will be three months (or ten years) from now. The choir can start practicing an anthem, and the artist can begin to create a banner. All members of the worship planning team know in advance (as far ahead as they need to, to plan) what the texts will be for any given Sunday.

The lectionary gives preachers the opportunity to address passages that we might not choose if left to make our own selections. When our country is at war, it may not be popular in some congregations to preach about peace, reconciliation, and loving our enemies. But when the lectionary text asks that of preachers, we are granted freedom to preach a much-needed message.

The lectionary provides many ways to collaborate with others. Groups within the congregation can meet to reflect on the lectionary passages for the coming Sunday. Many resources—in books and periodicals and on the Internet—are available to stimulate thinking about sermon ideas; these sources also suggest prayers and hymns based on the Sunday texts.

The lectionary helps the pastor and other worship planners stay connected to the larger faith community. In many small churches, pastors do not have ministry colleagues with whom they can work and study. The lectionary makes it possible for them to have fellowship with others engaged in a common task. In a similar way, the lectionary (which is used around the world) gives us a connection to the believers throughout the globe. It serves as a helpful reminder that the church is bigger than any particular congregation or denomination.

The lectionary is an aid in integrating the sermon and worship. Our services sometimes seem to bifurcate, with worship going in one direction and the sermon going somewhere else entirely. Using the lectionary does not guarantee that this bifurcation will not happen, but if all worship leaders and preachers are consulting regularly with one another as they use the lectionary, it should happen less frequently.

Lowry's assessment does not fail to note some potential problems with using the lectionary to plan worship and preaching. One notable problem is that the biblical text is sometimes cut into small portions. Because time in our worship services is limited, these small portions are more useable, but the congregation does not get the whole picture. For example, the Gospel reading on the fourth Sunday of Lent in Year C is the story of the forgiving father. We don't read the other parables that accompany this one, the stories of the lost coin and the lost sheep, until the nineteenth Sunday of ordinary time in that annual cycle. These three stories in their setting in Luke 15 inform each other, with each contributing to our understanding of the others. A related problem is the lectionary's inclusion of summary verses in a text, without including the verses that help us get to that summary. Psalms are often presented in selected segments rather than in their entirety. This text trimming can have a distorting effect.

Sometimes the connections among the four texts are superficial at best. Planners note a recurring word or image, and suddenly the service is shaped by "hills," when in none of the passages is "hill" a significant focus. Worship planners may ask the Bible to say things that it does not intend to say, just because of the juxtaposition of passages. On the other hand, there are often significant connections among the passages, and these connections can point to useful preaching and worship themes.

The many resources available to people using the lectionary constitute a temptation. We may turn to them before we have done our own work of internalizing the passage and listening to what the Word is saying. With certain lectionary helps, the call to worship, prayers, hymn and anthem selections, and sample sermons are all provided. Preachers and worship planners need not think about the texts and our particular context. The delicate question is, when does a help become a crutch?

The lectionary can become something of a deterrent to the sermon series. One can use the lectionary to preach a series on a set of texts from a Gospel, an Epistle, or an extended Old Testament narrative. Although the lectionary can lend itself to a Bible book study, it is less helpful if the congregation needs a series on stewardship, or prayer, or hospitality.

Some biblical texts that are difficult, which merit our attention, are not found in the lectionary. Certain texts that congregations do not want to hear are conveniently absent from the lectionary. The story of Tamar has only recently been added as an alternate text. Pastors and planners need to do careful assessments, and they may need to add some dietary supplements.

The overwhelming advantage of the lectionary is that it is rooted in scripture and makes long-range planning easier. A major drawback is that some big biblical themes simply cannot be adequately preached from the brief texts included in the lectionary.

A denominational calendar. Although a denominational calendar may have merit in offering ways to guide our worship during the year, this calendar is not the Christian year. The days this calendar sets aside as special—education Sunday, stewardship Sunday, missions Sunday, peace Sunday, and more—are so designated in order to get the work of the denomination on the worship calendar, and to increase each congregation's awareness of denominational priorities.

Combinations

Planners can effectively mix the various plans. The Christian year can lend itself to thematic planning, and ordinary time can be devoted to study of a book of the Bible, or to another kind of sermon series. External guides and internal guides can complement one another; combining them may bring helpful variety to the congregation's worship. Whatever the approach, our goal is to find ways to plan the worship menu to meet our congregation's needs for theological nourishment.

Thanksgiving dinner at our house has a set menu, and we all know better than to tamper with it! Congregations have times like that, too. One church has a long-established Christmas Eve practice of singing "Silent Night" as candles are lit throughout the congregation. One year the pastor decided to omit the candle lighting. The children were outraged; the sense of special privilege that came with holding their own burning candle was vital to their experience of the mystery of this night. Worship planners ignore the congregation's traditions at their peril. Not every service is the time for innovating.

The responsibility for knowing the congregation well rests with the worship planners. Not that our fondness for tradition means that we should resist all change. But change and flexibility come easier when we introduce them with an awareness of our congregation's investment in established patterns, and when we care for the needs those traditions address.

One dilemma for the cook arises when people in the same family have different tastes. When your family includes vegetarians and carnivores, for whom do you cook? If some like their curry spicy and others prefer it bland, how much seasoning do you add? Some cooks opt for preparing two meals to accommodate the different tastes, and some congregations do the same. They provide a contemporary service and a traditional service, or they have a youth service and a service for older people, or they have a single service that is "blended." In some cases, the blended service starts with a praise band leading choruses. The words are projected on an overhead screen, and people clap and dance in the aisles. Later in the same service, the congregation sings hymns from the hymnal. Some participants raise their hands in praise and shout "Amen," while others sit quietly with eyes closed in prayerful meditation. Worship with a clear structure and unified theme can better carry a variety of styles in the same service. Small servings of a variety of dishes make it possible for many to eat at the same table. Planners must be careful not to expect worshipers to eat meals full of items for which they have no appetite.

Conclusion

As our meals are planned by someone, so our worship services are planned by a person or a group of people, in a process that is more or less deliberate. As guests then choose items from the dinner menu, so worshipers make selections from the worship menu, in a process that is more or less conscious. Not all the worshipers take in all that is served on Sunday morning. For a variety of reasons and in a variety of ways, we may participate selectively in what has been prepared. Sometimes our attention is focused on worship, and sometimes it drifts. Sometimes we are wrestling with God privately about something. One piece may address our hunger, and another may not be to our taste. The task of worship planners is to plan a healthy and well-balanced menu and entrust the matter of selection to those present, trusting that God is at work in each person's life.

When we use any of the planning guides we've considered, we enjoy the advantage of being able to work ahead and prepare for worship several Sundays in the future, giving the Spirit ample time to work through us. External and internal guides also aid us in preparing services that cohere, worship in which scripture readings, music, visual focus, prayers, and sermon all speak to the same theme. The parts we plan can reinforce each other, rather then being experienced as fragments pulling our attention in different directions. The experience of the whole enhances our ability to enter into each element, and the individual pieces move us toward a grasp of something larger. Planners' prayerful efforts to integrate a service around a central text or motif can be used by the Spirit in a sweet and ineffable way to increase worshipers' sense of personal and corporate integration. We leave the table of our Sunday worship empowered for our work in the world, feeling less fragmented and broken, more centered and whole.

When we plan worship without using a guide, our hit-and-miss approach means that preachers will tend to preach the same old topics. We are likely to avoid uncomfortable texts and themes that the congregation needs to hear. We are less likely to have at our disposal the resources of the wider church. We read familiar texts, and once again we sing "Holy, holy, holy," while would-be worshipers register "same-old, same-old" instead of engaging anew with Spirit and Word.

If left to what we can grab on the run, without forethought and careful planning, our worship is apt to be theologically and biblically out of balance. We will find ourselves dining on the same fare Sunday after Sunday. Parts of our spiritual lives will not be nourished, and other parts will be over-fed. For our growth in faith and for the spiritual well-being of all in the congregation, we must plan Sunday dinner with care.

4

DESIGNING THE COURSES

Make a joyful noise to God, all the earth.
Say to God, "How awesome are your deeds!"
Come and see what God has done.
Bless our God, O peoples.

I come into your house with burnt offerings;
I will pay you my vows.
Come and hear, all you who fear God,
and I will tell you what God has done for me.
I cried aloud to God and extolled God with my tongue
Blessed be God!
(adapted from Ps 66:1, 3, 5, 8, 13, 16, 17, 20)

Formal dinners usually consist of several courses, each with its own character and purpose. Appetizers—cheese and crackers, stuffed mushrooms, shrimp with cocktail sauce—wake up our palate. Salads or soups, foods of light texture, get our digestive juices working. The main course pleases our awakened appetite and satisfies our hunger. Desserts top things off, leaving a lingering sweetness. As each course is presented, the meal unfolds amid conversation with family members or friends. A meal, usually routine, becomes an occasion.

Societal conventions dictate the sequence of courses. Green salads come early in a meal in our society and just before dessert in some European countries. In France, several kinds of cheese are often served at the end of the meal rather than as an appetizer. In some parts of China, rice is the final dish. "Eat dessert first—life is short" is humorous advice to North Americans, because we're brought up to think it's naughty to fill up on sweets that leave no room for healthier food.

Knowing the sequence of courses helps us relax. We're free to enjoy one another's company as well as the food. A mystery supper, where the courses are rearranged, may be amusing every once in a while, but before long the edginess of uncertainty—what *is* coming next?—would eclipse the fun. Wondering about the food would distract us from enjoying the company.

Good cooks plan the big picture of a dinner, arranging the courses for the occasion. A birthday supper has social requirements different from those of Thanksgiving dinner. An evening with friends carries expectations different from a retirement celebration. When they have the big picture in view, cooks plan how the preparation needs to unfold. Their choices depend in part on what is available, what kinds of preparations will enhance the flavor of the raw materials at hand, and the time set aside for the meal itself. Visual presentation issues come into play. Preparing a special meal is a big job, one that requires a good grasp of food basics, a dose of imagination, and a love of conviviality.

Worship planners work with the basic actions of worship in much the same way that cooks plan the courses of formal dinners. Each action has its own purpose and essential characteristics. Each creates an opportunity for the body to encounter God, for its members to engage one another and be empowered for ministry in the world. Worship orders that constantly rearrange the basic actions are as confusing and disconcerting as a mystery supper—what *is* coming next?

The need for courses: Worship as action

Theodore Jennings claims a significant worship reformation would result from our simply figuring out *whom* we were talking to *when*.[1] In many Protestant congregations, particularly those that do not follow a set liturgical order, the distinct character of the basic worship actions is often muddled. Words for gathering the congregation are reduced to a "Good morning" greeting. Praise may use upbeat music but include no words addressed to God. Prayers of confession may name all the problems of the world but not corporate and individual sin. Benedictions may instead be closing prayers.

Talking and acting toward another person are primary ways of creating, maintaining, strengthening, or ending a relationship. Imagine a conversation with a friend who suddenly begins talking about you in the third person, as if you were not there. Wouldn't you wonder what happened? Or what if your friend thanked you for a favor you had done but was looking over your shoulder at someone else while he expressed his gratitude? Would his thank-you count as an expression of appreciation? What if your friend tried to apologize for offending you but never named what she did that had hurt you?

Is her apology offered in good faith? What if your buddy assured you that you could use his car but never made it available? Does that promise count? When our communications with friends, family members, co-workers, or acquaintances are confused, our relationships suffer.

Communication is at the center of each worship action. God communicates with the congregation. The congregation communicates with God. At times, worshipers communicate with one another. Each action communicates intentions and desires particular to these relationships. If the communications are repeatedly confused, our relationships with God and one another suffer.

The title of Robert Webber's book, *Worship is a Verb,* demonstrates something of this wisdom.[2] Worship is a series of actions through which the congregation responds to the living God present in our midst in Christ and the Holy Spirit. Worship is not primarily a feeling, although joy, peace, and well-being are outcomes of worship. Worship is not an intellectual exercise, although new knowledge, insight, and clarification of beliefs may result. A coherent arrangement of worship actions opens a way for God to communicate with the congregation and gives the congregation ways to respond to God.

It is the responsibility of worship planners and leaders to understand the essential dynamic of these actions and arrange them in a way that our congregation can follow with ease. Unfortunately, worship planners sometimes serve desserts before the main course!

The courses: Basic worship actions

The Bible does not dictate a structure of action for congregational worship. Yet the psalms repeatedly describe a variety of actions that characterized Israel's worship. Each action has a distinctive quality, a specific direction of address, and a discernible quality of communication. Here we will examine each of the biblical worship actions with an eye to the unique purpose of each.[3]

Basic worship actions	
Gathering	Proclaiming
Praising, adoring, thanking	Affirming faith
Confessing sin	Witnessing, testifying
Receiving assurance	Praying
Offering	Sending

Gathering: Drawing the body together

The Holy Spirit gathers the congregation for worship, but the first stage in the action of gathering draws us into awareness that we are worshipers in a *congregation*. The imperative voice permeates the action: Come! Enter! Sing praise! Worship the Lord! These words and actions are directed to the members of Christ's assembling body. They remind us of the purpose of our gathering: to honor God, who has saved us.

Psalms 95, 100, 148, 149, and 150 are biblical models for the first stage of our gathering. They sound the imperatives and recite the reasons God is worthy of worship.

> O come, let us sing to the LORD;
> let us make a joyful noise to the rock of our salvation!
> Let us come into his presence with thanksgiving;
> let us make a joyful noise to him with songs of praise.
> O come, let us worship and bow down;
> let us kneel before the LORD our Maker. (Ps 95:1–2, 6)

The song "Come and Rejoice" not only summons us to worship but reminds us that we are a holy nation (1 Pet 2:9), serving Jesus the king:

> Come with rejoicing, the Father is calling,
> those who would worship in spirit and truth;
> come with your singing, come with thanksgiving,
> Jesus, our Savior, has made all things new.
>
> Come and rejoice, O holy nation,
> come and sing praises to him;
> come and bow down, worship before him,
> Jesus, the King of all kings,
> Jesus, the King of all kings.[4]

Songs, biblical greetings, or psalms focus our awareness that we are an assembly of God's people.

The second stage of gathering consists of an opening prayer or invocation directed to God, asking for empowerment to worship. We ask for the leading of the Holy Spirit, for Christ's presence in our midst, for open hearts and minds to hear God's Word. We pray that God will find pleasure in our praise and prayer.

"Gather us in" prays that God will continue the work of drawing the congregation into a unity that includes even those who may be at the edges of the church's social world:

> Gather us in—the lost and forsaken,
> gather us in—the blind and the lame.
> Call to us now, and we shall awaken,
> we shall arise at the sound of our name.
>
> Gather us in—the rich and the haughty,
> gather us in—the proud and the strong.
> Give us a heart so meek and so lowly,
> give us the courage to enter the song.
>
> Gather us in—and hold us forever,
> gather us in—and make us your own.
> Gather us in—all peoples together,
> fire of love in our flesh and our bone.[5]

This song stands against the notion that worship leaders lead the congregation into God's presence, as is occasionally implied in opening prayers. God in Christ is always present. But through their words and actions, worship leaders help God's Spirit make the congregation present and alive to God.

Early Christians believed that worship is directed to God, mediated through Christ, and empowered by the Holy Spirit. During the two stages of gathering, reminders of God's triune nature help us orient our worship to the fullness of God.

Often congregational worship is preceded by music: an organ prelude, informal congregational singing, a vocal ensemble, or recorded music. This music prepares worshipers to encounter and be engaged by God. It may be upbeat or reflective, classical or contemporary. But music alone does not focus attention on our presence in the body of Christ that has gathered to serve our God.

Praising, adoring, thanking: Remembering the why of worship

The actions of praising, adoring, and thanking flow naturally from gathering the body. The congregation directs these speech acts to God, acknowledging who God is and what God has done. A speech act accomplishes the action that it names.[6] "I praise you, Lord" fulfills the action of praising. "I thank you, Lord" accomplishes the act of thanking. "Christ, we do all adore thee" fulfills the act of adoration. The actions of praise and thanksgiving are intensified through lifting our hands. Kneeling and bowing down deepen the act of adoration. Often a speech act names specific actions or qualities that make God worthy of worship.

Praising, thanking, and adoring are three different moods that are too often collapsed into the single action of praise. We do well to maintain the distinctive communication quality of each action, evident respectively in the three examples below.

> Praise, I will praise you, Lord, with all my heart.
> O God, I will tell the wonder of your ways, and glorify your name.
>
> Praise, I will praise you Lord, with all my heart.
> In you I will find the source of all my joy. Alleluia.[7]
>
> We give thanks unto you, O God of might, for your love is
>   never ending.
> We give thanks unto you, the God of gods, for your love is
>   never ending.[8]
>
> Holy, holy, holy Lord, God of power and might,
> heaven and earth are full of your glory.
> Hosanna in the highest.
> Blessed is he who comes in the name of the Lord.
> Hosanna in the highest.[9]

In the Psalms, *in the action of praise, Israel remembers what God has done in love through creation and for their salvation and restoration.* Christians praise God by remembering these saving acts and our redemption through the life, death, and resurrection of Jesus. Praise gathers up our acclamations for God's loving-kindness for all generations across time and space. The action of praise is grand; it transcends our personal experience, our time and place, and encompasses all of creation. When we consider what God has done and continues to do, we are reduced to wonder and love.

> It is good to give thanks to the LORD,
>   to sing praises to your name, O Most High;
>   to declare your steadfast love in the morning,
>   and your faithfulness by night,
>   to the music of the lute and the harp,
>   to the melody of the lyre. (Ps 92:1–3)

The action of *thanking expresses our gratitude for what God has done* for us as individuals and as a congregation. In Psalm 118, for example, we thank God for steadfast love, for hearing our prayers and responding to them. Thanksgiving stems from God's saving grace felt in a personal way, which connects us with God's saving work throughout history.

> I thank you that you have answered me
> and have become my salvation. (Ps 118:21)

Many psalms connect lament with praise and thanksgiving. This combination seems strange to many contemporary Christians, who tend to separate their enthusiastic praise from their own suffering and the suffering of the world. The psalmists are far more realistic. Although written and sung primarily by men in temple worship, the Psalms express universal feelings, experiences shared by men and women, rich and poor, Jew and Christian. Psalm 22, for example, begins in despair as a cry of alienation: "My God, my God, why have you forsaken me?" The singer feels abandoned—an outcast, with dogs licking his wounds. His body is broken. All he can do is cry out to God. Although the psalm does not tell us exactly what God did for him, we know that God intervened. Deep anguish is replaced by a testimony of praise.

Psalm 30 recounts the transformation from mourning because of despair and abandonment into a grateful dance. In Psalm 57, the singer is beset by difficulties: storms, lions, and those who want to interfere with his just cause. Each time God saves him from destruction. Thanksgiving and praise are the worshiper's response.

> Be merciful to me, O God, be merciful to me,
> for in you my soul takes refuge;
> in the shadow of your wings I will take refuge,
> until the destroying storms pass by.
> I lie down among lions
> that greedily devour human prey;
> their teeth are spears and arrows,
> their tongues sharp swords.
>
> I will give thanks to you, O Lord, among the peoples;
> I will sing praises to you among the nations.
> For your steadfast love is as high as the heavens;
> your faithfulness extends to the clouds. (Ps 57:1, 4, 9–10)

Few congregations make lament a regular part of their worship, but without expressions of grief and loss, our testimonies and witness to the world are anemic. The hard-won wisdom that comes from honest lament can give our acts of praise and thanksgiving greater integrity and vitality. Our worship then springs from a deeper place within our being, and we proclaim our dependence on God for all that gives us life and salvation.

The action of *adoring names God's character and qualities* that we know through God's gracious activity revealed over time, recorded in scripture, told by faithful disciples, and experienced in our own lives. Adoration claims God's glory, holiness, righteousness, justice, beauty, steadfastness, graciousness, and greatness. In the presence of these qualities, we are humbled and awed.

These actions are rooted in our acknowledgment of what God has done and continues to do in creating, saving, and sustaining human beings and the natural world. In many congregations, the action of thanksgiving is missing, except on Thanksgiving Sunday. Much contemporary praise music adores God but rarely recounts God's saving acts in history. When the distinctions between praise, thanksgiving, and adoration are honored, our ways of engaging God are deepened and enriched.

Confessing sin and limitations: Telling life's truths

When Isaiah encountered the awesome grandeur of God enthroned, his first response was confession. "I am lost, for I am a man of unclean lips, and I live among a people of unclean lips" (Isa 6:5). Like Isaiah, when confronted with the overwhelming glory, mercy, and graciousness of God, we confess to God—and admit to ourselves—what we are and what we are not. Confession tells the truth. In worship, we tell the truth about the condition of our lives and of the world in which we live. We tell the truth about our choices that exalt ourselves and turn away from God and God's saving purposes. We name our broken and damaged relationships. We own the truth about our participation in societal structures that dehumanize other people and misuse the natural world. We acknowledge our limitations as creatures who are incapable of supplying our most fundamental needs. And we recognize that there are sins of which we are not even conscious, because of our capacity for self-deception.

Some truths that we must tell are deeply personal, particular to our own lives. Prayers of confession need spaces of silence for us to name the sins with which we struggle personally. Some truths name problems of unchristian behavior in the congregation. Inhospitality, lack of charity, ingratitude, spiritual pride, and impatience are among the sins frequently found in our congregations. Whether spoken by a worship leader or by the entire congregation, prayers that name these collective sins are essential for congregational health and spiritual growth. Some truths acknowledge the institutionalized sins of our societies that destroy the well-being of others at home and abroad.

Psalm 51 stands as a classic example of confession. In a straightforward way, the psalmist (David, according to tradition) confronts the reality of his sin. Although the specific occasion of sin is not named, the fact of the sin remains. The psalmist tells the truth, so that God's reconciling work can begin.

> Have mercy on me O God,
> according to your steadfast love;
> according to your abundant mercy
> blot out my transgressions.
> Wash me thoroughly from my iniquity,
> and cleanse me from my sin.
> For I know my transgressions,
> and my sin is ever before me.
> Against you, you alone, have I sinned,
> and done what is evil in your sight,
> so that you are justified in your sentence
> and blameless when you pass judgment. (Ps 51:1–4)

God creates new hearts and renews right spirits within us, but not until we have told the truth.

Steve Merkel's song "Lord Have Mercy" is structured correctly. We name our sin and pray for God's mercy. While we pray, we wait for God's Spirit to continue its work in us:

> Jesus, I've forgotten the words that You have spoken;
> Promises that burned within my heart have now grown dim;
> With a doubting heart I follow the paths of earthly wisdom;
> Forgive me for my unbelief,
> Renew the fire again.
>
> Lord have mercy;
> Christ have mercy;
> Lord have mercy on me.[10]

Other musical settings of the Kyrie (Lord have mercy/Christ have mercy/Lord have mercy) cause us to slow down, wait, and listen for the deeper truth of our confession, or in Charles Wesley's words, for "the depth of inbred sin."

> Show me, as my soul can bear, the depth of inbred sin;
> all the unbelief declare, the pride that lurks within.
> Take me, whom thyself hast bought, bring into captivity
> every high aspiring thought that would not stoop to thee.[11]

In a society that finds personal confession of wrongdoing nearly impossible, the act of confession is truly counter-cultural.

Too often our truth-telling prayers have not gone deep enough and have not been specific enough for God's Spirit to begin the work of transformation. Many of our hymns speak of sin, but singing about sin in general is not enough. Such songs can open our consciences to reflect truthfully on our lives, as the text by Charles Wesley demonstrates. But it is in the specific failures and deceptions of our relationships with others and with God that our sin entraps us. Wise worship leaders provide regular opportunities for us to name our sin, to call out for God's forgiveness, so we are freed to know God's mercy.

Receiving assurance: Hearing good news

The goods news of biblical faith is that God does not break relationship with us because of our sins. With great love, God offers us forgiveness time and time again. Worship leaders and preachers proclaim the biblical words of assurance on God's behalf. This is one action of worship in which we receive God's word to us; our response is gratitude. We may respond to this profound gift with songs and offerings, but these acts are not substitutes for hearing God's reconciling words.

> God is merciful and gracious,
> slow to anger and overflowing with steadfast love;
> who does not harbor indignation forever,
> whose resentment lasts only a short time.
> We are not treated as our guilt and sin deserve.
> No less than the height of heaven over earth
> is the vastness of divine love for those who fear God's holiness;
> as far as east is from west, God removes our sins from among us.
> As a child receives the tenderness of a compassionate parent,
> so we receive God's mercy, who knows our frame and remembers
> that we are dust.[12]

One possible reason that prayers of confession have fallen out of favor in congregational worship is that our confession has not been followed routinely with assurance of God's steadfast love for each person. If we focus exclusively on what we do wrong or are incapable of correcting on our own, we are left with a sense of failure. We need to hear that God, in love and compassion, invites us to start again.

Confession requires repentance if we are to gain power to live differently. Without the will to change sinful patterns, our desire for God's assurance becomes an exercise in cheap grace. Our confessions provide an opening for God's Spirit to begin and continue the work of renewing our hearts, of transforming our spirits. Hearing God's words of forgiveness is essential if we are to entrust ourselves to the Spirit's work.

Offering: Giving ourselves

Offering is an act of gratitude that grows out of our praise, thanksgiving, adoration, and confession. This free response expresses an abundance of grace. Offering in the biblical tradition is linked directly with worshipers' gratitude for what God has done in specific ways in their lives. In the Psalms, such offerings take the form of an animal or grain sacrifice given in fulfillment of a vow or out of gratitude for rescue from danger.

> With a freewill offering I will sacrifice to you;
> I will give thanks to your name, O LORD, for it is good.
> For he has delivered me from every trouble,
> and my eye has looked in triumph on my enemies.
> (Ps 54:6–7)

In the New Testament, Paul calls on Christians to offer themselves as living sacrifices to God (Rom 12:1). Our offering entails giving back to God something physical—something tangible—from our resources. One Sunday, a young Kenyan woman with two small children came to worship. Their little family had few resources. As the congregation started to pass the offering baskets, the young woman removed her foot coverings. When the basket came to her, she set it on the ground. Reverently, humbly, she stepped into it and stood praying. A respectful hush came over the congregation. She stepped out, picked up the basket, and passed it on.[13] Our offerings make us—our whole being, as Frances Havergal's hymn proclaims—available to God for use as God requires.

Take my life and let it be, consecrated Lord to thee.
Take my moments and my days; let them flow in ceaseless praise.
Take my love; my Lord, I pour at thy feet its treasure store.
Take myself, and I will be ever, only, all for thee.[14]

In most Protestant congregations, the offering would be more
properly called *the collection*. We collect money to pay pastoral leaders and to do God's work in the world. This act is not insignificant,
but our understanding of offering is limited if we think only of giving
money. In many middle and wealthy class congregations, worshipers
contribute their pledges to the offering plates once a month or once a
quarter. The size of the pledge may be generous, but the practice may
have no greater significance than the task of writing the monthly
check for electrical or telephone service. One congregation allows
people to make an electronic transfer of funds into its account on a
weekly or monthly basis, eliminating the need to offer anything concrete during worship.

In contrast, Christians of the early church brought food, clothing,
and other goods that were distributed to the poor of the congregation
or in the community. Many congregations have food and clothing
offerings several times during the year. Mennonite Central
Committee's health kits and school bag projects express this kind of
generosity. What if every Sunday, worshipers brought offerings
besides money for distribution in their communities? What if these
gifts were carried into the center of the congregation each week with
songs of thanksgiving and blessing? We would certainly need more
deacons and more volunteers to move the goods to their places of
need! And we might need greater awareness of and stronger connections with those places of need in our congregations and communities. Singing Robert Edwards's hymn as our goods and money are
gathered would reconnect our acts of offering and service, aspects of
discipleship that are more and more often severed.

God, whose giving knows no ending from your rich and endless
    store—
nature's wonder, Jesus' wisdom, costly cross, grave's shattered
    door—
gifted by you, we turn to you, offering up ourselves in praise.
Thankful song shall rise forever, gracious Donor of our days.
Treasure too, you have entrusted, gain through powers your
    grace conferred—

ours to use for home and kindred, and to spread the gospel word.
Open wide our hands in sharing, as we heed Christ's ageless call,
healing, teaching, and reclaiming, serving you by serving all.[15]

The act of offering does not have a standard place in the worship order of many Protestant congregations. It floats to whatever spot seems convenient, or it serves as a transition between other actions. Here is another unfortunate disconnect. At the base of the church's praise, adoration, thanksgiving, and offering is gratitude. Offering is integral to the expression of our thanks. Many congregations mirror the ingratitude of our North American culture. Why be grateful, if we credit ourselves with having achieved the good life? Worship leaders and preachers play an important role in expanding the congregation's understanding of offering and providing ways to practice gratitude and generosity in the context of worship.

Proclaiming: Receiving God's Word

Proclaiming is God's loving action toward the congregation. As God's ambassadors, preachers announce God's good news of salvation in Jesus, the Lord over death and life. We invite all people into relationship with God and declare God's covenant of everlasting love in Jesus. We announce the presence of God's kingdom, which will have no end.

You that are Israelites, listen to what I have to say: Jesus of Nazareth,
a man attested to you by God with deeds of power, wonders, and signs
that God did through him among you, as you yourselves know—this
man, handed over to you according to the definite plan and fore-
knowledge of God, you crucified and killed by the hands of those outside the law. But God raised him up, having freed him from death,
because it was impossible for him to be held in its power. (Acts
2:22–24)

God speaks through scripture and the preached word. We hear and receive this word, chosen for this particular moment in the life of our congregation and in our own lives. The Holy Spirit helps us interpret its importance and discern ways to act on what we have heard.

Although foundational truths are presented in all scripture readings and sermons, the Holy Spirit works with the preacher and with the congregation to communicate what is most needed to draw people into deeper fellowship with God. Scripture poorly read, snippets of text pulled from their context, and sermons poorly conceived diminish the Spirit's capacity to move hearts and minds. As preachers, we carry a primary responsibility for communicating God's message. We must continually work to know our congregation, so we can focus compassionately on the people whom we are addressing on God's behalf.[16]

Some worship leaders read the scripture texts on which the sermon is based. Some preachers prefer to read the texts themselves to give special emphasis to parts central to the sermon. Whoever reads the scriptures should do so with clarity and good sense. Too often, scripture readers simply pronounce the words without care for phrasing or for how the story flows. For listeners, the jumble of words conveys little meaning and no importance. Scripture readers announce and interpret the Word of God every bit as much as preachers do, and they must take their responsibilities seriously.

Singing can be a means of hearing God's Word proclaimed, particularly through psalms and words that narrate a biblical story. With the refrain of the song "Two Fishermen," we are taken up into the story, which invites our response.

> Two fishermen, who lived along the Sea of Galilee,
> stood by the shore to cast their nets into an ageless sea.
> Now Jesus watched them from afar, then called them each by name.
> It changed their lives, these simple men; they'd never be the same.
> "Leave all things you have and come and follow me."[17]

But care must be taken to preserve the clarity of God's message to the congregation. In "Here I am Lord," the verses name God's compassion and desires, conveying a sense that we are hearing God's voice. The refrain is the congregation's response that commits us to serve God as we serve others.

> I, the Lord of sea and sky,
> I have heard my people cry.
> All who dwell in dark and sin
> my hand will save.
> I who made the stars of night,
> I will make their darkness bright.
> Who will bear my light to them?
> Whom shall I send?

Refrain
Here I am Lord. Is it I Lord?
I have heard you calling in the night.
I will go Lord, if you lead me.
I will hold your people in my heart.[18]

When congregations sing the entire song, the interplay between God's voice and our response is obscured. The verses are better sung by a soloist or small group, with the congregation joining in a heartfelt response on the refrain.

Many Protestants consider the sermon the most important action of corporate worship. Indeed, hearing God's living Word is a primary reason for the congregation to gather. But proclamation—the sermon—is not worship. The congregation's response to the proclaimed Word, to God who is revealed through the Word, is worship.

Affirming/confessing faith: Claiming God's truth

Affirming faith or confessing faith is the second action in which worshipers intentionally speak truth. This time we name the truth we know about God.

> The LORD is my rock, my fortress, and my deliverer,
> my God, my rock in whom I take refuge,
> my shield and the horn of my salvation, my stronghold.
> I call upon the LORD, who is worthy to be praised,
> so I shall be saved from my enemies. (Ps 18:2–3)

We affirm our faith in who God is, what God has done in Jesus, how God continues to work through the Holy Spirit. Philippians 2:5–11 is an example of a faith confession that affirms Jesus's divine nature and human form. Several of Paul's letters open with greetings that summarize basic beliefs about Jesus that Christians commonly shared. The church's historic creeds (the Apostles' Creed and the Nicene Creed, for example) have a structure that outlines basic Christian belief.

> I believe in God the almighty, Ninasadiki [I believe].
> who created earth and the heavens, Ninasadiki.
> and in Jesus, the Son from heaven, Ninasadiki,
> of eternal love was begotten. Ninasadiki.
> Nasadiki, nasadiki, Ninasadiki.
> Nasadiki, nasadiki, Ninasadiki.[19]

Our confessions of faith are not limited to these biblical or historical forms. Martin Luther's hymn "A Mighty Fortress is Our God" is a robust affirmation of faith.

> A mighty fortress is our God, a bulwark never failing.
> Our helper he amid the flood of mortal ills prevailing,
> for still our ancient foe does seek to work us woe,
> his craft and power are great, and armed with cruel hate,
> on earth is not his equal.[20]

Using the metaphor of a fortress, Luther names an aspect of God's protecting nature. He names our hopelessness in overcoming the powers of Satan by ourselves, and he claims the power of Jesus, chosen by God, to defeat evil.

In a contemporary musical idiom, "Shout to the North" asserts the lordship of Jesus over all the earth's peoples.

> Shout to the north and the south
> Sing to the east and the west
> Jesus is Savior of all
> Lord of Heaven and earth.[21]

The basic speech act of an affirmation is "I believe . . ." or "We believe . . ." Not all statements of faith begin with either of those phrases, yet these affirmations undergird our actions. Our confessions of faith bind us, together, to the trustworthiness of God's revealed truths. In saying "I believe . . . ," we pledge to orient our lives toward these convictions.

Affirming faith is an action we direct to God as our personal commitment, our expression of loyalty. But it is also a sign of our shared faith. In this act, too, we recognize ourselves as the body of Christ. Our affirmations also proclaim to the world the beliefs around which we orient our lives. It may seem strange to think this action is directed to the world, because we don't necessarily broadcast our beliefs outside the church walls during worship (although radio, television, and Internet broadcasts take some congregations' services beyond their walls). Our presence in worship is a sign to the world of our allegiance to God and God's work in the world. Our practices of worship, our lifestyles, and our ethical decisions are extensions of the faith we confess.

Witnessing/testifying: Telling God's faithfulness

Our action of witnessing or testifying is directed to the other worshipers of the congregation. We tell how God has been active in our lives, in our congregation, in our community.

> I have told the glad news of deliverance in the great congregation;
> see, I have not restrained my lips, as you know, O LORD.
> I have not hidden your saving help within my heart,
> I have spoken of your faithfulness and your salvation. (Ps 40:9)

Testimonies take the form of story. Like the psalms of lament, our witnessing tells about a trial or crisis, a perplexing problem, a moral failure, or a situation of conflict in which God intervened in a discernible way.

> My lips will shout for joy
> when I sing praises to you;
> my soul also, which you have rescued.
> All day long my tongue will talk of your righteous help,
> for those who tried to do me harm
> have been put to shame and disgraced. (Ps 71:23–24)

Or we tell of an amazing turn of events, a sign of new life, or a deepened awareness of God's love and power.

> When I was sinking down, sinking down, sinking down,
> when I was sinking down, sinking down,
> when I was sinking down beneath God's righteous frown,
> Christ laid aside his crown for my soul, for my soul,
> Christ laid aside his crown for my soul.[22]

As was true for the psalmist and for many hymn-writers since, witnessing and testifying are actions that grow out of our personal experiences of God's steadfast love in the joys and challenges of our everyday lives.

> Redeemed! Oh the bliss of this glorious thought,
> my sin—not in part, but the whole—
> is nailed to his cross, and I bear it no more,
> praise the Lord, praise the Lord, O my soul!
> It is well with my soul, it is well, it is well with my soul.[23]

The words *testifying* and *witnessing* can be used interchangeably because their meanings are similar. They both entail giving evidence of what is true, evidence we have seen, heard, or experienced. Some worship traditions limit *testifying* to telling personal experience in the context of the congregation, while *witnessing* refers to what God has done for humankind in Jesus; it happens with people in the world. These distinctions are needlessly confining.

Witnessing strengthens the congregation in faith by confirming that God cares for us individually and as a people serving in the world. From adults they know and love, children and youth of the congregation hear about God's faithfulness. They learn to look and listen for God's Spirit moving in their own lives. New believers may relate their experiences of newfound faith or be encouraged by the faith of mature believers who are facing difficult situations. People with Christian friends in other parts of the world share stories of God's work in those places, expanding our awareness of and deepening our gratitude for Christ's body around the globe. Without stories of God's faithful activity in our lives and in the world, we are not adequately equipped to share in God's mission.

In many congregations, the time for joys and concerns is the natural place to testify, but seldom does what we say reach the level of witness. Some people and some congregations value the warm chumminess of this time and use it as a verbal newsletter, to bring the congregation up to date about their lives and their families. Sometimes someone tells a story so personal that it is inappropriate for a public event such as worship, and those present become embarrassed and uncomfortable, particularly if guests are in attendance. Perhaps what we relate rarely rises to witnessing because many believers are uncertain about how God is moving in their lives, or they are tongue-tied in their attempts to talk about what they do perceive. Perhaps we feel discomfort about claiming God's activity in our lives because we might seem to imply that what God has done for me, God will do for you. (And if God does act differently in your life, something must be wrong somewhere.)

Leaders can guide the period of sharing in a different direction by having worshipers tell their joys as part of the congregation's praise, thanksgiving, or offering, as the psalms suggest. The day's concerns could be mentioned as part of the congregation's intercessory prayer. Leaders could ask one or two people to open sharing time with testimonies from their experience.

Songs and readings can begin periods of witnessing, but they cannot replace the stories of people who know God's Spirit moving in their lives and in the world.

Praying: Speaking the depths of need and compassion

When we pray, we talk with God, naming the deepest needs and desires of our lives and the world. We speak to God in a variety of moods, in much the same way that we talk to significant people in our lives. We might express ourselves with words that are intimate and personal, expansive and jubilant, formal or casual. We usually talk to co-workers with politeness and perhaps deference (depending on our positions and responsibilities). We communicate more casually when we're with our families and friends.

Our primary images of God affect our choice of language register. If our dominant image is of God as an omnipotent almighty king, sovereign judge, and righteous father, we are likely to address God in formal language that respects the gulf between God's greatness and our smallness. If our primary image of God is reflected in Jesus as a compassionate healer, friend of sinners, dying lamb, or risen savior, our language will likely be more informal, resembling conversation between good friends and close relatives. We use a range of language registers to communicate our thoughts, feelings, hopes, and needs, in ways appropriate to the situation in which we are communicating. We talk more intimately with God in our times of private prayer and Bible reading, and more formally when we pray in public on behalf of the congregation.

We communicate with God in a variety of modes, like those we use with other people. We ask for help. We thank people. We admire the work they have done. We compliment them. We let them know when we are frustrated, tired, or afraid. Praise, adoration, thanksgiving, confessing, and offering, which we have been examining in this chapter, are modes of prayer that Jews and Christians have used throughout the centuries to communicate with God. In this section we turn to the modes of petition and intercession.

Prayers of petition (the formal term is *supplication*) begin with the recognition that we human beings have limited power. In spite of our technological mastery and scientific achievements, in fundamental ways we are helpless. We cannot cause rain to fall or make the sun shine. We cannot create air, water, or light—the basic elements that sustain our lives. Our ability to avert disasters, whether climatic, economic, or health-related, is partial, at best. We cannot root out the spirit of violence in the world, or put an end to evil. We cannot escape suffering. So we pray. We call on God to respond to our needs—

for physical, spiritual and emotional health
for physical and emotional safety
for adequate food, clothing, and shelter
for family and friends who care for us
for meaningful work
for resources to live humanely and justly
for opportunities to serve others
for deepening faith, purity of heart, wisdom, righteousness, trust, and obedience
for protection when temptation looms

We bring our petitions using words as old as the psalms.

Be gracious to me, O Lord, for I am languishing;
O Lord, heal me, for my bones are shaking with terror.
Turn, O Lord, save my life;
deliver me for the sake of your steadfast love. (Ps 6:2, 4)

Hear my cry, O God;
listen to my prayer.
From the end of the earth I call to you,
when my heart is faint. (Ps 61:1)

The Lord's Prayer remains the model for petitions. Its requests are those that Jesus taught are of greatest importance in our lives: the reign of God, daily bread, to be forgiven and to forgive, protection from temptation, and rescue from evil. These are our deepest needs. We cannot pray this prayer often enough.

Christian hymnody also carries our prayers. Hymns by the seventeenth-century German Pietists, Charles Wesley, gospel song writers, and today's contemporary worship composers are deeply personal. They focus on our individual relationships with God. A song such as "Hungry (I'm falling on my knees)" expresses heartfelt spirituality, which has an important place in congregational worship.

Hungry, I come to you
For I know you satisfy
I am empty, but I know
Your love does not run dry

And so I wait for you
So I wait for you

I'm falling on my knees
Offering all of me
Jesus, you're all this heart is living for.[24]

As we sing these songs, their meaning expands beyond our personal experience; the congregation claims the desire for a closer relationship with God. "Fount of love, our Savior God" voices a petition for guidance, which we need personally and collectively in the midst of competing values and temptations.

Fount of love, our Savior God,
Light on baffling ways we've trod,
your cross is our compass sure,
your love keeps our vision pure.
Lord, we thank you for your grace;
darkness flees before your face.
Fount of love, our Savior God, be our guide.

Many paths before us lie, many voices to us cry.
Which of all these shall we choose?
Here find peace or there all lose?
Jesus, take our hands, we pray,
show us your divine true way.
Fount of love, our Savior God, be our guide.[25]

The public nature of congregational worship makes it necessary to frame petitions in general terms, like those of the Lord's Prayer. But as with our confessions of sin, we must make our petitions specific to our individual needs. The presence of other worshipers can give us courage to name our deep longings and fears. Ideally, worship leaders include a period of silence in each service so we have opportunity to name our personal petitions.

Our *prayers of intercession* lay before God the needs of other people—people we know, people we do not know, people who pray, and people who cannot pray. We identify with their needs and recognize the limits of our knowledge, wisdom, and resources to address those needs. Praying for people who are ill or suffering may be the only thing we can do.

Our commitment to intercessory prayer may be tested if we seek to follow Jesus's instruction to pray for our enemies. How can we identify with people set on destroying us or bent on making us suffer? In a chapel service at Associated Mennonite Biblical Seminary, just hours after the terrorist attacks on September 11, 2001, the worship leader led the community in a prayer that included an intercession for those who perpetrated the attacks. It was hard to hear this prayer when our first responses were anger, fear, and despair. Later this leader said it was hard to speak that part of the prayer; we sensed this as we heard her voice crack. Praying for our enemies, whoever they may be, refines and expands our capacity for prayer.

Whether we are praying for ourselves or for others, our prayers in public worship should not whine. When we pray, we should not seek to avoid responsibility for our thoughtless actions. Our prayers should not treat as a need what is merely inconvenient for us. Prayers should focus on situations that are important and on people whose physical or spiritual welfare is at risk. We should not pray for personal, congregational, or social change we are unwilling to undertake.[26] If our prayers tell the truth and speak of real need, then they will have integrity and be worthy of God's response.

We rarely sing prayers of intercession except in the most general terms, as in this verse by Albert Bayly:

> Still your children wander homeless,
> still the hungry cry for bread.
> Still the captives long for freedom,
> still in grief we mourn our dead.
> As you, Lord, in deep compassion,
> healed the sick and freed the soul,
> by your Spirit send your power
> to our world to make it whole.[27]

We may sing a refrain such as "O Lord, hear my prayer" or "Oyenos, mi Dios" in response to petitions or intercessions that are named.

> O Lord, hear my prayer.
> O Lord, hear my prayer.
> When I call, answer me.
> O Lord, hear my prayer.
> O Lord, hear my prayer.
> Come and listen to me.[28] (based on Ps 102:1–2)

Oyenos, mi Dios, oyenos, mi Dios,
Listen to your people. Oyenos, mi Dios.[29]

These examples point to an important feature of prayers of petition and intercession. Worshipers' petitions and intercessions need to be specific. We pray for particular people, particular situations, and particular needs. Our singing should open our minds and hearts to pray verbally with clarity and focus on what matters most.

There are times when we do not know how or what to pray—when situations or events are overwhelming, when all the available options for action seem deeply flawed, or when we are so numb with grief or in such turmoil that we cannot focus or quiet our spirits to pray. We find ourselves speechless with horror and sorrow before large-scale calamities: school shootings at Columbine, terrorist attacks on 9/11, the U.S. invasion of Iraq and its aftermath, genocide in Kosovo and Rwanda and Sudan. Sometimes music with words shaping timeless truths provides the needed opening for corporate prayer. Thomas Troeger's hymn "Through our fragmentary prayers" creates a space for the stuttering of our hearts to find voice.

Through our fragmentary prayers, and our silent, heart-hid sighs,
wordlessly the Spirit bears our profoundest needs and cries.

Deeper than the pulse's beat is the Spirit's speechless groan,
making human prayers complete through the prayer that is God's own.[30]

On the Sunday after the Indian Ocean earthquake and tsunami in December 2004, Belmont Mennonite Church, in Elkhart, Indiana, began their service with Troeger's words and Carol Doran's music. In the face of such devastation and loss of life, the song allowed the congregation to lay its care and empathy for the victims before God.

Since the Protestant Reformation, the pastoral prayer has gathered up the congregation's modes of praise, confession, thanksgiving, offering, petition, and intercession. Usually these prayers are long, and sometimes they are formal. Many pastors and worship leaders carefully prepare their prayers. To offer petitions that express the worshipers' needs, we must know the members of the congregation well. We listen deeply to the spirit of the congregation and the life of the community that surrounds it. When prepared with care, whether it is written out or not, this prayer can be an important means of pastoral care for the congregation, because it names our deeply felt needs and yearnings.

Some pastors and worship leaders do not fully understand the purpose of the pastoral prayer form. They pray whatever comes to mind, with little attention to the range of ways the congregation relates to God in prayer. Often one prayer mode (e.g., praising, confessing, or interceding) is skipped or skimped in a congregation's worship life. Worship leaders in one congregation routinely used the pastoral prayer to name intercessions and occasionally to offer thanksgiving. Because the pastoral prayer was the only time the congregation prayed in the service, the vitality of its prayer began to diminish. Pastors and worship leaders must continually evaluate our practice of pastoral prayers. If the congregation is not given opportunities throughout the service to praise, thank, and adore God, or to make confession of sins, then the pastoral prayer must include these modes of talking with God.

A public prayer's Amen rightfully belongs to the congregation. It voices our affirmation—So be it—for what our leaders have prayed. Instead, worship leaders or pastors sometimes say "Amen" as they conclude a prayer. More liturgical churches rarely make this error; their set texts maintain clarity about the roles of leader and congregation. African-American congregations keep the spirit of the Amen alive in their responses to preachers and testimonies. Recovering the congregation's Amen voice would deepen our prayer and testimony by giving clear expression to our solidarity with what our leaders have spoken on our behalf.

Blessing/sending: Confirming God's good wishes

In Isaiah 6:8, God asks, "Whom shall I send, and who will go for us?" Our response, like Isaiah's, should be, "Here am I, send me!" Our encounter with God through worship empowers us to serve God in our work, in acts of kindness and generosity, and in relationships with family, friends, and strangers. We leave worship prepared to be agents of God's purpose in the world. The action of sending can take two forms: blessing and commission.

Blessings, or benedictions, extend to all worshipers the hope of God's shalom, God's desire for our well-being, peace, and salvation. The keywords "May God . . ." mark the pattern of blessing.

May the Lord bless you and keep you.
May the Lord's face shine upon you.
May the light of the Lord's countenance shine upon you, and give
you peace.
(adapted from Num 6:24–26)

May the grace, mercy, and peace of God,
who is our creator, our redeemer, and our sanctifier,
carry us safely through all the days of our lives and beyond life.[31]

Traditionally worship leaders and preachers serving in their priestly roles have offered blessings to the congregation with arms outstretched. But we who are part of the priesthood of believers all have the authority to bless one another. We bless the world through our service and acts of compassion. The practice of passing the peace of Christ to one another is rooted in this impulse to offer blessing to one another. Giving and receiving blessing are powerful expressions of love.

Go, my children, with my blessing, never alone.
Waking, sleeping, I am with you, you are my own.
In my love's baptismal river, I have made you mine forever.
Go, my children, with my blessing, you are my own.[32]

Sometimes what is named as a benediction in church bulletins is instead a closing prayer. Rather than being an extension of God's empowerment to us, our closing prayers direct our desires for empowerment back to God. These prayers have an appropriate place as part of the sending action, but they are not an act of blessing. Our congregations and communities desperately need the lavish potential that the act of blessing—the extension of God's best wishes for reconciliation, peace, grace, and shalom—can unleash.

The Lord lift you up;
the Lord take your hand;
the Lord lead you forth,
and cause you to stand.
Secure in God's Word,
seeking God's face,
abounding in love,
abiding in grace.[33]

Words commissioning us for service in the world are also frequently misnamed benedictions. Blessings are offered to us as gifts. They describe something we can have. Commissions take the form of a command or exhortation. They identify something we are called to do. Commissioning is an appropriate sending action. It focuses the demands of the sermon or the theme of the day into specific action we take in our families or communities. Or these words can summarize a vision for ministry.

The action of sending should be strong, clear, and bold. Generally, our blessings and commissions should be spoken rather than sung. They need to be crafted for the specific ministries of the congregations and its members. Too often our services close with limp words that we receive with eyes closed and heads bowed, paltry fuel to convey us out to do God's work in the world with confidence. We should leave worship feeling empowered and directed for our priestly work in the world. Closing prayers, whether sung or spoken, are our response to the blessing or commission we have received.

Considering the meal

The basic worship actions we have examined are found in all styles and patterns of Christian worship, with the exception of silent Quaker meetings. It is possible to analyze the worship structure of a Roman Catholic mass, a contemporary praise and worship service, or a traditional evangelical service with these basic actions in mind. Some worship traditions place more emphasis on certain actions and practice others only occasionally. The actions of praise and thanksgiving have been under-represented in many Mennonite congregations in the last several decades. Some contemporary style worship services do not include confessions of sin. They frequently omit the "collection" and may or may not provide another opportunity for worshipers to offer themselves to God.

Many worship planners and leaders rely on a scriptural theme, image, or theological idea, frequently provided by the sermon, to hold a service together. A central theme or image is useful for planning, because it functions in a multivalent way and can be open to a number a possible meanings. It may offer worshipers an idea to contemplate, provide a point of integration, or give a sense of flow from one worship action to another. However, the theme is secondary to the pattern of actions, which gives the service direction and momentum.

Many of us have experienced worship services in which everything said or sung pointed to the theme in some way, but our responses of praise, thanksgiving, or offering were indistinct or confused.

Several common features of congregational worship are missing from the list of basic actions.

Singing is an activity of worship. As the examples above demonstrate, singing is an expressive medium that can accomplish specific worship actions if hymns and songs are selected mindfully. Nearly every worship planner agrees that the congregation should sing, but the idea that our song could aid the momentum of our worship is new to many. Too often congregational singing has been used to keep the congregation participating (as opposed to sitting and listening) or to give worshipers a brief exercise break, rather than as a medium for carrying out particular acts of worship.

The *musical prelude* serves an important role in gathering the congregation's energies. It may share in the action of gathering, but it is not a primary worship action. Neither is the *postlude,* though the energy released in the music can carry us out to serve in the world.

Special music can elaborate on the day's scripture text, making it part of the proclamation, or it may voice a prayer on the congregation's behalf. To have a "special" musical performance for its own sake is not warranted. Instrumental music should serve the movement of the worship; it is not an opportunity for the congregation's children to rehearse their recital pieces for the congregation's enjoyment. One congregation was subjected to a novice saxophonist's rendition of "Home on the Range" as the day's special music. Needless to say, the piece had no connection whatever with the rest of the service. Leaders who incorporate special music into their planning should have a clear sense of the worship action it serves.

The *children's story* or *children's sermon* will usually be part of the proclaiming action that brings God's Word to children, and to the child in all of us, in ways they and we can appropriate.

Silence is not one of the basic worship actions, yet it is increasingly important for worshipers whose lives are constantly on the move. Silence stops everything, so we can be still and know that God is God. Silence can also provide space for us to frame our particular personal prayers of confession, thanks, or petition, in the context of the congregation's prayers. It can give us opportunity to reflect on and respond to the day's proclamation, or to shape our testimony to God's work in our lives.

Announcements are important for congregational life but by no means essential to our worship. Often they add verbal or visual clutter. So where can they fit in the service? The first step is deciding what the purpose of announcements is: Giving information? Generating support and enthusiasm? Requesting discernment? Reporting outcomes of congregational projects? Not all announcements have the same purpose; not all of them are created equal. To the extent that worship leaders know the announcements in advance, they can link these words with an appropriate worship action. Reporting outcomes might become part of the congregation's thanksgiving or prayer of petition. Announcements requesting discernment can be incorporated into prayers of petition. Those generating support and enthusiasm could be part of the congregation's witness and testimony. Giving information might also link with the action of witness. Worship leaders and pastors do well to determine which of the announcements serve the congregation's worship of God and which are best communicated in other ways.

Announcements may be made as part of the congregation's gathering time, before the formal call to worship or gathering music. Some congregations find that they fit well just before the congregation's sending. Wherever the announcements are made, their location must be considered carefully and appropriate arrangements made for communicating them.

Ordering the meal: Developing worship orders

Worship planners and leaders order coherent patterns with these basic worship actions, in much the way that a skillful cook organizes courses of a large meal. A cook who recognizes the character of the salad course can place it at the beginning or end of a meal, with mindfulness of its relationship with other courses. A worship leader who knows the purpose of offering can place it as part of the congregation's praise, as a response to the proclamation, as an extension of the congregation's affirmation of faith or its testimony. Whether worship is reordered every week or follows a structure that is revised once a century, determining the courses of worship requires theological artistry akin to the culinary artistry of a good cook. Congregations and denominations often develop worship patterns that serve their particular theology and ethos.

Several combinations of worship actions emerge in natural and deeply satisfying ways. Praising and thanking naturally lead to offering. Affirmations of faith flow easily from praising or proclaiming. Prayers of petition and intercession reasonably follow affirmations of faith. Praising—adoring—confessing—testifying—thanking—offering is a chain of action often found in the Psalms.

The arrangement of the actions gives a shape to a worship event that is much like a dramatic form. A service may build to a particular high point, or it may have several high points. Arranging a series of actions under a broad general heading (for example, Hearing God's Word) helps worship leaders and worshipers alike feel the connections between actions. Sensing these interrelationships aids musicians and other worship leaders in making informed choices about congregational responses that help the actions of corporate worship flow more smoothly.

The following worship outlines from several Christian traditions demonstrate how the actions can be arranged. Keep in mind the essential communication dynamic in each action. No theme has been identified in any of these outlines, which makes it easier to see how the actions shape the service.

Basic outline (Marlene Kropf)

Gathering	Responding to the Word
Praising God	Affirming faith
Confessing and reconciling	Petition prayers
Offering ourselves and our gifts	Intercessory prayers
Hearing God's Word	Sending
Scripture reading	Commissioning
Sermon	Blessing

This basic outline by Marlene Kropf places hearing and responding to the Word at the center of the service. Gathering primarily addresses the congregation. Praising and confessing are distinct actions through which the congregation addresses God. Reconciling stands as God's action toward us in assuring pardon for our sins. Offering follows as a celebration of God's grace.

These various actions prepare the way for us to receive God's Word first in the form of scripture and then as interpreted through the sermon. The congregation responds to the Word preached with an affirmation of faith and then with prayers rooted in trust and loyalty. The sending action consists of a commission related to the sermon and a blessing of empowerment. The action of witnessing is not specifically placed in this outline. It could occur in conjunction with the actions of praise or offering, or after the affirmation of faith. Each of the actions could be elaborated on or extended as necessary.

Blended (Robert Webber)

Gathering	Sharing the Table
Praising, adoring	Offering
Confessing	Thanksgiving prayer
Hearing the Word	Sharing bread and cup
Scripture proclaimed	Sending to serve
Sermon	Blessing
Prayers	

Robert Webber, in *Planning Blended Worship*, identifies four broad types of action—gathering, hearing, sharing, sending—which are made up of several distinct actions.[34] Hearing the Word and Sharing the Table are at the center of this outline, reflecting the basic movements of worship in the Western church since the fourth century. Webber advocates a "blended" worship style that includes the traditional services of Word and Table of liturgical churches, and uses contemporary music and expressive arts (such as drama, visual art, dance).

Praising, adoring, and confessing are all addressed to God in the church's gathering. The scripture proclaimed and the sermon are God's Word to us; our prayers are shaped by what we have heard and are offered in confidence of God's response. The offerings of money, bread, wine, and self begin the preparation for communion. The prayer of thanks expresses gratitude for God's salvation and asks blessing for the bread and wine about to be shared. Members of the body breaking bread and sharing the cup together participate in communion with Christ.[35]

This outline ends with a blessing for service. Webber does not include a specific place for an affirmation of faith, which could be placed after the sermon, before the prayer. Testifying also does not have an identified place. This action could be more difficult to fit into the service, because it introduces a different congregational dynamic. However, witnessing could be part of the sermon or introduced after it, depending on the sermon theme; it might also be placed as a response to the sharing of bread and cup.

Contemporary (Judson Cornwall)

Outside the camp: Personal testimony
Through the gates: Thanksgiving
Into his courts: Praise
Inside the holy place: Adoration; Complete focus on God, Jesus, or Holy Spirit
In the Holy of Holies: Silence, individual prayers, singing in the Spirit
Scripture reading
Preaching
Dismissal

In *The New Worship*, Barry Liesch discusses two contemporary worship patterns: free-flowing praise, which follows a five-phase pattern developed by Eddie Espinosa and John Wimber, and journey into the Holy of Holies, developed by Judson Cornwall.[36] Both patterns maintain clear separation between an opening song service and the preaching that follows. The journey to the Holy of Holies uses the model of the Old Testament temple to order the worship actions. It relies heavily on Pentecostal and charismatic expressions of faith.

Music "outside the camp" draws us from the cares of the world and from our personal needs, moving us toward thanksgiving. Thanksgiving for God's gifts and blessings that we have experienced personally shifts us to praise and eventually into adoration of God. Here the songs often have a more intimate quality, which leads into personal prayer. In Pentecostal or charismatic congregations, this intimate prayer may include silence, singing in the Spirit, or speaking in tongues. This prayer time is frequently the high point of the entire service, not just the climax of the song service.

Proclamation consists of scripture texts and sermon. Closing prayers may include petitions and intercessions as well as specific prayers for healing. The corporate action of affirming faith is not specifically included but could be part of the song service. Witnessing/testifying may be incorporated as part of the service of prayer.

United Methodist basic pattern (without Holy Communion)	
Entrance	Confession, pardon, and
Gathering	peace
Greeting and hymn	Offering
Opening prayers and praise	Thanksgiving
Proclamation and response	Prayer of thanksgiving
Prayer for illumination	Lord's Prayer
Scripture	Sending forth
Sermon	Hymn/song and dismissal
Response to the Word	Blessing
Concerns and prayers	Going forth

The basic worship pattern among United Methodists has much in common with the Liturgy of the Word in Roman Catholic and Lutheran traditions. According to *The United Methodist Hymnal*, this pattern is provided as a guide for worship planners suggesting a variety of options for the congregation.[37]

Entrance rite. Gathering could include such activities as greeting one another, announcements, rehearsal of congregational music, informal prayer, singing, testimony, meditation, or musical prelude. Greeting in the Lord's name is offered by the worship leader, and is followed by a hymn, presumably a hymn of praise, although that is not specified. The opening prayer could be a collect,[38] a prayer of confession with words of pardon, or a litany such as "Lord, have mercy." If additional praise is desired, a setting of "Glory to God in the Highest" could be used, or a psalm, scripture song, anthem, or *Gloria Patri*.

Proclamation and response. The prayer for illumination takes the form of an invocation calling the blessing of the Holy Spirit on the reading, hearing, preaching, and doing of the Word. The order encourages reading two or three scripture texts, interspersed with sung responses and followed by the sermon. The response could take a variety of forms, including an invitation to discipleship, a hymn or song, incorporation of new members through baptism or membership transfer, or an affirmation of faith using one of the creeds. Joys and concerns may be expressed and then included in the prayer that follows. This prayer may take the form of a pastoral prayer or a litany of intercession and petition. Alternatively, the worship leader or members of the congregation may offer brief petitions, intercessions, and thanksgivings, and each may be followed by a spoken or sung response. If a prayer of confession and assurance of pardon was not included in the entrance rite, it may follow here, after which people offer one another a sign of reconciliation and love. The offering gathers monetary gifts or other gifts to be dedicated and is accompanied by vocal or instrumental music. This series of actions is clearly the central action or high point of the service. It reflects both the importance of hearing the Word and responding to what has been heard.

Thanksgiving. The prayer of thanksgiving is spoken over the offering and ends with everyone praying the Lord's Prayer.

Sending forth. The worship leader or preacher gives a blessing, and the congregation responds with a suitable hymn. The service may end with an instrumental postlude, momentary silence before the congregation disperses, or informal fellowship.

All the actions of worship described earlier in the chapter have a place in this outline, though testimony is only given as an option for the gathering. The period for joys and concerns could also include witnessing. This description also demonstrates the various ways worship actions can be accomplished: through spoken words, music, silence, formal prayer structures such as collects and litanies, or extemporaneous prayers. In most cases, a clear structure of actions can open a variety of possibilities for expressing them.

Placing the confession of sin after the sermon gives worship leaders the option of shaping this prayer as a response to scripture texts and sermon. The other outlines locate confession of sin prior to hearing the scriptures and sermon. Consider the implications of these placement choices. Putting prayers of confession early in the service may indicate that unacknowledged sin impedes our worship. And placing these prayers before the scripture texts and sermon suggests that unconfessed sin interferes with our ability to hear God's Word, that confessing our sins prepares us to listen as God's voice addresses us anew. Putting confession of sin after the sermon suggests that through hearing the Word we may be moved to repentance. Or this location for confession may imply that unacknowledged sin impedes our ability to receive or to do the Word we have heard. During Lent, preaching often focuses on confession and repentance, which makes confession after the sermon a logical choice.

Possibility #1

Gathering	Responding to the Word
Greeting	Affirming
Praising	Confessing/assurance
Witnessing/testifying	Offering
Adoring	Praying
Proclaiming	Thanking
Scripture reading(s)	Sending
Sermon	Blessing
	Commissioning

Worship planners in congregations that do not follow a prescribed worship order are often left with the responsibility of periodically organizing (or reorganizing) the worship order. A spirit of playfulness is invaluable in imagining different sequences of worship actions and considering the theological implications of each arrangement.

Possibility #1 uses four common categories of actions: gathering, proclaiming, responding, and sending. The action chain of gathering begins with a greeting that acknowledges the body that is present and moves into praising, a primary reason the body has gathered. Members of the congregation witness to God's presence in their lives, or to ways God has intervened in their behalf in difficult situations.

Adoration of God's nature and character, perhaps especially of God's steadfast love, follows the testimonies to God's tangible presence in our lives.

Proclaiming includes reading God's Word and interpretation of the Word through the sermon. This action focuses God's communication to the congregation, and the congregation's responsibility to be still and receive the message.

Responding to the Word opens with an affirmation of faith, a sign of our trust in God and our appropriation of the wisdom of the

Christian testimony over the centuries. With faith in God's unending love and mercy, we feel safe to confess our sin, shortcomings, and failures. The assurance of God's pardon frees us to offer ourselves more fully to do what God needs and wants from us. This offering includes our prayers of petition and intercession. Our final response is thanksgiving for God's Word to us, for God's mercy, for God's desires for us, and for God's steadfast love that allows us to entrust to God's care all that is troubling and destructive.

The sending blessing empowers us to abide in God's good will. We are then commissioned to work in the world to extend God's reign.

Possibility #2

Gathering in God's Power
  Gathering the Body
  Praising
  Adoring
  Affirming faith
  Offering
Hearing God's Word
  Proclaiming scripture

Proclaiming the sermon
Responding to God's Word
  Witnessing
  Confessing/assurance
  Praying
  Thanking
Sending on God's behalf
  Commissioning
  Blessing

This playful option again groups the basic actions into four categories, each with a specific relationship to God.

Gathering focuses the congregation's energies and attention for worship. Praise for what God has done and adoration of God clarify what the congregation has gathered to do. An affirmation of faith aligns our commitment and faith in God. We offer ourselves and our gifts to God whom we trust and adore.

We hear God's Word through the reading of scripture, preferably several texts, and the Word is interpreted in the sermon. The congregation receives God's Word in silence and then responds to it.

Witnessing immediately after the sermon allows us to confirm from our own experience the truth we have heard in God's proclaimed Word. Our confession acknowledges our failures and shortcomings in living up to God's purposes and desires. Prayers of petition and intercession gather up other needs that require God's attention and conclude with thanksgiving for God's enduring faithfulness and care.

Sending begins with a commission to live what we have heard and leads into a blessing of empowerment to carry out what we have been commissioned to do.

Seeing the whole meal

These outlines are painfully sparse; they don't seem particularly gracious or inviting. Yet, looking at the actions stripped of music, words, and gestures helps worship planners see the internal logic and movement of services we plan. Who is talking to whom in the action? What is the intent of the action? How do the actions fit together in a way that helps the congregation encounter God and engage our brothers and sisters? What could get in the way of receiving God's empowerment? These questions help us make choices that serve the basic communication needs each action requires.

Over time, the worship patterns of most congregations gather accretions. Special music pieces that have no clear worship purpose, long announcements, extended children's stories, or undisciplined sharing of joys and concerns add clutter. Sometimes the accumulation of these practices completely overshadows the congregation's fundamental actions of praise, offering, or confession. Many worship reforms in church history have been motivated by a simple desire to return to what is basic, to alter or eliminate practices that have become distorted or distracting, or that have acquired exaggerated importance. Isolating the fundamental worship actions—identifying the basics—clarifies what the congregation is doing in its communication with God.

Many faithful worshipers are unaware of how the organization of worship actions gives shape to the congregation's shared faith. We may experience worship as "one darn thing after another," with little sense of how actions relate to each other. Worship feels like an agenda, a list of things to get through before we can reassemble for coffee in the fellowship hall. Few people want to invest in an agenda. Dynamic worship has flow, energy, and momentum that an agenda rarely possesses. Worship leaders who are unclear about how each action communicates or about the overall purpose of worship cannot help us encounter God or engage one another. Planners must understand the basic action sequence of services they will lead, and choose words, songs, and gestures that will enable us to enter the action wholeheartedly, with confidence and anticipation.

Leading from one to the next, the courses of a satisfying meal stimulate conviviality, surprise, and pleasure among the diners. The courses announced by the cook are served with care. What we anticipate reaches fulfillment. Everything happens in its own time, with calm assurance. The meal progresses with ease, and we are filled with grace and gratitude. Worship that nurtures and nourishes the congregation's relationship with God requires the same attentive care to how the actions of worship are ordered and led.

5

PREPARING THE ENTRÉE

Jesus said to [Simon Peter], "Feed my sheep." (John 21:17)

In mainstream North American culture, the centerpiece of the meal is the entrée. Appetizers, soup, and salad are followed by the main dish, which may be accompanied by side dishes and followed by dessert and hot beverages.

The French word *entrée* means "entry," but the entrée is not the first course of a dinner. Rather, it is the entry into the menu. In planning the menu, the cook first decides on the entrée, and the rest of the meal then takes shape around it. If the main dish is to be Fettuccine Alfredo, perhaps the meal will start with a zesty antipasto platter of olives and artichokes, tomatoes and peppers, salamis and cheeses, which sets the stage for the subtle flavors of the creamy pasta entrée. Crusty Italian bread complements the pasta, and provides a way to soak up every last bit of rich sauce. The meal may conclude with moist, sweet tiramisu and a strong, dark espresso.

A standard restaurant bill of fare starts with appetizers, soups, and salads. Then comes the heart of the menu, the various entrées and their accompaniments, followed by desserts and after-dinner beverages. The entrées are listed in the middle of the printed menu, but most of us begin by making a choice from among them and then put together the other pieces in a way that complements that main-dish selection. The entrée is the center of the meal; the other parts of the menu are chosen to prepare for it and to follow from it.

At home we may eat haphazardly, grazing on one item and then another, as our fancy strikes us. But mealtime takes on a finer quality when we plan a menu and arrange the courses with the centerpiece—the entrée—clearly in mind. Even a simple breakfast can be served with care, with fresh-squeezed orange juice preparing the way for an entrée of oatmeal laced with plump raisins, drenched in warm milk and dusted with brown sugar, accompanied by a steaming mug of fair-trade coffee.

If Sunday worship is a metaphorical Sunday dinner, many Protestant groups regard the sermon as the entrée of this meal. Other denominations consider the Eucharist to be the entrée; still others see the entrée as including both the preached Word of the sermon and the reenacted Word of the table. In this chapter, our focus will be on the preached Word as the entrée.

The similarities between the proclamation course and the entrée are many. Although worship does not begin with preaching, the scripture text and the interpretation direction set by the sermon do constitute the point of entry for worship planning. The thought is laughable that we would plan worship by saying, "Let's begin at the beginning, by preparing a call to worship, and then we'll see what scripture reading and sermon would be fitting in light of it." Nor would we say, "Here is a beautiful benediction; let's work backward and see what kind of service we can put together that would lead nicely into it."

Among the parts of a worship service, the proclamation piece has a singular significance. In this part of our worship God speaks to the people. Singing, praying, confessing, and the other actions of worship are actions of the people. In the reading of scripture and the sermon, the action and initiative change, and God addresses us. When the Word is proclaimed, the Spirit of God speaks as we listen. For this reason, we need to give special consideration to this important action. In many respects, it is the heart of the matter.

Reading scripture

We often equate proclamation with preaching, but the first act of proclamation in worship is usually the reading of scripture. In some traditions, people are asked to stand for the reading of the Gospel. This act attests to and reminds us of the importance of this reading.

Every oral presentation of scripture is an interpretation of the text, and each public reading needs special care to communicate the intended meaning of the passage. If we begin to think of the scripture reading as an interpretation of a word from God, along with the sermon, our care for reading will intensify. Sometimes the proclamation of the scripture may be a dramatic reenactment, sometimes a group may offer a choral reading of the text, but always these presenters are undertaking an oral interpretation of the Word of God.

If we carry this intention with us, scripture reading will not be done casually or assigned at the last minute to whoever is handy.

Readers need training and practice. We would not think of asking someone who has never had a lesson to play the organ, yet sometimes we ask people to read scripture in worship without providing the preparation that could enable them to do so well.[1]

The following sequence for preparing a passage for reading in public worship will assist the reader as well as the other planners. First, we read the passage audibly several times. When we read silently, we slide sloppily over parts of the passage that are well known to us or that we don't understand. Reading aloud requires that we deal with every word. Effective readers take time to study the text, becoming familiar with the words and with the meaning of the passage.

Next, we talk with the preacher about the message of the text and the sermon. Because oral scripture reading, like preaching, is always an act of interpretation, preacher and reader need to agree on the focus of the passage for this worship service. If the reader and the preacher do not agree, it is the responsibility of the reader to defer to the message chosen by the preacher. Then, while the preacher continues to prepare the sermon, we look for ways to do an interpretive reading of the text that will aid listeners in hearing the intended message.

What is preaching?

The fact that there are many definitions for preaching presses us to address the question of what preaching is. Preacher and homiletics professor Erland Waltner taught a definition that is elegant in its simplicity: "Preaching occurs when a word from God intersects with human need."

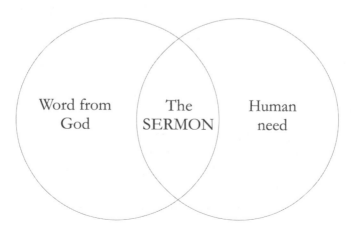

This simple definition includes basic components of preaching. "A word from God" tells us that through the Spirit and the Bible a message is given by God. "Intersects with human need" invites us to consider the ones who will hear the word and their particular needs. Implied in this definition is a preacher who receives a word from God and faithfully conveys that message to the point of the congregation's need.

As is immediately obvious, preacher and professor Deane A. Kemper's model is more complex.[2]

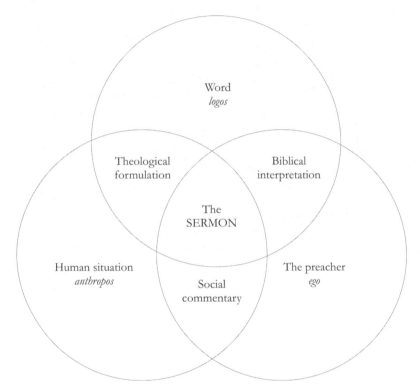

For Kemper, every sermon includes three major components: the word from God, which is communicated through the Bible and particularly through Jesus; the human situation, which includes the micro and macro contexts in which the listeners live; and the person and personality of the preacher. As these three circles of influence overlap, theological formulation, biblical interpretation, and sociological commentary result. The sermon is in the center, where all the parts intersect.

This model invites several observations. First, it is a model for the sermon, not for preaching. This model takes us from the larger circles to the center where the sermon lives. The sermon is important to preaching, of course, but the sermon is not preaching.

Second, we notice that the influence of the preacher on the sermon is as great as the influence of the Bible and the human context. Some preachers deny the extent of their influence on the sermon, while others overrate their role. The preacher's influence extends to the choice of text, how the text will be read, and how the text is interpreted. In addition, the preacher analyzes the congregation's needs and the interpretation of the world we live in. The preacher's personality and communication style also play significant roles. The influence of the preacher is substantial and not to be minimized. At the same time, the preacher's role is only one of three fundamental elements.

Third, Kemper's model expects balance among these three components. When one component takes over the majority of the influence, the outcome ceases to be a sermon. When the Word takes over, the sermon becomes a Bible study. When the human situation takes over, the sermon becomes a speech on a religious topic. When the preacher takes over, the sermon becomes a performance. Bible studies, speeches on religious topics, and performances are all legitimate, but they are not sermons.

My own definition includes aspects of these two definitions, with the addition of an *action* or *results* component: Preaching is the public-address form of ministry in which a word from God intersects with human need, and out of that meeting comes new life.

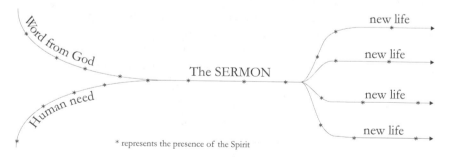

* represents the presence of the Spirit

To the influence of the Word, the human context, and the preacher, this definition adds a fourth dimension, the expectation of change.

The transforming power of the Holy Spirit is at work in the preacher, in the Word, and in the listeners as they hear and respond. No preacher begins to preach in the hope that everyone will be just the same after the sermon as they were before it. Preaching expects change. Through the Word, the analysis of the human context, the shaping of a message and its delivery—through all of this and into the ears and hearts of the listeners—the Holy Spirit participates in the preparation and delivery of the sermon.

So, what is preaching? Certainly no single definition can claim to be the correct one, but the question merits our consideration. How we answer it will shape our preaching in profound ways.

Sermon preparation styles

Considering a variety of meal preparation styles and dining events may help us describe and evaluate approaches to sermon preparation and sermon content.

Preparation styles	
Carryout food	Leftovers
Home cooked	Slow cooker

Carryout food. A carryout meal is prepared in a restaurant and picked up by the purchaser to take home and serve there. Carryout meals save time and energy. And frankly, some of us are not such good cooks. Deli carryout is often tastier and more interesting than what the cooking-challenged can prepare at home.

Some preaching might be called carryout. We can find prepared sermons ready to lift from the source and serve from our own pulpits. One preacher confessed that he devotes Thursday to finding a sermon. He does not use Thursday to work on a sermon, or to prepare a sermon, or to look for ideas to incorporate in his sermon; rather, he uses Thursday to *find* a sermon. His approach is carryout taken to the extreme.

If we understand a sermon to be the place where a word from God intersects with the needs of a particular people, then a diet of carryout is bound to be inadequate. In addition to including a full understanding of the biblical text, effective preaching incorporates the eyes and heart of the preacher and the eyes and heart of the congregation. A sermon prepared for someone else's congregation will not adequately nourish our own family of faith, however competently it has been prepared for delivery in another setting. The relationship between the scripture text, the preacher, and the congregation is so basic to effective preaching that a humble homemade sermon is superior to one too rich for the preacher or the congregation to digest.

At the same time, books, periodicals, and Internet resources can stimulate the preacher's thinking and may awaken ideas that can be effectively developed with our own congregation in mind. In a sense, these resources may serve as recipes which are consulted in our own sermon preparation.

Home-cooked meals. When asked to describe home cooking, people may begin to reminisce about Mom's meatloaf, Uncle Nate's matzo ball soup, Dad's barbeque, or Aunt Rosa's Christmas tamales. The common theme is food lovingly prepared for those who will share in eating it. Home-cooked food can be a vehicle for expressing love and care.

Roast beef with potatoes and carrots was the Sunday dinner menu when I was growing up. In my mind's eye, I see Dad peeling potatoes at the kitchen sink, his blue-and-white-striped apron protecting his Sunday-best clothes. Home cooking is intimate. When we gather at the table to eat it, we are fed in ways that go far beyond calories, proteins, fats, carbohydrates, vitamins, and minerals. An infant who is offered adequate nutrition may nevertheless lose weight—fail to thrive—because feeding happens in an environment devoid of such bonds of love and care.

The home-cooked sermon is also rooted firmly in love—for God, for the scripture, and for the congregation. Part of what enables people to thrive on our preaching is the care and attention that we invest in our preparations. When we maintain relationships of trust and affection, when we prepare our sermons with a loving mindfulness of the congregation's needs and concerns, people will listen with the confidence that something worthwhile awaits them and will move them God-ward. Like many meals, home-cooked sermons may be ordinary fare, nothing flashy, but they will nourish the spirits of the family of faith and help them grow strong in faith. The Spirit of God feeds people when they open themselves to God's loving care through the offices of the preacher who is a channel of that concern for their nurture and growth.

Leftovers. Leftover food has gotten a bad name, even though some dishes actually taste better the second time around. After a few days in the refrigerator, the flavors of last Tuesday's chili may be more subtly and satisfyingly blended. Yesterday's French bread may soak up the milk and eggs for tonight's bread pudding better than a fresh loaf would.

People love to sing old hymns and hear familiar Bible passages, yet congregations seem to expect a new sermon every week. But perhaps some sermons are worth preaching twice. When asked to state a purpose for the sermon, preachers will say the sermon is "to remind" the congregation of something. Some of the congregation may have heard the original message and then forgotten it. They may appreciate being reminded of a forgotten but important biblical truth. And others in the congregation are bound to have missed the message the first time it was preached, because they were absent or inattentive; they, too, may benefit from having it preached again.

That said, we preachers do need to watch out for practices that reflect simple laziness and lack of preparation. It is one thing to choose to preach again what needs to be heard again; it is something else to be "inspired" on Saturday night to dig a six-year-old sermon out of the file cabinet just because we have not done our work this week.

When Mom only takes time to cook on the weekend, her family will tire of eating Saturday's black bean soup all week. Sprinkling grated cheese on top for Tuesday supper does not fundamentally remake Sunday's chicken and rice casserole. For some preachers, despite a change in text, the sermon remains the same. It is always about the love of Jesus, or about sin and salvation, or about peace and reconciliation. When Sunday after Sunday our preaching returns to the same texts, the same themes, or the same messages, we are serving the congregation lazy leftovers. It's not enough just to add a new joke or illustration!

Slow-cooked meals. Some of the best food takes time to come into its own. A Crock-Pot stew may simmer for eight or ten hours, yielding moist, savory morsels of beef and vegetables. Marinating meat overnight tenderizes it, and the seasoning has an opportunity to permeate the whole roast. Bread dough rises for hours to produce just the right texture and yeasty aroma, and aging under the proper conditions enhances the flavors of fine cheeses and wines.

The making of a good sermon is a process of slow cooking. Preachers might consider time as a major ingredient in effective preaching. Microwave and stir-fry can be great for some kinds of creations, but they are not helpful images for sermon preparation.

Some preachers can prepare a sermon in eight to ten hours, but few create an effective sermon in less time than that. Sermon preparation—understanding the scripture text, reflecting on the needs of the congregation, and arriving at meaningful ways to apply the text to the lives of listeners—is a complex and time-consuming process. Some preachers routinely spend fifteen to twenty hours per week on preaching.

The best preachers usually do not do all their sermon preparation in one sitting. Preparation requires contemplation time and listening time. The words *simmer* and *marinate* are apt ones to describe the process. Some of the elements need to be put together in order for the process to begin, but then the ingredients are given time to do their work. A bread recipe may counsel the baker to "let the dough rest"; an interlude before loaf formation allows the gluten to relax and makes the dough more malleable.

Quality preaching begins long before the sermon is delivered. Preachers don't necessarily improve their preaching by memorizing their sermons, but we do improve our preaching by internalizing our sermons. If the message has worked its way deep into the heart of the preacher, that sermon will inspire listeners.

Perhaps we put off sermon preparation until Saturday night because we think we need a big block of time to prepare a sermon, and our days are crowded with commitments and our schedules frequently disrupted by pastoral care emergencies and other demands. Sermon preparation needs to be broken up into smaller tasks and spread out through the week(s), so one can get pastoral calls, committee work, and other administrative tasks done as well. But if one begins sermon preparation well in advance of Sunday, the marinating and simmering can be going on in the midst of other obligations. Like bread dough, the initially assembled ingredients can be resting, and when we resume work on the sermon, it can assume its ultimate shape with less effort or manipulation on our part.

Many preachers have discovered the value of devoting a few hours each day to sermon preparation. Some of us find that when we set aside time first thing in the morning, we are less likely to be interrupted. Others concentrate better late in the evening. Each of us must find the time that works best for us and then claim it for sermon preparation.

The old riddle asks, "How do you eat an elephant?" The answer is,

"One bite at a time!" Preachers get in trouble when we try to eat the whole elephant at one sitting. If we wait until Saturday night, we don't have enough time to chew on the text in light of the congregation's situation. We can divide sermon preparation into more manageable chunks by identifying tasks for each day. Doing each day's work relieves stress and allows us to move through the steps of sermon preparation in a way that leaves time and energy for other pastoral duties.

Recipe for preparing a sermon

What follows is an outline of the process of expository or exegetical sermon preparation. The intent is to analyze the steps, to foster awareness of all that needs to be done, and to remind ourselves to allow adequate time for what is yet to come. The fact that there are many steps may make this recipe seem unduly complex. But smaller tasks can fit into manageable blocks of time throughout the week and in the midst of other responsibilities.

A recipe for sermon preparation

Listening tasks
1. Draw near to God and listen to the Spirit.
2. Determine the text.
3. Discover the text's content.
4. Discern the congregation's needs with the Spirit's direction.
5. Develop a bridge between text and congregation.

Strategy tasks to design the sermon
6. Decide on a message.
7. Define the sermon purpose.
8. Discuss the text and ideas with others.
9. Decelerate—slow down and listen to God, text, and others.
10. Designate a sermon structure.
11. Draft a sermon.
12. Defer to the Holy Spirit.

Delivery tasks
13. Devote time to rehearsing.
14. Deliver with passion.
15. Demonstrate your gratitude.

Listening tasks

Listening is an essential task that occurs throughout the sermon preparation process, but it is particularly crucial in the beginning stages as the preacher seeks to discern what God is saying. The preacher becomes the listener and struggles to hear God, the text, the congregation, and the context. We are enabled to speak the Word by listening to God, to scripture, and to each other.

1. Draw near to God and listen to the Spirit

"Christians learn to speak the Word by hearing it, so a grateful listening is the habitual disposition that makes preaching possible," writes Stephen H. Webb.[3] According to Webb, "Karl Barth goes so far as to define preaching as 'the speech which obediently listens.' The preacher in a way is the church's chief listener. Barth expands this point by suggesting that the church should be understood as the 'listening church.'"[4]

Our discussion about communication in worship often focuses on the role of the preacher as the source and speaker of the message, and we forget that our role as receivers takes precedence. We must guard against presuming to work independently of the Spirit, and against an arrogant over-reliance on our own skills and creativity.

We do not have anything to say if we have not first heard something. We begin by listening intently to God. Our task is to put ourselves in the presence of God in prayer, in reading scripture, in solitude and meditation. Somehow we must find ways, appropriate to our time and place, to pay attention to God and to hear what God is saying to us. One of the most difficult things for preachers to learn is that preaching is not first of all about the preacher. It is first and foremost about God.

Turning to God at the outset of our preparation to preach displays our dependence on God; it is a sign of our trust in God's role in the preaching experience. The Holy Spirit is our collaborative partner in preaching. We are not soloists or competitors but partners.

In "Educating in the Spirit," Carol Lakey Hess writes about two ways of misunderstanding the relationship between Spirit and preacher. The first is the concept of "the Spirit of the gaps."[5] In this view, the preacher does whatever she can do, and then she relies on the Holy Spirit to fill in what is lacking. The Holy Spirit is the *x*-factor, that mysterious variable that accounts for what human efforts have not accomplished. In this relationship, whatever the preacher can do, the Holy Spirit does not need to do. The better the preacher is, the less frequently she calls on the Spirit and the less she asks the Spirit to do.

In this model, the preacher functions in the absence of a constant prayerful reliance on the Spirit, who waits at the margins. Lakey Hess uses the analogy of the relief pitcher who is called in to salvage the situation or seal the win only when the regular pitcher gets in trouble or wears out. Otherwise, the Spirit just sits on the bench in the bullpen and waits for the next crisis. Perhaps we envision God being especially busy on Saturday night—in the late innings when our own efforts fail and we start feeling frantic about tomorrow's sermon.

The opposite extreme is an equally problematic way of understanding how the Spirit works with us in the preaching process. In this view, the Holy Spirit is in charge of the whole sermon event, and the preacher takes no credit or blame for the sermon. The preacher is the one at the margins in this scenario.

This understanding of the Holy Spirit's work in preaching is familiar among the Amish. The ministers meet just before the service to decide who is going to preach that morning and what the text or emphasis will be. Under these circumstances, the preacher of the day must completely turn the event over to the Spirit for inspiration and a message, and he carries little immediate responsibility for the effectiveness of the sermon.

In contrast to these two approaches, preaching at its best is the work of both the human being and the Holy Spirit. It is a genuine partnership. The preacher collaborates with God. Thus, the first preaching task is to cultivate a healthy listening relationship with God.

2. Determine the text

Sometimes the step of determining the scripture text on which the sermon will be based is straightforward, because it is given by the lectionary or set by the worship committee. But often the task is not so simple. If the congregation or denomination follows a lectionary, preachers may still need to choose from among four (or more) passages. We decide which of these lections will be the sermon's primary text.

Sometimes lectionary readings are abridged from longer passages—parts of a larger narrative or prophecy, or selected verses of a psalm, for example. We should at least consult that context before deciding on the text, to ascertain how the piece selected relates to the larger whole.

But sometimes choosing a text involves focusing narrowly on a strong verse or phrase that conveys a needed message. In time of catastrophe, we may be drawn to preach from Isaiah 40:1—"Comfort, O comfort my people, says your God"—while setting aside the rest of the passage. Or we may use the phrase that recurs throughout the book of Deuteronomy, "Remember and do not forget," without preaching on any of the specific passages in which this phrase appears.

The point here is that the preacher must define precisely what the text for this particular sermon is. The boundary of the text for the purposes of the sermon must be clearly delineated. The selection may be a chapter, a pericope, a verse, a phrase, or a word. A system for deciding on the text can be a great advantage.[6] In the absence of such a guide, the preacher can waste valuable preparation time trying to select the text.

3. Discover the text's content

As we continue to be mindful of God's presence, we begin to spend time with the text that has been selected. Intimacy with the text is the goal. We may work from the original Greek or Hebrew, constructing a clause layout and making our own translation. We may consult other translations, versions, or paraphrases.

We read and reread the text. *Memorization* connotes a process that may seem rote and mechanical, but the expression *learning by heart* conveys a more organic process of taking the scripture into the core of our being. The desired outcome is to know these words so well and so thoroughly that we make them our own and they live in us. So we read the text often, out loud, and listen to it. Perhaps we write it out on a card and carry it with us. Or we inscribe it on a sticky note and post it on the bathroom mirror.

A two-stage approach helps us discover the content of the text. First, we notice things about the text, ask questions of the text, observe the customs and the rituals of the times, notice the feelings we have toward the text, and contemplate why this text has been included in the Bible. If it is a narrative, we reflect on whom we identify with in the story.

In *The Practice of Preaching,* Paul Scott Wilson outlines questions that preachers can address to a biblical text during this period of study.[7] His list is extensive and covers several pages. While we need not ask of each text every question he suggests, these questions can assist us in discovering what a passage holds.

After asking questions of the text, we are ready for the second stage of discovery: listening to the experts of the ages. Only now do we read commentaries and examine the history of the interpretation of this text. What have Bible scholars said about it? At this stage, we attend to knowledgeable voices of the past and present and collaborate with these authorities.

As listeners to the text, we want to know both about what is happening in it and also about what it means. Considering why this passage was included in the canon helps us begin to ask and answer important questions of meaning. Most texts have a variety of possible messages, which need to be identified.

At this stage, too, we identify theological ideas in the text. Most texts have several themes, and listing them can help us begin to clarify what the action of God is in this text. What is the face of God that is being portrayed? What is the major concern or movement of the text? The answers to these questions will aid us as we begin to formulate the message or central idea for the sermon.

Discovering the text's content is a vital stage in developing a sermon. This step is important, time consuming, and complex. If one is not careful, this stage in sermon preparation can devour huge amounts of time. We do well to confine this study to a fixed number of hours each week. To establish limits is not to say this step isn't important. It is only to say that other important tasks remain. Students who sit in theological libraries surrounded by books filled with interesting information and opinions can sometimes develop analysis paralysis, which may result in preaching our study notes. A sermon is not a book report. Rather, the purpose of studying the text is to enable its message to speak to the lives and hearts of our congregations.

4. Discern the congregation's needs

In order to move through the next step in sermon preparation, we must know the congregation.[8] Demographics, perspectives on life, theological preferences, and social circumstances of people in the congregation all play a role in shaping the sermon, but here we focus on the congregation's needs. If a sermon is defined as the intersection of a word from God and human need, the sermon will scratch where the congregation itches. The sermon will speak to something that listeners sense is amiss in their lives or something that is not right with the world.

Identifying the needs of the congregation is one of the preacher's tasks. Sometimes these needs are obvious. If a tornado has devastated your town, or if your congregation has experienced three deaths in the past week, it will be obvious to everyone what the needs are. People will come with their grief and turmoil in the forefront of their minds and hearts, and the preacher must speak to their pain. To overlook these obvious needs would be thoughtless and uncaring.

Sometimes the congregation is experiencing a need of which they are scarcely aware. Sometimes a particular problem has been identified, but the real need lies below the surface. The wise preacher will look deep for underlying fears and longings that should be spoken to.

Universal human needs must also be addressed in preaching from time to time. Guest preachers who do not know the congregation well often address universal human needs, needs that touch everyone at some time. The need to be loved, the need for security, the need to be forgiven—these are needs that everyone has. Effective preachers devote sermons to these big themes from time to time.

On any particular Sunday, the congregation will include people with a wide variety of concerns. Some are personal and cannot be appropriately addressed from the pulpit. Some will touch a portion of the congregation; others will be present throughout the congregation. An awareness of these needs will inform our preaching, even as we recognize that not every concern can be spoken to in every sermon. Part of what brings people to worship is the hope of finding solace for a wounded spirit, a balm to help heal what hurts. We dare not overlook this longing. It is our responsibility to be constantly aware of what is troubling the congregation and to evaluate what needs ought to be addressed in our preaching.

Some of what concerns people in the congregation will not be suitable fodder for our sermons. Some matters simply do not rise to a level of significance that merits giving them attention in the pulpit, and we should not trivialize our preaching by devoting time to issues that do not belong there. On the other hand, significant needs and concerns must be addressed in preaching, and addressed in a way that constitutes an authentic meeting of a word from God with human need. Through such sermons, the Spirit will draw people into deeper relationship with their creator, redeemer, sustainer.

5. Develop a bridge between text and congregation

In step three, we immerse ourselves in the scripture text, and in step four we are attentive to the congregation and their needs. Somehow these two worlds—the world of the text and the world of the congregation—must now come together.

The next task is to identify the relevance or application of the text for today. Preaching is sometimes defined as speaking an interpretation of the ancient text in light of the contemporary context. How can we bring together the long-ago-and-far-away and the here-and-now?

We want to understand how the messages or important ideas of the text will connect with the lives of the listeners. This is the place for a generous helping of congregation analysis. How will the listeners hear this ancient text? As we serve a congregation, each passing year increases our fund of knowledge about these people, yet every day new experiences shape how they hear. Coming to know the congregation is an ongoing responsibility.

Sometimes it helps to prepare two lists, one of possible messages that the text addresses and one of needs in the congregation. What most concretely connects the two lists? What messages seem most central, and which of the congregation's needs seem most urgent, or most widespread, or most neglected? In moving back and forth between the text and the congregation, the sermon begins to emerge. In this process, we pay particular attention to the nudging of the Spirit.

Strategy tasks

The next set of sermon preparation tasks are the steps of creating the sermon. In these steps we take what has been given to us in the listening time and piece together what will become the preached sermon.

6. Decide on a sermon message

One of the most significant problems in preaching is that often preachers try to do too many things in the same sermon. Texts contain a number of messages, and congregations need to hear a variety of messages, but a sermon can seldom do more than one thing well.

The task in this step is to decide on a message that can be written as a simple statement. Here we distill the essence of the sermon into a crisp, straightforward, declarative sentence.

Often we have an easier time identifying the sermon topic than clarifying the sermon message. If asked, we may say we plan to preach "about God's love." But the message might be "God loves you," or "God's love is a miracle," or "God's love is never-ending," or "God's love is greater than our sin" or "God's love sustains us in our loss." Any of these could be the message. But "God's love" is a sermon topic rather than a sermon message, and the statement "God's love is a miracle and it is unending" covers two messages, not one.

7. Define the sermon purpose

Defining the message quickly leads us to the discussion of the sermon purpose. In the above example, the preacher might want to *remind* us of God's love, or *convince* us of God's love, or even *inform* us of God's love. Sermon text and message and purpose are each extremely important, and they must line up with each other. So what is the sermon purpose? If the theme is what the sermon is about, and the message is what the sermon wants to say, then the sermon purpose is what the sermon intends to do. What does the preacher want to accomplish with this sermon?

Preaching assumes that listeners will somehow be changed. We do not preach so people can leave the service no different than when they entered. So the question is, How will these people be different after they have heard this sermon? The sermon purpose lays out what the sermon will do.

Preachers must decide on a single sermon purpose. How can one know what kind of sermon to create, if it is unclear what the sermon is to do? The sermon purpose focuses on results. The preacher contemplates the text and the message and decides how the congregation will be changed. What are the results that I seek? The sermon is designed to accomplish that mission.

Many preachers find it difficult to make a commitment about what the sermon is to do. They want to leave the results to God. The desire to allow the Spirit to accomplish whatever is right and good seems reason enough to refuse to identify a sermon purpose. But do not fear for the Holy Spirit! People often thank us for preaching words we did not say. God will provide a message for those who need a particular message. The point is that we will have trouble knowing what to put into the sermon and what to leave out if we do not know what the sermon is meant to accomplish.

For example, one preacher has decided that the scripture text is about stewardship and so is trying to decide what the sermon purpose might be. If the preacher wants *to teach* the congregation about stewardship, then he must assess what they currently know and give them good biblical instruction that will help them know more. If the preacher wants *to invite* the congregation to participate in the joy of giving, a mark of the life of faith, then the sermon will have a different form and content. If the preacher wants *to urge* the congregation to give in a way they are not now giving, for the sake of the congregation's survival and mission, then the sermon will have another form and content. If the preacher wants *to insist*—we can just see the blood vessels standing out in his neck—that people tithe in order to be part of the congregation, then the sermon will have yet another form and content.

Purpose is basic to deciding what goes into the sermon and what does not. A sermon without a purpose lacks direction and often ends up going nowhere and accomplishing nothing. If we who are preaching don't know what the sermon is to accomplish, how do we expect listeners to figure it out? Far too often, people come away from a sermon with no clue what it was about. And even if they know what the topic was, they may not know what they are to do in response. Every preacher needs to ask every time she preaches, "What do I want to accomplish with this sermon?"

In order to identify a useful sermon purpose for a particular sermon, the preacher revisits the work that has just been finished:

- •We recall that the study of the text is the primary base from which the purpose is developed.

- •We remember what our analysis of the congregation has shown us. Keeping a church directory open nearby makes it easier to develop the sermon purpose for these particular people rather than for some imagined or idealized congregation.

- •We reflect on the particular needs of this congregation in light of the messages of the text; this exercise helps us identify an appropriate sermon purpose.

•We establish a purpose narrow enough to manage thoroughly in the space of one sermon, but big enough to matter. We can expect to move people only so far with one sermon, so we must have realistic expectations. Equally difficult and equally important, we set a topic big enough to have theological significance.

We sometimes find it challenging to define the scope of what we expect from a sermon. We may expect too much; alternatively, we may expect too little. A sermon can be transforming on a cognitive level, moving us somewhere on the continuum from ignorance to comprehension. Or a sermon can move us along the affective spectrum, from lack of awareness to affirmation. On the volitional continuum, we may move from resistance to desiring. Seldom can one sermon move us on all three scales.

Of course, a twenty-minute sermon can only take people so far. Generally speaking, the less time we have, the less we can accomplish. Congregations that expect a ten-minute homily ought to consider the implications for their nourishment of such small servings. On the other hand, the dictum that "No souls are saved after the first twenty minutes" reminds us that we can also lose impact by going on too long.

Another problem for preachers is the temptation to define the purpose too broadly. Beware of any statement of sermon purpose that comes in the form of a compound sentence! Take this statement of intent: "to inform and convict the congregation about sin in their lives." We may indeed want to inform and convict, but if we are pushed to name just one purpose, we usually discover that one part serves the other. The sermon purpose likely should read: "to convict the congregation regarding sin in their lives." Information becomes one of the ways we accomplish that central purpose. Informing is not the purpose; it is a strategy for attaining the purpose of convicting.

A third common problem is that bland verbs issue in vapid sermons. The sermon purpose serves as the spine of the sermon, and the verbs we choose can lend color, focus, energy, and clarity to the statement of purpose. "To talk about prayer" is an insipid goal, compared to "to compel people to their knees." A strong verb can set the tone for the entire sermon. Because preaching portrays an action, the effective preacher employs vigorous verbs.

After we have determined text, theme, and message, drafting a good statement of sermon purpose sharpens the focus of our sermon preparation. Then we work toward making everything in the sermon support the message and the purpose.

8. Discuss the text and ideas with others

Preaching is a multifaceted partnership. The preacher collaborates with the Spirit of God, to be sure, and also with scripture and with scholars and experts. But an often overlooked partnership is with the congregation. Two recent books address the collaborative relationship between the preacher and the congregation. These books describe a homiletics of inclusion.

Lucy Atkinson Rose, in *Sharing the Word: Preaching in the Roundtable Church,* invites preachers to conversational preaching that grows out of connections among the worshipers.[9] Her collaboration incorporates those marginalized by the usual isolated, individualistic process of sermon preparation. Her nonhierarchical roundtable includes everyone equally, and it fosters mutuality. Meaning is found through conversation among the participants. Although the preacher continues to preach with a solo voice in public address form, she gathers what she preaches from the roundtable church conversation. The sermon is designed to stimulate conversation in the congregation and in the world.

John McClure's *The Roundtable Pulpit* describes a similar desired outcome, with more structure.[10] Again, the goal is to move from a leader-centered style of sermon preparation to a style that is inclusive and dialogical. McClure advocates discussion with members of the congregation around the sermon texts, the needs of the congregation, and the experiences and insights of the group. Out of that conversation comes the raw material for the sermon.

The six to ten members who make up the group commit themselves to the process for an agreed-on period; when one leaves the group, someone new joins the roundtable. This plan provides a systematic way to hear the voices of all members of the congregation. Everyone is empowered to contribute, and all are taken seriously.

Another benefit of this collaborative process is that pastors come to know members of the congregation more deeply. As people share from their reading of the text in light of their faith and their experience, good illustrations and other sermon material emerge. This process also helps the congregation understand the preaching task, and it enhances their abilities as listeners.

Collaboration between preacher and congregation is vitally

important. In these models, leader and ordinary readers become partners in hearing God's voice in the text and interpreting that text for the congregation. Imagine how attentively people listen to these sermons, knowing that the message has been discerned collaboratively by a roundtable that includes the preacher and members of the congregation.[11]

On Monday afternoons, I meet with Our Ladies of Perpetual Reflection to discuss the lectionary texts for the coming Sunday. In this small circle of friends, our engagement with and understanding of the Word is expanded and enriched. As we see the scripture through one another's eyes, the limits of our individual perspectives give way to a larger vision. We preachers need to stop doing everything alone and begin to talk with others about what we are working on and thinking about. We need to create structures like those McClure mentions.

9. Decelerate—slow down, listen to God, text, and others; then revise

No matter how busy we are, no matter how behind we may be in our sermon preparation process, we must resist the temptation to ignore this step. How often does someone at your house or office toss a bag of Orville Redenbacher's in the microwave, hastily punch the buttons, and dash on to the next chore, without pausing to listen as the popping of the kernels slows, signaling that the snack is ready? The aroma of burnt popcorn reminds us of the risks of rushing headlong through our chores. Sometimes our impatience to move things along backfires for cooks and preachers.

Step nine is a speed bump that we may be tempted to go over too fast. This step reminds us to take time to listen again for what the Spirit is saying. Take a walk. Go for a bike ride. Play the piano. Bake bread. Do whatever allows our mind and spirit to attend to God's Spirit.

10. Designate a sermon structure

A hard thing for some preachers to understand is the benefit of a clear and stable sermon structure. If the congregation is to be able to follow the message, the contents must be carefully organized. A coherent form makes it possible for listeners to track the preacher's words. Without organization, the congregation does not know how to listen or what to listen for.

Some preachers assemble a grab bag of interesting ideas that leaves listeners reeling. As the ideas emerge helter-skelter, listeners wonder, how are these thoughts connected? Around what purpose do they cohere? Even a potluck dinner has some organization! Plates, utensils, and napkins come first, followed by hot dishes, salads, and bread, with desserts at the end, and drinks off to the side. A modicum of structure allows the people proceeding down the line to assemble the pieces of a complete meal.

We might conceive of the organizational structure or outline as a skeleton. In one of Gary Larson's Far Side cartoons, a Boneless Chicken Ranch is populated with a surreal assortment of floppy chickens, shapeless blobs, scarcely recognizable except for their feet, combs, and beaks. Without bones, one mammal could hardly be distinguished from another; one pile of fur would look much like the next. And we have only to consider the effects of broken bones to realize how essential structure is to good function. So it is with the sermon. We must provide a clear structure so our listeners can follow, so the sermon can accomplish its intended purpose.

Although some structure is essential, no one kind of organization works best for every sermon. The particular structure or outline selected is the plan for presenting the contents and message of the sermon. Certain structures lend themselves to certain kinds of sermons.

Structures order the contents of the sermon, and they guide the movement through the sermon. In *Patterns of Preaching,* Ronald J. Allen catalogs structures that organize the sermon contents in a variety of ways.[12] These structures clarify how sections of the content relate to one another and help both the preacher and the listener know what ideas are central and what parts provide support.

The following catalog is not exhaustive but is an illustrative sampling of possible structures for organizing the contents of the sermon.

Sermons containing points. This old form has sometimes been dubbed "three points and a poem." The structure, which might consist of two to five points, identifies several key ideas about which the preacher wants to converse with the congregation. The ideas are laid out in a plain, direct, propositional way. Sometimes artful alliteration gives the points punch and makes them memorable, although its ill-conceived and injudicious use can present problems! The sermon ends with a word of application or a conclusion (the poem).

The sermon that is shaped by points holds potential for variety as well. The number of points is one variation, but there are others. The points could be sequential, like the rungs of a ladder: one negotiates the first rung before proceeding to the second and then the third. Or the points may be random and interchangeable, like pegs on a board. The order of the points is not important; what is essential is their relationship to the board.

As sermons get shorter, a preference for the one-point sermon has been emerging in North American churches. In this sermon, the preacher addresses one clear point from several angles. The point remains constant throughout, but the perspective changes. A sermon on the story of the forgiving father, for example, may deal with the theme of forgiveness from the point of view of the father, the older son, the younger son, and the hired hand. Some experts on homiletics suggest that a well-conceived one-point sermon is the form best suited to the attention span and expectations of congregations of our time and place.

Verse-by-verse. Verse-by-verse exposition is an ancient sermon form. The units may be verses or thought units such as sentences, phrases, or words. The writings of Origen (185–253 C.E.) and the Dead Sea Scrolls contain examples of this form. John Calvin preached in this style. The focus here is on exegesis and the hermeneutical connections between the verses. Sermons using this form sometimes conclude with more sustained theological reflection. Ron Allen's book *Preaching Verse by Verse* explores new ways to use this old form.[13] This organizational approach has strong teaching overtones, and sermons using it may feel much like Bible study.

Thesis–antithesis–synthesis. The thesis-antithesis-synthesis approach to organizing material draws on the philosophy of Hegel, whose dialectic describes his understanding of the contradictions in existence and history, which then lead to their resolution. A thesis gives rise to its reaction, an antithesis, which contradicts or negates the thesis, and the tension between the two is then resolved by means of a synthesis. Using this framework, the preacher presents an interpretation of an aspect of God or the Bible or the world. Then the antithesis exposes the limitations or inadequacy of the thesis. The synthesis mediates the two, often in a way that transcends both.

Journey to celebration. The journey to celebration is an old form, which preserves patterns from African religious traditions. The sermon moves from one block of material to another, but the last block is celebration of what God has done or is doing. This celebration section is designed to empower the community: although the journey through the wilderness may have been hard, arriving in the Promised Land brings great joy. Henry Mitchell's book *Celebration and Experience in Preaching* provides an important description of this form.[14]

Theological quadrilateral. This structure begins with a brief introduction, followed by the four parts of the quadrilateral. The first part examines *scripture* to see what it says about the theme and the message. The second part studies *tradition* to uncover how the church throughout history has addressed the subject at hand. Part three relies on *reason* to explore how the text and the tradition might elucidate the theological meaning of the subject. The conclusion, devoted to *experience,* considers the application to our lives. A sermon in this form gives attention to each of the four aspects, to a greater or lesser degree depending on the text and theme. Note that this organizational form involves much of the work of good sermon preparation, but in the quadrilateral approach more of this groundwork is presented as part of the sermon.

Narrative. Because about 80 percent of the Bible is story, a narrative form is particularly effective for preaching on many texts. In *The Homiletical Plot,* Eugene Lowry presents a five-stage design—drawing on short-story form—that is especially useful for narrative preaching.[15] It begins with *upsetting the equilibrium.* A great way to claim the congregation's attention is with conflict: this form begins by creating dissonance for the listeners as it introduces the subject of the sermon. Part two moves on to *analyzing the discrepancy.* The issues that were presented in stage one are unpacked and evaluated: the plot thickens. Then the preacher introduces a *clue to resolution.* Listeners are given a hint of the good news to follow. It is just a hint, but the story begins to turn the corner. The fourth element, *experiencing the gospel,* presents the good news in light of the problems that were part of step two. Faithful preaching interprets the gospel as it bears on the problems we face. In the sermon's conclusion, *anticipating the consequences,* the preacher describes the future in light of the good news that is brought to the dilemma. This step is the application, by another name.

Many Bible stories follow this form, so the translation from scripture text to sermon unfolds easily. Another strength of this shape is its inclusion of both problem and good news in one sermon. Some of us are inclined to preach that "Christ is the answer" without having clarified what the question is. This form requires delving into the question before an answer can be introduced. Other preachers are inclined to preach the evils of our times and the sins in our lives without articulating the good news of the gospel of Jesus Christ. Because this form demands both problem and solution, both question and answer, it is a balanced approach.

Persuasion organization. A good sermon has a clearly conceived purpose. Effective preaching intends to move listeners in the desired direction, to bring change to the congregation. A familiar and well-established form for persuasive speech is the Monroe Motivated Sequence.[16] Like Lowry's *Homiletical Plot,* it has five steps. The first is *getting attention.* To persuade people of anything, we must begin by getting their attention. The second task is to identify a *need.* What is the problem, and why is it significant? When the need has been carefully laid out, the listener will be eager to hear a *solution.* The speaker's responsibility will be to put forward a solution that listeners will find believable. The next step invites *visualization.* If the solution is applied to the need, how will life be different? In this step, the preacher helps us anticipate the new life that results from applying the solution to the need. Finally, the preacher introduces the *action* the congregation will undertake in order to make this new life a reality.

This form is particularly useful in evangelistic preaching.[17] But we can profitably turn to this method of organization whenever we desire to motivate significant change in the hearts and minds of the listeners.

Selecting an appropriate sermon structure is critical to achieving the sermon purpose. Too many sermons are structured around the string-of-beads concept. All the points are equally important, and we go around and around and never really arrive at the end. Sermons benefit from having a clear beginning and moving toward a clear conclusion. Such clarity in structure enables listeners to stay attuned and to follow our progression through the points to a satisfying ending.

11. Draft a sermon

Finally we have arrived at the step that most preachers think of as sermon preparation. Yet we are on step eleven of our recipe. Much has already been accomplished. At this stage, we begin to put words, ideas, and illustrations together. Here the major images begin to come into focus in a meaningful way. If the sermon structure is clear, the message is clear, the needs of the congregation are clear, and the purpose of the sermon is clear, the work of actually cooking the sermonic dinner will not loom large or be traumatic.

Let's review here, using an example.

> *Text: 1 Kings 17:8–16, the story of the widow of Zarephath.* This story comes near the beginning of a long section of 1 and 2 Kings, focusing on the prophets Elijah and Elisha. We have to consider the verses before and after before deciding on the boundaries of the text, which is a coherent if not complete narrative unit.
>
> *Need: People in our church have many worries.* We worry—far too much, about too many things, including safety, money, business, work, relationships, family members, the state of the world. This passage could lend itself to a sermon on another topic that would connect with people's lives, but we choose worry partly because it is so pervasive, and because individual listeners can go in different directions with it and consider it in terms of specific things that preoccupy them. Compelling illustrations can be drawn from those specifics. Note: ask others what they worry about.
>
> *Message: God provides for our needs.* If the congregation were to believe that message—were to trust that, no matter what, God cares for them—life would be different and they would worry less.
>
> *Purpose. To emblazon on our hearts the reality of God's providence.*

We ask what the sermon needs to say in order to bring the congregation from a life steeped in worry to the conviction that God will take care of them, will see them through any troubles they face. The structure will help us frame an approach, and the language and images of the text suggest possibilities for preaching. Maybe we will demonstrate the fickleness of all that we are tempted to put our trust in, or maybe we will offer a recital of the faithfulness of God, or maybe both. In any case, the sermon design will connect the ancient story with the stories of our lives, our experience with the experience of the widow.

Using the structure we have chosen, we begin to fill in the outline. Granted, the draft at this stage may be pitifully rough, but it is a beginning. The task is to move through the sermon. If the emerging sermon seems pedestrian, we remember that at this stage we are just beginning to walk through it!

When we have sketched an initial draft, we can begin the important work of refining and filling in. This step begins with checking for coherence and developing or smoothing transitions. Does the manuscript as it stands take the listening congregation where they are supposed to go? Do the transitions make it easy for everyone to follow? We review the structure to make sure the rough draft represents the plan for moving the congregation. Transitions are pivotal if listeners are to follow the sermon easily and move reliably from point to point.

Now we begin the polishing that makes a pedestrian sermon begin to dance. We search for action verbs and concrete and colorful language that will capture the interest and imagination of listeners. We consider images and words that are familiar to the listeners. We listen for language that carries not only the approximate meaning but the precise nuance that we desire.

Next, we add to the sermon illustrations that will appeal to people's senses, illustrations they will find moving. Effective illustrations create a concrete image for an abstract idea or bring clarity to the message, helping listeners see or feel the point or imagine themselves in the situation. The task of the illustration is to help communicate the message, to aid the congregation in taking in our meaning, to make that meaning tangible and memorable. A wonderful illustration that is not on target is a distraction. That one we file away for use when the right message comes along. And we always begin with the message and then look for apt illustrations. An approach that starts with engaging story and then creates a sermon to go with it gets the cart before the horse.

The introduction must capture listeners' attention, connecting with where they are and setting up where the sermon will take them next. But again, an interesting or amusing introduction that does not set up the rest of the sermon is not an apt opening. Getting the congregation's attention is necessary but not sufficient. The introduction must also deliver the listeners to the site of the sermon and its message. Often the introduction is best written last, when we have greatest clarity about where the sermon is going.

The reverse may be true for the conclusion. It starts with the end of the sermon body and delivers to the congregation the final word: what we want people to remember or the action we hope they will take. Often these words are a combination of the message and the sermon purpose. If the conclusion is the destination of the sermon, it may well be the first thing written. Then the sermon is developed in a way that helps the congregation arrive at that point. When we are traveling, usually we know where we are starting from and where we are going. We may get from point A to point B by a variety of routes, but we are clear about where we are going. Composing a sermon by beginning with the conclusion assures us that the proclamation will end decisively rather than just peter out.

In the composition phase, the final thing the preacher needs to do is go back and read the sermon from beginning to end for clarity and ease of flow. A strategy that starts with drafting the conclusion, then develops the body of the message, and ends by affixing an introduction sometimes leaves some bumpy spots. We sand down the rough places and check again for clarity. Will the listeners hear what we intend?

One of the most difficult parts of the sermon preparation process is knowing when to stop. Time may run out or other duties overtake us, and in any case, at some point we must give the preparation over to the Holy Spirit, who has been our coauthor all along.

12. Defer to the Holy Spirit

When we have finished drafting the sermon manuscript, we again take time to listen intentionally to what the Holy Spirit is saying to us regarding the sermon. In each major stage of sermon preparation, we need to take time to stop and engage the Spirit. Of course, the Holy Spirit is an ongoing partner in every step of the preaching task, but designating a distinct step for encounter with the Spirit reminds us of our reliance on this dynamic and creative relationship. The temptation is great to push on to do the next task, but stopping just to be in God's presence and reflect again on what God wants to do with this sermon is an essential part of good preparation. Holding our work-to-date lightly, we prayerfully check back to see that the chosen message and purpose, the congregational need we have identified, and the structure selected still seem right. We can rest assured that collaboration with the Holy Spirit will bring us comfort and energy. God will provide for our needs!

Delivery tasks

Preaching is an oral event and an event in time. Public address is part content and part presentation. A written text communicates in a way quite different from the proclamation that happens on Sunday morning. A sermon is not finished until the spoken word has left the mouth of the preacher in the presence of the congregation. It is not completed until the ideas have at last ceased to resonate in the minds and hearts of the listeners. Even then, it is not over and done with. For these reasons, we give great care to how we will deliver the sermon.

13. Devote time to rehearsing

Some of us breathe a sigh of relief when the words of the sermon have been crafted, thinking our preparation for Sunday's service is complete. But after giving careful attention to planning and preparation of Sunday dinner, the cook still has work to do. How will the table be laid? With what tablecloth, napkins, dishes, glassware, and tableware? Will there be candles or flowers? And how will the meal be served to the guests? Buffet or family style? In how many courses? What serving dishes would be appropriate? So, too, important tasks still await the preacher before the sermon is ready to present to the congregation. If the sermon is written by Thursday, we have Friday and Saturday to internalize the message and prepare for delivering it.

Effective communication involves not only careful preparation of a text but delivery of the message in a way that will most effectively enable listeners to hear and understand.[18] Our hope as preachers is that those who listen will receive a message that is as close as possible to our intended one. Although we cannot control all the factors that affect transmission of the message, our concern is to attend to as many as possible.

Rehearsing the sermon is vital to its successful delivery.[19] I am assuming the preacher has produced a manuscript in the previous steps and is now seeking to become familiar with the text, in order to deliver the words effectively. Is it better to preach from that manuscript or to distill it in notes or as an outline? The power of the communication lies in speaking directly with the congregation. To converse eye-to-eye will communicate best. In so doing, we address these words from the core of our being to the very souls of the congregation.

Rehearsing is the process of getting the message from the manuscript into our heart so it can be delivered with passion to the congregation. Rehearsing well will entail a generous amount of time; the process cannot be rushed.

First, we read the manuscript aloud so we can hear the sermon in our ears. We attend to the cadence of the sentences and the choice of words. We saturate ourselves with the text by reading it aloud in the worship space where we will preach. We read it aloud as often as we need to (three to ten times) until we begin to feel that we know it.

Second, we look again at the structure around which the sermon is organized. If we cannot isolate the structure, we back up a few steps and prepare a structure that works for this sermon. Then we learn the structure. We commit that structure—those three points or five points or that single point—to memory. We identify the illustrations and other supports we have put in place to make those points.

Third, we memorize the opening sentences, the supporting points, and the concluding words. Strong eye contact with the congregation is essential to effective preaching. If the opening words are presented verbatim from the heart rather than from the paper, the sermon will start with strength. We will also deliver the concluding words directly to the congregation. Weak conclusions that seem to dribble off the edge of the pulpit do not stay with our listeners. By now we also know the structure of the sermon. The preacher who is this well rehearsed could give the sermon to anyone on the street corner or in the grocery checkout line. It has become part of us.

There is only one more step to rehearsing: making notes from the rehearsal manuscript to jog the memory along the way. We write down key points, phrases that will remind us of illustrations, and phrases we want to present verbatim. These notes will go with us into the pulpit.

A confident and experienced preacher may well be ready to go into the pulpit with just notes. That preacher is able to look directly at the congregation throughout the sermon, speaking as person to person. Preachers who want to enhance communication with the congregation will conquer their hesitations and push themselves to move in this direction.

An exception to the practice of preaching from notes is the controversial sermon. Although we will give the same generous attention to rehearsing this sermon, staying close to the manuscript will assure that we speak exactly what we have so carefully scripted. All week long, we will give serious, prayerful time to study, analysis, and preparation for this sermon, and to reviewing it. This kind of sermon definitely requires a slow-cooker process.

14. Deliver with passion

By this time, the preacher may be tired of the sermon. We have spent so many hours with the ideas and illustrations that it may feel distinctly unexciting. This response is entirely normal. What we want to remember now is the excitement that we felt about the sermon idea when we first began to work with it. Our task is to reclaim that initial enthusiasm. But if the bored feeling arrives early in the preparation process and does not depart, it may signify that the sermon is in fact dull. In that event, we will check it with listeners whom we can trust to give honest response, to speak truth to us in love!

Many of the things we do in delivering a sermon are actions. We stand up and raise our voice and pronounce the words. But what we always remember is that preaching is first about God, then about the listeners, and only last about us. Much of the work we as preachers do in rehearsing is aimed at preparing so thoroughly that the focus will be on God and the listeners and not on us.

Beginning preachers are often most concerned about themselves. Will I do a good job? What will the congregation think about me? Does my hair look okay? Will they be able to tell that I am nervous? "It's not about you!" could well be posted on many a pulpit to remind us that our best work will get us out of the way.

More experienced preachers are often concerned about content. Is my theology correct? Will they get my joke? Are these ideas too complicated for the congregation to engage with? These people want to read their manuscripts to be sure that everything is exactly right.

Still more seasoned preachers are concerned about the congregation. Are they hearing what I am trying to say? Are their needs being addressed? Why are some sleeping? Or weeping?

The most effective preachers are ultimately concerned about God. Am I being faithful to the text and to God? Is God being glorified and honored? Will people come to know God better through this sermon?

The most effective proclamation of the Word is used by the Spirit to draw the congregation into encounter with God. It is to that end that we humbly and prayerfully devote our time and skill and practice.

If we sense that the message is important, we will bring an urgency to our preaching that will captivate our listeners. If we feel the message is unimportant, we have no reason to preach it. We must listen to our hearts. Is there passion or intensity or urgency about this word? Does it matter if people hear this message? Are the people who are absent missing anything? We are called to preach as if our souls depended on it. We are called to preach out of such love for these people that we would not have them miss this word that God has given us.

15. Demonstrate your gratitude

When we have finished preaching the sermon, it is time to express gratitude to God for the many ways the Spirit has accompanied and led us in preparing and bringing this word to the congregation. Because we have been listening to God, because we have been trusting and depending on God, because we believe that the Spirit of God is communicating with the listeners, the appropriate response is gratitude to God. We offer our gratitude for God's work in the preaching event; we give thanks for the privilege of being called to preach; we bring our gratefulness for the ways the Word is working in the lives and hearts of the listeners. It is not about us! Thanks be to God!

Topical sermons as preparation variation

The recipe above begins with a Bible passage and progresses to a delivered sermon. Not all sermons start with a biblical text. Theological themes (Christology, atonement, eschatology), ethical issues (marriage and sexuality, care for the environment, domestic abuse), church practices (women in leadership, baptism, congregational discernment)—these and many more issues are important, and the topical sermon can be a helpful way of speaking to them.

In *Preaching the Topical Sermon*, Ronald Allen observes that "the topical sermon is a vitamin supplement to the nourishing fare of regular preaching from the Bible."[20] Allen's statement indicates that while topical sermons can sometimes be helpful, they do not constitute a complete diet. Preachers who rely only on topical sermons might want to consider the health of their congregations.

The preparation process that Allen proposes begins with the topic. After the preacher has identified the topic, the first eleven steps in preparation are different angles on the topic. They include consideration of the preacher's knowledge and pre-association with the subject, biblical perspectives, denominational perspectives, listeners' perspectives, the preacher's position, the congregation's experience with the matter, and the mindset of the listeners. Only at this point does the preacher identify the message and the purpose and prepare to design the sermon.

In our society, we face issues not addressed explicitly in the Bible but on which biblical teaching and Christian faith may be brought to bear in preaching that offers benefit to our congregation. Topical sermons do serve a useful function in preaching, but they must be prepared with great care.[21] It is tempting—and perilous—to draft a topical sermon message and then go looking for a text to serve that message: under the circumstances, we risk trying to make the text say things it was not intended to say, adapting it to serve our need of the moment. When I see signs outside churches advertising sermons on "Raising Successful Teenagers" or "The Dangers of Drugs," I wonder what texts the preacher plans to use, and I hope that they are not being distorted to serve the preacher's message.

Conclusion

The steps we have traveled provide a sequence for moving through preparation of a sermon. Although it is a sequence, the process is also a fluid one. We all discover, with practice, what patterns work best for us. In general, though, preachers are encouraged to practice all of these steps somewhere along the way. Perhaps we see the various tasks as a dance, with movement and rhythm, rather than as rigid rules to be followed to the letter.

With experience, these steps become second nature. What looks like a cumbersome process begins to flow smoothly. As with a favorite recipe, we can set aside the cookbook, so we can follow these steps from memory, improvising and creating variations as the need arises and inspiration strikes.

6

CHOOSING INGREDIENTS

"To what should I compare the kingdom of God? It is like yeast that a woman took and mixed in with three measures of flour until all of it was leavened." (Luke 13:20–21)

The foods that have graced the everyday meals of my life have been unremarkable. Nourishing? Yes. Balanced, hearty, plentiful? Yes. Interesting? Rarely.

When we lived in California, my husband and I discovered the neighborhood Thai restaurant. The bold flavor of Thai basil and the subtlety of lemon grass awakened my tongue and my interest. *Hot* took on a whole new meaning. We loved this food.

Then we moved to the Midwest, where Chinese restaurants are plentiful, but Thai restaurants are few. After several years of deprivation, I began learning to fix our favorite Thai dishes.

Five primary flavors define Thai cooking. Fish and soy sauces provide the salty taste; palm or coconut sugar, the sweet. Limes and tamarind juice contribute a sour jolt, while dark green vegetables offer the bitter. A wide variety of chilies and other peppers supply spicy hot seasoning. Shallots, garlic, ginger, fish sauce, and chili or curry paste form the base of most main dishes. Sweet basil, a distant relative of Thai holy basil, is no substitute for it. Chicken and fish provide primary protein sources, but pork and beef appear often. Pad thai (a rice noodle dish) calls for one type of rice stick. Spring rolls require thread noodles. Jasmine is the only variety of rice served.

I am a novice in using the ingredients required for Thai cooking, but my dabbling in this cuisine has awakened my respect for how ingredients make foods tasty and attractive. I'm more curious about what is in dishes I eat—the ingredients' natural characteristics, various uses, and compatibility with other ingredients.

Story, God's story, is the primary ingredient of Christian worship. Music, poetry, rich words, drama, visual art, movement, gesture, and dance serve the story that unfolds as the congregation worships. Each artistic medium has a distinctive character, with unique possibilities. When joined together, these media stimulate our senses, body, mind, heart, and spirit to experience God's story more fully.

Story: Worship's main ingredient

The story of God's love for all that is created, of God's redemption for all that is fallen, is the main ingredient of Christian worship. Our praise and thanksgiving are rooted in the ongoing story of what God has done. Our testifying is grounded in what God is doing now. The rituals of communion and baptism are foretastes of God's story fulfilled. Each time Christ's body gathers, we tell God's story and add our chapter to the story of redeeming love that continues to unfold.

Our exploration of worship ingredients opens with an overview of characteristics of story, then looks at specific qualities of God's story.

What is a story? What does a story do?

Stories recount events that change peoples' lives. Aristotle contended that stories have a beginning, a middle, and an end. In the beginning, life for the characters is normal, predictable, running smoothly. Then something messes things up. Now the characters confront a problem that must be resolved. Sometimes they can rely on their own ingenuity or chutzpah to regain control. More often, they need help from other people or powers that intervene to set things right. By the end, when the dilemma has been resolved, the characters and their world are forever changed.

What does a story do? Stories create a world of possibilities. They shape identities as they are retold. William Bausch identifies a number of story characteristics that integrate faith and imagination.[1] Several are especially relevant for our exploration.

Stories help us remember. A story sets important events into an order; it gives them a form that lends itself to retelling. It creates coherence by weaving together the actions, intentions, moods, or desires of the characters. In telling a good and true story,[2] listeners relive the event. We enter into it and become part of the story's tradition. As we retell the story, it becomes our own.

Deuteronomy 6:20–25 summarizes Israel's Exodus from Egypt. This story is explicitly designed for repetition to instruct future generations.

When your children ask you in time to come, "What is the meaning of the decrees and the statutes and the ordinances that the LORD our God has commanded you?" then you shall say to your children, "We were Pharaoh's slaves in Egypt, but the LORD brought us out of Egypt with a mighty hand. The LORD displayed before our eyes great and awesome signs and wonders against Egypt, against Pharaoh and all his household. He brought us out from there in order to bring us in, to give us the land that he promised on oath to our ancestors. Then the LORD commanded us to observe all these statutes, to fear the LORD our God, for our lasting good, so as to keep us alive, as is now the case. (Deut 6:20–24)

Stories are a bridge to our culture, our roots. Family stories, community stories, histories, legends, or myths shape the identity of individuals and of groups. They reinforce shared, commonsense ways to approach problems, or they demonstrate how the characters use resources of money, knowledge, wit, or wisdom to resolve crises. Such stories can show cultural strengths as well as liabilities. The children's story *The Little Engine That Could* [3] tells of the determination of a little engine who saves all the toys through his willpower and positive thinking: "I think I can . . ." The story reflects quintessential Western—North American—values of individual heroism and a courage that risks failure. The parable of the good Samaritan (Luke 10:29–37) highlights the hardheartedness of leaders of God's chosen people, and the generosity of a despised neighbor.

"A man was going down from Jerusalem to Jericho, and fell into the hands of robbers, who stripped him, beat him, and went away, leaving him half dead. Now by chance a priest was going down that road; and when he saw him, he passed by on the other side. So likewise a Levite, when he came to the place and saw him, passed by on the other side. But a Samaritan while traveling came near him; and when he saw him, he was moved with pity. He went to him and bandaged his wounds, having poured oil and wine on them. Then he put him on his own animal, brought him to an inn, and took care of him. The next day he took out two denarii, gave them to the innkeeper, and said, 'Take care of him; and when I come back, I will repay you whatever more you spend.' Which of these three, do you think, was a neighbor to the man who fell into the hands of robbers?" (Luke 10:29–36).

Stories restore the original power of the word. Words embodied by the storyteller communicate directly with listeners (or readers), drawing us into the drama of vivid actions with energy and emotional strength. In this story, Jesus's words to two blind men restored their sight:

> As Jesus went on from there, two blind men followed him, crying loudly, "Have mercy on us, Son of David!" When he entered the house, the blind men came to him; and Jesus said to them, "Do you believe that I am able to do this?" They said to him, "Yes, Lord." Then he touched their eyes and said, "According to your faith let it be done to you." And their eyes were opened. Then Jesus sternly ordered them, "See that no one knows of this." But they went away and spread the news about him throughout that district. (Matt 9:27–31)

Words activate our imaginations, creating pictures in our minds. Voice inflections, tempo, and silences of spoken stories impress on us the power of specific words to shape meaning. Stories provoke curiosity and compel repetition. Good and true stories raise questions in the listener's mind: How did that happen? Why did that person react that way? What if this would have happened instead? How could the story have ended differently? What wisdom does this story hold? By their nature, stories induce us to tell them again until we have considered many possibilities. Conclusions show us a way out of the story's dilemma. We retell stories until we find the satisfactory ending.

Stories bind us to all of humankind, to the universal human family. All peoples tell stories. Personal and social identity are grounded in the capacity to tell and retell stories. We hold stories in common with people who are like us. We tell these stories to people who differ from us. By doing so, we reveal something about our character and way of being in the world. Hearing stories from other peoples and places opens new worlds of possibility. True stories are grounded in the essential questions of what it is to be human. Different cultures manage human failings, foibles, and calamities in various ways. Listeners and readers learn something about their shared humanity as they consider the contrasting worlds the stories create.

Stories provide a basis for hope and morality. Stories allow listeners and readers to stand apart from the remembered event and to consider the characters' actions. Through stories we can witness the display of virtues such as hospitality, as in the case of Lydia.

We set sail from Troas and took a straight course to Samothrace, the following day to Neapolis, and from there to Philippi, which is a leading city of the district of Macedonia and a Roman colony. We remained in this city for some days. On the Sabbath day we went outside the gate by the river, where we supposed there was a place of prayer; we sat down and spoke to the women who had gathered there. A certain woman named Lydia, a worshiper of God, was listening to us; she was from the city of Thyatira and a dealer in purple cloth. The Lord opened her heart to listen eagerly to what was said by Paul. When she and her household were baptized, she urged us, saying, "If you have judged me to be faithful to the Lord, come and stay at my house." And she prevailed upon us. (Acts 16:11–15)

Our imaginative wonderings allow us to envision endings that ensure the achievement of justice and reconciliation. Heroic stories, in which good, mercy, or kindness triumph, bolster our hope for a just, peaceful, and loving world.

Telling stories is a human need. A shared narrative creates community. It shapes identity, because our stories reflect who we are and what we do, what we value. It inspires imagination; through this process we can ponder a variety of possible ways of being and acting. It sustains hope, as we seek endings in which justice, reconciliation, peace, and love prevail.

How does God's story function?

God's story of creation, redemption, and final fulfillment is the main ingredient of Christian worship. The congregation's praise, prayer, proclamation, and testimony of God's steadfast love is told from the past to the present moment. Worship draws the stories of God's people into the biblical story unfolding throughout time to redeem the world and all who have lived in it.

Imagine a line spiraling through time, gathering within it all that has happened since the dawn of creation: God giving order to the earth and creating all living things—Adam and Eve's expulsion from the garden—the Exodus from Egypt and wandering in the wilderness—the kings and prophets of Israel—the exile to Babylon and eventual return—Jesus's birth, life, death, and resurrection—the coming of the Holy Spirit at Pentecost—the beginnings of the church—Constantine's declaration making Christianity the state religion—the formation of monastic communities—the ecumenical councils—the Crusades—the Reformation—the achievements and agonies of the twentieth century—until this moment. The theme that binds all these stories of faithful and flawed communities and individuals is God's persistent love that desires to set things right. Because God addresses each of us and each community in our particular situation, the story has many facets and angles. God uses any means available to restore us to our original blessing. Each time a congregation worships, its story is incorporated into God's story that continues until time will be no more.

Many postmodern thinkers claim that "the master narrative" is dead.[4] Gone are the political, economic, and social controls that dictated which parts of the story could be told. These thinkers maintain that many aspects of contemporary life simply cannot be addressed or answered by such narratives. Indeed, the Bible does not seem to answer some of life's most perplexing issues. Why does evil persist? Why do bad things happen to upright and righteous people? Why do the unjust prosper? These thinkers rightly notice that many important stories in Christian communities have been suppressed, particularly stories about women, the poor, and others who have been marginalized by society. The idea of the master narrative has taken a beating. But Christian worship, expressed by a community of faith, has no foundation apart from the redeeming story of God. Told in a thousand variations, the restoration of all creation to the abundant love of God is worship's unending theme.

The arts in worship: Ingredients that serve God's story

Humans have always used music, poetry, drama, visual images, movement, and dance to tell their most important stories. These arts engage the senses, stimulating thought and moving our hearts. Artistic expressions confirm what we already know or believe to be true. They can also challenge these assumptions. They have the power to expand our experience and transform our perceptions, thinking, or action.

The arts used in worship can reveal aspects of God's redeeming story in ways that are accessible and relevant to contemporary worshipers. They can disclose the hidden dimensions of God's presence. They provide expressive channels through which the congregation can enter God's continuing story of redeeming love.

Some art forms have had a privileged status in Christian worship. Music, for example, has been highly valued. Dance has been undervalued. New art forms or adaptations of older forms require changes in worship patterns. The unique characteristics of each medium must be taken seriously. They are a good starting point for determining how that art form can serve God's unfolding story and help the congregation enter into it.

In the remainder of this chapter, we will explore the characteristics of arts that are particularly appropriate for worship. Along the way, we'll consider some possible uses for specific worship actions and the potential dangers of indiscriminate use. As is true for all other aspects of worship, the arts must communicate in accessible ways in local congregations. What communicates in one setting may not work well in another. Wise worship planners, leaders, and preachers who know their congregations are able to use the arts effectively to gather a people into God's story of saving love.

Music

Pitch, tempo, rhythm, melody, harmony, and timbre—qualities grounded in the physics of sound—make music a basic medium of worship. Human bodies and souls respond deeply to the textures and movements of sound unleashed by voices or instruments. Our voices and bodies attune to one another. We create a powerful blend of physical force and soulful sensitivity as we breathe and release sound together.

Tempo and rhythm draw us into the intimate language of our bodies and of the body of Christ. These are media through which we can move together. Just try standing still during the singing of a Black Gospel hymn or a catchy praise song! We feel the deeper pulses of life and of our congregations when we move in common to the beats of a song. Music synchronizes our breathing, speaking, harmonizing, and moving as no other art form can.

A melody arranges pitches into contours that can stir the mind and heart. Minor keys tend to turn our moods inward. Major keys draw us outward. To sing freely with joy or with gut-wrenching anguish is to know ourselves as profoundly physical beings. As Anne Lamott observes, "Music is about as physical as it gets. . . . We're walking temples of noise, and when you add tender hearts to this mix, it somehow lets us meet in places we couldn't get to any other way."[5] The need to physically release ourselves in worship is almost impossible to resist. If dance has been suspect, at least we could sing.

Although singing is an embodied experience, and although sound resonates through our bodies, music is primarily an art for the ear. The pleasure and pain of sound waves are literally taken into our bodies, organized by our brains, and interpreted as deeply felt experience. When musical sound is paired with evocative words that engage our minds and hearts, deeper meanings slip into our awareness. Perhaps this quality is what gives congregational singing pride of place as an enduring expression of worship. Hearing music, whether performed by vocal soloists or choirs, instrumentalists or organists, is qualitatively different from creating our own vocal sound. Listening rarely involves our whole body.

Skilled musicians use music's powerful resources to lead worshipers in praise, prayer, and other acts of worship. The psalms invite us to create new songs. Words that recount God's saving deeds constitute a large body of the church's song. Such songs of praise, adoration, and thanksgiving often are matched with major melodies that call for moderate or quick tempos. Songs of praise are often upbeat, bright, and joyful. When accompanied by organ, band, piano, drums, or guitar, many hymns and songs of praise call forth our energies. Hymns such as "Joyful, joyful we adore thee," "Earth and all stars," "Cantemos al Señor," "Asithi: Amen," "Great is the Lord," "Immortal, invisible, God only wise," "Now thank we all our God," "O Lord, our Lord, how majestic is your name," and "Oh, for a thousand tongues to sing" exemplify this wedding of evocative words and strong music to praise God for deeds accomplished, adore God's character, and thank God for mercies shown.

Some songs of praise express a quiet dignity or stark simplicity that tempers our exuberance. "The God of Abraham praise," paired with the tune LEONI, draws us with solemnity and reverence into the vastness of God's character.[6] (See Appendix 9 for musical notation.)

> The God of Abraham praise. All praised be the Name,
> who was, and is, and is to be, is still the same;
> the one eternal God, ere all that now appears,
> the First, the Last, beyond all thought through timeless years!
>
> God's Spirit flowing free, high surging where it will—
> in prophet's word it spoke of old—is speaking still.
> Established is God's law; and changeless it shall stand,
> deep writ upon the human heart, on sea and land.
>
> God has eternal life implanted in the soul,
> God's love shall be our strength and stay, while ages roll.
> Praise to the living God! All praised be the Name,
> who was, and is, and is to be, is still the same!

The melody spans more than an octave, rising with deliberate motion and falling with some unusual downward leaps. The music, set in a minor key, carries us through dissonances and surprising flashes of bright major harmony, conveying musically the message that we cannot predict the outworking of God's ways. The eighth notes that sometimes pass between chords, as well as the chords themselves, suggest a slow but not ponderous tempo. Interesting tensions are set up between the top line of the melody and the bass line, as they move in opposite directions from each other, then find resolution as they move closer together.

"Praise the Lord," set to the Japanese tune SAKURA, expresses praise in a plaintive, austere voice.[7]

> Praise the Lord, praise the Lord,
> for the greenness of the trees, for the beauty of the flowers,
> for the blueness of the sky, for the greatness of the sea.
> Praise the Lord, praise the Lord, now and forevermore.
>
> Thanks to God, thanks to God,
> for the gift of friends in Christ, for the church, our house of faith,
> for the gift of wondrous love, for the gift of endless grace.
> Thanks to God, thanks to God, now and forevermore.
>
> Glory to God, glory to God,
> for the grace of Christ, the Son, for the love of parent God,
> for the comfort and the strength of the Spirit, holy God.
> Glory to God, glory to God, now and forevermore.

The simple structure of the verses draws our minds deeper into the wonder of creation; the gift of human relationships made possible through Christ; and the grace, love, comfort, and strength offered to us by the triune God. *Hymnal: A Worship Book* provides no harmony or accompaniment, so our attention stays focused on the simplicity of the words and melody. Within the phrases of SAKURA, the melody moves from one tone to its neighbor, with occasional leaps over a tone. But the leaps between phrases can be large, up to seven tones away. These jumps may make singers feel uncertain about whether they will land on the correct tone. And it is precisely this vulnerability that the words and melody are intended to help us feel. Before the vastness of creation, the wonder of Christian unity, and the glory of God's grace and love, we recognize our limits, our finitude.

This quality of fragility means the tempo cannot be fast. Our awe is expressed here in slow, measured, and delicate ways.

Gathering songs for the congregation require strong rhythm, matched with accessible or familiar melodies. Rhythm and melody focus the congregation's attention and aid the Spirit in drawing the body into a sense of our unity. Words and melodies that are too complicated distract from sensing ourselves in a body.

"Shout to the North" uses melodic repetition and a driving dance-like rhythm to call us to worship.[8]

> Men of faith rise up and sing
> of the great and glorious King
> You are strong when you feel weak
> in your brokenness complete
>
> (Refrain)
>   Shout to the North and the South
>   Sing to the East and the West
>   Jesus is Savior to all
>   Lord of heaven and earth
>
> Rise up women of the truth
> Stand and sing to broken hearts
> Who can know the healing power
> Of our awesome King of love
>
> We've been through fire
> We've been through rain
> We've been refined by the power of his name
> We've fallen deeper in love with you
> You've burned the truth on our lips
>
> Rise up church with broken wings
> Fill this place with songs again
> Of our God who reigns on high
> By his grace again we'll fly

Men and women and the entire church are invited to acknowledge their brokenness and the refining trials that deepen our dependence on God. God will empower and enliven our worship. We in turn shout our faithful affirmation to the world: Jesus is Savior and Lord. The major key and the buoyancy of the refrain carry the hope of this song. The downward, almost restless movement of the melody of the verses creates a welcome contrast to the refrain, which is introduced by the leap of six tones. The repeated notes on "Shout to" and "North and" suggests the voices of a herald or trumpet or bell. The pattern of tempo and strong sense of two beats to the measure lend a sense of suspension to these repeated notes. The bridge section ("We've been through fire") introduces another rhythmic pattern and moves into a minor key, signaling the difficulties through which we have passed.

A radically different musical prayer for gathering comes from the Cheyenne people. "Jesus A, Nahetotaetanome" (Jesus Lord, how joyful you have made us).[9]

> Jesus Lord, how joyful you have made us
> to come together here with you now!
> In your mercy you have called us.
> You say, "I am the way." We hear you call us.
> We ask you, "Come lead us day by day."
> We follow your way.

The remarkable melody spans an octave and a half. The first three notes maintain the same pitch, then the melody leaps up five tones, then it slowly works its way back to the starting tone. That pattern is repeated, but the second time, the melody continues moving below the opening tone, ending an octave below it. The final phrase opens with a leap of five tones and again works back to the lowest tone. The melody recognizes the ascended Christ who is beyond us and who has humbled himself to come to us. A medium tempo effectively calls us to worship.

Prayers of confession and petition need melodic and rhythmic sounds that still the activity of our minds, hearts, and souls by quieting our bodies. These sounds open the way for our intimate talk with God. A steady tempo and inspiring melody open spaces, allowing the deepest desires of our souls to find voice. "Lord, listen to your children praying" demonstrates how repetition in the melody, rhythm, and harmony serve this quieting function.[10]

> Lord, listen to your children praying,
> Lord, send your Spirit in this place.
> Lord, listen to your children praying,
> send us love, send us power, send us grace!

The melody of this song covers a span of only four tones. It moves continually, but in small steps rather than large leaps. The tone that opens the song is sung for two long beats, as is the last note of the first phrase. One long beat of rest follows each of these phrases. The third phrase begins like the first phrase, and the fourth launches into a different rhythm, as we implore God to send us love, power, and grace. The long notes and deliberate rests settle this piece into a stillness that is unperturbed by the relative quickness of rhythm of "listen to your children." Several flatted notes give the music a blues sound that creates a sense of space for prayer. This song cannot be rushed—the final tone, which we hold for four long beats, assures an unhurried pace.

These examples demonstrate how the resources of melody, rhythm, harmony, and structure can be used effectively by wise music leaders to open the way for gathering, praise, and prayer. Songs for congregational singing should be chosen with an ear to their purpose at a particular place in worship; this process requires that we give as much attention to the music as to the words. Music skills needed for the sensitive selection of songs for congregational singing in worship will transfer to choosing other types of vocal or instrumental music.[11]

Choral music works best when it extends the scripture text of the day—providing another version of the passage, offering another interpretative angle, or giving musical commentary. J. S. Bach was a master at using melody, harmony, and rhythm to break open new meanings for the words he set. Vocal groups or soloists at times may sing the prayer of the congregation, using melody, tempo, rhythm, and harmony to express our heartfelt desires and longings.

"Special music" can often be a distraction in worship. It may fulfill an aesthetic need but often does not further the worship action. However nice the piece and the performance are, special music that does not promote the congregation's engagement with God has no legitimate place.

Of all the arts the church practices, music—particularly congregational song—is the most powerful. One study has shown that the effects of Parkinson's disease can be lessened temporarily as the affected person listens to music.[12] Another study provides evidence that students get better scores if they have listened to music—especially classical music—just prior to taking a math test.[13] Science is finding evidence for what people have known for a long time: music stirs emotions, stimulates the mind, and organizes the body.

Throughout the Bible, singing is inextricably linked with expressions of gratitude, joy, wonder, and praise for God's astounding love. Too often congregational music leaders do not recognize how tempo or the shape of a melody can deepen the congregation's expression of praise, confession, and other worship actions. Their leadership fails to bring out the expressive qualities of the song. As a result, everything—hymns, contemporary praise music, or a blend of many styles—sounds the same. Skilled musicians and worship leaders understand the physical and emotional power of music and steward these precious resources well.

Poetry and rich words

Beginning with the treasury of the Psalter, the prayer of God's people has been rooted in poetry. The psalmists' images, turns of phrase, and urgent cries spring from experiences of life. The poetic imagination recasts these experiences into hymns, songs, and prayers that speak the deepest desires of the human soul. The tapestry of worship is woven through such words. Delightful rhymes, word plays, consonance, and alliteration create memorable patterns. Images and metaphors surprise us by showing to our mind's eye relationships between things which our physical eyes cannot see. Searing knowledge and new insight come from "seeing" such things for the first time.

Hymns, songs, and prayers capture images, ideas, and sentiments, and wed them with the powerful musical resources of melody, rhythm, and harmony. Word and tone merge, resonating deeply in our bodies. When eloquent text and powerful tune join, the Spirit uses them to change people's souls; we are stirred, grounded, connected, and transcended. Poetic words linked with melody connect our wills with our passion. Notice how a sense of quasi-religious solidarity emerges when people sing their country's national anthem or their school song. After the terrorist attacks of 9/11, people in many communities of the United States sang "God bless America" as a prayer for God's care and an affirmation of trust. For many North American Mennonites, singing "Praise God from whom all blessings flow" ("606") confirms our praise and expresses our enjoyment of four-part a cappella singing.

Poets distill experiences into arrangements of words that focus our attention on what is essential. We see through the poet's eye and consider deeply what we perceive. From this perspective, we may recognize the truth of what the poet depicts. The poet's idiom may name something in our experience for which we have not found our own words. Or perhaps we imagine how to name in new ways the truth of our lives.

Preachers and worship leaders practiced in distilling experience into powerful words stand in the tradition of the biblical prophets and storytellers. They speak with a precision that may be close to God's heart. Sometimes the economy of God's words is frightening:

> Let there be light.
> I AM WHO I AM.
> Hear, O Israel: the LORD is our God, the LORD alone.
> Who do you say that I am?
> I am the bread of life.
> I am the way, and the truth, and the life.
> Our Father in heaven, hallowed be your name.
> Blessed are the pure in heart, for they will see God.

Sermons also open spaces for strong, evocative, and imaginative language. Preachers who hear poetry read or sung develop an ear for rhythm, alliteration, word play, irony, metaphor, and sharp images. A sermon in rhyme or in regular meter would sound strange to many of us, although the rhetoric of many an impassioned Black preacher comes close to poetic speech. In any case, a preacher's delivery can be informed by these poetic qualities. The economy of words demanded by poetry is a welcome alternative to the verbosity of some preachers. Preaching informed by poetry uses the repetition, phrasing, accents, and tempo found in oral traditions of storytelling. These qualities help listeners hear the shape and emphasis of the sermon. Whether one preaches from a manuscript or from a mental outline, a love for vivid words and a respect for their power to evoke fervent response separate powerful preaching from sermons that are bland and mediocre.

Congregational prayers also create space for language that can move the soul. Using a variety of biblical names for God expands our awareness of the many ways God is present with us each day in Jesus and the Holy Spirit. Naming many, varied qualities of God's character might encourage us to pay more attention to the kindliness of the supermarket checkout woman, the helpfulness of our car mechanic, or the playfulness of our children, all of whom are created in God's image. Our thanksgivings might overflow with joyful wonder—maybe even giddiness—as we recount God's unending blessings. Confessions might name our sinfulness in images of broken glass, torn fabric, wilted plants, overflowing trash, virus-infected computers, or coffee-stained clothing. The point is not to stuff prayers full of mismatched metaphors or to be clever and cute. But expanding our capacity to see ourselves in relationship with God in the experiences of ordinary life is a primary goal as we select words for worship.

Silence in poetry, preaching, and music is essential. In and around the words, silence allows us to listen and ponder. Through silence we find places to let the truth of what we have heard resonate in us. Many people now, even Christian worshipers, shun silence. Often public worship is crammed with words and music. Poets and those who practice the art of distillation can teach us how to be still and know that God is God. Silence helps us confront truth in our inward parts. Many of us fear the truth we might find there. When worship is active, upbeat, engaging, and flowing, we can evade silence. And in the midst of so much activity, we might avoid the truth about our lives that needs to be acknowledged. Truth can endure the test of silence.

Much Western religious poetry is consigned to the printed page, so that it can be read again and again. Hymns and printed liturgies that rise to the level of poetry are too rich in image and thought to be taken in all at once. We repeat them so their wisdom has time to seep into our being. But poetry throughout much of the world's history has been performed orally, recited as memorized verse, or improvised in the moment of performance. In worship traditions not bound by printed texts, the poetic qualities of worship language resemble the structures, patterns, cadences, and rhymes of oral poetry. Written prayers, readings, and songs enrich the language of worship deeply, but preachers and worship leaders also do well to rely on the simplicity, economy, strength, and color of oral speech traditions.[14]

Using language with poetic qualities is a skill that is cultivated over time. Prose talk, which is often oriented toward conveying information, prevails in contemporary North American culture. Words clutter our minds through media that are omnipresent in our lives. We forget most prose talk, because it is trite and unimaginative. Language that forms us in faith is strong and vivid. It evokes our feelings, shapes our thoughts, and motivates our wills. Every word matters. Distilling, being still, listening, and imagining—these essential skills characterize preachers and worship leaders who use oral and written language well.

Drama

Human sin, orneriness, and rebelliousness have created all kinds of conflict in God's story. Conflict leads to drama. Drama elevates, extends, and intensifies the action of stories by slowing it down. We feel the heightening tensions and eventually the resolution. Good stories draw us into the center of the conflict and skillfully guide us to a reconciliation. Many biblical stories of conflict follow certain themes:

> order overcoming chaos (creation)
> reconciliation overcoming betrayal (Joseph and his brothers)
> beauty overcoming what is grotesque, ugly, or unbalanced
>   (Revelation, new Jerusalem)
> love overcoming indifference or hatred (Jesus and later his
>   disciples)
> relationship overcoming alienation (Ruth and Naomi)
> truth overcoming falsehood (Ananias and Sapphira)

Many dramas are like rites of passage. We make a transition from one way of understanding ourselves in the world to a new self-understanding. We move in the story from a place of orientation, where things are normal and predictable, through disruption and disorientation, to a place of reorientation, with a new sense of what is normal.

Biblical narratives read, told, or dramatized in worship make us feel the conflict of human waywardness and God's reconciliation. Drama uses our minds to address matters of the heart. Scripture readers who highlight the drama of the assigned passage often provide the first interpretation of the day's text. Undue vocal emphasis, elaborate gestures, or exaggerated movement distract us from the dramatic elements of the story, although good diction, appropriate emphasis, and correct pronunciation are essential. Good interpretations follow the contours of the passage, giving voice to what needs to be heard at this particular moment of God's unfolding story. Worshipers yearn for simple, clear, and intentional reading of the Bible; indeed, they respond when the reading of scripture is a proclamation of the gospel.

When several readers bring the scripture texts alive, the sense of drama heightens. We hear multiple voices and points of view that often signal conflict. We perceive new layers of meaning, and perhaps a tension of interpretations or perspectives that challenges our thinking. The scripture texts must be suitable for several readers to proclaim; otherwise, the primary story or message of the passage can be obscured.

A storyteller, recounting the story verbatim or in paraphrase, brings its pathos into the immediacy of the moment. She is fully present, addressing the congregation face-to-face. Gestures, movement, vocal color and modulation, volume, and walking intensify the story's action and mood. The story lives, embodied in ways that stir a response in us.

The acting team of Ted (Swartz) and Lee (Eshleman) have given many audiences new insights into biblical stories through the production of *Fish Eyes, Creation Chronicles,* and *DoveTale.*[15] They find the critical points of the Gospel and Hebrew scripture stories they enact. Using humor, they nudge us to confront our reactions to the tensions these narratives raise. The stories seem fresh and modern, even when Ted and Lee are in rustic costume. We laugh heartily at the disciples' reactions, often revealing our own mixed motives, uncertainties, and wavering commitment. Sometimes their stories do not reach resolution and so invite us to find an ending in our lives. Children, youth, and adults of all ages see ourselves in these stories, enjoying their vitality and sometimes squirming with the truth they show us about ourselves.

Full-scale productions of plays have a place in the church's worship at times other than Christmas Eve and Easter. Bringing stories alive with characters, motion, and perhaps music engages worshipers with sights and sounds that draw us in. The line between the actors and the congregation can blur, bringing us all into the action.

The film *Jesus of Montreal* is the story of a motley group of actors preparing to reenact the passion of Jesus during Holy Week in Montreal. Each of the actors is experiencing personal turmoil. As the play begins to take shape, the actors move deeper into their roles, and we begin to notice subtle transformations in their lives. They start living their parts outside the play as well as in it. On opening night, the audience, gathered in a park, follows the actors from station to station as the passion is acted. When Jesus is presented to the crowd after being flogged, a Black woman breaks through the imaginary wall that separates the actors from the audience, runs to Jesus, and cries out to him. She looks delusional and seems utterly uncouth compared to the polite and cultured white people in the audience. But at that moment she enters the story of Jesus's passion, becoming a participant in his impending death. Like this woman, we may cross the line from audience to participant when a powerful story is dramatically enacted.

Stories from other cultures—and from popular culture—are appropriate for worship when they extend the biblical story. Much wisdom from the world's people demonstrates essential biblical faith or provokes a reexamination of personal commitments. Such stories challenge us to consider faith from a new viewpoint. Especially when these stories are connected with the day's sermon, new insights can emerge, and the impetus to act can result.

Well-told stories affect children and adults deeply. For this reason, stories and dramas for worship must have integrity. They will present truthful situations, explore vital issues, take seriously the temptations of real life, reveal the ambiguity of human choices, and present viable and believable conclusions. Unfortunately, many dramas created for worship do not reach this standard: the conflict of the story is contrived or simplistic, and the "right" conclusion is patently obvious. A worthy dramatic story for worship will avoid resorting to facile, uncomplicated conclusions for complex situations, nor will it let the questions and complexities of living overwhelm the narrative and the characters, so that no resolution seems possible. Biblical stories provide excellent guidance for identifying characteristics of engaging stories with straightforward dramatic power. We need to steep ourselves in these scriptural narratives.

Christian rituals are important dramatic forms that the church practices routinely. Baptism and the Lord's Supper, in particular, use words, gestures, movements, objects, and often music to enact these central actions of Jesus. In tangible ways, the congregation embodies the mystery of covenant love. Celebrations of baptism and the Lord's Supper demonstrate how God's saving story encompasses the story of a particular congregation and of the individuals who are its members.

The blessing of children and anointing for healing also catch the congregation in the saving spiral as these acts align with the special needs, desires, and blessings of its members.

Dramas, storytelling, and good scripture reading help the congregation see the stories of God's people enfleshed, taking place in our presence, now. Making the drama of stories live helps us envision ourselves embodying God's story in the world.

Visual art

Since the time of the Reformation, statuary, icons, stained glass, and murals in worship spaces have made many Protestants uncomfortable. Fear of idolatry abounds where visual images are concerned. However, with the availability of inexpensive reproduction methods, cheaper projection equipment, and increasing interest in visual art, Christians of all types are rediscovering the potential of visual art in worship. When our eyes see new aspects of the biblical story, our imaginations are opened to new questions and possibilities in God's unfolding story.

Shape, line, color, light, texture, movement, harmony, rhythm, organization—these visual design elements draw us into a scene, mood, or idea. Whether realistic or abstract, these art forms show us something about the world and the nature of how things are—or how they could be. We begin as observers and, if we look carefully enough, eventually we are taken into the work: we dwell in the image and the image begins to dwell in us.

Three broad types of visual art are found in present-day Christian worship spaces: (1) pictures, icons, photographs, stained glass, banners, tablescapes,[16] or architectural features that remain stationary; (2) slide shows; and (3) images that move—film, video, multimedia, or real-time projection. Each medium addresses worshipers in unique ways that make significant demands on our abilities to see and interpret.

Stationary images and figures create a space that focuses our attention. Our eyes come to rest on a work and slowly take in its details. We are drawn into the work's mood. With a quieted eye, contemplation is possible. Seeing beyond the surface features of a work, we discover a number of possible meanings, which we discern within our particular social and culture contexts. Margaret Miles claims that visual images, while rendering identified themes, do not point to specific conclusions. Visual images are multivalent and cannot be definitively interpreted.[17] Nor do images evoke the same thoughts or emotions in all worshipers.

Images do "picture" an order or structure in relationships among God, humans, and other created things.[18] David Morgan describes how popular religious images, such as Salman's "Head of Christ," inspire assurance of Jesus's presence when they are seen in the midst of everyday activities. Images repeatedly viewed begin to create a sense of social and religious orderliness. In times of disruption and chaos, they recall an earlier orderly existence and represent hope. Such images offer reassurance and reaffirmation of belief.[19]

A Roman Catholic church in northern California painted a large, brightly colored mural across the front of the sanctuary behind the altar. The upper body of Christ is pictured in the center of mural with his right hand extended toward the congregation. The planet earth sits in his palm. In the background are the stars, moons, and planets. Everything that takes place around the altar and pulpit is seen against the backdrop of this cosmic Christ holding the world. Every gathering of the congregation is a reminder that they are part of a mystery beyond comprehension, which is nonetheless made human in the person of Jesus Christ. The mural places life in proper perspective.

The contemplative gaze of the worshiper is what Protestants have feared. Rather than seeing through the image to sense the truth or presence of God lying beyond it (as the Orthodox understand the role of icons), many Western Christians fear that the worshiper will see only the object—the art itself—and worship its aesthetic qualities alone. Equally troubling is the possibility of mistaking aesthetic qualities with divine reality. This problem is not trivial, because visual artwork cannot tell us exactly what it means.

Miles claims that visual art in worship spaces fulfills a formative function. It shapes religious feelings by "drawing the worshiper[s] to imitate and participate in the qualities and way of life formulated by the image." She contends that language trains the mind effectively but does not engage the emotions as powerfully as images do. Contemplation of the subject of the work, which is a form of meditative prayer practiced in the company of other worshipers, has been underdeveloped since the Reformation.[20] Sitting in the presence of large paintings, statues, or stained glass windows depicting biblical stories or themes begins to shape the spiritual sensibilities of the congregation.

Golden Gate Lutheran Church in San Francisco has several large stained glass windows depicting Gospel stories. The largest one, closest to the altar on the congregation's left, shows the women coming to the empty tomb and encountering the angel; at the turn of the twentieth century an immigrant congregation of Scandinavians gave the witness of these faithful women prominence in their worship space. Women who worshiped there in the late 1980s and 1990s found this choice empowering. The stories of women's faithfulness have not received as much attention as those of men.

The range of visual images or visual elements in a worship space can span the spectrum from the iconic, to the representational, to the impressionistic, to the abstract.[21] *Iconic images* follow traditional conventions and can be "read" to gain particular scriptural or historical meaning. These images may also have an educational function, but frequently they point the worshiper beyond the images themselves to the biblical or historical story they depict. They usually reinforce widely held beliefs; they provide visual reassurance of basic tenets of faith. *Representational images* depict scenes with visual accuracy and invite worshipers to connect them with their own experiences of spiritual encounter. *Impressionistic images* capture the feeling, tone, or mood to which the artist wishes to draw worshipers. *Abstract images* suggest religious meaning but require worshipers to draw on their own interpretive understandings to determine meaning. Inquiring believers are often drawn to representational, impressionistic, and abstract images to extend their religious understanding or challenge distorted beliefs.[22] Miles asserts that viewers interpret an image according to their own interests, which are shaped by their personal experience, place, or status within their communities, their education, and their spirituality.[23]

Visual art often establishes the boundaries of the congregational worship space. Art that depicts biblical stories or evokes a theological theme defines the worship area as story space. Stained glass, seasonal banners, and painted or projected images identify the congregation as a body with a story, as pictures displayed in a home reflect and shape the identity of the family that dwells there. Unfortunately, some visual media have been domesticated, and their potential to communicate in public worship is therefore diminished. They take on decorative functions rather than theological ones. For example, flowers may be beautiful on the dining room table at home, but if they have no theological or storytelling purpose in worship, they do not belong in the worship space. Decorations fitting for a living room coffee table rarely deepen our worship responses. Banners, tablescapes, or fabric installations may mark a season—a Sunday, a few weeks or months, perhaps years—in a congregation's life. They are transient, serving to focus attention on specific themes or images found in the scripture texts of the season.

Women of First Mennonite Church of Hillsboro, Kansas, created six four-by-twelve-foot quilted banners for the seasons of Advent, Christmas, Lent, Easter, Pentecost, and planting-harvest. The brightly colored geometric banners were coordinated to complement the stained glass in the worship space. Each banner has several dominant images that provide clues to the season it represents; no words appear on the banners. The process of creating the banners revealed a number of unexpected things; not the least was that "beauty has transforming power and can take you beyond yourself."[24] Indeed.

A stationary image imaginatively communicates openings into its theme or story. Whether it is a literal image that depicts a biblical story or an abstract image that provokes deeper thought, it invites worshipers to enter its presence to find meaning. Viewing these images contemplatively is a form of prayer. They define space in which the congregation's story continues to unfold in a way that complements the reality depicted.

Slide shows stand as a midpoint between stationary images and video animation. Words on slides interpreted by images, colors, or background texture add further interpretation to songs, scripture readings, or sermon illustrations. In these examples, we are addressed by the projected images. We are given time to register the image's impression and experience a response to it, but we lack time to think deeply about what we are seeing. The range of possible meanings is controlled by the relationships between the visual images and themes, and the language and/or music paired with them. Rarely are slide shows organized as experiences of prayer, although one could do so with longer exposures on each image.

Video and multimedia programs present controlled narratives. Clips of popular films, collages of daily life in the neighborhood, scripture-based shorts, or locally produced documentaries of church activities may draw worshipers into an edited story. These films, with or without music and other enhancements, can illustrate a particular biblical or theological theme, or present an ethical dilemma. But the visual story runs at its own pace, with its own energy, which may be different from the momentum created by the congregation's worship. The combination of language and moving image mimics our integrated sensory experience, which explains its power. When handled poorly, a film clip or other multimedia presentation is intrusive, hijacking the real-time experience of the congregation with the urgency and intensity characteristic of film. The film's story must be addressed by what surrounds it in the service; otherwise its narrative thread cannot be woven into the story unfolding in congregation's worship. Film does not open a space for prayer; it can serve illustrative or educational purposes in corporate worship.

The real-time projection of unfolding events such as sermons, baptisms, and children's stories may occur in large gatherings where worshipers cannot be close to the centers of action. This raw footage can be highly invigorating and highly distracting.

Each of these visual media demands certain interpretive dispositions from the worshipers. The effectiveness of stationary images, banners, or tablescapes depends on our capacities for reflection and contemplation. They require that we look through the image and into its depths—as we gaze at someone who is deeply beloved. They also ask us to be seen, to be held in the image's presence. They call forth a relationship. Slide shows demand a capacity to hold an image in focus long enough to feel its presence, then to let it go, ready to receive the next image. The felt quality of the set of images is what persists. That feeling may be enhanced by words that focus particular interpretations of the images.

Video and other moving images demand the capacity to follow a narrative visually, to witness a story parallel to the one unfolding in the immediate worship setting. The capacity to go with the images and words that weave the story is required. In later reflection, we find the film's deeper meanings. Real-time video demands that worshipers be present in the moment, interpreting the projected images against the backdrop of the actual time and space in which they are participating. This type of video is always larger than life but must be kept in proper perspective. Preachers or worship leaders see the congregation in true scale as they look out. But because the background is scaled down, the congregation sees preachers and worship leaders as larger than life. This distortion can skew perceptions about leaders' power, persuasiveness, and authority.

Protestant congregations that would have avoided visual images in their worship spaces in the past now routinely include projected images, film clips, and banners. The challenge for worship leaders lies in using visual media wisely for the sake of deepening the congregation's response to God.[25]

Movement, gesture, dance

All worship is grounded in the movement of bodies. Speaking, singing, and offering require bodies in action. Several Hebrew concepts, which are translated with the English word *worship* are primarily body actions: bowing down, giving reverence and honor by bending at the waist, serving God or a revered human being.

We train bodies for worship. Eyes are closed and hands are folded for prayer. Voices shout or mumble "Amen." Hands clap or are lifted in praise. Hands are clasped for passing peace. Hands are laid on heads or raised in benediction. Feet are washed or move with the music. We stand to sing or affirm shared faith, and we are seated for sermons. We may kneel for prayer, blessing, and baptism. Most worship postures or movements quiet the body, freeing the mind and heart to concentrate. Other movements, planned or improvised, arouse the body to express love, ecstasy, intention, or commitment. Corporate worship teaches our bodies the gestures and postures of receiving, offering, sharing, listening, and responding.

Most Protestant worship spaces reflect small regard for the body as an expressive medium for engaging God. Space is usually plentiful for movements of the upper body (hands, arms, and heads). But space for walking, kneeling, or dancing is often severely limited. Aisle and pulpit areas are scarcely large enough for a few people to walk, let alone dance or process.

Dance emphasizes the ordinary movements of worship, highlighting what we might not notice otherwise. Literal or abstract dance movements act out the congregation's common gestures: arms uplifted, heads bowed, kneeling, hands folded. Set to music, they flow with ease. Hymns, songs, stories, and scriptures accompanied with sign language communicate an added gracefulness and another interpretive dimension.

Abstract dances, usually choreographed and rehearsed, ask worshipers to see more deeply into the action and tensions presented by a story or song. Like video and film clips, dance requires capacities for going with what is portrayed. Some dancers effectively mime scripture passages as they are read or recounted, telling the story through their actions. Members of one congregation created a series of *tableaux vivants* to portray moments in the story of the prodigal son. Two people moved through a series of poses, holding each about thirty seconds. This approach gave the congregation time to absorb how the reunion of parent and child occurred. Such movement can give shape to important meanings of stories, biblical themes, human conflicts, and reconciliations. Often, dancers and their witnesses form a sympathetic connection. We feel with each other. Drawn into the dancers' movements, we discover what it might mean to offer ourselves fully to God and God's ways.

InterPlay® is a community of dancers and players who use the wisdom of their bodies to improvise movements.[26] InterPlay® founders Phil Porter and Cynthia Winton-Henry have developed an approach to prayers of intercession called "dancing on behalf of . . ." Dancers listen to the prayer requests of members of the congregation. Then, with or without music, they dance a prayer, using what their bodies know about the specific situations that have been named. Sometimes the dance is a series of solos; other times it is a group dance drawing on an improvisational form. The movements can be representational or abstract. They are not choreographed or polished. This prayer in motion is often deeply moving at an emotional and spiritual level, for those who dance and for those on behalf of whom they dance.

Dance is a series of shifting images that gives human shape to the stories we recount in worship. It can move us through God's story, isolating, highlighting, and extending its saving wisdom. Sharing many characteristics with drama, visual art, and music, dance honors what bodies know about the faithfulness of God. Dramatic conflict is felt through large, fast, aggressive, or tense movements; the calm and stillness that come with resolution restore our hope. As with visual art, dance movements can span the range from the literal through representational to abstraction. Without words accompanying the dance or surrounding it, the movements can give rise to many possible meanings. As with music, the rhythm, phrasing, and texture of movement give it shape and momentum. For good reason, peoples throughout the world have told their most important stories through the combined media of music, poetry, drama, and dance.

Summary

Each medium makes a unique contribution to the congregation's worship expression. Together they break open the boundaries set by spoken words in isolation. A careful blending of music, visual elements, poetry, drama, and dance to achieve the primary actions of worship is the worship planners' responsibility.

The examples in the table in Appendix 10 suggest how the various art media might focus a particular worship action. The artistic media described in this chapter open channels by which worshipers move deeper into God's story. Sally Morgenthaler calls these "contact points," through which the soul makes contact with God.[27] When arts are introduced in worship, "specialists" or "professionals" too often become the congregation's performers. Worshipers become spectators, watching what happens rather than participating. Whenever possible, the congregation should move, sing, and speak on its own. Art should not make worshipers passive.

Our bodies were created with five senses through which we come to know the blessings of God's love, grace, and mercy. We see the glory and grandeur of God in creation and the light that darkness can not overcome. We hear God's voice in burning bushes, whirlwinds, and naming us "Beloved." God's word is proclaimed when scripture is heard aloud. Like Mary and Thomas, we sometimes must touch the truth with our hands to believe. The epistle of 1 John opens, "We declare to you what was from the beginning, what we have heard, what we have seen with our eyes, what we have looked at and touched with our hands, concerning the word of life . . ." The psalmist invites us to "taste and see that the Lord is good." And Paul declares that the aroma of Christ is spread in every place where he and other witnesses of Christ go. We take into our being the physical sensations of daily life. Our hearts and minds interpret their meaning. Faith begins with what we hear, see, taste, touch, and smell.

Our senses also powerfully shape our ability to interact with other people in the course of our activities. The loss of any single sense radically affects our ways of knowing and interacting with other people, and surely with God as well. We cannot afford to privilege one sense over another.

In this chapter, we have not explored taste or smell.[28] Sensitivity to smells is an issue for any people in our congregations. Perfumes, incense, and scents of all sorts aggravate allergies and asthma. At this point, cautious use of all aromatic substances needs to be the rule.

Good cooks respect the unique qualities of the ingredients they use to create nutritious, tasty, and imaginative dishes. A simple dish of mashed potatoes comes alive with the addition of a flavor enhancer such as salt, pepper, garlic, horseradish, butter, gravy, cream, sour cream, or cream cheese. The right combination of textures and tastes awakens our sense of smell, excites our taste buds, and arouses our appetites. Worship leaders and pastors do well to use the rich variety of arts appropriate for worship with a similar respect and imagination, to serve our telling of God's saving story.

7

COOKING COLLABORATIVELY

Now there are varieties of gifts, but the same Spirit. (1 Cor 12:4)

When it comes to planning and leading worship, experience disproves the old adage that "too many cooks spoil the broth." Inspired by the Spirit, this work at its best is a communal act, led communally, and meant to engage the entire congregation. The time, energy, and communication we invest in collaborative planning yields rich rewards in the lives of those who lead and in the congregation as a whole.

In our household, my husband and I share cooking responsibilities. Generally, I take the lead in menu planning. When we have a special meal to plan, I sit down with an array of cookbooks and the latest food magazines on our shelves. Keeping in mind who the guests will be and the particular requirements of the occasion, I flip through the pages, seeking creative inspiration. After gathering an assortment of options, I read recipes aloud and ask, "Does this sound good to you? What do you think of this combination? Would an Asian cabbage salad go well with this savory pork chop recipe? Or would you rather serve an apple salad with pork?" As my husband offers responses, we gradually organize a menu.

Along the way, we engage in a fair amount of negotiation. Although we enjoy many of the same foods, he tends to prefer a more highly spiced menu than I do. If he were designing the menu alone, we might end up with two or three "hot" dishes; if we plan a menu together, a less highly seasoned recipe will replace at least one of those choices.

When it comes to cooking the meal, my husband takes the lead with the appetizers, vegetables, and entrée. He also decides what we will drink with the meal. Usually I take responsibility for the bread, salad, and dessert. Although neither of us particularly enjoys washing lettuce or spinach, I get the job. And although he doesn't often give me advice, I sometimes hover nearby when he's crushing garlic and suggest that six cloves will probably be quite enough. I defer to him when it comes to garnishing and presentation, because his sense of color and style is more imaginative and daring than mine.

Most of the time, such creative collaboration produces a colorful, flavorful, satisfying meal. As we clean up afterward in the kitchen, we evaluate the meal—the number and balance of courses, flavor combinations, texture contrasts, and overall appeal. I sometimes record our evaluation in the cookbook or magazine where we found the recipe, making notes for suggested changes or occasionally writing, "Don't bother trying this again!"

No doubt, it's possible for too many cooks to spoil the broth, but the wisdom in our kitchen points to the rewards of cooking together. Now that we've come to know and appreciate each other's strengths and have improved our negotiating skills, the kitchen is no longer a place of stress or conflict. In fact, we delight in the collaborative creative process and consider cooking together one of our more satisfying accomplishments. What's more, the meals we produce together are better than what either of us could cook on our own.

Introducing the collaborative process

A collaborative approach also has rich potential when it comes to preparing Sunday morning worship. And just as cooking a meal together involves many layers of cooperation, so a planning process that engages a team of people requires multiple levels of collaboration.

Obviously one level of collaboration involves key people who will be engaged in leadership on Sunday morning: the preacher, the worship leader, the music leader, the children's leader, and those involved in visual or dramatic arts. But behind the scenes are other layers of collaborative input or engagement. For example, a pastor may work with a team of lay leaders, such as elders or deacons, to develop the preaching diet. Preachers might meet formally or informally with selected members of the congregation for counsel during sermon preparation or for response afterward. They might also meet with members of their local ministers' group for collaborative conversation regarding the scripture texts for the week.

From time to time, music leaders will work with a wide variety of people in the congregation—children, youth groups, choirs, ensembles, individual musicians—in preparing music for worship. Both the children's leader and visual artist may meet with the preacher and worship leader to discuss the biblical texts, overall theme, and creative ideas for a season such as Lent. If children or youth are involved in the service, the worship leader may need to be in touch with parents, Sunday school teachers, or youth group leaders. Scripture readers might rehearse in advance with the worship leader, so their interpretation of the text coheres with the rest of the service. Interactions between those who provide pastoral care and those who plan worship will affect overall planning as well.

How does such collaboration occur? In the midst of hectic schedules and the unrelenting necessity of planning worship every week, how do busy people find time for such intensive engagement with one another? One answer is the team approach to worship planning. Although the definition of *worship team* varies from one congregation to another, the basic idea is that people with a variety of gifts are called to work together to give overall leadership to the worship planning process. Whether the group is appointed for a season or for a term of service of a year or more, participants work closely together, drawing on the strengths of each member for the sake of healthy, well-balanced congregational worship. In the end, such collaboration pays rich dividends for the spiritual life of the congregation, our sense of community, and our capacity to respond to the challenges of worship in faith and obedience.

A planning case study: Advent season

What might an effective collaborative planning process look like? The set of guidelines below suggests a series of simple steps for a planning process. It is followed by a case study describing the process as it is experienced collaboratively by a worship planning team.

Imagine that the fall season of congregational life is in full swing. Because Advent will arrive by late November, the worship leader for that season calls together the pastor/preacher, music leader, children's leader, and visual arts leader for a meeting in mid-October, about six weeks before the beginning of Advent. Prior to that meeting, each leader is given a copy of the scripture texts for each Sunday of Advent season with instructions to read and meditate on them. They are encouraged to mark up the pages, noting vivid images, dramatic movements, recurring themes, or other insights or questions. (In Appendix 11 is a sample sheet, with four lectionary texts for a Sunday in Advent that have been marked in preparation for the initial worship planning meeting.)

Guidelines for planning worship

1. Do homework in preparation for the planning session. What is the scriptural focus for the service? What images or concrete details are found in the text? What movements do you observe (for example, from fear to peace, or from despair to joy)? What theological themes seem important? If you are planning for one of the seasons of the church year, how has this season been celebrated before? What traditions have been meaningful or important for the congregation? What new practices might enliven worship?

2. Choose a focus and message on the basis of the group's discussion of the homework responses. In light of the community's current experience, what particular message is needed or desired? In other words, what are the connections between the text, the season, and the lived reality of the congregation? What is the chosen focus or purpose for this particular service? What will be the message of the sermon?

3. Consider how the arts might enhance worship. What resources—musical choices (vocal and instrumental); visual symbols; drama, movement, gesture, and dance; and silence—might deepen the congregation's worship?

4. Develop an order of worship that will facilitate the purpose of the service. Will the congregation's usual order of worship be suitable? How might the usual order of worship need to be adapted for this specific occasion? What issues of flow, simplicity, appropriateness, and feasibility need to be considered?

5. Involve the entire community of faith: varying age groups (children, youth, adults, elderly, etc.); other identifiable groups (newcomers, established folk, cultural subgroups, etc.). Assign leadership tasks to musicians, readers, artists, children's leader, etc.

6. Conduct an evaluation. Make evaluations a regular item on worship committee agenda, and solicit evaluation from the congregation.

Opening worship and scripture reflections

When the planning group arrives in the church conference room at 8:00 on the appointed Saturday morning, coffee, tea, and fresh muffins await them. Members of the group spend fifteen or twenty minutes chatting and eating and then sit down to engage in the ministry task at hand.

As leader of the planning process, the worship leader reads one of the appointed texts and offers an opening prayer. She makes a few introductory comments about Advent, reviewing its overall purpose and inviting those present to share a meaningful memory from last year's Advent season. Then they turn to the texts. Each member reflects on what they noticed in the texts, what captured their attention, what questions emerged. On a chalkboard or flipchart, a member of the group briefly notes each of these contributions; posting these discussion notes where everyone can see allows each participant to keep track of what is unfolding. Another team member records these notes on a computer, later sending them to each participant.

By 9:00, the pastor/preacher is asked to present possible preaching themes or messages emerging from the texts. Earlier in the year, the pastor discussed an overall preaching plan for the year with the elders, deacons, or other congregational leaders; now the pastor describes how the emerging themes might connect with or augment the overall theme for the year.

Listening to the congregation

Next the team turns a pastoral ear to the congregation. With the array of potential themes and preaching messages in view, they ask: What is currently happening in the congregation? What might God want to say to us? What unique message of the Advent texts might nourish the faith of worshipers? What focus would speak to the congregation's priorities for the year? What events in the community or world might affect the choice of themes for the season? How will decisions regarding Advent worship connect with other ministries of the congregation?

Discerning an overall theme and weekly focus statements

With these observations in hand, the team spends ten or fifteen minutes in silence, listening for the Spirit's direction. Out of the silence, members describe what they have heard and what themes or priorities may be emerging. Again a member of the group writes the responses where all can see.

Music and worship specialist Ken Nafziger has observed that "there is an important parallel between a work of sculpture and a central idea in worship. Both stand in the middle of the assembly, and many walk around them. Each observer will have a point of view differing slightly from all others."[1] The group approaches their discernment with an appreciation for the importance of selecting a central idea that can function in this way. After more reflection and discussion, they identify an overall theme for the season, choose a primary text for each week, and develop a focus statement for each worship service that grows out of the intersection between texts, potential preaching focus, and perceived congregational needs.

Planning the worship service

Around 10:15, the group takes a refreshment break. By 10:30, they are engaged in creative brainstorming. Team members make a list of possible ways to proclaim the texts and themes—in song, visual art, worship actions, children's time, or preaching. At this point, no ideas are rejected; rather, the team seeks to cast as broad a net as possible. One good idea stimulates another. A sense of abundant possibilities emerges as each member of the team adds insights.

Somewhere along the way, the team reviews the congregation's typical order of worship (the "courses" normally served) and decides whether the usual ordering of actions will serve the emerging theme. How should worship begin during Advent—in a contemplative mode or in a spirit of expectant hope? Do the acts of praise and confession belong together before the scripture reading and the sermon? Or should confession follow the sermon? How will the offering support the theme? And where will it be placed in the order of worship? How will the Word be proclaimed to children or young people? How will they be involved in the acts of worship? What acts of prayer might be most meaningful during the season—an extended time for silence because of the typical stress of the season, a sung prayer response that is used throughout the season, or a movement prayer that invites worshipers into a posture of waiting for the birth of Christ into their hearts and the world?

As these ideas are tested, the team tentatively selects an overall order of worship that will best provide a sense of unity and coherence for the season. They revisit the selected theme and test it with the emerging direction. By 11:30, they scatter for a half hour of individual work in silence and prayer, inviting the Spirit to move in their midst, guiding each individual leader to discern what is needed in their particular area of responsibility, whether it is worship leading, music leading, preaching, children's time, or visual art. As part of their work, they imagine particular individuals in the congregation who might be invited to fulfill certain assignments.

Wrap-up and closing

Around noon, the team gathers for wrap-up and conclusion. They share what they have been hearing and further refine the overall direction. Specific assignments are made for the coming weeks, and planning meetings are scheduled for those directly involved in each week's worship service. The person who will give primary leadership for each week is identified, as are the music leader and preacher.

By 1:00, the meeting concludes with prayers of thanks and prayers for the congregation. As team members leave, they are keenly aware that they have experienced God's presence in the midst of their work. They are empowered with a sense of direction for the season and know how they will proceed with their individual tasks. And they have been nourished by the experience of shared leadership and community in which they have participated.

Gifts of collaboration

When it comes to preparing worship for Sunday morning, a collaborative approach has abundant potential. Although leaders obviously need to respect one another and must learn to work together, the benefits of such partnership are plentiful.

First gift: Richer vision of God

Collaborative planning offers a more wholesome theological balance and a broader, more expansive vision of God's character and activity. Although each worship planner has favorite images of God and particular theological understandings that arise from scripture and experience, the dialogue that emerges from a broader range of experiences strengthens worship planning.

For example, two people who are planning a Lenten renewal service may bring quite different understandings of God's mercy toward sinners. A leader who has witnessed the harmful effects of coerced confession may be wary of the value of corporate confession of sin. Another leader who has experienced confession as liberation may be eager to offer the experience to others. As they discuss their differing experiences, they might discover a way to offer a more genuine and less threatening experience of confession than either would have planned alone.

Second gift: More needs met

Another gift of collaboration is that worship can meet a wider array of pastoral needs, both individual and congregational. Although the primary purpose of worship is to serve God rather than to care for the congregation, worshipers' needs for comfort or challenge or assurance are a valid part of what planners consider as they make choices of theme and direction. The wider their circle of contact, the more likely worship leaders are to make wise and sensitive choices. One individual cannot realistically be in touch with all the needs of a congregation.

A pastor may be aware that several members are grieving the deaths of family members who lived many miles away. Another leader may know of young couples who are struggling with infertility. Still another leader may be aware of a painful conflict in a local business that employs several members. When a focus on lament is proposed as a possible theme in a summer series on the Psalms, each of these leaders will bring a different and useful sensitivity regarding what needs to be lamented in worship.

A congregation that is grappling with a decision about whether to build a new building needs to bring such concerns to Sunday worship. Those who lead during these times must care both for those who are anxious and reluctant to move ahead, and for those who are enthusiastic about future possibilities. The prayers of intercession might actually be led by two people, with someone who supports moving forward being invited to pray for those who are anxious, and someone who is fearful being invited to pray for those who are eager to proceed.

Third gift: Expanded engagement

The use of more gifts in worship planning and leading enriches worship for both the congregation and its leaders. Because individual worshipers experience and respond to God in unique ways, worship leaders need to provide various modes for engagement in worship. For some worshipers, musical or visual proclamation of scripture will be paramount. For others, the sermon will be the center. For still others, the children's time will be the most vivid moment of engagement. Depending on whether worshipers process their experience in primarily auditory, visual, or kinesthetic ways, they will tend to connect more readily with one or another of the typical modes of presentation.[2] Over time, however, worshipers can expand their capacity for responding to many more modes of engagement if worship leaders and preachers offer them a varied diet.

Related to the matter of preferred modes of processing our experience is the matter of varieties of styles in worship—musical styles, preaching styles, prayer styles, formal-informal styles, language styles, and even visual styles. The worship leadership team needs to have a clear grasp of the preferred styles or modes of the congregation. They must also be able to offer critique and evaluation of the theological and communal implications of various choices.[3]

In the midst of diversity, what is required of leaders is an ability to respond wisely and compassionately to varied preferences but also to remain committed to the congregation's central biblical and theological convictions regarding worship. Often congregations need encouragement to engage in conversation regarding worship styles and preferences between generations, racial-ethnic groups, and groups of varying theological understandings. When members hear directly from others about why a particular practice or style is meaningful to them, the group is much better equipped to appreciate and value diversity.

A caution or two

Because the free-church tradition does not prescribe worship forms as precisely as some other traditions do, much more responsibility for planning falls on the worship leadership team. A benefit of such freedom is that a high degree of creativity and participation can enrich worship for all; an obvious disadvantage is that worship may become chaotic free-for-all, lacking unity and coherence, or it may become tired, bland, and predictable.

Thus some cautions are also in order. Much time and emotional energy can be wasted if the "cooks" interfere with each other or subvert the overall purpose in favor of personal agendas. Regrettably, worship sometimes ends up being a hodgepodge of competing flavors and courses instead of a satisfying meal. Therefore, when worship is being planned by several people, they need clearly designated leadership and clarity of purpose and focus. They must keep the central scripture text or texts before them. A high level of trust and respect will enable people with varying opinions to make difficult choices while maintaining good relationships.

Sometimes collaborative groups become chummy. They talk together as insiders, perhaps unintentionally excluding others, and they become less objective about one another's contributions, sometimes failing to confront issues that need attention. When collaboration deteriorates, the congregation soon feels the loss of energy, and worship becomes a focal point of stress rather than a Sabbath experience of challenge, joy, and renewal.

Another caution relates to congregational size. Whether a congregation is small, medium, or large, the team approach will work well. In tiny congregations, however, where the pastor gives major leadership to worship planning, it may take time to train lay leaders to become part of the team. But pastors should make this a high priority in order to gain the gifts of collaborative worship planning for the entire congregation.

Questions for collaborators
How is a collaborative worship planning team organized? Who is the central leader?

The basic collaborative worship planning team for ordinary Sunday morning worship consists of at least three people: the worship leader, the preacher, and the music leader (who might function as an individual or represent a team of musicians).

In the case study above, the chair of the worship committee or the chair for a particular season is in charge of the planning process. In a multi-staff situation, the minister of worship might well be the central leader, but in most cases, the chair of the planning process should not be the pastor or preacher (except in a very small congregation, by temporary necessity). Why not? The task of preparing a sermon is demanding and time-consuming. Because the pastor or preacher is usually the person best trained and equipped for preaching, those gifts and skills should be devoted to preaching, not to chairing a worship committee. In addition, the planning meeting is an important step in the preacher's own sermon development process. If preachers need to divert attention to chairing a meeting, they will not derive as much benefit from the meditation time or group discussion time.

Nevertheless, the preacher's advance study of the texts is an essential piece of the process. The planning group could flounder indefinitely or spend a disproportionate time trying to settle on a theme if the preacher has not already discovered some potential directions. Especially in congregations with a solo pastor, that person has most access to the needs and vision of the congregation and is equipped to bring that comprehensive perspective to the planning process.

How are roles on the team differentiated?

In a worship planning team, each member has distinct leadership gifts and responsibilities. Each team member also knows clearly who carries which responsibilities. The worship leader cares for the overall focus, flow, and coherence of the service, giving special attention to scripture, prayers, and congregational participation. The music leader cares for the sounds of the service, the integration of word and music, and the rhythms of prayer expressed in song. The preacher cares for the sermon, taking special responsibility for the way the proclamation of the Word expresses the particular biblical focus of the service, responds to the congregation's needs, and supports the congregation's call and vision.

From time to time, one element of worship may assume more or less importance. A sermon series might take precedence during the Sundays of ordinary time. The ritual of confession and assurance might take priority during Lent. Or music might become the most significant element of worship during festival times such as Christmas, Easter, or Pentecost. Other leadership roles, such as the children's leader or visual art leader, might also take on increased importance at certain times. In each case, the team works together to discern the rhythm and flow of emphases.

What specific skills and preparation are needed for fruitful collaboration?

A variety of gifts are needed for an effective collaborative worship planning team. Worship leaders need gifts of organization and skill with language, especially a good ear for the language style and context of the congregation. They must understand the historical structures of worship, be well grounded biblically and theologically, and be thoroughly familiar with the role of ritual in worship, and with particular rubrics in their setting. They must be warm, prayerful, and trusted as reliable spiritual guides. A special leadership skill needed is the capacity to interpret a particular purpose for worship to others and inspire their collaboration. This role might be called *pastor of the process.*

Preachers also need gifts of organization and skill with language. They need to be good students of the Bible, be reliable interpreters, and especially be able to make vital connections between the Word of God and the life of the people in the congregation. They need to be clear, persuasive, authentic, and trustworthy. In addition, they too must understand the historical structures and purposes of worship so the proclamation of the Word serves the larger purpose of the congregation's corporate spiritual formation and engagement in God's mission of love in the world. A special leadership skill needed is a capacity for tending the connection between scripture and congregational vision. This role might be called *pastor of the Word.*

Music leaders need good musical skills, a capacity to inspire others to make music, and the ability to critically evaluate music choices. They must be well aware of the congregation's musical desires and potential and have a good sense of what will engage people effectively in worship. They must also understand the biblical purposes and historical structures of worship and especially the role of music in fulfilling those purposes. Particularly, they must understand how singing functions as prayer in worship and its significant role in shaping people's encounter with God. A special leadership skill needed is a capacity for calling forth the congregation's voice. This role might be called *pastor of sound.*[4]

Not just one aspect of the pastoral role but many dimensions are needed for worship to fulfill its purpose in congregational life. Sometimes these gifts and capacities are clearly differentiated on a team. In other cases, gifts overlap—as when a worship leader also has strong musical gifts or when a preacher has gifts for leading prayer. If they respect and honor one another's gifts, such teams are twice blessed, because they instinctively understand one another's modes of working and can more easily integrate their work. Most of all, though, the team needs sensitivity to the Spirit's direction and the capacity to respond as a team as they make and carry out specific plans for worship.

While each member of the team is responsible for the integrity and harmony of the worship planning process, the chair or leader carries responsibility to guide the process and to be attentive to group dynamics. When members are struggling to clarify their ideas or to communicate with one another or others in the congregation, the chair attends to those difficulties. The worship leader should be equipped with a variety of tools to facilitate the planning process. The leader should know when to interject ten or fifteen minutes of silence, when to suggest singing a song, when to pause for prayer, or when to call a halt to discussion and ask the group to pay attention to their interactions with one another. The chair should also set aside time for evaluation of the group process and arrange for whatever follow-up is needed.

How are leaders affirmed or credentialed for their ministries?

When worship teams include both credentialed and lay leaders, congregations will need to give attention to the ways all leaders are affirmed for their ministry. Credentialed leaders, who are more often seen in highly visible public roles, are likely to receive more affirmation. Someone who faithfully and creatively leads the children's time in congregational worship or who accompanies singing every week may not receive as much affirmation. Team leadership is best nurtured when all members of the team are publicly blessed and affirmed for their role.

A lay leader who chairs the worship committee or who leads music may gradually grow into a significant spiritual leadership role in the congregation. When the congregation understands the pivotal role of worship in congregational spiritual formation and in its mission, they may choose to license or otherwise credential or affirm the individual for that specific leadership ministry. If they move in this direction, they will need to conform to the policies and procedures of their credentialing body. They will also continue to care for the quality of relationships among all members of the team.

Do collaborative worship planning teams actually work?

Yes, collaborative worship planning teams work! They work especially well in congregations where pastors are clear about their own role and where they are committed to developing and empowering a leadership team. As team members are being formed in faith through the collaborative process, the entire congregation benefits from their spiritual growth. A plentiful harvest of spiritual fruit is gathered as the worship planning team regularly meditates on the Word, listens for the Spirit's direction, prays together, and learns to communicate well within the team and beyond.

Obviously, the congregational size has an impact on collaborative planning. In multi-staff congregations, staff members often carry more responsibility for worship planning and leading. In small congregations, pastors and key leaders carry more of the load. Whatever the size of the congregation, a collaborative approach offers benefits not only for the leaders but also for the spiritual vitality of the congregation.

Who takes responsibility to care for the process and for team members when collaboration breaks down?

In situations where the planning process breaks down or relational problems divide the group, the team leader may meet individually with members to clarify the issues and then bring a report to the group. Together they will decide whether they can resolve their difficulties or whether they need to invite an outside facilitator, from within the congregation or beyond, to assist them.

As such leadership teams work together, the issue of respect is critical. Although each role is vitally important in the service, even more important is the unity and collaboration of the team as they work together to fulfill a single purpose. The sermon is not the main thing, music is not the main thing, nor is leading worship the main thing. The main thing is a Spirit-guided worship service in which the team has done its best to listen to the Spirit's leading and discern a particular focus for the service; and in mutual respect, they have offered their leadership gifts for the sake of guiding the congregation's encounter with God in worship.

Unfortunately, too many examples can be found of unharmonious, unfruitful relationships or competition between members of worship leadership teams, which resulted in ruptures that brought harm to congregations. To minimize the risk of such difficulties, clear leadership must be established, and the team leader must carefully and prayerfully tend the group process.

How do collaborative teams keep growing and improving?

To keep growing as leaders, the team needs to be well equipped with resources for their ministry. Such resources may include a growing library of books, videos, and other material. Regular training at carefully selected conferences, retreats, and workshops is also valuable. Especially helpful are seasoned mentors who can guide the individual growth of leaders. An annual retreat provides opportunity for planning, reflection, and renewal.[5]

What is the relationship between the seasonal planning team and the congregation's worship committee? Between leaders for any particular Sunday and the worship committee?

Depending on the size of the congregation, the worship committee may take direct responsibility for weekly worship planning, or it may delegate that work to seasonal or monthly planning teams. Because of the time involved in planning and leading, more and more congregations are moving toward the monthly or seasonal approach for weekly planning. In those situations, the worship committee oversees the congregation's vision for worship, establishes overall themes and procedures, trains and guides new leaders, and supervises the work of seasonal or monthly planning teams, thus providing focus and continuity for the congregation's experience of worship.

Seasonal or monthly planning teams have the advantage of bringing fresh, creative energy to the ongoing ministry of worship leading. Picking up the overall themes and patterns established by the worship committee, they develop plans for weekly worship and lead those services, along with others they have invited for specific roles. If the congregation has a solo pastor, she meets with each of the seasonal or monthly planning teams and functions much as described in the case study. The worship committee chair provides orientation for the group, sees that they have the resources needed, and oversees evaluation. It can be very helpful for the seasonal or monthly planning team to meet with the entire worship committee during or after their stint of leadership to discuss what they are experiencing and to participate in evaluation.

What is the relationship between the worship committee and other leadership groups in the congregation?

Those who plan and lead worship bear responsibility for a major piece of the congregation's spiritual formation. With the pastor or pastors as regular members of the team, the team has a direct and vital connection to the central leadership structure of the congregation. While this connection is essential, links need to be created with other leadership groups as well. Because worship overlaps with and intersects with every arena of congregational life—including pastoral care, education, and mission—such links are indispensable.

Ministry teams, combining pastoral and lay leadership, are one way congregations provide for these links. A lay minister of mission and a lay minister of worship, for example, can have regular conversation as members of the ministry team, thus assuring a healthy flow of ideas and planning between these two arenas.

In other settings, the links may be less formally constructed or may be developed as the need arises. A representative of the mission committee may be invited to join the worship committee when plans are being made for mission Sunday or for a special worship series on mission. Or the leaders of the children's Sunday school department may meet with the worship committee on occasion to make connections between education and worship.

How far in advance do leaders need to work in order to enhance the collaborative process? What communication structures or processes are needed?

One of the very real struggles in week-to-week worship planning is scarcity of time. Although a seasonal worship committee may meet six weeks in advance to lay the groundwork for a season, a great deal of work remains to be done each week. And because most congregations do not have a minister of worship on staff and many do not even have full-time pastors, lay leaders must be prepared to give considerable time to planning and leading.

Advance planning is extraordinarily valuable. It gives leaders time to pray, gather resources, listen to others, rethink their plans, and invite others to collaborate in leading the service. It allows time for creativity to flourish and for more complex plans to be implemented.

What is ideal is for a pastor/preacher, in collaboration with other congregational leaders, to establish a yearly calendar of biblical texts and themes for worship as well as other arenas of congregational life. Although these plans can be changed as needed, they provide guidance for the work of other leaders and encourage more thoughtful, better integrated planning.

What happens in weekly planning sessions?

Keeping in mind the vision and purposes of the worship committee as well as the monthly or seasonal planning team's goals, the leaders for a given Sunday should be able to comfortably accomplish their work by meeting a week and a half or two weeks prior to that date. If the group waits until Tuesday or Wednesday to plan next Sunday's worship, it's usually too late to involve other people in leadership (many people decline if asked to do something in worship just a couple days before Sunday). It's also too late for the leaders themselves to be as creative and responsive as they could be.

By the time of the weekly meeting, the members of the planning team have already considered the scripture texts and participated in the development of overall themes for the month or season. The preacher has already chosen a tentative focus for the sermon. The children's leader has already been considering possible approaches. A worship center may already be in place, having been developed by the visual art leader for the month or season. What is left for the weekly meeting is review of the initial preparations and developing a specific plan for the service.

Weekly worship planning agenda

1. The group begins with worship and prayer.
2. The preacher for the service reviews the message of the sermon.
3. The team restates the overall theme or focus of the service.
4. The worship leader suggests an overall design for the flow of the service.
5. Team members offer ideas for specific elements of the service: music, presentation of scripture texts, prayers, rituals, offering, children's time, visual center, and dismissal.
6. Together the team makes final choices, editing and reworking as needed, and assigns tasks for leadership.
7. The worship leader invites the group to reflect on how they have worked together and concludes with prayer.

Although it can be tempting for the weekly planning team to dive directly into their business, a better way to begin is with worship and prayer. The leader reads one of the scriptures for the coming Sunday and suggests a time for silence or brief reflections—in this way connecting immediately with the nourishing spiritual center of the task.

After prayer, the worship leader goes over the previous planning and the focus for the assigned Sunday. The preacher provides an update on how the sermon is developing, and the music leader reports on plans for music. Then the worship leader presents a possible outline for the service, and the group works together to develop the service. Each leader has freedom to comment on the direction of the sermon, on music choices, on prayers or rituals, and on the overall flow and shape of the service. Now the collaborative approach really pays off. Because several heads and hearts are better than one, response from trusted co-leaders helps all sharpen and clarify their choices. When something must be added or cut, each one sees the necessity and willingly engages in rethinking the service. The result is a far more integrated, cohesive service, one that has received careful critique in advance.

A good habit is to end the meeting by asking how the team is feeling about the way they are working together. If misunderstandings or hurt feelings are reported, they can be quickly repaired. Or if more time is needed, those involved can arrange a time to talk, and the group can encourage and bless them. There is simply no substitute for giving regular attention to healthy relationships on the team.

Although weekly planning sessions may include the children's leader, the visual art leader, and those who are involved in dramas or other parts of the service, so many people may find it difficult to coordinate their schedules. The presence of these leaders is more critical at the monthly or seasonal planning session. Furthermore, the detailed work of outlining the service is more efficiently accomplished by a smaller group. It is essential, though, for those leading the children and those working with visual art to be integrally connected with the planning process. The significance of what they have to offer will be considerably diminished if they are overlooked in the planning.

After leaders become accustomed to the collaborative way of working, their weekly planning can normally be accomplished in sixty- to seventy-five minutes and can usually fit into a time slot before work or immediately after work, so as not to tie up precious evening hours. After the meeting, each person finishes assigned tasks and reports back to the others by telephone or e-mail. By Wednesday or Thursday before Sunday worship, they have communicated all the necessary information for the service to the church secretary, who prepares the church bulletin, or PowerPoint presentation, or whatever other format is used.

Although shortcuts such as planning by telephone or e-mail may seem appealing, these approaches do not yield the desired results of collaboration. Nothing can substitute for being together in person, struggling with the shape of the service, being inspired by someone else's idea, sensing the creative flow of the Spirit in the group, and yielding to a commonly discerned plan. The spiritual formation and transformation of leaders in the context of Christian community requires such an investment of time and energy.

It's true that the collaborative approach takes time. If one counts the preparatory meeting in which an entire month or season is planned; the weekly planning session; and the individual time spent in prayer, reflection, planning, practicing, and contacting other people, it may well be that thirty-five or forty hours—a week's work—will have been invested in an ordinary Sunday morning worship service by the collaborative worship planning team. Is worship worth such an investment? Although each congregation will need to decide for itself whether worship is a priority, this investment does more to nurture the congregation's spiritual vitality than any other investment of time. The hours spent planning and preparing for Sunday worship are hours devoted directly to the heart of the pastoral task: leading the congregation into God's presence, strengthening their life as a loving community, and empowering them to love and serve God in the world.[6]

What needs to happen each Sunday morning before worship begins? How does the leadership team ensure that all parts of the service have been prepared for? How are last-minute snarls untangled?

In the sample scenario described above, the collaborative worship planning team completes its preparations by mid-week. On Sunday morning, they arrive an hour early and quickly check in with one another. From then on, they function independently until about fifteen minutes before the service begins. The pastor/preacher may spend most of that time in the foyer greeting people as they arrive, engaging in conversations with them; the hour before worship is a prime time for connecting with a wide variety of people. The music leader will likely be rehearsing with individuals or groups and accompanists. The worship leader may be rehearsing scripture readings, dramas, or rituals, and checking in with others involved in the service (children's leader, visual art leader, ushers, people running the sound system, for example).

About fifteen minutes before the prelude or gathering music

begins, everyone involved in leadership gathers in the prayer room, the pastor's office, or some other suitable space. Here the worship leader reviews the entire sequence, invites any last-minute questions, suggests some moments of silence, and then guides the group in a relaxed time of prayer, offering all their planning to God. If something has been overlooked that should have been prepared, the team decides whether to include or omit it. On leaving the room, they take their places, and the service begins.

How do other people in the congregation, including youth and children, become involved in leading and participating in worship?

Although the collaborative planning team is central to Sunday morning worship, it is not alone. Throughout the planning process, the members of the planning group seek to include others in leadership. Their first consideration is the gifts in the congregation. Both formally and informally, they encourage the development of gifts and call people to use those gifts in worship. Because no good purpose in worship is served by a democratic approach, in which everyone takes a turn reading scripture, acting in a drama, or leading music—whether or not they have gifts—those who invite others to lead spend time discerning whom the Spirit may be calling and gifting for leadership.

Several kinds of grids are regularly consulted as choices are made. For example, the team considers age groups in the congregation: older and middle-aged adults, young adults, youth, and children. They think about those who are new to the congregation and those who have been around a long time. They take notice of various ethnic, cultural, and economic groups.[7] They reflect on the streams of spirituality and theology represented in the congregation. The planning team especially considers those who could help the congregation hear certain texts or heighten their awareness of particular actions in worship.

Good planning will give careful attention to the role of youth and children in worship leadership. Again, the motivation is not democratic inclusion. Rather, the pertinent consideration is what actions of worship may be effectively and appropriately led by youth and children. If the congregation will hear a scripture text best if a child speaks it, then a child should be invited to lead by reading and be given whatever guidance is needed to do so well. If a role in a drama or musical work would be enhanced by having a teen fill it, then that teen should be invited to do so.

The planning team needs to think outside the box about ways to engage children and youth in worship leadership. Although the act of confession is not normally a good place to involve children as leaders, one congregation found a meaningful way to engage children in leading the prayer of confession on the first Sunday of Lent. On the Sunday before Ash Wednesday, the children's Sunday school classes constructed small crosses by joining two crossed bare twigs with purple yarn. During worship the next Sunday, these palm-sized crosses were distributed as part of the time of confession: worshipers came forward and passed by a large standing cross while they sang, "Take up your cross and follow Jesus." The worship leader encouraged all to put their crosses in their place of prayer at home. Throughout the Lenten season, the congregation spent time reflecting on Jesus's call to follow and shared those commitments in worship each week.

The leadership visible in worship should, over time, reflect the composition of the congregation. Although planners need not develop a quota system or approach the matter as a mathematical exercise, if worshipers see that worship leadership reflects the congregation's demographics, they will recognize that their voices are being heard.

When and how does evaluation occur? How do leaders receive response? How does the congregation receive feedback?

When response and evaluation are neglected, worship deteriorates. Because worship is a communal experience, people who participate must be given ways to respond to what is planned and led. If leaders do not organize a way to regularly solicit response, they will get it anyway—and, human nature being what it is, they are most likely to hear from people who have complaints. Leaders must take the initiative here, as in other ministries, to invite response from the congregation and to create contexts in which it can be offered constructively.[8]

But just as important as congregational evaluation of worship is the worship committee or worship team's own internal evaluation. At least once each year, the team must pause to reflect on their goals, commitments, and working relationships. A set of evaluation questions can be given to members in advance of an annual meeting; these questions become the focus of discussion. Selected elders or deacons might also be invited to join the committee for such evaluations. Questions might include the following:

How is new leadership encouraged and called forth? If the potential for team leadership does not exist because of the size or gifts of the congregation, how might a pastor or lay leaders initiate some parts of such a vision?

One way congregations expand the pool of those involved in worship and music leading is by offering occasional training workshops. Someone with special expertise in worship drama, oral interpretation, or leading in public prayer can be invited for a Saturday morning or Sunday afternoon training session. Those who participate in the training can then be called on regularly in the following weeks to lead that action in worship.

Another way to expand the leadership pool is to provide mentors for those who have gifts for worship leading. In one congregation, the worship committee selects a gifted teenager to work alongside a master worship leader for a month or season. The teen attends the overall planning session and watches how the process works. Then he participates in the weekly planning session. On the first Sunday or two, he may read a scripture. By the second Sunday, he assists in inviting others who will be involved in the service and rehearses with them before the service. The next Sunday teen and mentor co-plan and co-lead the service. By the fourth Sunday, the youth plans and leads the entire service. Each week, the mentor and the teen meet immediately after the service to evaluate the service. If the young person's interest is confirmed and continues, he is invited to lead on suitable occasions through the rest of the year and is given response and encouragement.

In churches where lay leaders have previously been given little responsibility, a simple but significant place to begin is to invite congregational members to participate as readers of scripture. Another starting place is the children's time. Nearly all congregations have people who work well with children. The pastor can mentor these folks, helping them understand that the children's moment is part of the flow of worship, not a time for instruction or entertainment. Another obvious beginning point is music. Children, youth, and adults have musical gifts that can be developed further for worship ministry.

Whatever the size of the congregation, intentional regular efforts must be made to discern gifts and call forth lay leaders for the ministry of worship planning.

What is the connection between collaboration and the spiritual formation of leaders?

Although collaboration in worship leadership may seem complex, it is actually an efficient and fruitful way to accomplish two important goals at once. A significant and central ministry task of the congregation is carried out at the same time that faith is being formed among those who are leading. Encouraged, supported, and mentored, team members grow to maturity both as individuals and as leaders. If we consider all the spiritual benefits to be gained by the team in the case study described earlier in this chapter, we might be astounded:

Biblical engagement. Each person delved into the scriptures before the meeting, becoming acquainted with a variety of texts.

Prayer. Both before and during the planning meeting, listening prayer was vital.

Pastoral care. All members of the planning team took responsibility for discerning the needs of the congregation and responding in appropriate ways.

Creative thinking and planning. Stimulated by one another's creative ideas, the group had more than enough ideas to choose from as they moved into the planning stage.

Dependence on God. Because no single person was responsible for the outcome, the group together practiced depending on the Spirit's guidance.

Relational growth. As they worked together, the group refined their listening and communication skills, deepened their trust in and respect for one another, and discovered the treasure of abundance that is uncovered when people collaborate instead of working alone. Along the way, they also learned how to speak the truth in love and to offer forgiveness when differences or misunderstandings arose.

Thus collaboration in worship planning and leading builds up the body of Christ even as it accomplishes an essential ministry of the congregation. Rather than serving up bland, monotonous, or non-nutritious meals, a collaborative team prepares and serves colorful, flavorful, and satisfying meals that appeal to the whole body of Christ. With the Spirit's many and varied gifts in use, the congregation is nourished and strengthened each week for their life in Christ, their love for one another, and their witness and ministry in the world.

8

HOSTING THE GUESTS

Welcome one another, therefore, just as Christ has welcomed you.
(Rom 15:7)

At most meals, someone is in charge. Even at a potluck, where every-one brings a dish, someone gets things started by organizing the table. Main dishes are grouped at one end, followed by salads and bread, and at the end come the desserts. Another table is laden with hot and cold drinks. Someone calls the group together, offers a prayer, and invites people to help themselves.

Different kinds of meals require different styles or degrees of hosting. A picnic may be as uncomplicated as calling a few friends and meeting at an appointed time at the local park. When folks have located a suitable spot out of the sun and under the trees, they spread blankets and open picnic hampers. The food appears: crisp fried chicken, baked beans, dill pickles, potato chips, and wedges of water-melon. Relaxed and informal, the meal proceeds without much obvi-ous direction, yet someone got the whole event started.

In an office lunchroom, the employees take turns hosting a monthly one-dish meal. The person in charge brings a slow cooker full of soup, which simmers all morning. At noon, a table is spread simply, with soup bowls, a loaf of bread and some butter, and the slow cooker. Some months, a bouquet of flowers from someone's gar-den graces the table.

At ordinary family meals, Mom and Dad are typically in charge. Nowadays, when parents often share cooking duties, they dish up the food after one of the children has set the table. Mom or Dad offers a grace, and the food is passed family style. Parents pay attention to the flow of conversation, making sure each family member is included and arbitrating when disagreements occur. At the end of the meal, everyone pitches in to clear the table and load the dishwasher.

On more formal occasions, such as holiday feasts or special celebrations, hosting becomes more complex. Often several people get involved. One sends out invitations, another oversees menu planning, someone else is in charge of decorations, another greets guests at the door, and still another provides guidance for table conversation. The courses of the meal are carefully orchestrated: sometimes planners set an overall theme, arrange a pleasing combination of tastes and textures and colors, and provide an interesting balance of traditional and new foods.

Worship leader as host

Viewing the worship leadership team as hosts for Sunday morning holds potential for helping us understand the ministry of leading worship. Whenever people gather—whether for worship or some other social experience—someone must give attention to hosting the event. People need to be welcomed and sent. They need to feel connected with what is happening and with others who are present. They need to feel that someone is guiding the event toward its purpose. They need to know their needs are being considered and cared for. Without such attentiveness, any social gathering disintegrates. People feel disconnected, become irritable or withdrawn, and eventually stop participating.

Although the call to serve as host can at first seem daunting, most people already know a great deal about hosting. Functioning as a host of worship means drawing on what we already know and making appropriate inferences and connections. Building on this foundation, an inexperienced leader can develop the capacities and skills for leading people into an encounter with God. As we gain more experience, we function less and less self-consciously and eventually are able to create hospitable spaces for meeting God.

Who can host the meal?

It used to be that only ordained ministers, deacons, or elders led worship. Today, in free-church worship traditions, almost anyone may stand before the congregation and guide worship on Sunday morning. Beginning in the late 1950s and early 1960s, as more egalitarian patterns of communal life emerged, lay leaders of worship began joining or replacing ordained leaders in this role. While more direct involvement and wider participation in leading worship have offered many strengths and greater creativity to worship, churches have also sustained some losses.

Those who lead worship carry enormous responsibility for guiding people into awareness of God's presence and into the spacious place where transformation happens. If worship leaders do not understand their role and do not inhabit it with conviction and grace, they will have difficulty creating a space where the Spirit can move. When Christians do not regularly encounter God and one another in life-changing ways in weekly worship, the body of Christ suffers and the church's witness is weakened. As a result, the gracious reign of God in the world is less visible and less potent. But when worship leaders do understand their role and are equipped for this leadership ministry, they join God's Spirit in extending the invitation to transformation in remarkable and fruitful ways.

John Bell, composer, musician, and preacher of the Iona Community in Scotland, tells the story of how he began exploring his call to leadership ministry. As a teenager, he confided to an elder in his congregation that he was sensing God's call to ministry. The wise elder told him, "You will need three things if you want to become a minister: a love for God, a love for the people, and a love for language."[1] These three arenas require the careful attention of any who aspire to leadership in worship or preaching.

Our love for God is nourished by participating in worship, by our own personal prayer, by diligent study of scripture, and by opening ourselves to many streams of Christian spirituality.

Love for the people of God is nourished by wide and deep acquaintance with the body of Christ to which we belong. This love entails paying close attention to what people care about, what moves them, what inspires them. It involves watching how people do significant things in daily life, for the rituals of the church are grounded in the ordinary actions of eating, drinking, bathing, washing, touching, and embracing.

The third arena, love of language, also calls for thoughtful consideration. Although the levels and styles of language vary from church to church, all worship is enhanced by clear, apt, vigorous, rhythmic, and passionate language. Those who aspire to lead worship should listen closely to the patterns and cadences of local speech. We should also read broadly—the Bible first, and then fiction, nonfiction, autobiography, and poetry. We do well to pay attention to spiritual autobiographies, especially the accounts of people who have found their way back to the church or who have come to the church for the first time as adults. The sensibilities of these people about religious language can be unusually instructive, as we notice how new Christians describe the power of vivid and passionate language to lure them into God's presence.[2] Poetry, with its earthiness and colorful images as well as its concern for what is at the heart of reality, strengthens our love for language.

Some religious traditions are suspicious of anything but the plainest speech. That God might be pleased with an exquisite line of poetry, a sparkling image, or a skillfully turned phrase seems beyond their grasp. Walter Brueggemann makes a case for public prayers being "well said," not to call attention to the artistry but "to mobilize and sustain the attention of the praying community." He writes, "Such prayer must be porous, in order to allow the words uttered to be access points for other members of the praying assembly who may take these utterances as their utterances."[3] If we think beauty is merely decorative, then our hesitation may have some merit. But if beauty is a language for the ineffable, creating space for deeper encounter with mystery, then it surely belongs in worship of the most high God.

Fifty years is a short span in which to develop a new leadership role and train people for it. Proceeding mainly by trial and error, some congregations have discerned helpful ways to call and train worship leaders, while others struggle to find their way. Gaining clarity about the purpose of leading worship, understanding its role in the congregation, and assessing the gifts required are critical steps toward renewing the church.

Using the image of host as a central image for worship leading can open a territory for fruitful exploration and prepare the way to empower leaders for more effective ministry in the church. To that discussion we now turn.

What does it mean to host the people of God in worship?

Perhaps the most obvious place to begin our assessment of what it means to host God's people in worship is with the horizontal dimensions of hosting. Part of the identity and role of the worship leader is similar to the task of being a host at a dinner or banquet. If worship leaders take their cues from what we already know about ordinary hosting in our homes and other social settings, we will discover a bountiful treasury of insights.

A recent visit with my extended family in Oregon inspired the idea of hosting an Oregon meal for friends in my current home in Indiana. As I pondered the idea, questions came to mind. Whom should I invite? What should we eat? Would we eat in the dining room or outside in the garden? How should the table be set? What might we talk about at the meal?

Before any cooking happened or before any guests arrived, I needed to think my way through these questions and many more. Because of my attachment to Oregon, I wanted to share this meal with especially good friends, people who would appreciate the significance of my devotion to my home state and be willing to put up with my ridiculous love for it. I knew immediately that several Oregon specialties would be on the menu: rich, robust Tillamook cheese, flavorful hazelnuts, and fresh Dungeness crab or Oregon salmon. In addition, I would go foraging for several varieties of crisp, sweet lettuce for salad, as well as for fresh berries to create a memorable dessert.

Because the natural beauty of Oregon has been such a significant part of my attachment to the state, I chose the perennial flower garden in our backyard as the outdoor setting for the meal—and hoped for a warm, rain-free evening. That choice also meant the garden had to be weeded and the grass cut. We had to carry tables into the garden and cover them with festive cloths (weighted down at the corners, so they wouldn't blow away if the evening was windy). And we had to select dinnerware appropriate for outdoor eating.

During the meal, I invited our guests to tell stories of their native territories. As each course was served, I recounted memories of eating the special foods of Oregon when I was growing up. That prompted other food memories from guests, and we spent a delightful evening recalling stories and telling one another about our homes in faraway places.

Offering hospitality that evening was a labor of love. By carefully thinking through the task of hosting, and by considering both my own desires for the evening and what our guests would find enjoyable, I was able to plan an event that all of us found satisfying.

Clearly, the task of hosting a meal is complex. It begins long before guests arrive, moves into high gear as soon as the doorbell rings, and requires ongoing attentiveness throughout the meal. It is a time-honored way of expressing love and care for people we cherish and with whom we want to share a special time.

Hosting the community's engagement with one another

When it comes to worship planning, the same complexity applies. The hosting duties of the worship leadership team begin long before Sunday morning, they are vitally important during the service, and they continue even after the service is over. Although the worship leadership team will definitely not carry out all these tasks alone, these responsibilities are part of the role.

Host	pastoral presence who
	cares for the community as a whole
	is attentive to context
	is able to think through order and process
Role in worship	to care for context and comfort of the
	community
Axis of attention	horizontal

In planning, we first consider who will be worshipping together on a particular occasion. Those who lead are called to pay loving attention to all who are present: children, young people, adults, those who are struggling, those who are rejoicing, the lonely, the new folk, and the faithful regulars. All our choices will be informed by an awareness of who will be present at worship.[4]

Paying attention means greeting everyone who comes; the ministry of greeting and ushering may, in fact, be the most underestimated ministry on Sunday morning. Certainly, good hospitality requires a friendly smile and words of welcome at the front door. It may also require well-placed outdoor signs as well as the presence of a greeter in the church parking lot to ensure that people find their way to the front door. Those who have problems with mobility and those herding small children into the building may need assistance. People with special needs may be grateful for a large-print hymnal, help with an elevator, or space for wheelchair seating in the worship area. After worship begins, the ministry of hospitality continues—making sure people can hear or have found the right hymnbook, and providing spoken or written directions adequate to guide them through the logistics of the service. When worship is over, people are available to converse with worshipers and to hear concerns or joys.

In addition to greeting those who come, the host considers other elements of welcome. What about a visual welcome? What will people see when they approach the church doors and when they enter the foyer? Is the area clean and cared for? Can people readily find information about the church and its activities?

An under-explored dimension of the welcoming ministry is the presence of an appropriate visual center in the foyer that draws people into the scripture focus for the day. Even before people enter the sanctuary, their attention may be captured by what greets their eyes. For example, during Lent one year, Jesus's story of the prodigal son was a central feature. A congregation placed a large print of Rembrandt's *The Return of the Prodigal Son* on an easel in the entrance, where children as well as adults could pause to look closely at the painting. Throughout the season, children's time considered the various characters depicted in the painting.

Inside the sanctuary, other visual elements can welcome worshipers and prepare them to receive the Word of God: an artful display on a central worship table, banners on the walls, or other symbols.

Related to the visual elements is the larger issue of the space in which worship takes place. What arrangement of chairs and benches will best encourage the congregation to worship God? Is the temperature appropriate? How do the acoustics serve or hinder worship? Can everyone hear and see what is going on? Can people comfortably move forward to receive communion? Can they actually see a baptism? One congregation invites children forward to sit on the floor nearby whenever a baptism occurs. The congregation baptizes adults, and they want children to grow up seeing and knowing what the ritual of baptism looks like, thus preparing them for the day when they will be baptized.

A less tangible dimension of the space question is the issue of emotional space. Do worship leaders create a spacious place for the congregation? Do we communicate a genuine welcome to all—young and old, rich and poor, joyful and grieving, and those with more and less formal education? Do we lead in a way that is both purposeful and relaxed? Is there a leisurely quality about the time the congregation spends together in worship? Do we make transitions thoughtfully? Can we join the congregation's pace?

Sometimes the opening words of worship feel exclusive. If the worship leader is overly upbeat and enthusiastic, those who are discouraged or depressed may feel disregarded. On the other hand, a too-solemn leader can suppress the joy and excitement of those who come feeling especially invigorated. One way of offering hospitality at the opening of worship is with words that acknowledge this variety.

> If you are delighted to be here, and if you are tired or troubled,
>   you are welcome.
> If your faith is strong, and if your faith is battered or frail,
>   you are welcome.
> If you are eager to offer praise to God, and if you just need to be quiet,
>   you are welcome.
> God welcomes us all to worship today.
> God promises to meet us here.[5]

Considering who is present when making choices for worship also extends to the resources used—the task of creating the menu. Hospitable worship leaders forage for the very best resources we can find to enrich worship. We look for language and images that are understandable, inclusive, and accessible to the congregation. At the same time, we are alert to choices that may gently stretch the congregation's awareness and offer fresh ways of speaking or praying.[6]

As an open-ended, creative process, such searching goes on week in and week out. Keeping files of stories, images, prayers, or bits of poetry or song that might contribute to worship provides us with valuable resources for future planning.[7]

When an array of resources has been gathered, we give thought to how the ingredients will work together and how the meal will be served: How will the service flow? What is its overall shape? What should come first or last?[8] Sometimes a particular element of worship—a song, for example, or a dramatic presentation of scripture, is so powerful that everything else that happens must be arranged to give this element central place. When the beloved communion hymn "I am the Bread of life" is sung, it often becomes the climax of the service.[9] Because of the narrative quality of the text and the rising crescendo of the refrain, the song builds toward a powerful climax. To sing anything afterward tends to feel anti-climactic.

The texture and character of resources is another issue. What will be familiar and well-loved? What will be fresh? Flavorful? Spicy? Colorful? What is ephemeral? What has staying power? Worship leaders must tend the balance and interweaving of what is familiar and what is new, paying attention to what a congregation needs in order to feel secure in worship but also opening up the edges to fresh experiences.[10] Discerning an appropriate diet for worship—whether in singing, preaching or praying—requires creativity and vigilance.

Throughout the service—in the choice of music, in the sermon, in the prayers—we express or inhibit hospitality in the choices we make. A song leader who disregards the favorites of elderly worshipers will not be able to lead the whole community effectively. A preacher who uses exclusively male examples in sermons sends an inhospitable message toward women and girls. A leader of prayer who never prays for the concerns of children or who ignores the needs of the poor excludes these groups from the congregation's awareness. Worship leaders and preachers do well to keep an internal grid in mind, composed of all the groups in the congregation they need to care for. Although such a grid cannot be used in a mechanical fashion, it can aid reflection on the quality of hospitality we offer in worship. And while the practice of hospitality reflects the community's commitment to valuing differences, its main focus is to enlarge what the community holds in common.

A hospitable worship leader may be required, on occasion, to intervene in delicate or difficult circumstances when the quality of worship for the community as a whole is in jeopardy. In one congregation, where sharing of joys and concerns is a regular feature after the sermon, some worshipers occasionally came to the microphone and spoke as though they were oblivious to the amount of time they were taking, or they included intimate details inappropriate for a public setting. Pastors spoke privately to these people, encouraging them to keep others' needs in mind as they shared their concerns. From time to time, leaders offered gentle reminders to the entire congregation regarding ways to share appropriately.

Even after receiving such courteous feedback, however, one or two individuals continued to struggle to find appropriate ways to share. After a stirring service one Sunday morning, a woman stood to speak, first sharing her appreciation for the service and then relating a long list of concerns about a friend. After she spoke for several minutes, repeating herself, and disclosing more and more intimate details, the congregation became uneasy, even embarrassed by her apparent inability to bring the recital to a conclusion. The wise worship leader on duty that day left the platform, walked to the microphone where the woman stood, and gently asked, "How can we pray for you today?" The woman was able to state her desire simply, and the worship leader offered a heartfelt prayer on behalf of the woman and her friend. The hospitality of the worship leader transformed a potentially distressing incident into a moment of compassion and care.

A hospitable worship leader can also help the congregation remember its manners. Because some changes are annoying or inconvenient or simply uncomfortable, worshipers may need encouragement to be patient long enough to understand and receive what is unusual or strange. A worship leader who was being especially attentive to teenagers in the congregation chose to use a popular song as part of the call to worship. Knowing that some of the older folks would likely be put off by this style of music, he invited a teen to lead worship with him that day. In a carefully prepared call to worship, the two spoke of the dazzling variety of ways the natural world gives glory to God. Then they shifted and spoke of the many ways human beings praise God. Finally, the teen said, "As we enter worship, let us listen to a song of praise that holds significant meaning for many young people today." After the service, people expressed appreciation for the thoughtful leadership. A bridge of communication and respect had been built.

The worship leader as host of the gathered body provides a vital form of pastoral care. Caring for the community as a whole, the leader is aware of all the groups in the congregation, remains attentive to the context, is able to think through a suitable order and process, and guides worship in a way that invites wholehearted participation, thus recreating and renewing the body of Christ each week. What we as worship leaders must remember is that hospitality is not about the host. It is all about the guests and about offering the best possible service and attention. Although the host often experiences a blessing as well, the ministry of worship leading does not focus on the host's desires or needs. Worship leading is a servant ministry, building up the body.[11]

Hosting an encounter with God

The horizontal axis of attention is, however, just one dimension of the ministry of the worship leader as host. Worship leaders are also called to care for the vertical axis of attention. When Christians meet for worship, they gather for the purpose of meeting God together. As important as the horizontal dimensions of gathering are for the community's sense of well-being, the body of Christ cannot be sustained or renewed without regularly experiencing an encounter with the living God.

Shaman	person of spirit who
	has encountered God
	knows the ancient stories and ritual pathways
	is trusted by the people
	is equipped to guide others on the path to God
Role in worship	to guide the congregation's encounter with God
Axis of attention	vertical

In traditional societies, such as some Native American groups, the person who guides the community's encounter with the sacred is sometimes called a shaman. Although this term is not usually used in church, the role is known and experienced all over the world. In fact, Jesus could be considered a shaman in his priestly role of guiding people into an encounter with God and God's vision for the world. Just as the image of dinner host contributes important understandings for worship leading, so the image of worship leader as shaman can contribute to an enlarged understanding of this leadership ministry.

The shaman is a person of spirit, one who has encountered the divine, knows the ancient stories of the faith and its ritual pathways, and is trusted by the people. One could also appropriately use the term priest for this role; however, many Protestants go blank when they encounter that term, or they immediately resist it. A shaman is a priest—but a priest with a difference. Not just an institutional representative of the church, the shaman knows God intimately, knows the ways of God in human experience, knows the stories of God handed down from one generation to another, and knows the role and function of symbol and ritual in worship. In ancient Celtic druid religion, for example, the shaman leader spent twelve years in training before being entrusted with leadership of the community's sacred rituals.

During that time, the apprentice shaman learned the songs, stories, poetry, dances, and symbols of the tradition—all by heart. In addition, the apprentice learned the habits of the heart, the attitudes, and the spirit required of a leader. Only after such extensive training could a shaman assume the role of spiritual leader.

Even today it may take twelve years—or more—for a worship leader to learn to inhabit the role: to get beyond the need to be the center of attention; to recognize what a community needs in worship; to understand the importance of pacing, time, space, structure, and anti-structure; to develop the courage to lead and to be trusted to guide the community into God's presence.

Sometimes worship leading is assigned to people who are not yet ready for this ministry. In a mistaken attempt to be inviting to all, congregations indiscriminately pass around the assignment. Although it is certainly important to invite broad participation in leading worship, the role of worship leader cannot be sacrificed on the altar of inclusivity. Those who lead must think carefully about what ways of leading are appropriate for people in the congregation. At the same time, congregations must ensure that those who lead worship have been carefully trained and are able to bear the weight of the responsibility.

In one congregation, a teenager was invited to lead the congregational prayers of confession during Lent. Because of the significance of the act of confession during this season and the naked vulnerability required for such intense soul-searching, the congregation needed a trusted guide for such prayers. Although the teenager could have offered effective leadership of other parts of the service, his lack of experience and discomfort with the role made it difficult for worshipers to open themselves to God's cleansing work during the prayers of confession in Lent.

Another congregation focused on the theme "longing for God" during Advent. Each Sunday, a psalm of longing was read by someone in the congregation who had experienced an unfulfilled longing. One Sunday, a couple who had experienced years of infertility read the psalm; another week, a man who had spent nine years in prison read it; another week, it was read by a woman who suffered a chronic illness. In each case, the readers were not people who ordinarily functioned in leadership roles during worship; rather, their authority as leaders arose from their firsthand experience of longing. Their willingness to be vulnerable effectively expanded the congregation's awareness of its longing for God and God's reign.

The operative principle here is that for the sake of the congregation's encounter with God, we must exercise care in selecting and training worship leaders. This statement is not an argument for excluding younger or less experienced people from the role; rather, it is a plea to create a context for their development. When a twenty-eight-year-old asked in a workshop, "How can I stand before the congregation as a shaman when I have so little experience?" the leader responded, "Do you truly want to lead your congregation in worship?" When the young adult answered affirmatively, the leader replied, "Then do it when you're invited—and ask for feedback. Ask for feedback often—because the way you will grow into a mature and trusted leader is by listening to what helps your congregation worship."

A significant dimension of this capacity to lead hospitably is the worship leader's own life with God. While the leader's spirituality is essential for this ministry, it can also be misused. Sometimes, for example, worship leaders are tempted to draw attention to their own spirituality. Such efforts are usually counterproductive, because they deflect attention away from God, thus creating an unhealthy dependence on the leader. These efforts may also discourage worshipers who feel they cannot measure up to the standard portrayed. The balance we seek here grows out of two sources: the leader's own intense and careful spiritual preparation to lead, and the leader's capacity to put that preparation at the service of the congregation. When the leader experiences God's presence in the process of preparation, that encounter will inevitably shape and color the leadership she provides for the community.

Preachers must care for this intersection between the personal and the public, too. No congregation wants to hear sermons that are unconnected with life. Nor do congregations want to hear sermons that only reveal what the preacher is thinking and nothing of the preacher's personal faith. The congregation's experience of God's presence in worship is enhanced when the preacher's own faith enlivens but does not dominate what is preached. If the preacher tells a story one week about a personal experience of prayer, the congregation will be grateful for this glimpse into his piety. In the same way, if he tells a story about a grandchild, the grandparents in the congregation (as well as parents and grandchildren) will identify. If, however, the personal prayer stories or the grandchildren stories begin to dominate his sermons, they will soon create a barrier for worshipers. The stories must serve the purpose of the sermon; they must also be drawn from the life of the whole community, so the spirituality of the congregation is expressed in worship.

What we desire is a combination of transparency and translucence, of letting light shine through us but not drawing attention to ourselves as mediators of light. In order to guide others into God's presence, the leader's own spiritual life becomes the animating energy for words, silence, and gestures. The attention of the shaman worship leader, however, remains focused on directing the community's encounter with God.

In *Liberating Rites*, Tom Driver describes an hours-long initiation ritual he witnessed in Haiti. Although he had been introduced to and welcomed by the shaman leader at the beginning of the evening, he was surprised to discover how inconspicuous the leader remained throughout the event. "Had I not met him earlier and kept my eye out for him, it would have taken me a long time to figure out who, if anybody, was in charge. Excellent host of the party, he moves about quietly, making sure that everything is all right, that everyone who needs greeting gets it. He also gives signals to the drummers from time to time. He does not speak much to me, but I soon realize he is aware of my every movement, and this reassures me."[12]

Perhaps one of the best compliments anyone can pay to a worship leader or preacher is "You didn't get in the way of the community's worship." With respect to the vertical dimensions of hosting worship, less is definitely more: the less one sees or notices the leader and the more one sees or notices God, the better the congregation is served.

One moment in worship during which the shaman quality of the leader is evident is in the opening words. Although the degree of formality or informality varies from place to place, the opening words of worship always set a tone for the worship service that follows. If the worship leader says "Good morning," and continues with folksy conversation regarding the weather or last night's basketball scores, people will settle into an amiable comfort. If worship begins with words such as those that follow, however, the shaman leader is directing the people's attention immediately and effectively to God's presence:

Leader	You are home to the exile
	touch to the frozen
	daylight to the prisoner
	authority to the silent
	anger to the helpless
	laughter to the weary
	direction to the joyful:
All	*Come, our God, come.*[13]

Through much of the history of the church, worship has opened with words known as the *sursum corda* ("lift up your hearts"):

Leader	The Lord be with you.
People	*And also with you.*
Leader	Lift up your hearts.
People	*We lift them to the Lord.*
Leader	Let us give thanks to the Lord our God.
People	*It is right to give our thanks and praise.*

Here the decision about whether to start with the horizontal or the vertical dimension is neatly circumvented. In this text, both the horizontal axis and vertical axis are evident, but with the vertical taking precedence. We do well to heed the wisdom evident in this opening.

Another important expression of the shaman capacity of the leader occurs during congregational prayer. Although it would be ideal for any Christian to be able to offer a public prayer when called on to do so, most leaders need to develop their gifts for such ministry. The act of addressing words to God may be the most vulnerable moment in public worship. As Annie Dillard comments, "I often think of the set pieces of the liturgy as certain words which people have successfully addressed to God without their getting killed."[14] The leader's own relationship with God is made evident at such moments; even more important, the leader's capacity to stand between the people and God is revealed. Does the leader know how to mediate the deep desires of the congregation to God? Does she know their spiritual struggles? Does she understand who God is to these people? Can the leader see beneath the surface and articulate unexpressed fears or longings? Is she able to inspire trust in God's faithful purposes?

While such leadership depends in part on one's command of the language of prayer, it depends even more on the worship leader's willingness to become a channel of grace. Offering oneself as a mediator between humans and God and between God and humans is costly work. It requires bearing the pain, guilt, fear, shame, and despair of human experience. It also requires trusting deeply in "the great shepherd of the sheep," the one who will "make you complete in everything good so that you may do his will" (Heb 13:20). Even when answers do not seem to be forthcoming or God seems very far away, a shaman leader persists in praying vulnerably and honestly.

Eventually, even the most faithful worship leader comes up short. Sunday morning arrives again, and it's time for the prayer of praise or confession or intercession. The worship leader opens his mouth and pauses. Doubts hang suspended in thin air: Is God really there? Do these people really want God? And what am I doing in this place—I who have failed miserably to live in love and charity with my neighbor (or spouse or children or friends) this week? How can I open my lips and not be struck dumb? At such moments, sheer courage and naked trust are all that keep the worship leader from abandoning his post.

The rituals of worship are another arena in which the leader's capacity to fulfill the vertical dimension of the role is tested. Here the leader's capacity to represent God is crucial. The actions of ritual—breaking bread, pouring water, serving the cup, committing a soul to God—must illuminate God's loving, generous action, which is more than human response.

When a baby is blessed, the minister stands in Christ's place, takes the child tenderly in her arms, looks directly into the infant's eyes, speaks the words of blessing with gentle strength, and then joyfully carries the child up and down the aisles of the congregation addressing the child by name and assuring him, "Here are your people."

At a baptism, the minister slows down the pace of speaking and action to indicate that this moment is sacred. Heaven and earth wait for promises to be spoken. He pours water slowly and gently, he extends a welcoming hand, and he speaks words of joyful conviction to the new Christian:

> In the name of Christ and the church,
> I give you my hand and bid you to rise and walk in newness of life
> by the same power that raised Christ from the dead.[15]

At the end of a funeral, the minister steps down from the pulpit and stands beside the casket, slowly turning toward it and then placing a hand on it. She pauses to wait for a moment of full and deep silence, and then she speaks the final weighty words:

> Into your hands, eternal God,
> we commend your servant.
> Receive unto yourself, we humbly ask,
>   a sheep of your fold,
>   a lamb of your flock,
>   a sinner of your redeeming.
> Receive [name] into your arms of mercy,
>   into the company of your saints,
>   into everlasting peace. Amen.[16]

These are human words and actions, but they are also God's words and actions. The one who leads in these moments bears the burden of embodying God's love and care. Fortunately no single worship leader needs to carry such responsibility alone. When worship leading is a collaborative ministry, the entire team shares the call to represent God's presence. Such leaders carry the community's mantle of authority, the weight of history, the repository of memory. Only over time and with the accumulation of experience can worship leaders both represent God to the people and represent the people to God.

Hosting God's vision for the world

There is yet another dimension of the worship leader's role as host. In this role, the worship leader's capacity to see into the heart of reality —the pain and joy, the hope and despair of life—and the ability to name and speak the truth are essential. The worship leader stands before the community as a prophet, holding up a mirror to the world beyond the community and at the same time holding up God's vision for the world. The axis of attention is outwardly focused.

Prophet	passionate truth teller who
	sees into the heart of reality, both the heights and depths of human experience
	cares deeply for the world God loves
	inspires and motivates transformation
Role in worship	to inspire and empower action in the community and the world
Axis of attention	outward

Even while the worship leader is functioning simultaneously on both the vertical and horizontal levels of attention, he is also required to give attention to the Sunday morning newspaper, weekly news magazines, current issues in the community, and larger global concerns. Without these dimensions of attentiveness, the words and gestures of worship become self-serving, insulated, atrophied, and barren.

But it is not enough just to bring the world into worship. The worship leader must also keep alive a vision of God's desires for the world. Caring deeply for the world God loves, the leader's passion for justice and shalom become amply evident. Trusting in God's good purposes and God's power to bring new life, her faith in the triumph of love is revealed and undergirds the community's response.

It would be easy for some worship leaders to be satisfied with the horizontal and vertical dimensions of hosting. To care lovingly for the community and to be in touch with God may seem adequate, may even seem like appropriate pastoral responses. But biblical faith requires more. If our eyes have not been opened to the injustices and needs of our world, then we will not have offered true worship. God's question, "Who will go for me?" will remain unanswered, and we will not have fulfilled the purposes of worship.

The prophetic dimension of leading worship can be described as a discerning role. The worship leader is a seer, a careful observer, a loving critic. Not everything that happens in the church neighborhood or larger community needs to be brought to worship. Rather, as host of worship, the leader's task is to listen carefully to the scripture texts for the day and perceive the relevant and productive connections.

Just as a good cook pays attention to what fruits and vegetables are in season and brings them to the table at the moment of ripeness, so a discerning worship leader-prophet knows and understands the seasons of God's working. When God is speaking and the congregation recognizes God's activity, then they can hear and act on the call to mercy and justice. If the worship leader has not carefully discerned these connections, they can seem overwhelming or insincere or even irrelevant. The congregation's capacity to respond to prophetic words and actions is proportional to the aptness and relevance of what leaders bring.

During the days after the September 11 attacks, many pastors and worship leaders struggled to discern how to lead their communities in prayer. That people wanted to pray together was abundantly evident;

how to pray faithfully wasn't always as clear. How was God seeing what had happened? What was God's call to the Christian community in the midst of disaster? How could Christians pray for the fearful and grieving as well as for enemies?

One ambiguous but understandable public response was the sprouting of "God bless America" signs in yards and businesses and on billboards. While the desire for God's blessing is always appropriate, too often the sentiment that accompanied the signs was a demand that God withhold blessing from those deemed to be America's enemies. The double meaning of the slogan was present even when Christians gathered.

In the chapel at Associated Mennonite Biblical Seminary (Elkhart, Indiana), when the seminary community gathered for prayer during those days, the dean startled worshipers one day when he prayed with great passion, "God, bless America!" After a dramatic pause, he continued, "God, bless Iraq! God, bless Afghanistan! God, bless Northern Ireland! God, bless Canada!" In that moment, he stood courageously in the role of worship leader as prophet, speaking God's truth into a confusing and turbulent situation.

Like the vertical and horizontal dimensions of the leadership role, the outwardly oriented dimensions of worship leading must be cultivated. They do not necessarily come naturally, especially to those who may be drawn to the more nurturing aspects of pastoral leadership. One of the first requirements is a courageous truthfulness. It seems as though speaking the truth should be easy to do in worship, but often things aren't so simple. Sometimes the truth isn't clear, or God doesn't seem to speak clearly. Sometimes the congregation is divided about what is true; sometimes human limitations prevent us from seeing truth; sometimes the leaders and the congregation don't want to see God's truth. Often, of course, what is true can only be seen in hindsight. Thus those who inhabit the role of worship leader as prophet will require a certain humility to keep company with their courage.

We will also devote time, energy, and prayer to becoming discerning people. Jesus promised that the Spirit of truth will guide us into all truth (John 16:13). In company with other members of the body, leaders can study scripture, open themselves to God's Spirit, and test their understandings of what the Spirit is saying to the congregation. Part of this ongoing testing is noticing not only who God is but also what God is doing. Is God speaking judgment? Offering comfort? Calling for repentance? Liberating? While the congregation may prefer only comforting or encouraging pictures of God, the faithful worship leader will cast a wide net in the search for truth.

Prophetic worship leaders and preachers must pay careful attention to local, regional, national and worldwide news—movements, events, and people. As noted above, the task is not to overwhelm the congregation with news but rather to make relevant connections so that what God is doing can be seen more clearly. During an Advent season, worship leaders in one congregation structured a prayer sequence in two parts: bad news and good news. In the first part, they read bits and pieces of news from the week's newspapers—stories that focused on injustice, violence, poverty, and discrimination. After a pause for silent prayers of confession, they read from the beautiful prophetic texts of Advent that describe God's vision for the world—a place of peace and plenty and joy for all. The prayer concluded with a song expressing the congregation's longing for the coming of God's day.

The prophetic role is uniquely expressed in worship in the acts of confession, lament, and intercession. At heart, acts of confession and lament ask worshipers to name and confront their human failings and limits in the light of God's mercy and grace. The acts of intercession call on God to respond to human needs. Each of these actions is diminished if it is not straightforward, realistic, and truthful. What is not named and brought for cleansing cannot be healed. Thus the ongoing health and maturity of the Christian community depend on the willingness and capacity of worship leaders to be truthfully prophetic.

At the same time, the words of the worship leader or preacher cannot be harsh or unfeeling. An extraordinary example of sensitive truth telling can be found in the collected prayers of Ann Weems, a liturgist and workshop leader who wrote Psalms of Lament after the death of her young adult son. Although worship leaders need to borrow prayers carefully, the following pain-filled lament (patterned after the Hebrew psalms) might be adapted for use just before communion during a time when a congregation's sufferings have accumulated and seem to have no end:

It is not fair, O God!
Everybody knows we belong to you.
We declared it in the sanctuary.
Why, O God of mercy,
do we sit at the table of death?
Move us, O God of power; move us
to the table of life!
Give us bread and give us wine;
in the name of your son
let us live again!

If you would just
break the bread of life
over our heads,
the crumbs would be sufficient.
If you would just pour the wine
close to us,
the splash would revive us.

O God of glory,
our dead hearts beat again.
The hosannas rush out of our mouths,
and we bow down
in the presence of our God
who is life eternal.[17]

To fearlessly name our failings—personal, social, economic, political—in worship or prayer can be risky, yet worship leaders need to find ways to do so. In a collection of prayers called *Awed to Heaven, Rooted in Earth*, which he offered in classroom settings, Old Testament professor Walter Brueggemann demonstrates such praying with admirable sensitivity and skill. Before a baptism class, he prayed,

You mark us with your water.
You scar us with your name.
You brand us with your vision,
    and we ponder our baptism, your water,
                        your name,
                        your vision.
While we ponder, we are otherwise branded.
    Our imagination is consumed by other brands,
                —winning with Nike,
                —pausing with Coca-Cola,
                —knowing and controlling with Microsoft.

Re-brand us,
> transform our minds,
>> renew our imagination.
> that we may be more fully who we are marked
> and hoped to be,
> we pray with candor and courage. Amen.[18]

Although it may be easier for us to see the prophetic role expressed in the spoken word, musicians and visual artists or dancers also participate in the prophetic dimensions of leading worship. A more revolutionary song than the Magnificat does not exist; it is Mary's passionate declaration of God's justice. What we are invited to see in worship can also speak prophetically. At Christmas one year, a visual artist created a wreath for worship that consisted of metal scraps—crushed soda pop cans, knives, wire, and other debris. Although the overall effect was not pretty, the wreath was a striking addition to worship and especially to prayers of intercession about the brokenness and violence of the world.

Paying attention to three things at once

The task of worship leading is surely complex. Just as planning and hosting a successful dinner party is a multidimensional juggling act, so the ministry of leading God's people in worship requires a nimble dexterity. A hospitable worship leader must be attentive to the community that has gathered, to God who has called the community together, and to the Spirit's desire for transformation of the world and of the context in which the gathering takes place.

A community of faith that achieves a remarkable integration of the vertical, horizontal, and outwardly focused dimensions of worship is the Iona Community of Scotland. Drawing on the rhythms and images of Celtic Christianity, the Iona Community creates fresh, simple, beautiful worship resources with an amazing breadth of inclusiveness, a clear focus on God, and keen prophetic insight. The following prayer of intercession and confession, for example, exhibits both warm compassion and bold honesty in its description of Jesus's comforting welcome of sinners and his stern judgment of sin. It thoughtfully explores a wide range of human situations, and it clearly describes God's vision of liberation.

In you, gracious God,
>the widowed find a carer,
>the orphaned find a parent,
>the fearful find a friend.

In you,
>the wounded find a healer,
>the penitent find a pardoner,
>the burdened find a counselor.

In you,
>the miserly find a beggar,
>the despondent find a laughter-maker,
>the legalists find a rule-breaker.

>>In you, Jesus Christ,
>>we meet our Maker,
>>and our match.

>>And if some need to say, "Help me"
>>and if some need to say, "Save me"
>>and if some need to say, "Hold me"
>>and if some need to say, "Forgive me"
>>then let these be said now
>>in confidence
>>by us.

>>*(silence)*

>>O Christ,
>>in whose heart is both welcome and warning,
>>say to us,
>>do to us,
>>reveal within us
>>the things that will make us whole.

>>And we will wait;
>>and we will praise you.
>>Amen.[19]

Another example, a short closing response, offers a similar wholeness of vision:

Leader   For all that God can do within us,
            for all that God can do without us,
All   *Thanks be to God.*

Leader	For all in whom Christ lived before us,
	for all in whom Christ lives beside us,
All	*Thanks be to God.*

Leader	For all the Spirit wants to bring us,
	for where the Spirit wants to send us,
All	*Thanks be to God.*

Leader	Listen,
	Christ has promised to be with us
	in the world as in our worship.
All	Amen.

| All | *We go to serve him.*[20] |

Rarely can one individual successfully hold together all three dimensions of the hosting role of the worship leader. Nor is any individual expected to do so. A collaborative team of leaders is needed to embody all the dimensions. Further, within the faith community, the Spirit provides a variety of gifts "to equip the saints for the work of ministry, for building up the body of Christ, until all . . . come to the unity of the faith and of the knowledge of the Son of God, to maturity" (Eph 4:12-13).

What is essential is that the primary worship leader on any given Sunday be able to care for and coordinate all three dimensions of worship. Working alongside musicians, preachers, visual artists, ushers, and other leaders, the worship leader as host ensures good communication. Each one involved in preparing for the worship service will possess a clear understanding of the central image or theme, will apprehend the desired flow of the elements of worship, and will be aware of how their particular part fits with the whole. Their contributions will be valued. As the service proceeds, they will be empowered to lead because the host has created a spacious place for the gifts of all. And when the service is over, the worship leader as host will care for whatever evaluation needs to take place, so leaders will be able to serve more faithfully and effectively in the future.[21]

Christ as host at the table of worship

Worship leaders who work diligently to develop their hosting abilities support the threefold purpose of worship: a transforming encounter with the living God; honest engagement with self and community;

and lively empowerment for faithful response. Yet more than human effort is required to accomplish these purposes.

When all is said and done, at this Sunday dinner Christ is the true host. Our Lord prepares a table before us, welcoming us to the feast of love. Worship leaders are given the extraordinary privilege of cooperating with the Spirit who draws worshipers into God's presence and makes of them one body. And when God's presence is honored and known, then the whole community grows toward the fullness of God's dreams and desires for the church and the world. Worshipers go out in the power of the Spirit to love and serve in the name of Christ.

9

PRESENTING THE MEAL

The Lord GOD has given me the tongue of a teacher, that I may know how to sustain the weary with a word. (Isa 50:4)

In my mind's eye, one of my childhood memories is almost as much Norman Rockwell as reality. When I was a third grader, we went to Grandma and Grandpa's house for a traditional holiday dinner. Aunt Frances, Uncle Paul, their four children, and Uncle Wayne were already there when we drove into the lane. My brother and I jumped from the car, leaving Mother and Dad to find a place to park. Breathless and bright-eyed, with ear-to-ear smiles, we ran to the house to greet everyone.

In the dining room, the table was stretched out as long as any table I had ever seen. And it was covered with a beautiful white tablecloth that had not a wrinkle except for the carefully ironed crease that went down the middle for the length of the table. The table was set, and chairs had been gathered from around the house to provide seating for each person. Still awed by the sight of that dining room, I rushed into the kitchen to greet Grandma. After giving me a hug, she turned away from the stove, cleaned up the cooking dishes a bit, and then announced that she thought everything was ready.

But she still had one thing to do. As we children went to call everyone to the table, Grandma wiped the beads of perspiration from her brow and gently put her hair in place. Then she took off her cooking apron and put on her Sunday apron. Now she was ready to join us at the table. Changing that apron transformed Grandma. She had been a kitchen worker, and she became one who presided at the table. She had been the cook, and she became the host. In changing her apron—out of respect for her guests and in recognition of the special celebration—she changed, too.

We tend to think that dinner is about food. Certainly, it is about food and cooking. But the eating space, aromas, tastes, colors, textures, table coverings, centerpieces, dishes, style of service, conversation topics, and the attitude of those serving all contribute to the meal and to our enjoyment in eating and even to our ability to eat.

Something similar is true about worship. Many of us think that worship is just about the words spoken, the songs and hymns sung, the prayers prayed. Granted, these are important. But they are not the whole worship experience. Many other aspects of the worship event either assist us in worship or distract us from worship.

Worship as communication

Communication is a basic building block of our faith. In Genesis 1, we hear God's words summoning the world into existence. Christians also refer to scripture as the Word of God. John 1 calls Jesus "the Word that was with God"—that "was God," that "was in the beginning with God" (John 1:1–2). God's spoken words, God's Word written, God's Word incarnate: in all these aspects and more, communication is fundamental to Christian faith.

Christian faith is a relational faith. Our faith is rooted in a relationship with God through Jesus, and it also depends on our relationships with God's people. Our faith shapes how we live with each other. Relationships require communication of some kind. As Christians, we are in relationship with God and with people. Therefore, we acknowledge the possibility of and the necessity for communion with God and with one another.

We look for ways that God communicates with us, and we seek ways to communicate with God. The first chapter of this book mentions one major movement of worship as a "transforming encounter with the living God." The basic actions of worship in chapter four invite communication with God. Chapter five repeatedly reminds preachers to listen to what the Spirit of God is saying, so we can become vehicles through which God can speak to our congregations. Communication with God is a primary action of worship.

But our communication with God differs from our communication with people. In *The Journal of Communication and Religion*, Quentin J. Schultze writes about the "God-Problem" in communication.[1] He defines the God-Problem as how to consider the speech agency of God within human interaction. How is it that we hear God speaking to us? We can scarcely understand the "human-being problem" in communication—the complexities of communication between people—let alone comprehend how God addresses us or is addressed by us.

Before we proceed to discuss communication in worship, we must remember that both the human and the divine are involved in worship communication. As worship leaders, it is our job to be aware of both dimensions. We are human, and human means of communication are the ones we understand. But we also know that, in ways that defy description, God communicates through the Spirit to us and to those who worship with us. This exchange marks a great instance of collaboration between the human spirit and the divine Spirit. But because we are human, we rely on human models to examine what happens in communication.

Communication theory

Although many theoretical models of communication have been developed, the one below is perhaps the easiest to grasp. All communication can be reduced to this simplest of forms.

According to this model, the source communicates a message to the receiver by encoding it. The message is then decoded by the receiver or listener. Success in communication is achieved when the message decoded by the receiver is close to the message the source intended to encode.

Many communication acts are part of the process of planning and participating in worship. At every intersection, the possibility of misunderstanding arises. Consider the communication that goes into planning alone. Each of many acts of communication has a source who encodes messages, intended and unintended, which others decode. The opportunities for miscommunication are countless. Such miscommunication occurs most frequently in one of two ways. Either a source sends a message that the intended receiver does not receive, or the source unintentionally sends a message to which the receiver responds. Both kinds of miscommunication are problematic; wherever possible, source and receiver ought to exercise care to minimize them.

In worship, the leader might be the *source* who *encodes*—speaks with vocal sounds and gestures—the scripture lesson. The text becomes the *message* which the person in the congregation *decodes*—

sees and hears—and thus *receives*. The process sounds simple enough, but rarely are things as straightforward as they seem. Each of the five components of the process—source, message, encoding, decoding, receiver—is multifaceted, and each is often surrounded by noise that interferes with the communication. We will look at these five elements in turn, and then we will reflect on noise.

The source

The source originates the message being encoded. But in worship, who or what is the source? One might say the preacher is the source in preaching. But she prepares by studying the biblical text, so perhaps the Bible is the source, or the writer of the passage, or God, or the translators, or the writer of the commentary she consulted, or the sermons on that text which she has heard. All of these are potentially sources, and at each exchange, possibilities for miscommunication are present. With regard to the source of the communication event of preaching alone, the complexity of the picture is almost overwhelming.

Or consider the singing of a hymn. Is the composer the source? Or the writer of the text? Is the Bible the source of inspiration for the poetic text? Or is the source the worship planner who selected the hymn? Or the song leader or the organist who leads it? Or is the source the congregation that sings the hymn? Or the God who gives the singers breath? All of these are possible sources.

In public worship, the human sources in the actions of worship are agents of God's Spirit. They seek to communicate the messages of praise, prayer, and preaching.

The message

Every communication action includes a message. Consciously or unconsciously, the source sends a message. In worship, the source decides what the message is and then finds ways to encode it. If the worship leader has selected the message "Welcome, people of God," he still has many choices to make. He has just selected the words. Only when the tone of voice, the rate of speech, the facial expression, and the posture and attitude of the worship leader have encoded the words does the congregation know whether the message is "I am tired this morning" or "Here we are again for another Sunday morning" or "Isn't it wonderful that we can gather together to worship God!" If the source does not consciously decide these aspects of the message, his voice and body will decide for him. The words are only part of the message.

Usually, multiple messages are being conveyed at the same time. Our task as worship planners is to decide on the dominant messages we want to communicate and to find ways to minimize the cluttering messages while maximizing the intended messages.

Encoding

A careful communicator will leave as little as possible to chance in the communication process, because sloppy encoding obscures the message. Indeed, because the source controls only the selection of the message and its presentation, not its reception, the source must work hard to make sure the desired message is clearly encoded. Of course, this process involves precise understanding of the content of the message. But it also involves a particular vocabulary, and a certain rate, volume, rhythm, and intensity of speech. Other factors include tone of voice, attitude, and gestures. Facial expression also enters in: eyes, posture, tilt of the head. Pronunciation, enunciation, and vocal and physical energy and passion also play a part in encoding the message. Sometimes a leader says that the worship of God is important just by her posture, or by her shined shoes and neatly pressed clothing, or by well-rehearsed music. Warm smiles and gentle words and gestures to the children let all know that children are an integral part of the congregation.

Decoding

The next task in communication belongs to the receiver. Decoding is the process of taking the signals given by the source and translating them into ideas and feelings. I can talk, but until another person decodes the message, it has not been received. When listeners give careful attention to the words and sounds and gestures, and all the other codes that the source has prepared to communicate the message, decoding happens.

At the decoding stage, lots of cross-cultural miscommunication occurs. What one person sees as a gesture of welcome is another's gesture of disdain. One who seeks to communicate a message of care and friendship by standing inches away from another is understood as conveying a lack of appropriate boundaries. The person in the process of decoding is looking for signals that can be understood and read with clarity and certainty. The encoder must think carefully about how to send the message in a way that will produce accurate decoding. In other words, the source has to think like the receiver in order to ensure the safe delivery of the message.

The receiver

The work of the receiver is to pay attention to all the signals that are coming his way, to sort out which ones communicate together in a cluster, and to interpret or decode what the meaning of that communication cluster is. The role of the receiver has typically been undervalued. When miscommunication occurred, the source has often been held to be at fault. In fact, both the source and the receiver bear significant responsibility in the communication process.

If the receivers are dozing off, or preoccupied about something at work—if for any reason they are not bringing their fully alert, observant selves to the worship experience—then they are unlikely to receive the entire message the preacher intends to convey. If the receiver is not expecting God to speak, she is unlikely to hear the message God's Spirit is bringing.

People who listen to sermons have limited power to control the preacher's prepared content, but their power to affect preaching is not negligible. Receivers' engagement or lack of it has an impact on the whole communication event. Just as a classroom of eager listeners energizes the teacher, receivers can improve preaching by improving the effectiveness of their listening.

Noise

Noise in this context refers to unintended sounds and sights, movements, thoughts, and other extraneous elements that make communication unclear. Noise is communication clutter, comparable to static on the radio or the cell phone, or to snow on the television screen. In the worship setting, attention to minimizing this clutter is a never-ending task.

We often think of clutter as the papers covering the desk or the dirty dishes on the kitchen countertop. The resulting confusion prevents us from using the space as it is designed to be used. The same is true of noise or clutter in worship.

Some of the noise in worship comes from the worship leader in the form of unnecessary words, throat clearing, and vocalized pauses. What some of us experience as an informal friendliness, others find distracting.

Noise in the worship space comes in the form of candles that burn too close to a cloth or someone's hair. The child playing with little cars on the hymnbook rack is making noise, literally and figuratively. The platform light with a bulb out, so you can't see the face of the speaker, creates interference. The tattoos on the worship leader's arms produce noise, as does the preacher's dress fabric, covered in big bright flowers, and the worship leader's Mickey Mouse tie. The beep of someone's pager, the ringing of a cell phone, and the hum of ceiling fans cause distractions. The typo in the bulletin and the announcement of the wrong hymn number produce noise. The possibilities for noise in the worship space are almost endless.

Our desire for effective communication in worship means we pay careful attention to what we intend to communicate. But we also look and listen carefully for unintended messages that obstruct worship communication. In the worship leader's role as host, managing noise is a significant task.[2]

A more complex communication model

Having looked at each of the elements of communication, let's reconsider the communication model in the worship setting. Based on the discussion above, we can now envision a model in which many sources are encoding many messages, and these many messages are then decoded by many receivers. And in decoding the messages, each receiver relies on a different set of experiences and expectations.

One might also map the communication in terms of a single source, a worship leader who is trying to communicate one or more messages. The congregation hears a variety of messages—perhaps even the intended one. (See examples on page 242.)

All these messages and more may be transmitted simultaneously. The same person at the same moment can be communicating conflicting signals, and the result is confusion among the receivers about what they are to hear. The worship leader thinks the congregation is hearing the formal content: "For God so loved the world that he gave his only Son, so that everyone who believes in him may not perish but may have everlasting life." But others are hearing that this message doesn't matter or that God's love is not really good news.

This portrayal may make worship communication seem utterly chaotic, as though to believe that significant interchange could take place in public worship is absolute folly. But remember that we trust

SOURCE	encoded	MESSAGE 1	decoded	RECEIVER RECEIVER RECEIVER
worship leader	speaks words	John 3:16	hears words	God loves the world

SOURCE	encoded	MESSAGE 2	decoded	RECEIVER RECEIVER RECEIVER
worship leader	low energy	I'm tired	sees low energy	the message doesn't matter

SOURCE	encoded	MESSAGE 3	decoded	RECEIVER RECEIVER RECEIVER
worship leader	scowls	I have a headache	sees unhappy face	God's love is not good news

SOURCE	encoded	MESSAGE 4	decoded	RECEIVER RECEIVER RECEIVER
worship leader	shuffles papers	I didn't prepare	sees lack of preparation	worship is not important

in the gracious indwelling of the Spirit of God. For the Spirit touches not only the source but also the receivers and prepares each for the communication relationship.

Distance and space

Another important communication concept addresses distance between speaker and listener. The following guidelines apply to North American readers. And all of us may use them as a reminder to notice the guidelines appropriate in other cultural contexts.

Four distance categories mark different behaviors for usual inter-actions between North Americans. Note that these labels and distances are generalizations and approximations.

intimate space	0–18 inches
personal space	1.5–3 feet
social space	3–10 feet
public space	10 feet +

Intimate space is very private. We want only a few people to be this close to us, and we want them to wait to be invited into this space. We resent people who get in our faces. In worship, we often sit this close to one another, but we relax when the person already sitting on the bench or in the row welcomes us into the seat beside them. We notice that having enough space for a Bible or a hymnbook between us feels good. We prefer not to sit arm-to-arm close.

Studies indicate that churches without some excess seating do not grow. North Americans like to have some space around them. Some preachers like to leave the platform to move about the congregation during the sermon. The experience of immediacy and directness this practice lends to communication may be offset by the sense some congregants may have that their intimate space has been encroached on. Preachers do well to notice what distance feels comfortable and what volume of speech and tone of voice seem appropriate.

Personal space is handshake and over-the-counter distance. We are accustomed to this distance in the bank and the store. It is possible to extend the arm and touch the other person, to see each other's eyes, and to hear slight variations in the voice. Most of our personal relations happen in this space. In personal space, we speak just a little louder, and the gestures are a little larger—although still not big.

Social space describes the variety of distances that would be available in a typical living room, classroom, or lounge. Everyone can see and hear everyone in the space, but communication is not private here. In the larger space, vocal volume increases, as does the size of the gestures, and the expressiveness of facial features, so all communicate across a greater distance.

Public space is standard platform distance. Generally speaking, this category encompasses distances including everything from the front row of seats in the auditorium to the last row of the top balcony. Sound amplification systems increase volume, but they do not enlarge gestures. Those addressing a crowd in public space need to adjust their gestures and speech to this distance. Everything becomes stylized—bigger, slower, louder—so everyone can pick up the signals. Increasingly, large worship spaces make use of huge closed circuit television screens placed so that worshipers can see as well as hear. However, part of the amplification the listeners must do for themselves.

Sensitivity to these various distances informs preachers and worship leaders as they decide how to interact with the congregation. Leaders need to evaluate the nature of the space the congregation uses during public worship. Depending on the congregation's size and people's placement in the worship area, they may be sitting in personal, social, or public space. If the leader is speaking in a style appropriate to people in personal space, those in public space may find the presentation bland. Alternatively, those seated nearby may perceive as exaggerated or theatrical a preacher speaking in a stadium voice and gesturing expansively.

Presentation

Every meal includes both the food and the presentation of the food. The "fast food" designation refers to a popular style of presentation. This revolution in presentation affects how America eats, how much we eat, and what we eat. Indeed, the very shape of Americans has altered in part as a result of this transformation in the way food is presented. While this change in presentation is not necessarily a good thing, we do need to notice the phenomenon. In addition to the care they give to food preparation, successful restaurants and cooks pay close attention to issues of presentation.

Worship setting

Presentation in the worship setting is complex, partly because what contributes to one person's worship may be noise for another. Still, some general principles can aid our discernment.

Let's begin with the platform area, the focus for the eyes of the congregation. What do worshipers in our congregation see? What does this area communicate? A wall-mounted cross, lifted up as a triumphant expression of Jesus's resurrection victory? In one African tradition, the cross that worshipers face is not suspended in midair but connected with the ground, graphically symbolizing the God who comes to us on earth and is present in solidarity with us.

As planners and preachers, we need to leave our usual places and sit where the congregation sits. We move from place to place in the worship area, and we contemplate the part of the room from which the service is led. Do extension cords scramble like spaghetti across the floor? Do we see banners, posters, pictorial or abstract stained glass, representations of Jesus? Are the images sentimental or striking, evocative or prosaic? Does the communion table always look the same, functioning almost unnoticed as an anchor, or does it sometimes hold communion elements and at other times a tablescape? Do we observe a pair of ferns posted on plant stands flanking the organ?

Does a Christmas tree shelter a manger scene? Does a flag declare and define what we give our allegiance to? Do silk daisies adorn the piano? Is the carpet clean and cared for, or does it show the effects of lots of traffic across it?

My purpose is not to make judgments but to invite attention to all the visible elements and careful deliberation about the purposes they serve or fail to serve. A worship space filled with many things to look at may make it hard for those present to enter into worship. After all, everything at the front of the church has potential to assist or hamper the congregation's hearing of the message. Flowers and greenery, symbols of all kinds, banners, and table displays all require evaluation in light of this concern: do they aid or interfere with the intended communication in worship? Visual elements in the sanctuary should be defensible in terms of worship!

We consider removing whatever is likely to present a barrier to worship. One way of undertaking the necessary evaluation would be to strip everything from the worship space, down to bare walls and windows. Then we restore or add only what will assist our worship for the Pentecost service next Sunday or the Advent season about to begin. We bring into the worship space only what will help us focus on the intended message for a service or a season. Space for worship is not like a living room: one does not decorate it once and leave it as is for ten years.

We begin to think of visual pieces as sources that communicate messages. What do the more permanent features of our worship areas—stone and brick and wood surfaces, for example—communicate? How does light, natural and artificial, enter the space? What do windows with views to the world outside or covered with heavy curtains say to us in the context of our worship?

The space speaks, and its communication is in harmony with the chosen message of the day and with the enduring faith of the congregation. Everything added to the worship space undergirds or assists the interpretation of the theme. Flowing cloths in shades of blue are set with clear vessels filled with water for a worship service focusing on Jesus's encounter with the Samaritan woman at the well and their conversation about living water. For a service on the good shepherd, green cloths hung from various heights represent the Judean hills. On one "hill" the Christ candle sits, surrounded by tea lights representing many sheep.

Who looks after the cloths used in worship, to see that they are hemmed and clean and ironed and neatly draped? In some traditions, those who serve in the altar guild provide dedicated behind-the-scenes care for fabrics, vessels, communion elements, flowers, and other aspects of the worship space. This service is vital but largely unnoticed when it is functioning at its best.

Many congregations miss the opportunity to integrate planning of floral pieces with the rest of the worship planning. Through no fault of their own, those in charge of flowers often operate like lone rangers, because we neglect to include them in the worship planning process. Beautiful as flowers may be, they do not aid worship unless someone gives thought to how and when they can contribute to the message of the day or the season. The joy of an Easter celebration may be intensified if its profusion of blossoms stands in dramatic contrast to the austerity of a Lenten season with no flowers. During the month of July one year, the worship commission of an Indiana congregation invited members to contribute something from their flower garden each Sunday, as part of an ongoing discernment process. People came to church carrying a long-stemmed red rose or golden daylilies, sea oats or bright-eyed phlox, nodding plumes of ornamental grass and vividly colored zinnias. Each week their flowers, ordinary and exotic, were gathered into a large informal bouquet and brought forward at the beginning of worship to reflect gratitude for the abundant and varied gifts with which God had blessed the congregation, and to shape its prayers toward using those gifts as God desires.

Each worship planning group will want to do an inventory of its own worship space. We look carefully and name what we see. What is showing wear and needs to be replaced? What do we need to clean or repaint? In one church, on the wall just above the preacher's head was a series of dirty boot prints. Talk about distracting! What is structurally not negotiable? What is movable and can be changed? How do we care for the feelings of those who have an attachment to what does not serve a valid function in worship? And how do we enhance the congregation's appreciation for what has the potential to contribute to their worship?

Worship leaders, preachers and song leaders

When worship leaders enter the platform space, more communication begins. People are living, moving beings and are "talking" even when they are not speaking. The research of Albert Mehrabian, a speech communication theorist, has shown that 55 percent of all meaning transmitted in a face-to-face setting is communicated by the body, 38 percent by the voice, and only 7 percent by the words spoken.[3] Because we are always communicating something, we need to be aware of what our behavior is saying to others. Mehrabian's research suggests that how we present ourselves carries more clout than our words. When our nonverbal messages contradict the verbal ones, people are likely to trust the unspoken ones.

If we return to the more complex communication model in the middle of this chapter, we notice that one message has to do with the words, and the other three messages have to do with something the worship leader is doing. Those three messages are likely to outweigh the message that God loves the world.

Worship leaders, song leaders, and preachers are being observed whenever we are in front of the congregation. Our wandering eyes, tapping toes, whispered conversations, dozing, note writing, even blank stares can distract those who want to listen. When we are in front but not leading, we carry responsibility to be model listeners, helping others attend to whomever is presenting at that moment. Anyone glancing at us should see nothing to catch their awareness; our total demeanor—posture, eyes, and energy—will guide attention to whomever is leading at that moment. We are right with the song leader, not singing half-heartedly or checking the bulletin, our thoughts on what is coming next. We can emulate the chorus in an ancient Greek drama. Those twelve to fifteen actors, placed on stage between the central actors and the audience, responded to the action on the stage, and their response guided the audience response. In the same way, when the congregation looks at anyone on the platform who is not currently providing leadership, they see in our attention and engagement a model for their own participation.

Movement

Movement is the single most powerful communication tool, and in worship it should be used purposively. Movement grabs interest more than sound; it commands attention more than anything a preacher or worship leader says. This realization should help us grasp the significance of the walking around that some preachers and worship leaders are given to these days: the movement itself captures our attention to such an extent that until the preacher stops moving, the congregation is unlikely to be able to hear his words clearly. In a recent study, one participant observed that a preacher pacing back and forth is "like a duck in a shooting gallery." The preacher's intent was probably not to inspire the listener's contemplation of that image.

A principle for shaping our movement in worship is that we ought to move only when we have a reason to do so. All movements communicate. Random movements also say something, so sometimes no movement is the best movement. We need to be comfortable standing still before we start to move. Perhaps we should try nailing our shoes to the floor! Every action is to be motivated by the message, carefully designed to help the congregation understand more clearly what we are saying.

Gestures

Gestures are a particular kind of movement, and they too may be purposeful or purposeless. Our preaching and worship leading will be most effective when we use gestures intentionally and eliminate the random gestures that speak only of our nervousness or agitation.

Purposeful gestures fall into several categories. *Descriptive* gestures provide a visual explanation to help the listener understand what is being said. When I say "Stop!" and simultaneously hold up my hand with palm out, I am using a descriptive gesture. The angler describing the one that got away—his hands stretched six feet apart—gives us a vivid picture of the fish he holds in memory.

Other gestures are *emphatic*. They help us grasp the importance of the message or the intensity of the speaker's feelings. A speaker who pounds her fist on the podium is underlining her words. A two-year-old's stamping foot communicates volumes about the definiteness of his "No!" A parent's scolding index finger may reprimand as effectively as a spoken "Don't you ever do that again!" Sometimes a gesture helps the listener recognize what deserves special attention.

Capable preachers and worship leaders understand *ritual* gestures and use them with assurance. The actions create the ritual. In worship, we break communion bread and pour the water of baptism with a care and confidence befitting these solemn practices. The worship leader who raises her arms in blessing at the end of the service is conveying God's own benediction: limp, half-extended arms will not get the job done.

As preachers and worship leaders, making our gestures maximally effective will require observing ourselves and practicing. Videotaping gives us opportunities to watch ourselves. We can monitor whether our gestures open from the shoulder, as they should, rather than from the elbow. We notice hands fidgeting with papers and paper clips, or moving from pocket to tie to glasses or beard. While larger gestures are a vivid addition to communication in a public setting, small movements that may serve to release energy for the preacher become distracting for listeners. Toes tend to wiggle when we are anxious or energized, and it may be wise to avoid sandals and other shoes with open toes when we lead. An awareness of how others see our movements can aid us in modifying them to draw attention away from ourselves and toward what matters.

An advantage of old-fashioned pulpits is that they masked the leader's many small movements. But in many of our churches, the talking head is a thing of the past. Listeners want embodied preachers. The challenge is to discipline ourselves to maximize the advantages that come with bringing our whole bodies to communication, while minimizing the problems.

Voice

There is more to communication than being heard, but being heard is not insignificant. The voice helps shape the emotional content of words and ideas; it brings another dimension to verbal communication. The same words spoken with different rates, pitches, volumes, or inflections may have vastly different meanings. Depending on how it is spoken, "I'm sorry" may be an expression of deep regret or a reassertion of my right to do something despite your disapproval. When uttered in panic at top volume, the word *fire* acquires new meaning: "FIIIRRRE!!" Along with the sense of the words themselves, vocal expression has vast power to transmit meaning.

If, as Mehrabian's research suggests, the vocal portion of communication is 38 percent, we need to listen carefully to the way we talk. As worship leaders and preachers, we want our voices to serve the message of the worship service and the sermon. We will pay attention not only to the accuracy of the words that we use but to the nature of the voice that conveys those words.

Although we tend to think our voices are a given, speech is learned behavior. We acquire spoken language patterns like those of the people among whom we were raised, and later in life we can unlearn and relearn the ways we use our voices. Our speaking can be evaluated in terms of many qualities, including rate, pitch, volume, and timbre. We should invite this kind of assessment from those who listen to us regularly. If our vocal qualities weary our listeners, professional evaluation and intervention may be warranted to help us speak more naturally and dynamically. These qualities are more matters of habit than of biological endowment, and they can be retrained if they are not serving us well.

Articulation and enunciation have to do with clarity and expressiveness, while pronunciation has to do with accuracy. These factors are also significant in worship. Sloppy speech makes a congregation work hard to comprehend, and indistinct enunciation and improper pronunciation can cause listeners to hear words that were not intended. Sometimes a regional dialect will call attention to a worship leader or preacher. Worshipers bear some responsibility not to let such things become barriers, but sometimes it is the speaker's task to reduce vocal noise.

Like singers, worship leaders and preachers might think of their voices as musical instruments. Although every instrument has its own distinct qualities, each can produce many kinds of sounds and rhythms, and each benefits from disciplined use. Effective vocal presentations are the result of developing a wide range of expression, by varying factors such as rate, volume, and pitch.[4]

People whose vocation asks them to use their voices in public settings learn to think of voice and body as one; voice and body are in some respects the same instrument. Good vocal production is not just a matter of vibrating vocal cords; it begins with attention to breathing and posture. Professional singers see that they get appropriate hydration and sleep, exercise care about allergies and infections, and avoid smoke-filled environments and ingesting food and drink that impair vocal quality. We do well to adopt practices that enhance the health of our voices in particular and our bodies in general, in order to become better communicators.

Rate. Although English speakers on average can hear and decode about 400 words per minute, we can tolerate that speed for only a short time. We can sustain listening at 185 words per minute, but even this rate will become fatiguing if it is continues too long. The usual pace for public discourse is 120–150 words per minute. In personal or small group speech, the rate can be faster. In public address, though, if one speaks too quickly, people cannot understand.

Many worship leaders and preachers must work on slowing their speech so the congregation can understand without effort. Adrenalin tends to make us speed up our normal rate of speech when we should be slowing it. At the other extreme, people who speak too slowly sometimes lose their listeners. We can think much faster than we can listen, so if leaders fail to keep things moving along, listeners' minds may wander. Some speech teachers ask students to record their speeches and play them back, doing a per-minute word count to assess whether their rate of speech is appropriate.

Volume. A message cannot reach listeners if it is spoken too quietly. Adequate volume is a function of several factors, including the size of the congregation, the architecture of the sanctuary, and the availability and adequacy of amplification. Variation in volume gives modulation to speech and adds meaning to our words. No single volume is correct; some variation is desirable. But our voices must not become so quiet that listeners cannot make out what we are saying. An area that often needs attention is the tendency to let our voices drop at the end of the sentence; important ideas are lost because we neglect to sustain adequate volume.

Pitch. Generally speaking, people prefer to listen to a lower voice rather than a higher one. Perhaps lower voices are just more undemanding to listen to, or perhaps we have learned to accord male voices more authority and thus appreciate them more. But voices at both extremes—extremely high pitched and extremely low pitched—are difficult to hear and understand in public address. Altos, tenors, and baritones are in the range people find easiest to hear. Although pitch is largely a biological inheritance, we can move the pitch of our speaking voices some through exercise. Sopranos might try singing the alto line, and deep basses might work toward the baritone lines.

All spoken languages use differences of pitch. Tonal languages use pitch variation to signal a difference in meaning between words. English is a stress language rather than a tonal language, but variation in pitch is a factor in communicating meaning accurately—in conveying attitude or changing a statement (falling intonation) to a question (rising intonation). This movement in pitch not only adds meaning to our speech; it also creates interest. Monotonous speech drones on, taxing listeners' ability to stay engaged.

Body

Our physical presence as worship leaders communicates in a variety of ways. Posture conveys much about the conviction and energy we bring to leading worship and preaching. Good posture begins with distributing our weight evenly on both feet. From this neutral position, we move easily in any direction. Standing with all our weight on one foot gives the impression that the occasion is casual and informal, but it can also communicate discomfort with or lack of investment in the event or the message.

Closely related to posture is the angle at which we hold our head. Again, from an upright neutral position, we can gesture with our head as need arises. Holding it tipped to either side may communicate that the message or the speaker is not to be taken very seriously. Women more often fall into this pattern, but men are not immune. If we begin speaking with our head tilting off to the side, what might be a meaningful gesture instead becomes noise.

Facial expressions are valuable forms of body language. Almost simultaneously we read the smile, the brow, and the eyes of another. As a cluster, these features are strong communicators. In different combinations they convey different things. Leaders need to learn to communicate effectively using facial expression, and we also need to cultivate our ability to read the expressions and body language of our listeners.

Ancient wisdom asserts that eyes are the window to the soul; by looking into someone's eyes, we can see how things are with them. By implication, the more we make eye contact with our listeners, the more intently they will listen and the better they will understand what is on our hearts. Anything that interferes with this eye-to-eye communication will inhibit the depth of understanding that could otherwise pass between us. If we are constantly looking at our manuscripts or notes, our eyes are not available to our listeners. Repeatedly diverting their attention to projected images also obstructs this deeper interpersonal communication. Half-glasses may be all we require for reading, but if the rim cuts across our eyes, listeners will be frustrated in their desire to see these mirrors of our souls. Tinted glasses similarly interfere, as do reflective lenses and eyewear that calls attention to itself.

Social smiles begin to emerge when babies are just a few weeks old, and at a very early age we learn to read the body language of smiles. Ordinarily perceptive people can easily distinguish the smile of genuine joy that transforms our face when we meet someone we love, the slight smile that acknowledges a stranger on the street, and the forced smile we put on because social convention seems to require it. It is our job as leaders to make sure that our expression communicates clearly the desired message. If we are speaking authentically about joyful matters, or singing our praises enthusiastically, our faces will mirror that emotion. At the other extreme, when we speak of solemn subjects, a habitual smile seems out of place. Our communication is not served if we have been socialized—as are some people (especially women, but some men, too)—to smile ingratiatingly much of the time.

Grooming and clothing also deserve some consideration. In principle, we all agree that the fate of our souls does not depend on our hairstyle or clothing or glasses. But if we as worship leaders and preachers are the last people wearing polyester plaid suits, or a bouffant hairstyle, or cover-half-your-face glasses, we become a distraction. On the other hand, those leading worship will not generally be trendsetters whose garb attracts notice.

I am puzzled about into which category tattoos and body piercing fit! The issue is not whether tattoos are right or wrong. Although more and more people are sporting tattoos, and congregations are increasingly unlikely to take much notice of them, worship leaders and preachers with visible tattoos should seriously consider covering them while at the pulpit. Like words and images on a T-shirt, these pictures and inscriptions beg to be deciphered and so constitute a distraction.

Body piercings also require the use of some discretion. In many places in North America now, earrings for women are no longer a distraction, while earrings on men may be. The distraction factor of nose rings, tongue studs, and lip and eyebrow piercing is still relatively high. As the culture changes and congregational expectations change, so may the acceptance of tattoos and various kinds of body piercing. Perhaps the best approach is to sample some congregation members for a reading on how these elements affect the quality of our communication.

Hair presents different problems for men and women, but the question that deserves attention is the same: What assists in communication and what is a barrier? Styles may change, but hair should still be clean, appropriately cut, out of the eyes, and away from the face. Because the face and eyes are such important communication ports, they need to be accessible to listeners. Hair that covers the face and eyes makes it nearly impossible for listeners to hear. Those of us with big hair—long, thick, curly—need to assess whether it sidetracks attention from more important messages. In general my advice is, cut or coif!

Beards and mustaches also warrant care. Men with full beards and mustaches cover a significant part of the face, which is not available for communication. Worship leaders and preachers with beards that are well trimmed can communicate much better than those with longer, untrimmed beards. Mustaches present a particular communication problem. Being able to read someone's lips significantly aids communication, and shaggy mustaches make it appreciably more difficult for people to do so. Men who choose only a mustache and no beard will want to give thought to the line the mustache creates on the face. If the sides of the mustache reach too far down, a person may look perpetually grouchy.

Our clothing prompts people to relate to us in a particular way. In a sense, when we are selecting clothes we are choosing a costume and a role. Sorting out issues of appropriate clothing and accessories may be like walking through a minefield. What one church sees as fitting is unacceptable in another congregation. A good conservative suit and tie is expected in some settings and out of place in others. As is true with regard to all these issues of physical demeanor, there is no substitute for consulting trusted friends in our congregation. But while *context* is an important word, so is *communication*. In a congregation that tolerates or even likes having the preacher wear a tie festooned with cartoon characters, people may still be trying to figure out during the sermon what Dilbert is up to. After all, clothing and accessory issues are not just about the congregation's tastes but about what will help them worship.

Consider the anchors on the TV news. They are carefully dressed, but after the program we can't remember what they had on, because their clothing does not draw our eyes to it. Dresses made of splashy fabrics, dangling earrings that catch the light, holes in socks or the bottom of shoes, shirttails creeping out of waistbands, rumpled hand-kerchiefs poking out of pockets, pants with no belt in the loops: all this is noise or clutter that may cause people to dwell on the worship leader's appearance. Attire that fits us well, is neat and clean, appropriate to the congregation and the season, and considerate of the worship context will allow those looking on to dismiss what we are wearing and focus their attention on the worship event at hand.

Mind and soul

One of the most difficult places to control noise is in our own minds. Whether we are functioning as a source or as a receiver in the communication event, our goal is to be able to focus attention, to strain out the unhelpful thoughts that clutter our thinking and concentrate on what is being said or done.

When preachers who are gaining experience move from preaching with a full manuscript to using sketchy notes, they often fear that they will forget what comes next. If we have memorized the sermon structure and are listening to ourselves preach, we will not stray far from the path. But we need to listen: What have I just said, and what follows from it? I remember a preacher who stopped mid-sentence and confessed that he did not know what he had just said or what was to come next. I thought, if you are not listening to yourself preach, why should we?

The worship leader and the preacher concentrate vigilantly on what is being said and how it is being said. But a host of other stimuli also bombard our senses. Like triage specialists who must make split-second decisions about what urgently needs attention, what can wait, and what can safely be ignored, our minds are constantly assessing what deserves our attention, while our mental spam filters are detecting and deleting what is extraneous.

Memory is a major asset for preachers and worship leaders. The less we have to look at our notes, the more we can be present to the eyes of the listeners, and the stronger will be the communication relationship. Memory also eliminates purposeless repetition. In speech communication, repetition is a rhetorical technique that allows the listener to review an idea, as a reader might reread a sentence or a paragraph of written text. In spoken communication, when we restate an idea we can use different vocabulary—if we have a clear memory of our previous words. Framing the same idea in other words increases its impact on the listeners. Variety is vital to maintaining interest and reinforcing a concept. Simple repetition may suggest that the speaker is lazy or does not respect the listeners' intelligence.

As leaders, we attend both to the words that need to be said and to those that can to be omitted. Our words are our primarily tools with which we transmit essential feelings and ideas. These words are not filler; idle chatter has no place in worship. We select our words carefully, so they will inspire and satisfy and delight and comfort and challenge in turn, conveying just what we intend.

As preachers and worship leaders, we are quick to appreciate the need to listen to what is going on around us. It may take us longer to realize that we must also listen to ourselves, to what we are saying and doing. We speak and simultaneously attend to the sounds and actions around us, our own and others'. The messages being encoded and decoded are layered one upon another. Obviously, this communication event is demanding and multifaceted, and the quality of attention we as leaders bring to it substantially affects the experience of worship for those present.

The success of the presentation also depends on our passion and energy. In a thousand ways, we transmit signals about what we are feeling, so it becomes our job to manage our emotions as we lead. Passion means caring deeply and presenting with a sense of genuine drama. *Authentic, urgent, expressive, intentional:* these words cumulatively define passionate leadership. If we do not seem to care about the worship service, we can scarcely expect others present to invest themselves.

Even those at the back of the sanctuary must sense that the words matter to the preacher and the worship leader. Energy diminishes over distance, and what may seem passionate at a distance of three feet is limp and bland at fourteen feet. The urgency that the person at the pulpit generates and encodes needs to be both authentic and magnified to communicate with those in the last pew. As speakers, we must ring true if we are going to be believed, but in public address, the space requires us to perform using larger gestures, louder volume, and expressiveness far beyond what we consider natural in a smaller space and more intimate interaction.

The attitude of the worship leader or preacher changes to model for the congregation the attitude appropriate to what is being presented. A psalm of lamentation is read with a demeanor different from one appropriate to reading a psalm of thanksgiving. Actors are expected to name a motivating purpose for each line they utter. A discipline like this would result in worship leaders so thoroughly prepared that we knew what we wanted to accomplish with each sentence or paragraph that we speak. Then we would grasp the appropriate attitude, and listeners would know what they are hearing: presentation establishes meaning, and meaning is central to the message. Sunday worship would not just be set out there for the congregation to take and make what they can out of it. Nothing would be left to chance.

A subject that gets attention is the question of whether prayers and sermons should be written out or spontaneous. No one really argues about the content of these prayers or sermons. What congregations object to is a presentation style that gives the impression that the words are canned rather than fresh and heartfelt. The strength of having things written out is that worship leaders and preachers can give careful thought to what they will speak. The worship leader can check the theology of the prayer and not inadvertently end a prayer with "Jesus who died long ago." True, Jesus died long ago, but the theological truth that we want to echo in the ears of the congregation is that Jesus rose and lives again. The issue is to learn ways to communicate the written word in a manner that expresses authenticity.

Stage fright

Preachers experience stage fright in a variety of ways. The most profound is the stammering that comes with the thought of speaking on behalf of the Lord God. How can we mere mortals begin to utter speech as agents of God? Even if we see preaching as a matter of giving witness to what we have come to know rather than of speaking the words of God, the task is still an awesome one. Only those completely lacking in imagination and comprehension would feel no stage fright. And the role of the worship leader is no less remarkable. Our duty is to lead the congregation in conversation with the living God. If we stop to consider the nature of the task, we are awestruck or perhaps dumbstruck.

These leadership roles call for prayer and preparation, and stage fright is a fitting response, a sign that one understands the magnitude of the undertaking: Who of us is adequate to the responsibility of speaking to or as a representative of the living God? Stage fright is theologically sound preparation for the work of leading worship. When Moses was asked to speak for God, when Isaiah was invited to speak, when the angels approached the shepherds, there was always this stammering fear. In our preparation to communicate with and for God, we tremble. Preaching and leading worship should never become routine.

The other kind of stage fright that preachers and worship leaders face is performance anxiety about speaking in front of a group. This anxiety is so common that it is almost universal. Its manifestations include dry mouth, profuse sweating, trembling hands or legs, churning bowels, and a desire to run away. Whatever the symptoms, the engine of stage fright is fear, and the greater the fear, the greater the likelihood that one will experience some form of performance anxiety.

When fearful thoughts overtake us—I will fail, they won't like me, they will think I'm stupid, they will laugh at me, they will tell other people I'm a lousy preacher, they won't ever want to be seen with me again, they will be ashamed to have me as their pastor, I will lose my job—it is hard to stop them. It is best to manage stage fright before it gets started. We focus on our past successes, remember that the Spirit of God is with us and inspiring us, recall the passion we felt for the message when we first heard it, believe the listeners want us to succeed and that they are our friends. These memories provide comfort and help ease the symptoms. And we can learn the ways that our body responds to stress and prepare for those. Sometimes just making a few little preparations has a calming effect. When the symptoms become manageable, the distractions are minimized.

Conclusion

Presentation is important only to the extent that it serves the relationship between the worshiper and God. In other words, it is huge! Preaching is not about us as preachers; it is about everything we can do to bring God and the congregation together. For worship leaders, to inhabit the worship space is to give ourselves to the service of the Holy Spirit and the congregation. It does matter what we do and how we speak, so we give care to all aspects of the worship event.

That said, we cannot completely rid the worship setting of clutter; nor is it our task to control everything that happens there. Not everything is the worship leader's responsibility; we are responsible only for the things we can do something about. Worshipers, too, have some responsibility for the noise their minds and voices and bodies create. Whenever a group of people gather, someone will cough or sneeze.

And on any Sunday, something serendipitous may happen in which God is manifestly at work. We make our careful preparations and bring our best to presentation in worship and preaching, in confidence that the Spirit is at work to use them, in ways we expect and in ways we cannot anticipate, to nourish our congregation in its relationship with God.

10

ENRICHING THE FARE

Jesus said to them, "I am the bread of life." (John 6:35)

Flat breads—tortillas, pitas, injeras, chapatis and arepas
yeast breads—Jewish challah, Swedish tea ring, Ukrainian paska
wheat bread, corn bread, rye bread, barley loaves
breads with dark brown crusts, hard crusts, no crusts
biscuits, muffins, crumpets, scones, hot cross buns
tea breads, spiced bread, fruit bread, nut bread
daily bread

Kneaded by hand and allowed to rest and rise
rolled into balls, shaped into crescents, cut into rounds
poured like batter into pans

Fried or baked
in pans
in ovens
on stones
over open fires

Main dish of a meal
a bowl for soup or stew
a utensil for scooping up the rest of the meal
an accompaniment for other foods

Eaten in solitude
shared in company
every morning toast
lunchtime sandwich
dinner rolls
midnight snack with peanut butter and jelly

For Russians, bread on a journey is no burden
for the Danish, even crumbs are bread

for Spaniards, bread is relief for all kinds of grief
for Arabic Bedouins, the one who shares bread and salt is not an enemy
matchless gift of the Creator
nourishment for every place and time
broken and blessed.

The word *bread* refers to a complex reality. The possibilities for preparation are endless, and the shapes and forms of bread people create vary widely from one culture to another. Most often, great care and a significant investment of time are required to make bread. Occupying a privileged and essential place in both ordinary and festive meals of cuisines around the world, bread takes on a multitude of meanings. As Yvonne Young Tarr eloquently expresses it:

> In the act of creating bread, an honest loaf, an object with a presence, a fragrance, a substance, a taste, some would say even a soul, the baker has changed grain and flour and liquid into an entity. She or he has taken yeast, a dormant colony of living plants, and released and nurtured them in embryonic warmth, has sprinkled in sugar on which yeast thrives, has sifted in flour that builds the cellular elastic structure that holds the tiny carbon dioxide bubbles that raise the framework of the house called bread. And in that house is love, and warmth, and nourishment, and comfort.[1]

Worship is a similarly complex and multifaceted phenomenon. An infinite variety of design choices are available to worship leaders, musicians, and preachers. One set of choices will yield one kind of worship outcome for a congregation; another set will result in an entirely different experience of worship. And worship leaders who understand that each worshiper experiences meaning in a unique way know that our choices must offer the widest possible array of entry points, so every worshiper can meet God and be transformed in that encounter.

To make fitting and nourishing choices, worship leaders, musicians, and preachers must be aware of how worshipers perceive and make meaning, be equipped to analyze the multilayered textures of meaning in a typical worship service, and be knowledgeable about the relationship between design choices and outcomes in worship. While much of this process happens intuitively, a more systematic examination of these decisions and choices can be useful. Although the Holy Spirit is the major mover and actor in worship, human leaders have a part to play as well. The more we know and understand about how worship works, the more we will be able to cooperate with the Spirit. Becoming careless or inattentive to these dynamics in worship can lead to stale or anemic worship, or to overemphasis on one element of worship at the expense of others.

It is especially important for leaders to understand the role and function of symbols in worship. Because symbols bear significant power to engage worshipers physically, emotionally, intellectually and spiritually, they offer an exceptional opportunity for individual worshipers as well as the entire congregation to experience a vivid sense of God's presence. One only need think of the bread of communion to begin to understand this phenomenon.

The following chapter describes this territory, offering a pictorial representation, an analytical chart, and many examples for understanding what is, in fact, an enormously complicated reality, yet one that sustains and nourishes worshipers every week in amazing and fruitful ways.

But first, a word to the reader: If you find the following pages dense and complex, don't despair! As you take time to read slowly and reflect on your own experience, you will discover that you already know and understand what is being described. Often we don't stop to analyze the meaning of what we know, and especially what we know about what we do in worship. Be assured that if you persevere, you will be rewarded in the end with a valuable tool for planning and leading richer, more meaningful worship services.

Making meaning in worship

Our God-given capacities for perceiving the spiritual dimensions of life are varied and complex. We know God through simple words and see God in childlike images. We sense God's presence through the movement of story and preached Word. Through the blessing of material things—the water of baptism, the oil of anointing, and the bread and wine of communion—we touch, but cannot fully grasp, God's eternal presence in Jesus. Frequently we sense ourselves at the edge of mystery, whose power draws us into God's wondrous, unfathomable love, which holds the cosmos together.

Using our minds, hearts, bodies, and spirits, God draws us into relationship. Jesus—God's mysterious love made physical—revealed God's character through his teaching, eating, forgiving, healing, and miracle working. Jesus restored the life-giving processes of the physical world and thus showed us what God's reign looks like. His death, resurrection, and continual presence in the world are simple truths and perplexing mysteries. Our faith, inspired and sustained by the Holy Spirit, bridges the immense chasm between what we know with certainty and what we can barely imagine.

Christian faith is reasonable. But grounded in what we see and can explain, we also reach beyond sense to understand the wideness of grace, love, redemption, and shalom that is at the heart of God's character. Each day holds a range of experiences through which we find and interpret the meanings of God's movement. We pray, wait, listen, and test what God is communicating. Often when God's intentions are most hidden or perplexing, metaphors, stories, or symbols help us see through to what God desires.

The Holy Spirit works through many means to reveal God's presence and God's desire for relationship with us. We respond intellectually, emotionally, physically, and spiritually to God, regardless of whether we are alone or surrounded by a congregation at worship. Wise worship leaders and preachers use a variety of modes for encouraging us to know, interpret, and respond to God's active presence in Christ in our midst.

The following charts describe ways we interpret what we know through worship and preaching. At least six different ways of knowing can function simultaneously: literal, representational, narrative, metaphoric, symbolic, and universal.[2] As depicted in the following graphic image, these interrelated ways of knowing often do not occur in predictable patterns. Instead, they typically flow back and forth, interrupt each other, are repeated in endless variations, and, together, create the lively, complex experience that happens when worshipers' minds, hearts, and bodies are engaged in worship.

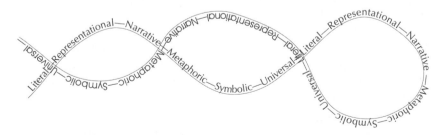

Another, more analytical description of the ways of knowing can be seen in the following chart.

Ways of knowing in worship and preaching

	Literal	Representational	Narrative	Metaphoric	Symbolic	Universal
Description	A=A • obvious meaning • one-to-one correspondence • common sense • limited interpretation • informational • concrete	A=A¹ • stylized or iconic presentation of idea • sign stands for original • mirror of idea in action • translation of idea into different medium	A→B→C→D • progressive development of action • plot	A is like B • concept set in a relationship with image, object, or experience • insight arises from comparison	A=B+C+D+E+F • condensed clusters of meaning • objects, themes, actions take on multivalent meanings • often multisensory	A=BxCxDxExF • experience of wholeness • transcendence • sense of expansion, union with all of life • felt experience of grace, love, shalom, etc.
How the concept is presented	Matter of fact • unadorned • straightforward • uncomplicated • explains how things are, • tells it like it is	Illustration of idea • demonstration of concept	Story • unfolds • develops • becomes more complex	As a relationship • parable • analogy • poem	Complexes of meaning • signified by codes (i.e., significant words, images, objects, gestures, actions) • opened through the senses	Interaction of scripture, foundational beliefs, expressive arts (particularly music), and ritual action
What the congregation does	Receives what is given • hears what is said • sees what is presented • accepts what is given • gains information	Sees connection between idea and new medium • enacts the translation	Follows the action • feels the story's tensions and resolutions • senses the story's significance	Observes relationship • considers • analyzes • reconsiders shared characteristics • discerns relevance	Participates in the symbol • enters the condensed meanings • gains access to the variety of possible meanings • symbols • interprets collective meaning	Experiences disclosure of the triune God • epiphany • revelation
What the presentation yields	Expanded information • foundational faith • vocabulary • basic concepts	Capacity to put a basic idea into action • to translate one experience into another	Common story • shared faith • identity • character formation • worldview (though often unconscious)	"Aha!" • surprise • insight • new way of understanding	Participation in the multiple dimensions of faith • active engagement • ignited imaginations • collective and personal meaning	Transcendent meaning • integration of thought, feeling, and action • unity • shared community
What the congregation experiences	Shared knowledge • shared meaning • explanations of essential matters of faith	Participation in idea through imitation • creation of inner desire and intention • sympathy • empathy	Entry into the story • suspension of disbelief • new possibilities for personal stories • redefined ending	New perspective or possibilities • expanded sense of God, self, or world	Self transcendence • access to reality (God) beyond the obvious, sensible level of experience	Congregational and/or personal transformation • *kairos* • depth of meaning • glimpses of fulfillment (e.g., fulfilled reign of God, unity in the Spirit, unending heavenly worship)

Not intended to be read as a developmental outline or a predictor of what will happen, the suggested structure for interpretation is more like a map illuminating the territory of meaning. Young children, for example, quite easily engage the literal level of meaning, but they can also intuitively grasp meaning in universal modes of knowing. On the other hand, many North American adults struggle with the metaphoric and symbolic modes. Vital worship and preaching move freely among these types of knowing. Few services or sermons remain entirely within one mode, but some modes tend to be privileged at the expense of others. Throughout this chapter, we will use the ritual of communion as a case study, including music and a sermon, with the hope of demonstrating how these types of knowing actually work.

Literal mode

Young children live in the world of the literal. They learn the names of people, objects, actions. They dwell in the basic and obvious facts of life. Juice is juice. A chair is a chair. Mommy is not daddy. Walking brings movement and lots of falls. Words have a one-to-one correspondence with specific things. Reality is concrete. Facts are rooted in sensory experience. Life is full of information simply to be received when people, young or old, operate in the literal mode. Interpretation plays little role in the process of understanding.

Literal understanding operates pervasively in news media and advertising. North Americans are bombarded continually with "facts" that they are expected to receive at face value. Many adults live their lives in the literal realm, rarely asking important questions or seeking spiritual or emotional realities beyond what they can see, hear, touch, taste, or smell.

At the literal level, worshipers understand stories, scriptures, sermons, and songs in the most basic and simple terms. What the text says, the text means. "The Bible says it—I believe it—That settles it" is the motto of the literal mode. Sermons functioning in this mode may expand worshipers' knowledge about particular facts or biblical concepts. People are to receive and accept these facts, considered "the truth," unquestioningly.

Because the foundational vocabulary of faith is developed in this mode, the literal should never be disdained. Every other category of knowing described in this chart depends on worshipers' capacities to understand at the simplest and most basic levels of experience. The danger for some preachers and worship leaders is to work in the literal mode too often, failing to challenge worshipers to expand their capacities to move to other levels of emotional, intellectual, and spiritual awareness. Moralism and didacticism are the prevailing temptations of the literal mode.

Representational mode

The representational mode expands the literal by translating the knowledge of that mode into a new form or into actions. For example, words represent objects or experiences that are not immediately present when two people converse. A hug represents feelings of love and care that cannot be expressed as effectively in words. Gifts given at Christmas or on birthdays express and celebrate the honor we have for our friends and family members.

In another way, a representative in the United States congress or Canadian parliament stands for all the people in her home district. She mirrors their values and needs; her presence is a sign of the interests in her region. She might be considered an icon or paradigm of her constituency.

Many words, gestures, and actions represent the relationship between God and the congregation in worship. Worship leaders, preachers, musicians, and scripture readers routinely represent Jesus as they guide the congregation's meeting with God. Musicians who "sign" hymns during congregational singing mirror with their bodies the meaning of the words. Passing the peace of Christ or shaking hands in greeting reflects Christ's welcome to all people. Monetary or service offerings translate our gratitude for God's gracious blessings. Our desire to serve others is embodied and focused in the sharp image of a foot-washing ritual. A central candle in front of the pulpit may represent the enduring presence of Christ in the midst of the congregation. Congregational singing in four parts stands as a sign of the congregation's unity and diversity.

The representational mode of knowing is nurtured through imitation. When repeated often, concrete, literal, and functional worship actions give shape to our internal desires or create outward intentions. David Morgan's descriptions of empathy and sympathy, although written about visual art in particular, are useful here.[3] Empathy stirs our desires to take on the qualities of character that we see or hear demonstrated in scripture, sermon, image, or movement. Sermon illustrations frequently create empathy. In many songs, worshipers sing their desire to be like Jesus. We picture biblical men and women whose steadfast love and courage carried them through uncertainty, suffering, and trial.

Sympathy stirs our hearts to action. Week after week we offer ourselves and our resources for others' sake. We intercede for the needs of the world. We envision a world of peace and well-being for all and commit ourselves to a way of living consonant with that vision. In this mode, worshipers see and do.

Because the representational mode of meaning is always dependent on the literal mode, we often experience a flow back and forth between these two modes in worship. When worshipers are invited to greet one another, they may turn to each other and say, "Good morning," shake hands, or in some cultures, give each other a hug. When, however, worshipers are invited to pass the peace of Christ to one another, their actions of greeting take on expanded meaning. Although they still engage in the literal-level action of shaking hands, they also become aware of Christ's presence in each other. On occasion, simple guidance from the worship leader, such as, "As you offer the peace of Christ to one another today, receive the other as Christ," can create a space for seeing and touching Christ in even richer ways.

There is always some risk in assuming that actions (such as passing the peace), objects (such as candles), or images (such as portraits of biblical people) represent only one thing or have a single meaning. When the relationship between the outward sign and its intended or prescribed meaning seems arbitrary, the power of the representation is greatly diminished. But when the action expresses an internal consistency or logic within the context of worship, then its meaning is communicated much more clearly.

What can diminish the representational level is naming or defining too narrowly what a particular action means. Part of the strength of the representational level is that more is communicated than the literal action. If a worship leader says to the congregation, "As you offer the peace of Christ to one another today, let your touch represent Christ's healing presence," the leader may have foreclosed the ways the Spirit can move in the ritual action. If Christ's healing presence is the intended focus of the service, the leader does better to surround the gesture of passing the peace with songs, prayers, or stories of healing than to prescribe exactly what passing the peace should mean on this particular Sunday.

Narrative mode

Narrative gives order and shape to the important things that happen in our lives. We ultimately forget what we do not weave into the stories we tell. Story is a way of knowing who and where we are.

The structure of worship itself provides a narrative framework for the biblical story to be heard through scripture and sermon.[4] The order of worship actions and the art media selected draw us into God's central story, which defines our worldview.

Over time, God's story shapes an inner world in us, which is often unconscious. Sam Keen tells a story from his childhood that illuminates the power of stories to shape our ways of seeing.

> It was in Tennessee that I first learned the history of my native land. Before I was six, I had walked through Judea, Galilee, Capernaum, Bethlehem, and Jerusalem, sharing a dusty road with Jesus and the disciples, finding at day's end the comfort of a footbath, bread and olives in a humble home. And what a rich time and place it was to which I belonged! Over these hills and desert places, my forebears roamed. From papier-mâché models, I learned the architecture of the Holy Land, and from bathrobe dramas its way of dress (and at recess there was milk and graham crackers). I learned of Deborah's heroism (but not of Molly Pitcher's) and of the judges and kings the Lord raised to lead and chastise his people (but not of the judges of Blount County who helped to keep whiskey illegal and bootlegging profitable). I knew the topography of Judea before I could locate the Cumberland Plateau, as I knew the road from Damascus to Jerusalem before I could find my way from Maryville to Knoxville.[5]

As we hear the Gospel stories again and again, the life of Jesus begins to live in us as his story gives structure to our lives with God. We increasingly see other people and the world as Jesus does: with compassionate love, grace, and self-giving service. We begin to live as though the reign of God is at hand.

The biblical story constantly surprises. God's ways with humans go against our natural inclinations or expectations. The mighty are brought low, the lowly lifted up. The meek, not the powerful, inherit the earth. God rejoices at the return of an errant child. Astonishingly, new life arises out of death. Time and again, God saves people in the face of disaster and graciously blesses the unlikely. To follow God's grand story into the immediacy of our lives, we must be able to suspend disbelief, as Samuel Taylor Coleridge says. By suspending our assumptions about how the story should go, we are seduced into its plot. God's possibilities seem plausible as a way of life.

Getting swept up into the story: this is the narrative mode of knowing. All the facts, ideas, precepts, and commands of religious practice must eventually get ordered into a story if worship and faith are to be vital and full of life.

The art of storytelling, because of its power to engage and transform, is crucial for good worship. A simple, clear telling of a story—without moralizing or interpreting—may be all that is needed. Other ways of telling the story, such as a memorized text or a readers' theater or simple drama, can also be effective if they serve the purpose of the service and do not distract from the overall flow of worship.

Metaphoric mode

Metaphors are relationships between words and images that provoke thought. If we were to hear for the first time these Gospel sentences—

> I am the vine; you are the branches.
> I am the good shepherd.
> The kingdom of God is like a mustard seed.
> The kingdom of God may be compared to someone who sowed
> good seed in his field.
> Now you are the body of Christ and individually members of it.

the relationships would seem unlikely. Our thoughts might proceed as follows: "Huh? There must be some mistake. I thought Jesus was a carpenter, not somebody that ran a vineyard. What's this about being a shepherd? Did Jesus farm? Couldn't he hold down a job? What's with the body stuff? I thought Jesus said we were branches."

On second thought, we might begin to remember everything we literally know about grapevines and branches, then all we know about Jesus. On third thought, we might begin to see that, just maybe, grapevines could show us something about Jesus that we had never considered before. We would turn these images round and round in our mind's eye. We would notice, for the first time, how dependent the vine branches are on the vine stalk for nourishment, water, and support. The branches cannot live without the vine. Jesus is the vine that nourishes, refreshes, and supports his disciples. He is the source of our growth. We depend on him for a fruitful life.

Scripture is full of metaphoric relationships that cause us to think—considering, reconsidering, extending what we know about life in Christ, God's character, or the Spirit's movement. Metaphors give rise to surprising insights—"Aha!" moments—that change the ways we see and think. Metaphoric relationships make us work, which may be why the disciples rarely understood Jesus's parables. They expected obvious, literal examples about the nature of God's kingdom; what they got were unlikely combinations of images—of mustard seeds, yeast, and banquets.

When we have little knowledge of one side of the metaphoric relationship, the metaphor cannot provoke insight. For many worshipers in North America, Jesus as the good shepherd may be a dying metaphor because shepherds are so rare. Sheep herders—an interesting shift in image—round up sheep with trucks or small all-terrain vehicles. Sheep dogs do much of the actual herding work. The images we have of herding sheep might not create the insights Jesus intended.

Overused metaphoric relationships also create problems. One biblical way of addressing God, as "Father," invites us to draw on our experience of fathers and to extend that image to encompass the best father-love we can imagine. But if we always address God as father, we miss other biblical possibilities for experiencing God as rock, shelter, fortress, still small voice, mother hen, creator, warrior, lover, and more. Worship leaders and preachers play an important role in expanding the congregation's capacities to think metaphorically.

Symbolic mode

The symbolic mode emerges when a variety of meanings are set in motion simultaneously. An action rooted in the present moment may trigger memories from many other times and places. Often congregational rituals or ceremonies provide a context for the interplay of condensed social, emotional, and theological meanings. The multivalent character of significant words, objects, stories, metaphors, gestures, sounds, and movements activated by the congregation weave new meanings that can ignite the worshipers' imaginations. A great deal is happening all at once. This mode addresses the whole person—body, mind, heart, and spirit—through the senses. Although worship leaders help guide the congregation in these moments, the Holy Spirit is the primary leader and interpreter in symbolic experiences with God.

Worshipers bring a vast array of personal meanings to worship in this mode. Some meanings are garnered, shaped, and refined by daily experience and personal stories that have deepened faith. Others are confused or ambivalent, having been shaken by daily life and stories that have assaulted faith. Regardless of what the church teaches about bread, wine, water, oil, the cross, the Bible, the preached Word, grace, forgiveness, love, peace—the primary images of Christian faith—these are always extended and supplemented by the experiences of individual members of the body of Christ. Worship leaders and preachers cannot control or mediate all the meanings the symbolic mode opens. We help the Spirit open the doors to draw the congregation through the sensible, tangible elements of worship to deeper knowledge of the grace-filled reality of God. Worship in the symbolic mode opens the congregation's awareness to reality beyond itself that ministers to its deepest longings.

Perhaps because of their multivalent nature, because they open to myriad interpretations, symbols have sometimes been suspect in Protestant worship. In traditions that value the literal and obvious, and in which didactic preaching has been popular, not all worship leaders or preachers will be equipped to use symbols well. As with metaphorical ways of knowing, leaders may be tempted to explain rather than to trust symbols.

When these leaders catch on to the power of symbols, however, they may be inclined to use them indiscriminately. A student pastor was assigned to be worship leader on one of the Sundays of the Easter season. Drawing from Luke 24:13–35 in the opening acts of worship, he broke a loaf of bread and shared it with worshipers, inviting them to open their eyes to the presence of Christ in their midst. A little later in the service, the fourth-grade Sunday school class presented a dramatic reading of the story of Jesus meeting the Samaritan woman at the well—a story full of water images. (The class had asked to present this reading, because they had recently studied the story in their class.) Still later in the service, the preacher preached a sermon about the vine and branches from John 15. By then, worshipers were reeling from symbolic overload—bread, water, and vine and branches. These strong biblical images became distracting and confusing when they competed with one another in the same service.

One good symbol is enough for any worship service. Far better to let one symbol permeate a service and do its work than to pile symbols upon symbols, making it difficult for worshipers to engage them. Worship planners need to remember that there are fifty-one other Sundays in a year, ample time to make use of a wide variety of symbols in worship!

Symbolic actions in worship should arise naturally out of the text or the focus for the day. They should not be imposed on a service. For example, in a service based on the story of Jesus's baptism (Mark 1:9–11), the worship leader and preacher chose the theme "You are God's beloved," emphasizing God's delight in each person. Sensing that the words spoken to Jesus are meant for all believers, they invited worshipers to come forward after the sermon to receive a water blessing. Dipping a finger in water, they marked the sign of the cross on each forehead and spoke words of blessing, "You are God's beloved daughter," "You are God's beloved son."

Such powerful symbols have potential to invite worshipers into Christ's presence and mediate love and grace, transforming the body of Christ into a blessed people who go out from worship to bless others.

Universal mode

The universal mode opens beyond the immediate moment of the symbolic to an experience of transcendence. Everything converges into a sense of wholeness. Worshipers may feel this mode as time out of time (*kairos*) or as the overwhelming love and grace of God. It may be experienced as shalom, the peace that brings all things together into a sense of common well-being. The Holy Spirit helps us glimpse an epiphany of the triune God's gracious glory, worship as described in Revelation. As a consequence of such communion, we are transfigured or transformed through a reordering of thoughts, emotions, and intentions.

In this mode, we experience knowledge of God in all dimensions of our being. Rationality, profound feeling, bodily expression, and spiritual depth are integrated. Taken beyond our normal capacities, we see God's intentions for the world, the church, and our own lives.

Worship leaders and preachers cannot plan for experiences in this mode, although we may choose words, music, or actions that prepare the way for this mode of knowing to emerge. It is the Holy Spirit's prerogative to lead the congregation into symbolic territory. Leaders must always be prepared for the Spirit to do just that and to assist the Spirit's guidance. The great temptation is to believe that experiences in this mode can be achieved through careful planning and manipulation. Nothing could be further from the truth.

A sample communion service and sermon: From literal to universal ways of knowing

Understanding these modes of knowing—literal, representational, narrative, metaphorical, symbolic, and universal—is important for planning ordinary Sunday morning worship. Any or all of the modes can be active in any of the actions of worship.[6] Further, each mode of knowing can function simultaneously with the others; together the various modes make it possible for worshipers—each at their own stage of perception—to grow in their awareness and experience of the mystery of God's presence. Because the Holy Spirit interacts uniquely with each worshiper and each congregation, the more modes of meaning that are available, the better. When a preacher makes use of a variety of modes in a sermon, more people are able to enter into what is said. When a song engages people at many levels, its power expands to unite the whole body, gathering everyone into God's presence.

If worship planners and leaders disregard the significance of any one of the modes, worship will be diminished. On the other hand, if worship leaders misunderstand the ways of knowing, seeing them as a list of items to be checked off, worship will not achieve its purpose either. The reality is that the ways of knowing are a unique intersection of the Spirit's mysterious moving and careful human planning.

One way to understand the modes of knowing is to examine them through the lens of ritual. Because ritual involves the body, mind, heart, and soul, the modes of knowing are especially active and varied. In addition, usual worship practices, such as singing, praying, and preaching, are also present and active in the many modes of knowing.

The following sample service, including a sermon, examines how each mode operates in the ritual of communion, a worship experience common to Christian churches. This case study also focuses on the special challenges of each mode, to which ritual leaders need to give focused attention.

O taste and see that the Lord is good (Ps 34:8)

Opening words	*Blessed are those who hunger and thirst for righteousness, for they will be filled.* (Matt. 5:6)
Song	Let the hungry come to me (v. 1) *HWB* 464
Prayer	
Psalm 34:1–8	Sung response: Taste and see (see Appendix 12)
John 6:48–51	
Sermon	"Jesus, Bread of Life"
Preparation for communion	I hunger and I thirst *HWB* 474
Invitation to communion	*As Jesus stood before the multitude, he saw their hungry, seeking hearts. Opening his hands, Jesus gave them bread, abundant bread, more than enough to satisfy every man, woman, and child. At a table with his friends Jesus shared bread—the gift of his life, living bread that comes down from heaven. Whoever eats this bread will live forever. If you are thirsty or hungry, come and eat. Eat the bread of life, and find strength for your soul.*
Song	Eat this bread, drink this cup *HWB* 471
Communion thanksgiving prayer and words of institution[7]	
Sharing bread and the cup	I am the Bread of life *HWB* 472
Closing words	*May the body and blood of Christ which alone can satisfy our hunger and quench our thirst, fill us with peace. May God bless us with daily manna for strength and sweet water for refreshment so that we may live in joy.*[8]
Song	Taste and see

Sermon: Jesus, bread of life

"Jesus answered them, 'I am the bread of life. Your ancestors ate the manna in the wilderness, and they died. This is the bread that comes down from heaven, so that one may eat of it and not die. I am the living bread that came down from heaven. Anyone who eats of this bread will live forever. This bread is my flesh which I will give for the life of the world'" (John 6:48–51).

These words were spoken by Jesus while he was teaching in the synagogue in Capernaum. Jesus refers to the manna that the children of Israel ate in the desert. In Hebrew, manna means "What is it?" We could call it the mystery morsel of the desert.

This daily food, this bread from heaven, is interesting for people like us to contemplate. It came every day, and for that the people were grateful. But the reason it came every day was so it would not be hoarded. You could not store it overnight. You gathered only what you needed for today. Any leftovers became spoiled and wormy.

Although the bread from heaven fed them on their journey, they died. Manna—what is it? The Israelite wonder bread is long ago and far away. So maybe it would be more helpful to look at our bread, which we refer to as enriched bread because it is made with "enriched" flour.

Since Roman times, bakers have been aware that flour stored a few months becomes whiter and has improved baking qualities. But storage time is expensive. About a hundred years ago, millers discovered they could get the benefits of prolonged storage instantly, by blowing nitrogen trichloride (chlorine nitride) gas into the flour as it descended the chute into bags. A 1945 study showed that dogs fed the treated flour developed hysteria.

Bread made from enriched flour has a remarkable shelf life. One reason for this extended shelf life is that some twenty-five chemicals are used in making commercial enriched bread. Another reason is that insects and rodents avoid it. In another study, rats were fed only bread made from enriched flour for ninety days. Two-thirds of them died.

In the process of refining enriched flour, twenty-two nutrients are taken out of the wheat grain, and four are put back in. Does that sound enriched? Imagine for a moment that a thief ordered you to strip down to your birthday suit. You had to give up your shoes and socks, shirt and slacks, underwear, wallet, glasses, jewelry, watch—everything you have on your person. Then suppose the thief took pity on you and gave you a tie and some shoelaces. Would you feel enriched? I don't think so.

When Jesus said, "I am the bread of life," I don't think he had in mind our "enriched" bread. Thomas Kelly in *A Testament of Devotion* writes about what "drove him from mediocrity into a passionate quest for the real whole-wheat Bread of Life."

Jesus declares that in him and through him we can know life in its fullness. Again, and with a deepened emphasis, Jesus claims that he—what he is and what he teaches—is the true food of the soul. Other good gifts can help for a while, but the grace of God for us in Jesus is inexhaustible. It will last forever.

In Jesus, we find what feeds us, what sustains us, what restores our spent vigor and renews our exhausted energies. To neglect regular seasons of devotion, to fall out of step with Christ, to lose touch with him, is to deny ourselves our necessary meals. To accept substitutes for the real thing is to contaminate ourselves and to become malnourished. Jesus requires only that we have an appetite for the whole grain bread of life. Bring that appetite, and you will be given what really satisfies.

Our lives are surrounded by urges to choose "enriched" bread. We are tempted to let ourselves be bamboozled into believing that what the world calls enriched is good for us. But let us come to Jesus with our appetite, our hunger for the whole grain bread of life. For Jesus is our hope for wholeness and life eternal.

Literal mode: We eat bread.

Give us this day our daily bread. (Matt 6:11)

At the simplest, most obvious level, what happens in a communion ritual is that food is eaten. That human beings must eat food regularly in order to survive is readily apparent, but because most people in North America have enough to eat, we may be mostly unaware of the direct connection between food and life. In other parts of our planet, however, where a crop failure one year results in food scarcity and famine the next, people know and respect the relationship between food and life.

To understand what happens in communion, theologian Monika Hellwig suggests that hunger is the place to start: "Before we can begin to understand the symbolism of the Eucharist or try to fathom the message it conveys, we need to remember hunger. Perhaps the older discipline in which the Catholic Church imposed certain fasts on its adult members should have been adjusted to modern conditions, rather than simply be allowed to be set aside."[9] "I hunger and I thirst," the first line of a communion hymn,[10] invites worshipers to an awareness of physical hunger as the simple entry point for the ritual of communion. Although the hymn goes on to speak metaphorically of the food offered in communion, it begins at the literal level, which is the foundation for all the expanded meanings to come.

Ritual implications. In a communion ritual, what is important at the literal level is that the bread be fresh, wholesome, and appealing. A tasteless wafer or a slice of highly processed white bread will not communicate the same significant life-giving connection as heartier, more substantial bread. In the same way, a tiny bit of bread does not serve as well as a sizable chunk. For the sense of life to be communicated, communicants must actually chew and swallow real bread.

In addition, a sense of abundance should be evident. Because this is the food that keeps us alive, servings should not be skimpy. A loaf of bread large enough for all to see and ample enough to serve everyone is important. Taking time for serving and eating is essential. No matter what words are spoken, if the food of communion does not speak nutrition and abundance, and if the ritual is rushed or pressured, the ritual will lose its meaning.

Music implications. The communion service opens with the first verse of "Let the hungry come to me":

> Let the hungry come to me, let the poor be fed.
> Let the thirsty come and drink, share my wine and bread.
> Though you have no money, come to me and eat.
> Drink the cup I offer, feed on finest wheat.[11]

This verse functions at a literal level, as does "Taste and see," used with the reading of the psalm. (See Appendix 12 for musical notation.)

> Taste and see, taste and see
> the goodness of the Lord.
> O taste and see, taste and see
> the goodness of the Lord, of the Lord.[12]

These are invitations to eat the bread and drink from the cup that will be served later. In subtle, graceful ways, these songs urge us to come and enter into the ritual of communion. The flow and shape of the melody emphasize the warm and genuine invitation that the words extend.

In this context, the verse of "Let the hungry come to me" is best sung by a solo voice, which becomes the welcoming voice of Jesus. If the bread and cup are already set before the congregation, the singer should stand near the table, so the song's words are clearly associated with the invitation to eat at this table and share this bread and cup. The congregation receives this invitation offered on Christ's behalf.

In most North American congregations, "hungry" must be understood to refer to spiritual hunger. Few people hearing this particular setting of the words are likely to be physically hungry, unless they have practiced fasting before sharing in communion. But many North Americans are spiritually hungry. They feel a pain and longing akin to physical hunger. This invitation, if it is offered in good faith, requires an abundance of bread and adequate nourishment from the cup. Hunger is not satisfied by crumbs. Communion should not be a feeding frenzy, but it should be a time when all who are hungry—physically and spiritually—can be satisfied.

The refrain "Taste and See" continues the invitation to eat, and to take in the trustworthiness of God. The melody, with its slow, gentle swing, lures us into the meal and directs our senses to the physical blessings of the bread and cup. By singing this continued invitation, the congregation is drawn deeper into the promise that the meal will satisfy our longing. Of course, the truth of this refrain requires attention to the quality of bread and wine or juice used for communion. Neither the bread nor the fruit of the cup need to be expensive, but they need to be tasty and pleasing.

The refrain at the end of the service could be played instrumentally or sung by the soloist who opened with "Let the hungry come to me." The waltz-like melody would carry the congregation out with the invitation to "taste" and "see" God's goodness in the multitude of blessings that life holds.

Sermon implications. The sample sermon begins in the literal mode. We hear about bread: the desert bread of the Israelites, ancient Roman bread, twentieth-century Wonder Bread. We hear how flour is milled, aged, enriched. Our understanding of these literal meanings prepares us to move to other levels.

Examples of literal preaching are sermons that move through a passage in verse-by-verse or even word-by-word fashion. Another literal sermon style uses many scripture quotations. Such sermons are concrete and direct; they contain much factual information. In style, they lean toward the didactic. Most sermons contain some literal portions as a point of common reference.

Representational mode: We break bread and share it with others.

And bread I broke with you was more than bread.[13] (Conrad Aiken)

The meaning of eating expands quickly when food is set on a table and a family gathers to eat. Slices of whole wheat bread, warm from the oven, spread with fresh butter and strawberry jam, become more than physical sustenance. Eaten in the midst of conversation and laughter, the bread that is broken and shared becomes inextricably linked with all that is good and healthy about loving relationships. While a slice of bread is no more nutritious eaten in company than alone, it seems more nourishing, because the experience of eating is infused with the joy of belonging and companionship. Thus what is eaten represents the joy of shared communion with others.

Ritual implications. Because the church gathers as a body to celebrate communion, the communion ritual also partakes of the atmosphere of a family meal. What is important at the representational level is that a warm and welcoming tone be set. Although communion may sometimes be a solemn ritual—during Holy Week, for example—it is still a meal eaten in company, not in isolation. The sense of belonging and companionship should be clear. Further, the action of breaking the bread should be clearly visible, because this is the specific action that makes sharing possible.

In many Mennonite churches in the past, it was customary for the bread and cup to be served to people in their pews. After it appeared that all had been served, the pastor always asked, "Is there anyone who has not been served?" If someone had been overlooked, everyone waited patiently while the deacons carried the bread and cup to them. This was a meal at which no one would go away unfed.

Speaking just such a warm welcome, the following invitation to communion highlights the Lord's Table as a place where the body of Christ is united in love:

> This is the Welcome Table of our Redeemer,
> and you are invited.
> Make no excuses, saying you cannot attend;
> simply come,
> for around this table you will find your family.
> Come not because you have to,
> but because you need to.
> Come not to prove you are saved,
> but to seek the courage to follow wherever Christ leads.
> Come not to speak but to listen,
> not to hear what's expected,
> but to be open to the ways the Spirit moves among you.
> So be joyful, not somber,
> for this is the feast of the reign of God,
> where the broken are molded into the Beloved Community,
> and where the celebration over evil's defeat has already begun.[14]

Music implications. The simple refrain "Eat this bread" from the Taizé community invites us to eat real bread and drink from a real cup representing Jesus's never ending spiritual nourishment of our souls.

> Eat this bread, drink this cup,
> come to me and never be hungry.
> Eat this bread, drink this cup,
> trust in me and you will not thirst.[15]

The invitation stirs our desire to reach out, come, eat, drink, and trust. This refrain is to be sung continuously, with additional singers adding verses above the congregation and instrumentalists layering other melodies. The invitation keeps working its way deeper into the mind, heart, and spirit, convincing us that with Christ we will not spiritually hunger or thirst again. Partaking of the bread and cup represents this basic truth.

Sermon implications. Just as a shared meal seems more nourishing than food eaten alone, so the sermon we hear in the company of God's people feeds and shapes the whole body. The sermon helps the congregation meet as a family to eat around the table.

In the sample sermon, manna is more than daily food. It represents God's provision for the people of Israel and the sharing of bread with the people. Jesus too represents God's provision for us—the bread from heaven, the very life of God given to us. Jesus is the one who sustains us, nourishes us, and restores us.

Narrative mode: We listen to the story in order to enter its reality.

> The real starting point of the Christian mystery is not the memorial of a death but the recognition of an enduring life.[16] (Evelyn Underhill)

Our scriptures are filled with stories of meals—from the roast calf, curds, milk, and cakes that Abraham and Sarah served to three unexpected guests by the oaks of Mamre (Gen 18), to the bread and fish Jesus blessed and his disciples served to more than five thousand listeners (Luke 9:10–17), to the daily breaking of bread enjoyed by the first Christians (Acts 2:42), to the Lamb's feast at the end of time (Rev 19:9).

Two meal stories, however, occupy a privileged place in scripture. The first is the Passover meal eaten by the children of Israel on the night of their departure from Egypt. Eaten hurriedly as families stood at tables, the meal consisted of roast lamb, unleavened bread, and bitter herbs (Exod 12:1–13). The story of that meal was told again each year at the feast of the Passover as the descendants of those liberated from Pharaoh's rule remembered their miraculous escape, gave thanks, and celebrated God's faithfulness.

Jesus and his disciples ate the Passover meal according to Hebrew custom (Matt 26:17–19). Although the same foods—roast lamb, unleavened bread, and bitter herbs—were served and the same songs were sung, the ritual meal by then carried the weight of additional layers of meaning, because of events that had transpired in the intervening years. The people of Israel had long ago gained their freedom from Pharaoh, but once again they were oppressed. Gathering around the same meal their ancestors ate, the Israelites experienced a deep connection with the ancient story. In the retelling of their story, they entered it again to remember God's faithfulness and to find renewed hope for deliverance in their own day.

This lively connection between a meal story of the past and present-day experience is familiar to those who celebrate Thanksgiving in the United States. Parents and grandparents tell children the story of the Pilgrims' first Thanksgiving, emphasizing the harrowing adventure of coming to a new land and the joyful celebration of their first harvest. Although roast turkey may not have been served at the Pilgrims' feast, it has become so firmly attached to the ritual that Thanksgiving cannot properly be celebrated without it.

In the biblical account, what began as a routine Passover meal for Jesus and his friends was transformed by the end—and thus became the second privileged meal in our scriptures. In 1 Corinthians 11:23–26, the earliest set of instructions for the Lord's Supper, the origin of this privileged meal is narrated. Ever since, the church has used these words to institute the meal eaten in memory of Jesus's suffering and death.

> The Lord Jesus, on the night when he was betrayed,
>   took a loaf of bread,
> and when he had given thanks, he broke it and said,
> "This is my body that is for you.
> Do this in remembrance of me."

In the same way he took the cup also, after supper, saying,
"This cup is the new covenant in my blood.
Do this, as often as you drink it, in remembrance of me."
For as often as you eat this bread and drink the cup,
you proclaim the Lord's death until he comes.

Ritual implications. Throughout the history of the church, Christians have held firmly to two basic requirements for communion: that bread and wine—the special foods—be served, and that the story of the Last Supper be told.

In the midst of the communion ritual, it is important that the narrative be told simply. This is not the time for complex or elaborate storytelling. Because action—not words—is the center of ritual, the narrative needs to serve the action. In fact, a sense of the story's importance is increased by using similar words every time. As worshipers return to a well-loved story, they enter more deeply into its meaning each time they hear it.

In the rest of the worship service, the sermon or songs or additional scripture readings may also tell the story. In addition, a homily or sermon offered in preparation for the Lord's Supper provides an unparalleled opportunity for illuminating the meaning of the story.

Music implications. The sample service does not use any musical examples of the narrative mode, although allusions to biblical stories are present, particularly in the words of invitation to communion. A hymn that could be used in a different type of communion service, "I come with joy to meet my Lord" illustrates the narrative mode.

I come with joy to meet my Lord,
forgiven, loved, and free,
in awe and wonder to recall
his life laid down for me.

I come with Christians far and near
to find, as all are fed,
the new community of love
in Christ's communion bread.

As Christ breaks bread and bids us share,
each proud division ends.
The love that made us, makes us one,
and strangers now are friends.

And thus with joy we meet our Lord.
His presence, always near,
is in such friendship better known;
we see and praise him here.

Together met, together bound,
we'll go our different ways,
and as his people in the world,
we'll live and speak his praise.[17]

The hymn incorporates a story within a story. Jesus's breaking bread with his disciples—whether with crowds in impromptu picnics on the hillsides, at the Last Supper, or in the intimate setting of the meal at Emmaus—are the primary stories underlying the text. In each of these stories, some truth about Jesus's divine power is revealed to his disciples and friends. This power draws people to him and to one another.

The secondary story is the one we create as we sing in a particular service of communion. We come in wonder. We come with others who are forgiven, loved, and free. We share the meal where Jesus is the host, and whatever divides us no longer has power. Together we bask in Christ's presence, sharing in his common life. We leave our physical meeting and move into the world, bound together by the experience of eating and drinking in the presence of Christ. The hymn defines the shape of our common life and names the benefits of being known in the community of Christ's friends.

This hymn works well when the verses are dispersed through the service. Verses one and two fit the beginning of a communion service of worship. Verses three and four end the period of table fellowship. Verse five makes a fine ending for the entire service. The way the hymn lends itself to marking the movements of the service is a demonstration of its narrative quality.

Sermon implications. The narrative mode describes sermons that are based on a story or follow the plot line of a story. The sermon might be heavy on illustrations, it could include a cluster of smaller stories, or it might engage one or two larger stories. In this sermon mode, the facts serve the stories. Although there may be many details, they will appear in service of the story.

Sometimes the biblical text itself is a narrative (as in the sample sermon). The larger narrative (which includes a plot, action, characters, dialogue, and conflict) from which the passage is taken is an account from the chronology of Jesus's ministry in which Jesus engages in an extended conversation with the crowd and those in charge of the temple.

A second narrative to which this sermon makes reference is the story of the people of Israel in the wilderness, with a particular focus on the story of manna which came down from heaven to feed and sustain the Israelites.

A different role for the narrative is illustration. In preaching, short illustrations are often brought in to give light to the point being made. In this sermon, both the brief history about milling and enriching flour and the imagined story about the thief help us understand the particular ideas they illustrate. They help move us toward the question of what kind of bread Jesus is.

Metaphorical mode: We consider how Jesus is like bread.

> Then they told what had happened on the road, and how he had been made known to them in the breaking of the bread. (Luke 24:35)

In the midst of a typical Passover meal, Jesus introduced a new set of meanings that extended beyond the literal level the ordinary actions of breaking, sharing, eating, drinking, and remembering. Taking a loaf of bread, Jesus blessed it, broke it, and said to his disciples, "Take, eat; this is my body" (Matt 26:26). With these words, he engaged the disciples' imagination by using a metaphor, juxtaposing the loaf of bread and his own body. As they ate, his followers probably understood only dimly that they were receiving a significant gift from their teacher, the one they loved and followed. Later, after Jesus's death and resurrection, they could see the connection between the broken bread and Jesus's broken body—both offered as a gift of life.

Ritual implications. For the metaphorical and symbolic levels of meaning to be active in communion requires giving careful attention to the literal, representational, and narrative modes. Metaphors and symbols only work when concrete experiences and human connections are already present. What ritual leaders can do to encourage engagement with metaphorical modes is to use parables, analogies, and poetic language that set up comparisons. For example, an affirmation of faith used in communion services makes these metaphorical relationships explicit for worshipers:

> I believe in God,
> the giver of grain and bread,
> and in Jesus Christ,
> the bread of life broken for us,
> and in the Holy Spirit,
> God's nourishing power in every grain and loaf.
> I believe that Christ is to be leaven in us,
> so that we may offer the bread of life
> to the hungers of every human heart.[18]

This affirmation of faith depends on familiarity with grain, leaven, and bread baking, and on at least a modest understanding of the science of nutrition, to invite worshipers to relate what they already know about bread to the ritual bread they will consume in communion. It leads them to expect that the nourishment received by their physical bodies in the eating of bread will be available to them spiritually as they experience communion.

In our post-Enlightenment era, attention is being given once again to the significant role of metaphor in scripture and in theology. Although literal and critical readings of scripture have dominated biblical studies for many years, today's renewed interest in metaphor and symbol has generated fresh appreciation for the ritual of communion and its potential for transforming our vision and our vocation in the world. When we add to this picture the significant anthropological work of the past century focusing on ritual, it should come as no surprise that many congregations are finding their faith renewed as they encounter scripture and ritual in new ways.

Music implications. Every phrase of the hymn "I hunger and I thirst" holds a metaphoric relationship, many of which are scriptural allusions.

> I hunger and I thirst; Jesus, my manna be!
> O living Waters, burst out of the rock for me!
>
> O bruised and broken Bread, my lifelong needs supply.
> As living souls are fed, so feed me, or I die.
>
> O true life-giving Vine, let me your goodness prove.
> By your life sweeten mine, refresh my soul with love.
>
> Rough paths my feet have trod since first their course began.
> Renew me, Bread of God, restore me, Son of Man.

For still the desert lies behind me and before:
O living Waters, rise within me evermore![19]

The overarching metaphor of the hymn suggests that the disciple's daily life is like Israel's forty-year sojourn in the desert, a time of relying on God's daily guidance and care for survival. That Jesus is named as manna makes a New Testament connection. Calling Jesus living water, an allusion to his encounter with the woman at the well, connects with God's provision of water when Moses struck the rock. Now we must stop and think, summoning everything we know about hunger, thirst, the cruel punishing life of the desert, the necessity of food and water, the unlikelihood of finding either, and what it means for Jesus to be the manna and water that satisfies our profound physical needs.

Next we consider Jesus as bread, with all its meanings, who nourishes even though he was beaten and broken. Yet, eating the broken bread he offers keeps us alive. His death prevents our death. We draw on what we know of grapevines to understand what it means that Jesus is a life-giving vine. We can be his branches, bearing good fruit. Our lives are renewed by his life.

Our wanderings through this earthly life, like those of the Israelites, have untold difficulties. Jesus nourishes like bread and strengthens like one who can save. The dangers and uncertainties of the desert remain, but Jesus, the life-giving water, is present forever.

For this prayer to work deeply into our minds and hearts, we must ponder the variety of metaphoric pairs the hymn holds. We cannot sing through the hymn quickly and grasp its meanings. Nor can we sing it just once to gain its spiritual truth. Some metaphoric insights come quickly, but most require contemplation with an inquiring mind and open heart.

Sermon implications. Metaphors help us think new thoughts by bringing two familiar things into a new association. We understand something new about Jesus when he is said to be a shepherd or a vine. Sermons are opportunities to explore metaphors.

This sermon is based on the metaphor that speaks of Jesus as bread. In this sermon Jesus is not enriched bread but whole wheat bread. Jesus is hearty, nourishing food for the soul. That gives us something to imagine and contemplate—something to chew on. As we bring our understandings of whole grain to the comparison, we expand our understanding of Jesus. Partly by way of contrast to enriched bread, we come to understand what it means for Jesus to be the whole wheat bread of life. Even as we cannot live without bread, so we cannot live without Jesus.

Symbolic mode: As we eat and drink, we receive the gift of life and are renewed in faith, hope, and love.

> Jesus said, "I am the bread of life. Whoever comes to me will never be hungry, and whoever believes in me will never be thirsty." (John 6:35)

After Jesus fed the five thousand, the crowd returned the next day with questions. Just who was Jesus? What did it mean that he had served them bread in the wilderness? They couldn't help remembering a central story in their tradition in which God had provided manna in the wilderness. What was the connection between what they had experienced just the day before with Jesus and the story they remembered about their ancestors?

In response to their request for a sign that would help them believe (a request at the literal level—which had already been granted in the previous day's miraculous multiplication of loaves and fishes), Jesus responded with symbolic language:

> I am the bread of life.
> Whoever comes to me will never be hungry,
> and whoever believes in me will never be thirsty. . . .
> Whoever eats of this bread will live forever;
> and the bread that I will give for the life of the world is my flesh.
> (John 6:35, 51)

Jesus used the image of bread to communicate God's care and sustenance. Inviting the crowd to go beyond the literal experience of eating and even beyond the story they knew so well (he told them explicitly that the bread of which he spoke was not like the bread their ancestors ate in the wilderness), Jesus called them to believe in him, to put their trust in him as God's Son, and to receive the gift of eternal life. Jesus challenged them not to put their trust in what is not ultimate; he summoned them to conversion and to new life. He promised them the gift of his own self in the eating of bread.

Although he couldn't have been much clearer, the crowd disputed what Jesus meant. Perhaps it wasn't so much lack of comprehension as resistance to committing themselves to Jesus's way. Even Jesus's disciples complained that the teaching was difficult, and some of them turned back and no longer followed him.

The difficulty Jesus encountered when he used symbolic language is not unlike what happens in worship today. As condensed and multivalent modes of communication, symbols require commitment on the part of the worshiper. They open up many avenues of response, asking the worshiper to engage personally and meaningfully with what is happening. Nathan Mitchell suggests that symbols are supple, flexible, and pliant, both influencing and being influenced by the very interactions that evoke them. He notes that "what we need today is not so much 'better symbols' but a willingness to let ourselves be grasped and explored by them. For a symbol is not an object to be manipulated through mime and memory, but an environment to be inhabited. Symbols are places to live, breathing spaces that help us discover what possibilities life offers."[20]

Thus if we open ourselves to symbols, receiving their power, our participation in a ritual in the midst of an ordinary worship service can precipitate transformation. A sip of wine or a taste of bread can initiate an encounter with the living presence of Christ, and the worshiper will not remain unchanged by such a meeting.

Ritual implications. Because of their power to form and transform, symbols must be handled responsibly in worship. Although some Protestants have dismissed the elements of ritual as "mere symbols," the experience of the church testifies otherwise.[21]

Handling symbols responsibly means being attentive to their multivalent character. Bread is served again and again in communion, but the physical properties of the bread chosen for a specific service must cohere with the symbolic meaning offered. For example, if a communion service is based on texts from the Exodus story and focuses on the theme of liberation from oppression, unleavened bread rather than sweet, yeasty Easter bread will better signify the experience of struggle. If a communion service is focusing on the unity of the body of Christ as members meet the Lord at his table, a braided loaf of bread will signify the presence of many members joined together in love and harmony. Even the utensils used for serving may contribute to or distract from the symbolic levels of meaning. Elegant crystal stemware and finely embroidered linen cloths may be appropriate for a table setting that celebrates the messianic banquet but not for a Maundy Thursday meal.

Handling symbols responsibly also requires treating the food and serving utensils with care and respect. If bread and wine are brought forward in a procession, they must be carried with dignity and arranged on the table in an orderly way. After the service, items should be reverently removed from the table.

One action that deserves special attention is the breaking of the bread. Because this action most clearly connects with Jesus's giving his own life for the salvation of the world, it should not be minimized. Holding the bread high, the celebrant breaks it slowly, letting its fragrance fill the air. Whatever words are being spoken need to coincide with the actions and not distract from them.

As the bread and cup are served to individual participants, a spirit of hospitality prevails. Those who serve look into the face of each communicant. They do not rush but offer the symbols as though this person is the only guest present. The spirit of hospitality is enhanced if someone has been appointed ahead of time to tend the table and make sure servers are supplied with what they need.

Another dimension of responsible leadership is providing pastoral care for those who experience the presence of Christ in profound or disturbing ways during the ritual. Not every worshiper will desire such personal attention, but pastors or servers who observe a communicant in distress should let the person know afterward that they are available for further conversation. In the same way, those who experience Christ's presence powerfully in communion may welcome a place to speak of their experience.

The following communion prayer illuminates the symbolic connections between the bread we eat and Jesus, the bread of life, as well as our transformation into Christ's body:

> God, food of the poor;
> Christ, our bread,
> give us a taste of the tender bread
> from your creation's table;
> bread newly taken from your heart's oven,
> food that comforts and nourishes us.
> A loaf of community that makes us human,
> joined hand in hand, working and sharing.

A warm loaf that makes us a family;
sacrament of your body,
your wounded people.[22]

Music implications. "I am the bread of life" re-echoes John 6:35–51
by placing the words in the congregation's voice. In the course of the
hymn, we move from physically eating bread to participating in Christ's
life here and now and into eternity, when we are raised to everlasting
life.

I am the Bread of life.
You who come to me shall not hunger,
and who believe in me shall not thirst.
No one can come to me
unless the Father beckons.

> And I will raise you up,
> And I will raise you up,
> And I will raise you up on the last day.

The bread that I will give
is my flesh for the life of the world,
and if you eat of this bread,
you shall live forever,
you shall live forever.

Unless you eat
of the flesh of the Son of Man
and drink of his blood,
and drink of his blood,
you shall not have life within you.

I am the resurrection,
I am the life.
If you believe in me,
even though you die,
you shall live forever.

Yes, Lord, I believe
that you are the Christ,
the Son of God,
who has come
into the world.[23]

Ideally, a soloist or choir would sing the first four verses, which would underscore this teaching of Jesus. It is a strong christological statement and a bold promise which the congregation is again offered through the rhythmic and dramatic quality of music. On the fifth verse, the congregation sings its affirmation of faith, which echoes Peter's confession, "Yes, Lord, I believe that you are the Christ." This soloist-congregation dialogue mirrors how God comes to us in Christ and invites our response of faith. Alternatively, in usual practice, the congregation sings all of Jesus's words as a testimony of faith.

The folk quality of the music, with its undercurrent of strummed guitar chords or running piano accompaniment, creates momentum. There is a dynamic restlessness in the music that continues to draw us toward the refrain. The melody of the verses does not travel beyond six tones, but the refrain has several dramatic leaps. One leap encompasses an entire octave—a bold leap of faith—that lifts us to the last day. This forty-year-old song still works exceptionally well in congregational settings. By now, many worshipers bring past experiences of singing the song to each new singing, which connects memories of communion across time.

This song, paired with the action of sharing the bread and cup, opens the symbolic mode by connecting the words of eating with the action of eating. It interprets that action—experienced here and now—in light of the promise of life beyond this moment. The reasons to taste and see the goodness of the Lord are sharpened and given a future fulfillment.

Sermon implications. The symbolic is a transforming action, and in the case of the sample service in which this sermon is preached, the most symbolic work will happen in the communion ritual itself when the congregation eats the bread. As we take Jesus into ourselves, our lives are changed.

However, the above comments do not dismiss the work of the sermon. Preaching in a ritual service such as this one carries the responsibility to enhance the senses and the imagination so that the symbols can do their work. The whole grain bread to be eaten in the communion service will have much more power if we have been helped to comprehend and imagine how nourishing it can be. That is the task of the sermon. By the end of the sermon, the congregation's appetite is whetted for this bread, as the symbol has taken on life and substance. We are eager to join in the ritual that will connect us physically with Jesus through this bread. The sermon also extends the experience of this connection into ordinary life: those present may think of Jesus again and again as they eat whole grain bread.

Universal mode: As our lives are broken and shared, we participate in eternal life, already experiencing the joy of the feast to come when all will be gathered at the marriage supper of the Lamb.

> Our life—to be eucharistic—must be wheat—
> seed and soil—light and darkness,
> growth and grinding—
> rhythm and season—now barren, now blooming,
> now barren again—
> eruptive force of faith and hoping.[24]
> (Jane Walker)

Describing God's ultimate intentions for the world, the prophet Isaiah uses the image of a festive banquet to evoke the splendor and glory of God's reign:

> On this mountain the LORD of all hosts will make for all peoples
> a feast of rich food, a feast of well-aged wines,
> of rich food filled with marrow, of well-aged wines strained clear.
> And [God] will destroy on this mountain
> the shroud that is cast over all peoples,
> the sheet that is spread over all nations;
> [God] will swallow up death forever.
> Then the LORD God will wipe away the tears from all faces.
> (Isa 25:6-8a)

The book of Revelation echoes this image in the angel's invitation to the marriage supper of the Lamb (Rev 19:9). Reflecting on the intimacy of being welcomed to this banquet table by Christ, our host, Horatius Bonar writes movingly—almost ecstatically—of union with Christ, in the hymn "Here, O my Lord, I see thee."

> Here, O my Lord, I see thee face to face.
> Here would I touch and handle things unseen,
> here grasp with firmer hand eternal grace,
> and all my weariness upon thee lean.

Feast after feast thus comes and passes by,
yet, passing, points to the glad feast above,
giving sweet foretaste of the festal joy,
the Lamb's great bridal feast of bliss and love.[25]

When Karl Rahner wrote, "The Lord gave himself to us precisely as food to be enjoyed,"[26] he was encouraging a richer, fuller experience of communion—not the fulfillment of a duty but a joyful participation in the mystery of Christ's life. Such a bountiful table, such blissful communion, and such joyful celebration represent the abundant reality toward which every communion table points.

As worshipers open themselves to be grasped by God's vision and God's desires for the world, the table also becomes a place of justice. The table that feeds us so abundantly is meant to feed all God's children, for this table is meant to transform all tables. And so as a foretaste of the meal to come, the communion ritual is a powerful stimulus for the church's engagement in ministry with the poor, the weak, and the oppressed.

When a pastor asked a young woman what moved her to become involved in a refugee program that demanded much of her time and resources, she replied that she had heard a call in the midst of a communion service. It happened one Sunday when the pastor used the image of Psalm 23—"my cup overflows"—as he poured the cup full, then allowed it to spill over into a plate beneath. In that moment, the Spirit moved in her heart and revealed to her the immensity of God's grace. As she rejoiced in the gift of salvation, she was filled with a desire to share God's grace with others.

Another woman who was discerning a call to pastoral ministry found that call became remarkably clear as she served communion in her congregation.

June 6

I turn,
bread in hand,
to find them leaning forward
in anticipation.

I hear the words—
familiar,
intimate,

holy—
being spoken in my voice.
I see the loaf break under the pressure of
my hands.

Celebration.
Mystery.
Remembrance.
The geographic crossroads of the already
and the not yet.

While the bread is passed,
I study their faces,
recall their stories,
lift them to God.

"Eat, beloved, the Lord's body broken for you."

With these words,
the YES,
resisted so long,
breaks free in my soul.

Yielding to grace,
the liminal becomes palpable.

Pastor.

Fundamentally changed,
I turn for the chalice.[27]

For these worshipers and many others, the communion table
becomes a place of transformation, a place where a fuller, more complete vision of God's purposes is revealed. When such epiphanies happen (and notice that the source of revelation in the two stories just cited
originated at the literal level—in a simple, concrete action of wine overflowing and in the action of looking intently into the faces of
worshipers), then the communion ritual has functioned simultaneously
on all levels of meaning. Such unity is the goal of all our worship.

Ritual implications. The universal level of meaning is not usually
the focus of worship on any given Sunday. Rather, this level of meaning accumulates over time. As we hear the familiar story over and
over again, as we share generously at the table, and as we open our

hearts and minds and bodies to the many ways the Spirit moves in rituals, we will be transformed by God's vision.

That said, worship planners and leaders do need to assure that space is created in our rituals for such revelation. Music, silence, visual arts, gestures, and movement are particularly powerful prompters. In addition, the worship resources we choose can also open or close a pathway to mystery. For example, if the words we speak in communion services always point backward to Jesus's suffering and death and never point forward to Christ's exaltation, we will miss opportunities for a more expansive vision.

Another way to open more space for God's vision is to include words and actions that connect with justice themes. As the gifts of bread and wine are brought forward in one congregation, a shopping cart filled with food for the poor is also wheeled forward. Each week, worshipers see this visible connection between the gift of Christ's body shared with them and the gifts they are called to share in the world.

Finally, to underscore the immensity of God's dream for the world, congregations need to celebrate communion periodically as a genuine feast. The table should be filled to overflowing with the breads of many nations and many pitchers of wine. Everyone must be invited to the table, for no one can be excluded from God's banquet. The words of invitation may come from Isaiah 25:6–8a or from Revelation 19:9b. The following prayer would be suitable for such a communion service:

> My God, I need to have signs of your grace.
> Serve me your sacraments,
> the first fruits of your Kingdom.
>
> I thirst for smiles,
> for sweet odors,
> for soft words,
> for firm gestures,
> for truth and goodness,
> and for triumphs
> (no matter how small)
> of justice.
>
> You know, O God, how hard it is to survive captivity
> without any hope of the Holy City.
> Sing to us, God, the songs of the promised land.
> Serve us your manna in the desert.

Let there be, in some place,
a community of men, women, elderly, children and new-born babies
as a first fruit,
as our appetizer,
and our embrace of the future.[28]

Music implications. Music is a powerful resource the Spirit uses to draw worshipers into the universal mode. Words, like those of "This is the feast," focus our minds on an image of fulfillment promised in Revelation.

This is the feast of victory for our God.
Alleluia, alleluia, alleluia.

Worthy is Christ, the Lamb who was slain,
whose blood set us free to be people of God. (R)

Power, riches, wisdom, and strength,
and honor, blessing, and glory are his. (R)

Sing with all the people of God, and
join in the hymn of all creation. (R)

Blessing, honor, glory, and might
be to God and the Lamb forever. Amen. (R)

For the Lamb who was slain
has begun his reign. Alleluia! (R)[29]

Part call to praise and part affirmation, the words we sing echo throughout time. Richard Hillert's tune, FESTIVAL CANTICLE, is a strong, stately, and expansive setting for John Arthur's words; the music lifts the spirit of the singing congregation. The words and music alone cannot guarantee an experience of transcendence, but when the Holy Spirit takes hold of the congregation, this is the type of song that can prepare worshipers to join their voices with believers across time and place in praising Christ.

Sermon implications. In the sample sermon, Jesus is the living bread that sustains us. Jesus gives us life and desires to be shared with others. Our hunger for and our allegiance to Jesus are demonstrated in our appetite for the living bread. If we eat this bread, Jesus assures us that we will live forever (John 6:51).

The act of preaching itself serves as an example of how the various modes of knowing interact. At the literal level, a preacher speaks words to the congregation. Because these words have commonly understood meanings, they communicate a message. Bread is bread, and words are words.

Viewed from another angle, however, preaching is representational. It is the preacher's task to translate the word that has been received from God into a message that the listeners can hear clearly. When the preacher breaks open God's Word (a metaphorical action) and shares it with listeners, they are offered bread, the manna of God, in every sermon. As listeners receive the bread and allow it to transform them, the sermon functions in a symbolic mode.

The universal quality in sermons is indeed a gift of the Holy Spirit. Although the sermon may help us see the wholeness of God, life fulfilled, and the glory of the beyond, such clarity of vision happens only by the Spirit. Sermons invite the Holy Spirit to speak to the listeners, to enter into their lives and transform them.

A word of encouragement

At this point, worship leaders, musicians, and preachers may feel that the task of preparing Sunday dinner is overwhelming. How could we ever remember and care for all these ways of knowing? And what difference does it really make?

No one promises that worship planning is easy! What we must bear in mind and heart, however, are two things. The first is that the Holy Spirit is the primary agent in worship—calling us to worship God, inviting us to respond to God's love and grace, and transforming and empowering us to be God's people in the world. We are not alone in this ministry.

The second thing to remember is that if we are called to the ministry of preaching or leading worship, we hold a rich resource in our hands—living bread that will feed and sustain God's people. We must bring all of ourselves, our best, to the task of feeding God's people. If we are true to our call, we will not serve just one food group in worship. Nor will we serve junk food. Instead, we will do our best to offer tasty, attractive, well-rounded meals. That entails learning as much as we can about worship, taking risks, learning from our mistakes, and trusting that the Spirit will continue to guide us. The modes of knowing are one tool for enriching worship. We already know a great deal about them from our own experiences of worship. The challenge is to become thoughtful and intentional in our choices, so worshipers receive abundant nourishment for faithful living.

11

MAKING OCCASIONS SPECIAL

On this mountain the LORD of hosts will make for all peoples a feast of rich food, a feast of well-aged wines, of rich food filled with marrow, of well-aged wines strained clear. (Isa 25:6)

In her unforgettable novella, *Babette's Feast,* Isak Dinesen tells the story of Babette, a French chef who uses her lottery winnings to create a sumptuous feast honoring the founder of her adopted community in Denmark. Securing the finest ingredients for each course, Babette executes each detail of the menu with skill and care. Although she remains in the kitchen throughout the meal, she serves a healing feast. Course by course, the exquisite food, fine wine, and grace-filled atmosphere ease the tensions between neighbors, which have accumulated over years of austerity. Astonished by Babette's extravagance, the founder's daughters slowly come to receive her generosity of spirit. As they express their gratitude, Babette returns the thanks. Using her artistic gifts for the people she has learned to love, Babette creates a feast that seems a foretaste of heaven.[1]

Although many cooks start planning just an hour or two before an ordinary meal, they begin planning weeks in advance for Thanksgiving or Christmas dinners. In fact, if they come across a great idea for a holiday meal during the year, they tuck it away in their recipe collections—ready to be retrieved during the holiday season. In contrast to everyday cooking, meals for special occasions require much advance preparation.

Such meals have other special requirements. A Christmas feast has more courses than usual, richer food, and a more elegantly set table. Certain favorite dishes—Mom's cranberry salad or a traditional coconut cake—are musts on the menu. We expect the meal to be the main feature of the day, and we devote a leisurely amount of time to enjoying each flavor, each dish, and every course. Conversation flows gracefully as memories and stories intermingle. Afterward, completely satiated and full of good will, we wonder if any other meal or celebration can match the one we've just enjoyed.

Although most Sunday morning worship is of the everyday variety, special occasions demand the kind of creative, thoughtful planning that a festive meal requires. Yet the basic understandings of worship that shape any ordinary service still apply on these occasions; worship on special days, as on any day, is a response to the living God. The same essential rhythms—encounter with God, engagement with self and the community, and empowerment for faithful response—are at work here. In addition, the role of the worship leader is still to serve as a shaman who guides the people's transforming encounter with God, a host who creates hospitable space for honest engagement with self and others, and a prophet who inspires an empowered response. What is true of ordinary meals is also true of special meals—only more so.

Sometimes special occasions are planned long in advance. My congregation spent several years in an intense process of constructing a new building. At long last, on a bright autumn morning, we processed into the new building, took our places in a sanctuary that still smelled of new building materials, and praised God with soaring trumpets, hearty singing, and fervent prayers. A less formal occasion, but also planned well in advance, occurred after several young adults completed baptismal preparation. On a sunny Sunday afternoon in late spring, we gathered at a nearby lake to rejoice in the ritual of washing and anointing new believers. We sang and prayed and committed ourselves to walk with these new Christians on their journey of faith.

Other special occasions come unbidden and unplanned for. Two World Trade towers are struck on a cloudless September morning, forever altering the landscape of a city and of our hearts. Numb and fearful, people find their way to churches, seeking solace and desiring to pray. The death of a child occurs unexpectedly, and a funeral involving hundreds of people must be planned in just two days. A frail 80-year-old calls his pastor and asks for anointing. The pastor invites an elder and several others to join her, and they go to his home to conduct an impromptu healing service.

Some special occasions are related to the Christian year. As the last dry leaves fall from barren trees, Advent worship planners convene and begin exploring the scriptures for the coming season. Or in the midst of winter dreariness, Ash Wednesday looms on the calendar, and the Lent worship committee goes to work to prepare this midweek service and the Sunday services to follow. Or Easter Sunday arrives, and the congregation desires a celebration worthy of the risen Christ. Coming around each year, the fasts and feasts of the Christian year offer familiar themes and emphases, yet the celebrations do not pall with repetition.

What unites all these occasions is heightened expectations. People long to meet God and desire support from the community of faith. They want to know they are not alone, that others share their joy or sorrow. They want the security of tradition to undergird these events, but they also want the day to be memorable, vital, and fresh.

Those who plan worship for these occasions rely on patterns and practices that are already well known and understood. Because of the sense of heightened expectations, however, a particular step in the planning process requires attention. To that piece of the planning task we now turn.

Discerning the face of God

Ordinary worship planning begins with reflection on the scripture texts for the day. Preachers, worship leaders, and music leaders read the texts carefully, meditate on them, and listen for the Spirit to guide them to a message that will meet the needs of the congregation. Because of the wide range of needs and desires present in a congregation on any Sunday morning, planners are always attempting to be responsive to that diversity. But what makes special occasions exceptional is the unity of the congregation's needs or desires. At a funeral, most everyone comes seeking comfort. At a baptism, most everyone comes eager to celebrate the commitment of a new believer to Christ and the church. On Christmas day, most everyone comes ready to rejoice in the incarnation of God in our world. Although there will be some variation in expectations, worshipers will experience an extraordinary cohesion.

With such clarity about the congregation's expectations, worship planners have a special responsibility to discern how God desires to meet the needs of the people who come to worship. In light of the unusual circumstances of the day, planners ask a set of preliminary questions, even before exploring possible scripture texts:

What face of God does the congregation need to see on this occasion?

What particular characteristic of God's activity or character needs to be illumined in order for the purpose of the day to be fulfilled?

When this critical step of discernment has taken place, the remaining decisions about the purpose, shape, and flow of the service follow naturally and logically.

If we look at such special services as weddings and funerals, this step of planning becomes clear. At a wedding, the face of God we always long to see is the face of faithful love. Because two flawed yet hopeful human beings have chosen to commit themselves to each other until death, worship needs to provide a sense of assurance that God's faithful love will empower these two to love each other and remain true to their covenant all their lives long. With that focus in mind, planners select scriptures, make music choices, and create a homily or meditation that will reveal this particular face of God. If a psalm text such as the following is chosen as the centerpiece for a wedding service, the bride and groom, as well as those witnessing their promises, will leave with renewed trust in God's love and a deeper confidence and hope for the marriage.

> Your steadfast love, O Lord, extends to the heavens,
> your faithfulness to the clouds.
> Your righteousness is like the mighty mountains,
> your judgments are like the great deep.
> you save humans and animals alike, O Lord.
>
> How precious is your steadfast love, O God!
> All people may take refuge in the shadow of your wings.
> They feast on the abundance of your house,
> and you give them drink from the river of your delights.
> For with you is the fountain of life;
> in your light we see light.
>
> O continue your steadfast love to those who know you,
> and your salvation to the upright of heart! (Ps 36:5–10)

Should the marriage ceremony be uniting two people whose previous marriages have failed, we may need to see another face of God.

Although God's faithful love could still be a strong theme of the wedding, God's desire to heal and forgive might also be an appropriate theme. If the bride and groom have faced their previous failures, repented of their sin, and taken the necessary steps to put this new marriage on a strong footing, they and their families and friends will also want to be assured of God's grace and God's promise to make all things new. A scripture text that might provide a suitable focus for such a wedding service is Isaiah 43:18–21:

> Do not remember the former things,
> or consider the things of old.
> I am about to do a new thing;
> now it springs forth, do you not perceive it?
> I will make a way in the wilderness
> and rivers in the desert . . . to give drink to my chosen people;
> the people whom I formed for myself
> so that they might declare my praise.

At the funeral of an elderly woman who has lived a long and satisfying life, the congregation's need to mourn will be tempered with a desire to give thanks for her faithfulness. The steadfast face of God, the God who sustains us in this life and the life to come, may be discerned as the focus, with Psalms 90:1–2 and John 14:1–3 as central texts. On the other hand, the unexpected death of a child may require a different face of God—one who weeps with us in our despair or who promises never to leave us or forsake us, comforting us with words such as those found in Isaiah 43:1–7.

An example of especially apt opening words—words that identified the most needed face of God as well as the deepest cry of the community—were spoken at the funeral of Marlin Miller, president of Associated Mennonite Biblical Seminary, after his unexpected and tragic death in November 1994. Gathered together in numbing grief, the community heard familiar words from the Gospel according to John: "Lord, if you had been here, my brother would not have died" (John 11:21). Martha's wrenching indictment startled worshipers, and then, in the silence that followed, we became profoundly aware that a grieving Jesus was present, sorrowing with us, lovingly offering us the hope of resurrection.

In the same way, baptismal services call forth different faces of God. Depending on their conversion experiences, the focus of God's activity in the lives of new Christians may be perceived differently. A classic image for baptism is new birth, the experience Jesus describes to Nicodemus in John 3. For some, conversion does indeed seem like the beginning of an entirely new life. For others, a clearer focus might be their incorporation into Christ's body, the church, as in 1 Corinthians 12:13. And for still others, the experience of being cleansed from sin and wrongdoing and being given a fresh start is primary, as in 1 Peter 3:21–22. What all of these experiences share is newness: God is at work creating a new life. Yet the particular way God works to bring newness varies. A different face of God—birth-giver, head of the body, or cleanser-forgiver—is revealed in response to the unique experience of each new Christian.

What is important in this step of the discernment process is to find a proper balance between the horizontal and vertical aspects of worship. Discernment begins with a careful assessment of the human situation: What do worshipers need on this occasion? But that awareness is a preliminary step to a still more significant question: In light of this particular human need, what face does God desire to show us? How does God desire to act? What does God desire to give? Although this may seem a small consideration, it is, in fact, the crucial element that determines whether our heightened expectations for worship will be fulfilled. Only God's presence can satisfy these desires. If we content ourselves with exploring only the human situation, we may end up feeling good about ourselves or others, but we will not connect with the Source who fulfills our deepest longings. In other words, the transformation that is the hoped-for outcome of any worship service will not happen.[2]

Understanding the role of ritual and ritual actions

Understanding the heightened expectations for worship on special occasions and knowing how to respond to them by focusing on God's presence and God's activity is the first requirement for effective planning of worship and preaching. A second requirement has to do with understanding the role of ritual and ritual actions. Because many worship services on special occasions also incorporate some kind of ritual action, those who plan and lead worship need to appreciate the significance of ritual and know how to effectively incorporate ritual speech and actions in worship.

Although rituals may be included in ordinary Sunday morning worship services, they usually play a more prominent role in special services. Whether it is the lighting of candles in Advent season, breaking bread in a communion service, marking the sign of the cross with ashes on Ash Wednesday, or anointing worshipers with oil in a healing service, the speech and actions of ritual communicate God's presence in dramatic ways. As our senses are touched, our whole body—mind, heart, and soul—comes alive to the Spirit's transforming energy. We find ourselves fed and nourished, restored and renewed, and deeply moved and transformed.

What defines ritual is *action*. More than speaking or listening to words, a ritual invites us to touch, see, smell, taste, and move. Leaders must take care to create a hospitable space in which such actions can occur. And although words are secondary, they are still important. Spoken words must be words of beauty and power, both tender and strong, able to bear many repetitions.

Although it is beyond the scope of this book to deal with the history of ritual in Christian worship, we notice in passing that the Protestant church, especially the free-church tradition, has had an ambivalent relationship with ritual.[3] Ritual is deeply embedded in human history and culture, but in these traditions until quite recent times, ritual in worship has been neglected and sometimes even seen as suspect. While these groups have practiced baptism and communion rituals, because Jesus mandated them, historically, free-church folks have invested little effort in other rituals. Furthermore, the emblems used in rituals have been dismissed as "mere symbols," a description depreciating the powerful potential of symbols and symbolic actions to reveal God's presence and to transform the worshipping community.

Some of our religious ancestors had good reasons to mistrust symbols and rituals because of abuses in the medieval Catholic church. The state church controlled access to the sacraments, deciding who could receive God's grace and from whom it would be withheld. The free-flowing grace of God was dammed up, hidden behind a barrier of ecclesiastical tradition, backed by the power of the state. In addition, because some of these reformers were influenced by the spirit of rationalism emerging in Western Europe, they turned away from mystical religious experience and embraced a rigorously practical faith that emphasized simple living and everyday expressions of charity to one's neighbors. With little interest in symbols and even less use for the arts, they devoted themselves to plain, unadorned worship and desired most of all to recreate in their own time the pure church of the New Testament.

Nearly five hundred years later, the world has changed. The disappearance of the sacred from daily life in North America has left a void, an emptiness. Although the early reformers likely could not have imagined how their descendants would hunger for the beauty and mystery of ritual and symbols, that is precisely what is happening in many churches today. We find ourselves returning to biblical stories such as Jacob's dream and his ritual response in Genesis 28:10–22, or to Jesus's baptism in Mark 1:9–11, and rediscovering in them ancient yet new understandings about ritual.

The story of Jesus's baptism, for example, reveals a theophany: "In those days Jesus came from Nazareth of Galilee and was baptized by John in the Jordan. And just as he was coming up out of the water, he saw the heavens torn apart and the Spirit descending like a dove on him. And a voice came from heaven, 'You are my Son, the Beloved; with you I am well pleased'" (Mark 1:9–11). Not a perfunctory practice lacking power and purpose, Jesus's baptism opened him to a revelation of God's presence and power with a never-to-be-forgotten message of love and blessing that surely reverberated in his heart and body: "You are my Son, the beloved. With you I am well pleased."

The richness of that experience stands in stark contrast to the neglect or devaluing of ritual. It also helps us understand the important role of symbols and symbolic actions in rituals. The word the church has used for these experiences is *sacrament*. Simply put, in a sacrament what is earthly becomes revelatory of the divine. Because God is the creator of the world and continues to be active in the world, any ordinary human action or experience can open a window that shows us something of what God is like and what it means to relate to God. And because such an encounter with the living God leaves no one unchanged, we are transformed by that meeting.[4]

Our worship rituals can be understood as incarnations of the gospel. They both proclaim the good news and shape us as Christians through actions in which we participate. To understand the incarnational power of rituals is to engage them at the deepest levels. For example, when the Jewish people observe Sabbath rituals by setting apart one day as holy, they are being formed in an understanding of all time as holy, able to be filled with a numinous sense of God's presence and activity. Through the incarnation of Jesus, God in human flesh, we come to see that everything human is redeemed. And in a communion ritual, when we eat and share bread and wine, we are being formed so that all our eating and relating reflect the love of Christ.[5]

Water, wine, bread, oil, and light have been the privileged symbols used historically in the church's rituals. Because they are linked to basic experiences of human existence—our thirst, our hunger, our need for comfort and healing, the cycles of day and night—they remain vital and meaningful. Our experience of these symbols in worship is enriched by our everyday experiences. Furthermore, as noted above, what we experience in the rituals of worship can also transform how we see and experience ordinary life. Barbara Brown Taylor writes about this crossover effect:

> I learned that the sacraments I practiced in church were patterns of countless ways that God uses material things to reach out to human beings in the world. The same pattern of rebirth that I learned in Baptism showed up in everything from bathing to watering plants. The same pattern of relationship that I learned in Communion was available in every meal eaten mindfully. The laying-on of hands took place as I held a crying baby or rubbed the shoulders of a tired friend. With a little oil, I could even offer the sacrament of a pretty good massage. When I walked outside and looked at the smoking compost heap, I saw a sacrament of death turning into life. When I used a bottle of white-out to correct a mistake, I remembered that my errors did not have to be permanent.
>
> Everywhere I turned, the most insignificant things in the world were preaching little sermons to me. Everywhere I turned, the world was leaking light.[6]

Rituals and symbols cannot contain, confine, or define God. But because human beings by nature are symbol-making creatures, our rituals become ways of touching or grasping the divine mystery. We *will* have our rituals. Thus the question for the church today is not whether to affirm or reject rituals but whether our rituals will be life-giving. Will we capitulate to the world's rituals—sporting rituals or political rituals or economic rituals—or will we invest creativity and energy in sacred rituals? Will our rituals invite and welcome people to Christian faith? Will they sustain us for the arduous journey of growth and transformation? Will they heal us when we are broken? Will they carry us when we are in despair? If they open believers to such transforming experiences, the church will not question the place of rituals.

Although it is true that rituals can degenerate into mere repetition—that they can become empty, that sometimes they may leave little room for the Spirit to move—they do not need to do so. What is needed for meaningful rituals is a deeper understanding of the nature and character of ritual and a willingness to explore, experiment, and learn from our rituals.

The gifts of good ritual: order, community, and transformation

In his helpful book on ritual, *Liberating Rites*, Tom Driver describes three essential gifts offered by good ritual to the Christian community: order, community, and transformation.[7]

The gift of *order* marks the capacity of rituals to establish security and boundaries and to inspire renewed trust in God. Good rituals not only remind us of an underlying cosmic order—that God created heaven and earth, and that we are in God's care—they reestablish that order. They participate in the making or restoring of order.

Perhaps funerals offer the most striking example of this gift. People old enough to remember the assassination of President John F. Kennedy vividly recall the great chaos that descended on the nation in the wake of that tragedy. Americans were not only outraged and bereft, they felt the very foundation of their lives was shaken. The world was out of joint. If presidents could fall, no one was safe. Amid this despair, the televised funeral service offered great comfort to the nation. A sense of stability and security began to return when the funeral cortege left the White House and moved majestically down Pennsylvania Avenue to the tolling of bells and the lament of bagpipes. The president's two small children, Caroline and John-John, walked beside their grieving mother, whose face remained hidden behind a black veil. At St. Matthew's Cathedral, the organ played solemn music, prayers were offered, and the words of the Roman Catholic mass were recited. When the requiem prayer was offered, peace settled over the nation: "Eternal rest grant unto them, O Lord, and let perpetual light shine upon them." Although the nation's grief was still raw, that powerful ritual made it possible to believe life could go on.

In our rituals, we gain a larger view of reality. We are reminded by scripture, songs, prayers, and homilies that nothing can separate us from the love of God in Christ Jesus—"neither death, nor life, nor angels, nor rulers, nor things present, nor things to come, nor powers, nor height, nor depth, nor anything else in all creation" (Rom 8:38–39). In the midst of such affirmations, God comes near. Thus our rituals become the occasion of numinous encounter, imbuing a profound awareness of who God is and who we are. With our trust restored, we can face the future.

A second gift of ritual is *community*. Rituals obviously bring people together in physical assembly, but they also tend to join us emotionally and spiritually. On these occasions, our emotions are permitted greater scope. In fact, Driver observes, "A ritual is a party at which emotions are welcome."[8] We weep tears of joy at a wedding or baptism; we succumb to our grief at a funeral; we solemnly remember Jesus's death when we break bread and share the cup on Maundy Thursday; we sing for joy and revel in the feast of the risen Christ on Easter Sunday. Within the safe confines of ritual structures, we laugh, weep, sing, eat, dance, and tell stories with more permission than usual. We enjoy a sense of freedom and solidarity, if only momentarily. And through these simple actions—washing, eating, drinking, anointing—experienced in the midst of shared sorrow and joy, a people is created, a new community is born.

The church needs to recognize and emphasize the amazing capacity of ritual to suspend the social and cultural divisions that otherwise keep people apart. When the Spirit of God moves within the powerful bonds of care and affection generated by good ritual, those who may not ordinarily recognize that they are sisters and brothers suddenly see that they are members of one another, members of the same body of Christ.

A young man in his first pastorate enjoyed good relationships with nearly everyone in the congregation. Yet he found himself at odds with one particular brother. This man took it upon himself to criticize the new pastor at every turn. Nothing the pastor could say or do seemed to help the situation, and gradually the two became estranged. Then the time came for the annual foot-washing service.

As fate—or God—would have it, the young pastor and his critic were paired for the foot-washing ritual. As they knelt wordlessly before each other, washed each other's feet, and offered each other the kiss of peace, a miracle of reconciliation occurred. Their enmity dissolved as they embraced and forgave each other. From that day forward, the church member gave his wholehearted support to the pastor, and the pastor was able to relate to him without defensiveness—two miracles in one ritual!

A third gift of ritual is *transformation*. Good ritual not only supports the order that has come down to us, it not only unites us with sisters and brothers in Christ with ties that are not easily broken, but it also offers the wondrous potential of transformation—a new life.

The transformative power of ritual happens in the words that are spoken and in the actions performed. In baptism, for example, we speak words and pour water, and God moves to recreate us, not in a magical sense, but in the moment when our intentions open us to God's transforming power.

> The new Christian is asked: "Do you, in the presence of God and this assembly, solemnly renounce the Devil and all his works, and declare the Lord to be your God?"
>
> The baptismal candidate replies, "I do."
>
> The minister proclaims: "Upon your confession of faith, I baptize you with water in the name of God the Creator, Redeemer, and Sustainer. May God baptize you with the Holy Spirit."

And just so—a new creature is born. Through symbolic words and actions, the transforming power of the Spirit becomes visible in a changed life. Both the congregation and the one baptized are aware that "the heavens have opened" in this ritual, and God's love and grace have become incarnate once again in the life of ordinary human beings.

We may not have a clue what God is doing, yet God's Spirit can still move in freedom and love to bring about the transformation needed, leaving us amazed and humbled. I remember leading a healing service during a weekend retreat. Many people came to be anointed, including a young woman who was weeping and being supported by a friend as she walked up the aisle. I had no idea what her story was or what in her life needed healing. I simply prayed the same prayer I had prayed for everyone else and anointed her with oil. Many months later, I learned that this experience was the first step in a long and arduous journey of healing in which God transformed that young woman's life and called her into ministry. As we faithfully offer the rituals of the church, God acts to transform and bring new life.

When rituals fail

We may also be humbled and amazed when rituals fail.[9] Although we may have planned carefully, sometimes it seems that no one has been touched, that God has not moved. What happens in rituals is always a mystery; we do not control God's actions. But more often than not, if we review what has happened, we will discover the failure is ours. Because ritual is about action more than about words, we may find we smothered the action with too many words. Someone has said that good ritual doesn't love paper, a dictum that we ignore to our regret. We may find that we failed to act hospitably, not giving people clarity about how they were to participate. Confused and ill at ease, worshipers were not able to enter into the ritual with open hearts and minds, giving the moment of encounter with God their full attention. We may have failed to take into account the very real needs of the people on a specific occasion, with the result that we alienated them rather than making a strong connection with them. Or we may not have thought through the service enough to make it cohere.

As a guest in a worship service, I watched a communion ritual fizzle. The service opened with a large choir singing exuberant, triumphant music. An energetic sermon reminded us that Christ promises joyful new life as we receive the Word—the living Word and the broken bread of communion. Loaves of bread were processed forward with lively guitar music. Everything in the service prepared us for a jubilant feast at the Lord's Table. Then two elderly men in black suits stood at the table and offered a solemn and lengthy introduction to communion, emphasizing the suffering and death of Jesus. As people came forward to receive the bread and cup, an organist played doleful music. All the sparkle had vanished. What should have been a joyful celebration—because of the way music and the spoken word had prepared us—became a confusing anticlimax. The leaders of communion may not have been adequately informed of the purpose or intended mood of the service. They were probably just doing it the way it had always been done. But the ritual failed. Although it had been properly enacted, it did not participate in the celebratory spirit appropriate to that occasion.

Sometimes the problem stems from failure to properly enact the ritual. After traveling thousands of miles to attend the funeral of three members of my family who were killed in a tragic automobile accident, we were in great need of comfort and care and expected the congregation's pastor to minister to the extended family. Unfortunately, the pastor was on sabbatical, and an inexperienced pastoral intern was on duty. We received only the sketchiest details about the committal service, which was to be held for immediate family members in the cemetery on Saturday afternoon. When we arrived, we were overwhelmed by the sight of three coffins in a row. Yet no one seemed to be in charge; no one was attentive to our pain. The simple service proceeded awkwardly—and then it was over. I realized with a shock that no words of committal had been spoken. The souls of our dear departed family members had not been commended to God. We left in a state of profound unease. Fortunately, the memorial service the next afternoon, which involved the whole church and the entire community, was much better planned and helped heal our distress, beginning to provide some of the closure so sorely lacking the day before.

Rituals can also fail because they gloss over the reality of a situation, perpetuating a fiction that all is well, when trouble lurks just beneath the surface. This failure happens when the parents of the bride and groom offer a public blessing at a wedding yet privately speak their regret about the union. It happens at funerals or memorial services when eulogies mask the truth about a person's life or about the family's relationship with the deceased. It happens when young people are pushed to receive baptism before they are mature enough to make authentic choices.

Rituals may even be destructive. Because the transforming potential of rituals is vast and may not always be directed toward the ends of God's gracious reign, rituals can unleash fearsome things. Gang initiation rites may transform young people into killers, as can the ceremonies of the American military. The uses of ritual in totalitarian governments give ample evidence that rituals hold the power to transform societies not into places of freedom but into engines of mass murder and even genocide. God's good purposes for the world can be thwarted by the misuse of rituals.

Ritual mapping guides for planning rituals

We can readily see that the three good gifts of ritual are closely related to the three essential movements or rhythms of worship described in chapter one. Rituals that create a sense of order and connect people with the holy are enhancing the first element of worship, *encounter with God*. Rituals that establish or support a sense of solidarity in the community, uniting people in a common purpose and place, are enhancing the second element, *engagement with self and community*. The third element of worship, *empowerment*, relates directly to the third gift of ritual, transformation. Thus the same understandings and practices that serve worship as a whole also serve the development of good rituals.

We can also readily see that the role leaders play in rituals is crucial for the truthfulness and effectiveness of these practices. When leaders inhabit the role of *shaman*, they are tending the community's encounter with God. When they inhabit the role of *host*, they are caring for the community's engagement with self and others. When they inhabit the role of *prophet*, they are functioning as seers who invite the community to envision a new, more just and peaceable future.

Each ritual makes particular demands on planners and leaders, with respect to actions, speech, music, preaching, and visual elements. These practical issues related to planning the most common rituals of the church (baptism, communion, weddings, funerals, and healing services) will now be considered, along with a series of suggested steps in the ritual planning process.

Determine the core ritual activity. A critical initial step in planning rituals is to determine the core activity of the ritual: What must happen—in terms of God's action and human response—for this ritual action to be accomplished? See the examples below.

Ritual	Core activity
Baptism	Sprinkling/pouring/immersing in water
	Using words, "I baptize you in the name of the Father, the Son, and the Holy Spirit . . ."
Communion	Prayer of thanksgiving Sharing of bread and cup
Wedding	Vows of the couple Pronouncement of "husband and wife"
Funeral	Eulogy, prayers Committal at graveside
Healing	Prayer of petition Anointing with oil or laying on of hands

Select the speech acts that are part of the ritual action. A speech act is one in which the speaking of the words accomplishes the action. Such words need to be spoken with conviction and grace: "I/we . . . praise, thank, remember, bless, declare, promise, pray, petition, intercede, invoke, baptize, pronounce, invite, offer . . ."

Find the mood, style, and tempo of music desired for each part of the service.

What moods, styles, textures, and tempos of music and text are appropriate at each stage of the ritual?

What specific musical settings are available? Do they fit the mood, style, and tempos for each stage of the ritual? How will they support movement or provide transitions?

Who will sing and/or play each of the selections (congregation, solo, ensemble)?

What kind of accompaniment is needed for each selection? What instruments are available? Can they be used unobtrusively?

How familiar are the selections to the average person likely to attend the service? What musical skills are required of the singers for each selection?

Choose the design and elements of the visual environment, including the sequence of movements.

Whom is the ritual for? Who is likely to be involved? How much space is needed for people to feel comfortable yet connected?

What visual design elements support the core action of the ritual?

What are the emotions, realities, and people who need to be considered—remembered, honored—in the space and performance of this ritual?

What are the biblical symbols and ritual requirements for this service?

What is God's action in this ritual? How will it be proclaimed or symbolized visually?

Be attentive to the rhythmic interplay of structure and anti-structure. *Structure* and *anti-structure* are concepts borrowed from anthropology to describe a continuum of ritual behaviors from the expected and predictable to the unplanned and unanticipated. Whenever humans gather in social situations, their actions and interactions are both planned and spontaneous. Effective rituals seek a pleasing, rhythmic, effective balance between these polarities. The following two columns summarize the essential characteristics of each pole. [10]

Structure	*Anti-structure*
What is secure	More elusive
Order	Mystery
Clear definition	Richness, depth of meaning
Thinking	Feeling
Word	Spirit
Certainty	Ambiguity
Sign	Symbol
Printed (church bulletin, PowerPoint, etc.)	Spontaneous
Doctrine	Story, narrative
Principle	Insight

A ritual that is too carefully scripted may seem cold and mechanical. On the other hand, a ritual that includes too many spontaneous elements may seem tentative and unfocused. The above listing offers a tool for recognizing and evaluating these elements. What can be far more challenging is experimenting with shifts of balance and finding the right rhythm for each ritual in its context.

Respect both tradition and innovation. We have noted that much of the value of rituals is their repetition. Because they connect with basic, universal human realities, they bear frequent repetition and continue to be meaningful. Nevertheless, a ritual that is repeated in *exactly* the same way quickly becomes a dead ritual.[11]

Just as structure and anti-structure create a dynamic rhythm in ordinary worship, so a rhythm of embracing what is old and what is new keeps rituals alive. Denominations have their minister's manuals or service books, guides that outline the essential elements of specific rituals. What makes a baptism valid is prescribed there; the rubrics for communion are stated; guidance is provided for weddings, funerals, and anointing services. These resources describe the basics, and anyone who plans and leads rituals within a specific religious tradition should study these guides carefully. What they don't do—and can't do—is show how to tailor a ritual for a specific occasion.

As noted earlier, the first step in planning any ritual is to discern what face of God is needed or desired on a particular occasion. As we listen to the needs of people and pay attention to what God wants to offer them, we engage in a creative process that directs us both to what is familiar and to what may be made-to-order just for this occasion. Frequently repeated rituals especially require such thoughtful attention if they are to remain fresh and meaningful.

If, in past eras, worship planners erred on the side of tradition and repetition, today's besetting sin is more likely to be thoughtless innovation and too little repetition. One way of maintaining a healthy balance is to regularly review the significant biblical themes related to each ritual. If, over time, a congregation is invited into an abundant array of these themes in connection with rituals, worshipers will be deeply rooted in images and insights the church has valued over the centuries. At the same time, a sense of freshness will pervade our rituals if leaders let the texts guide their choice of music, symbols, and ritual actions in response to specific contexts.

Explore a rich variety of biblical and theological themes. Two charts illustrate how significant biblical themes for the two most frequent rituals—baptism and communion—may suggest a variety of songs, symbols, and ritual actions, thus enriching the congregation's experience of God's presence and activity in the ritual.[12]

Major New Testament metaphors of initiation/baptism
Union with Jesus Christ in death and resurrection

Scriptures	Romans 6:3–6
	Colossians 2:12
Symbols	Baptism by immersion (descent into the water and ascent to new life)
	Baptismal fonts shaped like tombs
Hymns	O Jesus, I have promised (*HWB* 447)
	Who now would follow Christ (*HWB* 535)

Incorporation into the church, Christ's body

Scriptures	1 Corinthians 12:13
	Galatians 3:27–28
Symbols	Font at entrance of church
	Circle of blessing following baptism
Hymns	Will you let me be your servant (*HWB* 307)
	I bind my heart this tide (*HWB* 411)

New birth
Scriptures	John 3:5
	1 John 4:7–8
Symbols	Plunging paschal candle into water font (symbol of womb) at the Easter Vigil
	Posture of kneeling and being raised up
Hymns	New earth, heavens new (*HWB* 299)
	Mothering God, you gave me birth (*HWB* 482)

Cleansing/Forgiveness from sin
Scriptures	Acts 22:16
	1 Peter 3:21–22
	Hebrews 10:19–22
Symbols	Water
	New or white garment
Hymns	Amazing grace (*HWB* 143)
	There's a wideness in God's mercy (*HWB* 145)

Reception of Holy Spirit and empowerment for ministry
Scriptures	Matthew 3:16–17
	Acts 2:37–39
Symbols	Water poured out
	Anointing with oil
Hymns	Veni Sancte Spiritus (*HWB* 298)
	Here I am, Lord (*HWB* 395)

Major biblical eucharistic themes and images
Exodus from bondage in Egypt: justice for oppressed
Scriptures	Exodus 12–15
	John 1:29
	Romans 8:1–17
Symbols	Unleavened bread
	Pottery vessels
Hymns	I will sing the Lord's high triumph (*HWB* 261)
	Let the hungry come to me (*HWB* 464)

Jesus's suffering and death: memorial, thanksgiving, forgiveness of sin

Scriptures	Isaiah 53
	Passion narratives of Gospels
	John 6:47–51
	1 Corinthians 11:23–26
	Hebrews 10:19–23
Symbols	Hearty bread
	Earthenware vessels
	Communion served by "priest" figure
	Vertical emphasis—salvation is a gift
Hymns	My song is love unknown (*HWB* 235)
	When I survey the wondrous cross (*HWB* 259)

Risen Christ: Emmaus walk, living presence of Christ

Scriptures	Luke 24:13–35
	Romans 6:3–11
	2 Corinthians 5:16–21
	Galatians 2:19–20
	Ephesians 2:1–10
Symbols	Light, yeasty bread (pascha)
	Sparkling or homemade juice
	Festive table
	"Jesus" serves bread and cup
Hymns	Jesus, stand among us (*HWB* 25)
	Become to us the living bread (*HWB* 475)

Agape Feast: the church's meal, koinonia, unity of the body

Scriptures	Acts 2:46–47
	1 Corinthians 10:16–17; 12:12–13
	Ephesians 2:19–22
Symbols	Everyday table setting
	One loaf—hearty, home baked, or braided
	One cup
	People serve one another
	Horizontal emphasis
Hymns	Ubi caritas et amor (*HWB* 452)
	I come with joy to meet my Lord (*HWB* 459)

Messianic banquet: gathering at the Lamb's feast, eschatological hope, joy

Scriptures	Isaiah 25:6–10
	Luke 14:15–25; 22:14–16
	1 Corinthians 11:26
	Revelation 5:6–14; 19:1–10
Symbols	Elegant feast
	Bountiful table
	Fine bread, or the bread of many nations
	Gold, silver or crystal vessels
	Festive atmosphere
Hymns	At the Lamb's high feast (*HWB* 262)
	Now the silence (*HWB* 462)

As leaders make choices to emphasize one or another of these key biblical themes, they will also want to give thought to visual elements such as banners, sculpture, or other semi-permanent art in the sanctuary that evoke God's presence and illuminate the themes. As Nancy Chinn notes, "Art in ritual is not so much to make the Holy visible as it is to proclaim that the Holy is present."[13] If a congregation has people who are gifted in visual arts, and many do, these artists can be invited to create pieces that are regularly used in the congregation's rituals—a banner for baptism Sundays, sculpted earthenware for communion Sundays, or beautiful table coverings for weddings, or a funeral pall.

Related to biblical and theological themes is the role of the Christian year in rituals. For example, a communion service in late Advent or on Christmas becomes a festive experience if Christmas carols are sung while people come forward to receive communion. The joy of this ritual meal can barely be contained at such times. The justice-oriented texts of many Advent and Christmas songs also expand the meaning of the incarnation in surprising ways.

Be prepared to improvise on short notice. Recently when we discovered unexpectedly that we would have a guest for dinner and overnight, a five-minute phone call was the extent of time we had available for planning. We usually prepare in advance for such occasions, developing menus, going grocery shopping, and making sure we have items that guests will need, but this time we needed to improvise on short notice. We took stock of what we had on hand, figured out what could be purchased quickly on the way home from work, and made up the rest as we went along. A package of cheese-filled tortellini in the freezer would serve as the main course. A fresh loaf of Italian bread could be purchased quickly. When we got home, we stirred up an impromptu sauce for the pasta, assembled a simple green salad, and prepared a tray of fruit for dessert. A last-minute discovery was a stash of chocolate truffles tucked away in a cupboard, a gift from an earlier visitor. We served these with tea—and congratulated ourselves on providing a fine meal!

Because not every ritual can be planned in advance, leaders must be prepared to improvise on short notice. After consulting a minister's manual or service book, we draw on what is known and familiar: the Lord's Prayer or a favorite scripture passage or a simple kyrie that the congregation can sing from memory. We pay close attention to the features of the situation and in our prayers or brief homily make mention of what has brought about the ritual. Overall, such rituals are simpler than rituals planned well in advance; what they may lack in depth, they make up for in immediacy.

Evaluate the use of symbols and rituals. Although this chapter emphasizes the critical importance and fruitful potential of symbols and rituals, leaders must be judicious in their use of both. When those of us in ritual-and-symbol-deprived traditions first experience the power of rituals, we may be tempted to go overboard and make a ritual out of everything. Some rituals end up feeling as though they've been pasted onto a worship service just to make it more interesting or more exciting.

The following questions can help planners step back and evaluate whether the ritual or symbol is emerging naturally out of the intended focus of the service. The questions can be applied broadly—to individual symbolic elements such as banners, to a piece of sculpture, and also to an entire ritual action such as a baptismal rite.

With careful, thoughtful evaluation and a willingness to experiment and learn from failures and successes, our rituals can be improved. They can become privileged settings where people meet God, find themselves bound to others in ties of love, and are transformed to do the work of love in the world.

Questions for evaluating rituals or symbols
1. Is the ritual rooted in scripture?
2. Is the ritual rooted in Christian tradition?
3. Is the ritual consistent with our theology of the church?
4. Does the ritual witness to justice and compassion?
5. Is the ritual honest? Is it authentic?
6. Does it connect faithfully with the purpose of the worship service and flow from the chosen focus of the day? Does the ritual respond to the culture of the local community and its needs?
7. Is the ritual abundant and generous? Does it reflect God's gracious love?
8. Is the ritual transparent and multivalent? Does it have the capacity to point beyond itself to Christ?[14]

Ceremonies of love for the tongue-tied: Postmodernity and ritual

With all its potential for offering order, community, and transformation, ritual has many good gifts to enliven the worship of the church in any time and place. But if we consider the particular desires and characteristics of people in our postmodern society, we will find that ritual is especially needed today. A confession of many postmodern people is offered by Andre Dubus in *The Times Are Never So Bad*: "I cannot achieve contemplation, as some can; and so, having to face and forgive my own failures, I have learned from them both the necessity and wonder of ritual. For ritual allows those who cannot will themselves out of the secular to perform the spiritual, as dancing allows the tongue-tied a ceremony of love."[15]

The loss of the sacred in our highly secular world makes belief and commitment difficult. We long for robust faith, yet many of us have little capacity for sustained religious devotion. Cut loose from traditional moorings, we need more than words and concepts to experience and express our faith. If we are to meet God, our hearts must be touched, our imaginations grasped, and our bodies engaged. In such a situation, Dubus reminds us that ritual can be a path to genuine faith. Although personal prayer and other spiritual practices may seem futile, when we gather with the faith community and engage in the actions of ritual, we find ourselves reconnected with God and able to trust—even if only momentarily.

In a similar vein, Sam Keen writes about the remarkable power of the church's music to rekindle faith.

> I can't go back to traditional religion. Neither can I live within the smog-bound horizon of the secular-progressive faith. So I search for a way to unite the demands of the head and heart. Without falling into mindless faith or surrendering to authority, I want to find a way to lean on the everlasting arms. . . .
>
> The truth of the spirit, as I know it, is better conveyed in song and poetry than by propositions. The best of the Christian tradition, which continues to nourish me, is expressed in the music it inspired. Often, my mind is uncomforted by any set of beliefs that can stand the test of doubt, but when I listen to Bach's "Sheep May Safely Graze," my soul lies down beside still waters and a mysterious Lord is still my shepherd.[16]

The loss of a lively sense of community in the postmodern world is another reason people today are drawn to ritual. A community aids self-definition: we cannot understand ourselves without connecting deeply with others. And although we can be entertained alone, we cannot celebrate alone. We need others with whom to share our joys and sorrows, others with whom to sing and dance.

In his perceptive book, *Ritual: Power, Healing and Community*, the West African writer Malidoma Patrice Somé observes that the illnesses of American culture arise from our inattention to ritual and the absence of genuine community. Although we may depend on them, drugs and alcohol and shopping at the mall and being absorbed in television do not cure our alienation from one another. He goes on to explain, "Visible wrongs have their roots in the world of the spirit. To deal only with their visibility is like trimming the leaves of a weed when you mean to uproot it. Ritual is the mechanism that uproots these dysfunctions. It offers a realm in which the unseen part of the dysfunction is worked on in ways that affect the seen."[17] When postmodern people faithfully nourish their souls and tend the healing of their illnesses in ritual, they will not only find new life and meaning for themselves, they will be able to offer the gift of life to others.

Special occasions and the Christian year

> You gotta know what day it is.
> If you don't know what day it is,
>   the days just go right by and you lose them.[18] (Herb Gardner)

Just as specific rituals such as baptism and communion provide an external set of structures and expectations that need to be cared for in a worship service, so the Christian year also makes special demands on worship planners and leaders.

The Christian year is shaped by the story of Jesus—his incarnation, ministry, teaching, suffering, death, resurrection, and ascension. It includes the coming of the Holy Spirit at Pentecost and the birth and development of the Christian church. Like a well-chosen picture frame, the Christian year creates a structure that helps us see the story of Jesus more clearly. For many years, the Elkhart River has flowed through Elkhart between weedy, overgrown, trash-covered banks. Because of the unsightly setting, local citizens paid little attention to this natural feature of our environment. In recent years, a river walk has been constructed. With bricks, stones, and new landscaping now gracing its banks, the river itself has become the center of attention. In the same way, the Christian story stands out vividly within the framework of the Christian year.

In this central story of our faith, a fundamental rhythm of fasting and feasting flows through the year. Without the ebb and flow of the seasons, the Christian calendar makes little sense. And this reality provides the first challenge for worship leaders. In North American culture, where feasting (or at least overeating) is an everyday event, the rhythm of the Christian year can be difficult to achieve in a satisfying way. If every day is a feast, then no day is a feast.

Consider the task of menu planning for a weekend conference. Some retreat centers have a predictable yet pleasing progression for weekend menus. The Friday evening meal is soup and salad—light but satisfying. Saturday breakfast is sausage and scrambled eggs—a hearty beginning to a big day. Saturday lunch is a variety of breads and salads—nutritious and not too heavy. Saturday supper is pizza—spicy and simple, it leaves room for a late night snack. Sunday morning is bagels and cream cheese with fresh fruit—healthy but not too filling. And Sunday noon is a feast—roast turkey, mashed potatoes and gravy, green beans with bacon, a salad bar, dinner rolls, and several varieties of homemade pie. A whole weekend of heavy meals would leave retreat participants feeling sluggish and lethargic. Instead the cooks have learned to vary the amount and type of food in a satisfying rhythm. The result is enjoyable and healthy eating.

Worship planners need to give careful attention to the overall focus of each season—whether reflective, penitential, instructive, or celebrative—and plan accordingly. But they also need to be aware of the internal ebb and flow of each season. If leaders treat Lent as one long penitential season, they will have missed much of the drama. Lent will sound like a one-note dirge instead of a musical masterpiece of rich and complex harmonies.

What creates the ebb and flow of the Christian year is the scripture choices found in the lectionary. Although churches can observe the Christian year without using the lectionary, most congregations make some use of the lectionary if they follow the Christian year. When we understand the purpose and flow of the lectionary, we are well on the way toward planning appropriate and satisfying worship for the Christian seasons.[19]

What is the lectionary?

An ordered system of selected Bible readings, the lectionary provides four texts for every Sunday over a three-year period. The four readings are drawn respectively from the Old Testament and the Psalms, the Epistles (and Revelation), and the Gospels. The purpose of the readings is to provide a witness to the unity of the Old and New Testaments and to proclaim the whole story of salvation. God's plan for redemption is announced and initiated in the Old Testament and reaches its fulfillment in the death and resurrection of Jesus Christ. Through the witness of the church, the gospel is proclaimed to all generations.[20]

Because the lectionary and Christian year are organized around the story of Jesus, those who preach often focus on the Gospel story as central. While Christian worship always proclaims the good news of Jesus Christ, it is also important to preach from the entire Bible. Included within the lectionary structure are extended seasons of texts from the Pentateuch, Davidic narratives, Wisdom literature, the Prophets, Acts, the Epistles, and Revelation. Thus it is possible, even desirable, for preachers and planners to select other parts of the biblical story as an appropriate focus for Sunday worship.

What is the Christian year?

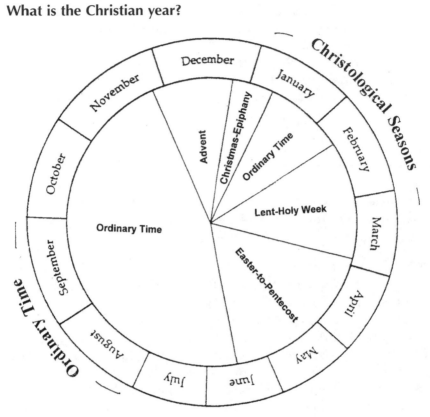

The Christian year begins with Advent, a four-week season of prayerful preparation for Christmas, a celebration of the incarnation of Jesus Christ. Although our culture hastens to the feast, the church pauses to reflect on the mystery of three Advents: the coming of Christ in glory at the end of time, the birth of Jesus as a babe in Bethlehem, and the birth of Christ in our own hearts and lives today. The purpose of the season is clarified by Meister Eckhart's question, "What good is it to us if Christ was born at Bethlehem on Christmas morning if Christ is not born in us today?"

The emotional-dramatic structure of the Advent season is reflected in the tradition of using three purple candles and one rose candle in the Advent wreath. When we light the rose candle on the third

Sunday of Advent, the color signals a shift in the mood of the texts. After the insistent call to repentance of the first two weeks, each text now foreshadows the joy of Christ's coming in the use of some form of the word *rejoice*. Mary's ecstatic song (Luke 1:46–55) foretells the upside-down kingdom Jesus will announce, in which the powerful are brought down from their thrones and the lowly are lifted up.

The Advent colors of rose and purple or blue give way to the whites and golds of Christmas, along with festive evergreens and brilliant poinsettias, as the twelve-day feast of Christmas begins, commencing with Christmas Eve and culminating in the feast of Epiphany. Observing Advent well leads to a glorious celebration on Christmas as the mystery of God's loving purpose is revealed in the coming of a savior for the entire world. Although January 6 doesn't often fall on a Sunday, many churches celebrate Epiphany on the Sunday closest to that day. Theologically, the feast of Christmas is incomplete without the feast of Epiphany, for it is on that day that the scripture texts clearly invite us to see God's ultimate purpose in sending Jesus, the salvation of the whole world. Without Epiphany, the church might settle into a cocoon of self-satisfaction, reveling in salvation for ourselves and neglecting to share the good news with neighbors near and far.

The following chart interprets the rhythmic flow and dramatic-emotional structure of the Advent-Christmas season, based on the lectionary scripture cycle. Notice how the season begins at a fairly low ebb, drops lower with John the Baptist's call to repentance, and then ascends to the fulfillment of the incarnation.

Advent-Christmas-Epiphany: Dramatic-emotional sequence

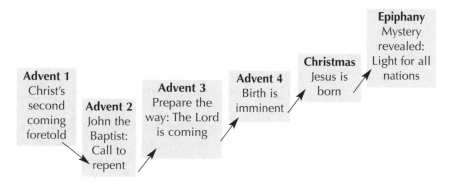

Epiphany
Mystery revealed:
Light for all nations

Christmas
Jesus is born

Advent 4
Birth is imminent

Advent 1
Christ's second coming foretold

Advent 2
John the Baptist: Call to repent

Advent 3
Prepare the way: The Lord is coming

A brief span of ordinary time occurs between the feast of Epiphany and Lent. During these weeks, the church encounters the story of Jesus's baptism, the call of the first disciples, and Jesus's early teaching and healing ministries. As Lent arrives, the stories of Jesus's life and ministry take on a more insistent quality as they become a personal invitation to renewal. Throughout the purple-hued weeks of Lent, Christians join Jesus in the journey toward the cross, fasting from distractions and counting the cost of faithfulness.

Of particular interest in the Lenten cycle is the specific focus of the call to renewal each year. Year A is the brightest year of the three-year cycle. The Gospel texts tell stories of people who meet Jesus for the first time and are transformed in that encounter—Nicodemus, the Samaritan woman, the man born blind. Lazarus is raised from the dead in a dramatic prefiguring of Jesus's own resurrection. Worship in Year A calls people to follow Jesus for the first time or to renew the excitement and vigor of their commitment.

Year B is more reflective. Salvation history is retold, beginning with Noah's obedience and continuing with Abraham's call, the wanderings of the children of Israel in the desert, and the giving of the law. The focus is the faithful—those who participate in the church regularly and who need to be reminded of their commitments and called to deeper fidelity and joy. A new heart is promised. God will revive our souls.

Year C is filled with passion as those who have wandered away are called to return to Christ and the church. Central to the season is the story of the prodigal father and son on Lent 4, in which we see the inspiring picture of God's outstretched arms and joyful reception of sinners. The other Sundays emphasize Jesus's teachings about the cost of discipleship.

As seen in the chart on page 331, the dramatic-emotional sequence of each year's texts is similar. Lent begins at a very low point with receiving the mark of ashes on Ash Wednesday and then moves into the desert with the story of Jesus's temptations in the wilderness. We are stripped of what is familiar and secure and are invited to begin a journey. As the season progresses, we enter more and more deeply into the mystery of God's love. As in a suspenseful drama, the fifth Sunday foreshadows the resurrection with a story of death and new life. When Palm Sunday arrives with its songs and jubilation, we may think we have arrived at the climax of the story. But we are wrong.

Holy Week plunges us into the depths of evil and despair. The one whom God sent to bring new life is sentenced to die. From the cross, Jesus cries out, "My God, my God, why have you forsaken me?" The earth trembles: "Creation shivers at the shock, the temple rends its veil. A pallid stillness stifles time and nature's motions fail."[21] Like the disciples, we face the bleak despair of what life would be like without Jesus and without hope. We drape our crosses in black. The emotional-dramatic structure of the season descends to its lowest point, the lowest point of the entire Christian year.

Lent season–Holy Week (Year A): Dramatic-emotional sequence

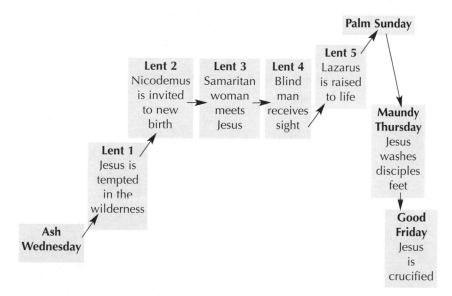

Although the illustration above notes the progression through Lent and Holy Week using the Year A texts, the emotional-dramatic trajectory is similar in Year B and Year C.

Before dawn on the third day, God's power breaks into our world. Death is vanquished; life bursts forth from the tomb. Because our Easter joy cannot be contained in one day, we celebrate for a week of weeks. Easter Sunday begins the "Alleluia season," a time for unbounded praise and setting aside our weekly confession of sin. Instead we confess or affirm our faith, expressing in all the ways we can find—sung, spoken, enacted—our trust in God's victory of life over death. After Easter Sunday, we revisit the stories of Jesus's post-resurrection appearances. On the second Sunday of Easter, we are comforted by the story of Thomas, who doubts Jesus's resurrection, and we know we are not alone in our struggles to believe. The third Sunday is always a meal story, and we find ourselves drawn into the circle of table fellowship where Jesus breaks bread in Emmaus or grills fish over a charcoal fire. The fourth Sunday of Easter season, a favorite of many, is Good Shepherd Sunday, in which we give thanks for the "good shepherd who gives his life for the sheep." Then begin three weeks of Jesus's teachings from the Gospel of John, during which Ascension Day occurs, and the disciples retire to wait for the coming of the blessed Holy Spirit. And finally, the day of Pentecost arrives. Easter white gives way to the blazing red of Pentecost as the church celebrates the gift of the Spirit's presence and power.

Easter-to-Pentecost season: Dramatic/emotional sequence

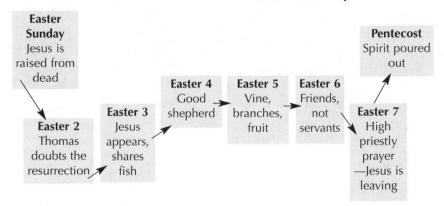

The day of Pentecost brings us back to ordinary time, and we settle in for a long stretch of Sundays in which the worshipping assembly rejoins Jesus in his journey of teaching, healing, and mentoring the disciples. The church is called to be the body of Christ and to do the works of Jesus in the world through the intimate companionship and strength of the Holy Spirit. As we come near the end of the year, we celebrate the communion of saints and look forward to the fulfillment of all things at the end of time. And then, just when we become weary in well doing, we return again to Advent and begin the renewing cycle again.

Special challenges of planning for the Christian year

The cycles of the Christian year provide a reliable structure and sequence for worship planning. Just as we know in advance that we will need to plan a menu for Thanksgiving or Christmas dinner, we know that Advent or Lent will arrive on schedule. Over time, a congregation accumulates customs and traditions for the seasons—the hanging of the greens for Christmas, a water blessing ritual on the Sunday commemorating Jesus's baptism, or a candle-lighting ritual of remembrance on All Saints' Day. Certain music may become closely connected with the seasons—"O holy night" on Christmas Eve or "Lift your glad voices" on Easter Sunday. Because we know when the seasons will come, we can even commission composers to write music for the congregation in advance of the season. Drawing on these well-established traditions creates anticipation and nourishes the congregation's faith.

Because of the familiarity and predictability of the seasons, however, worship leaders also need to be especially attentive to the particular needs and desires of the congregation as each season returns. Being thoroughly acquainted with the lectionary cycle sets planners free, for example, to listen for the ways this year's Lenten texts intersect with the congregation's experience. Although the Lent A readings are the brightest of the three-year cycle (telling stories of people who meet Jesus for the first time and are transformed), and the Year B readings, by contrast, are more sedate (reminding the faithful of their covenant with God), and the Year C readings are more poignant (calling all of us to see how we wander away from God and to return in repentance), these moods or emphases may not fit what the congregation is needing in a particular season. If, when Year C comes around, the congregation is rejoicing because of the vital growth in faith among their young people, worship planners will need to find ways to connect Year C texts with that exuberant experience—and not wait for Year A to roll around!

Advent, Christmas, and Epiphany present special pastoral challenges for two reasons: the church's calendar is out of sync with the shopping calendar (Christmas arrives in shopping malls long before Advent begins), and family gatherings often wreak havoc with worship attendance. Because many people are traveling and do not worship in their own congregations on Christmas, worship leaders may find it more helpful to focus on the feast of Epiphany as the climax of the season. By the time January 6 comes, most families have returned home and will be found in their regular places of worship.

What the Christian year does is tutor us in the image of Christ. Birth, growth, temptation, struggle, relating, failing, dying, rising—every human experience is recapitulated in the story of Jesus. Our lives are shaped and reshaped as we identify with God's purposes in the humanity of Jesus. Our lives become cruciform, and we rise daily to new life.

When we add life-giving rituals to this life-giving story, we experience a vital, potent combination that cannot be surpassed. Christian worship becomes the most powerful experience people ever encounter. In worship, we meet the God of life, our communities are shaped by a wondrous story, and we are set free in the power of the Spirit to love and liberate God's world.

Special occasions also call for particular attention to the role of preaching. Because of its interpretive function, preaching always helps the congregation make connections between God's story and our story. In the midst of a season of the Christian year or in worship services where a ritual is central, that interpretive function shifts slightly. During a season such as Advent or Lent, preaching needs to serve the overall theme or focus, guiding the congregation to the fulfillment of the season. On baptism or communion Sundays, preaching needs to serve the ritual action, illuminating its meaning and inviting our participation. In a different way in ordinary time, the sermon itself often becomes the center of worship. Even though all preaching is a proclamation of the Word and fulfills a needed function in worship, its role shifts on special occasions to serve the larger purpose of worship. Thus the need to collaborate becomes even stronger at these times. If preaching is to offer its unique gift in the midst of worship, worship leaders, musicians, and preachers must all understand the role of the sermon on special occasions.

Conclusion

Whatever special services are being planned—rituals, seasons of the Christian year, or marker events in the life cycle of the congregation, worship planners have amazing and abundant resources to guide them.[22] These occasions need never be humdrum or monotonous. Well-planned worship services on special occasions can truly become momentous experiences of God's love; they can unite the community, strengthening the bonds of trust and hope among the body; and they can open the way to a transformed future, a future in which God's will is done more fully on earth as it is in heaven. Like the special meals that friends and families enjoy, they will linger in the congregation's memory, providing illumination and grace for many years to come.

A final word to leaders: Rituals and special occasions require more than the usual wisdom, insight, and creativity of leaders. Because they play such pivotal roles in the ongoing formation and pastoral care of the congregation, they demand the very best planning and leadership. One seminary professor regularly tells students who are entering pastoral ministry for the first time, "Do the rituals well, and the congregation will forgive you for many other things." In other words, on these occasions when people's expectations are high and they are often needy or full of desire for a visitation from God, they need the richest possible experiences in worship. If we do our part faithfully—inhabiting the roles of shaman, host, and prophet with integrity and skill—we will have prepared a space where the Holy Spirit can move mightily, and the congregation will be blessed and transformed.

12

EXTENDING THE TABLE

"Go therefore into the main streets, and invite everyone you find to the wedding banquet." (Matt 22:9)

In my family, the familiar refrain "There's always room for one more" meant we expected to make our resources—whether beds, chairs, or food at the dinner table—generously available to guests. When all the extra boards were added to our dining room table, we could seat twelve people comfortably. On the occasions when we needed to stretch to accommodate a bigger crowd, we set up card tables at each end. My mother insisted that the card tables also be covered with fine tablecloths and small bouquets of flowers. In no way were the extra guests to be made to feel second-class.

While Christian worship is a gift for each faith community, nourishing its life together and its life with God, it is also meant to invite believers into an even larger, more compelling, more comprehensive worldview than can be contained in one place or time. As a universal reality, the body of Christ is a sign and foretaste of God's desires and dreams for the whole world and for all time. Thus when the body of Christ meets for worship, we participate not only at the table around which we gather today, but we join a much larger table, an extended table, at which all God's people gather, both now and in the world to come.

The prophet Isaiah glimpsed a vision of God's wider purposes when he noted that God's creative, redeeming work among the children of Israel was intended for more than their own benefit.

"It is too light a thing that you should be my servant
to raise up the tribes of Jacob
and to restore the survivors of Israel;
I will give you as a light to the nations,
that my salvation may reach to the end of the earth." (Isa 49:6)

A similarly expansive vision is found in Jesus's banquet parables, when he describes a dinner host who welcomes not just his friends but those who are poor, crippled, blind, and lame to a bountiful feast (Luke 15:16–24).

One way of conceiving this larger frame of reference with respect to worship is to imagine God's vision as a broad, beckoning horizon. While our eyes will always see what is close at hand most easily and clearly, they are also drawn to what is beyond. A distant mountain range or a river disappearing around a bend invites our gaze and attention. We wonder what more awaits our contemplation.

When we sing or pray in worship, it is altogether fitting that we should draw on the songs or prayers or images that are close at hand—what is familiar and what has been passed on to us. Our native vocabulary and customary practices create a comfortable, secure space in which to meet God. Teachers and parents are gratified when children learn treasured hymns and memorize well-loved scriptures, because the community is enriched by each one who receives and embodies the tradition.

But just as God entered into a covenant relationship with Israel for more than their own transformation, God intends for worship to meet more than our own needs. Our encounter with God is meant to create a larger space in the world for God to move and act. It is meant to transform our vision, so we begin to see the world as God sees it. In other words, through worship we begin to glimpse the wider horizon of God's purposes.

How can worship partake of such a vision? How can our Sunday morning gathering respect what is local and well known, and also be liberated from too-narrow, too-local, or too-traditional perspectives? How can the church discern an appropriate interrelationship of the near and far? How can Christians gather at a satisfying meal and also extend the table in worship, so God's vision can be known and shared with all who hunger for God's presence? In this chapter, the image of extending the table is offered as a way of understanding how worship can begin to participate in the expansive vision of God's realm.

How can Sunday morning worship extend the Lord's table?

Two Mennonite cookbooks, *More-with-Less Cookbook* and *Extending the Table*, have inspired several generations of cooks to expand their culinary horizons.[1] Traditional meat-and-potatoes dinners have given way to experiments with injera bread from Ethiopia, Vietnamese chicken soup, cucumber yogurt salad from India, baked plantains in orange sauce from Guatemala, and many other delights. Although the tastes and flavors of favorite foods remain appealing, a new territory of textures and spices beckons adventurous eaters.

It may be easier to expand menus at our dining room tables, however, than to extend the table of worship. To plan worship that includes people of all ages, differing cultural and economic groups, and varying theological perspectives can be a challenge for leaders. Yet the mission of the church—to be a sign of God's reign and to actively join God's creative, liberating work in the world—requires a hospitable community and hospitable leaders.[2]

Extending the table of worship by reaching across boundaries and traditions to welcome whomever God may call stimulates some practical questions about the day-to-day relationship between the congregation's worship life and its life of mission. How, for example, do worship and evangelism connect with each other? Is Sunday morning an appropriate time for evangelistic services, a time to invite people to commit their lives to Christ? And if hospitality is such an important part of the church's engagement in mission, how are the actions of worship affected? If people who come to worship are not familiar with scripture and do not know the songs of the church, how can we express hospitality toward them? And how does preaching participate in extending the table?

Some people argue that the answers to these questions focus mainly on style. They suggest that a certain style of worship is more oriented to mission than others, and the church's task is to discover that style and emulate it. Although churches should always be interested in strengthening and enlivening their worship, the question is more complex than style. Research shows that our experience of God in worship is the critical issue, not a particular style of worship.[3] Further, our hospitality and our life of faith are what attract seekers to the community. So how do we find our way to a set of questions deeper than style questions? What are the fundamental convictions that will guide us as we seek to extend the table of worship?

In *Inside Out: Worship in an Age of Mission*, Thomas Schattauer suggests that our fundamental vision of worship shapes our answer to questions about the relationship of worship and mission. He pre-

sents three possible views of worship as a way of exploring these differences. In an "inside-and-out" view of worship, worship is practiced primarily for the benefit of believers. As Christians worship
together, they are nurtured and energized for their lives in the world.
Worship indirectly serves the purpose of mission by empowering
believers to engage in mission in their daily lives. From time to time,
seekers may become part of the congregation and make a commitment to Christ and the community of faith—and then the cycle is
renewed as worship becomes, for them, a time for renewal and
empowerment.

A second approach, "outside in," envisions worship as a primary
setting for mission. Sermons become evangelistic as preachers proclaim the good news and invite people to follow Christ; or sermons
become a call to social justice, a proclamation of God's alternative
reign of peace and justice, and people are called to help save the
world. The music, prayers, scripture readings, and offering are all
selected with a focus on the particular group being evangelized or the
social commitments of the congregation.

In a third approach, which Schattauer calls "inside out," the worshipping community of faith is already located centrally within the
arena of God's mission. Thus there is no separation between liturgy
and mission, because the two arenas of action function simultaneously. "The seemingly most internal of activities, the church's worship, is ultimately directed outward to the world. The judgment and
mercy of God enacted within the liturgical assembly signify God's
ultimate judgment and mercy for the world. . . . This approach is both
thoroughly contemporary and radically traditional, and it moves us
beyond the conventionally traditional inside-and-out as well as the
radically contemporary outside-in approaches."[4]

What Schattauer is suggesting is that worship is the church's first
form of mission. It is a public ritual in which Christians participate
for the sake of the world and through which the Christian community is being formed into Christ's image. When our songs and prayers
and sermons glorify the God of shalom, and when our worship takes
place with a keen awareness of and in response to the world in need
of God's shalom, then the worshipping community of faith becomes
a visible locus of God's redeeming action in the world. And the community already begins to participate—first by worshipping together—

in that redemption. Worship is thus both the source of mission and active participation in mission.

If we examine our worship practices with this paradox in view, we will discover much useful direction for our planning. Each element of worship has the potential either to become an act of hospitality, or to create barriers; each has the capacity either to create a vision of God's feast and to extend the table, or to make the feast inaccessible. In this chapter, we will explore how the inside-out view of worship helps us discern appropriate and hospitable choices, so our worship is both faithful and welcoming as it extends God's table of justice and peace.

Inside-out worship: Choosing language to extend the table

When guests who speak an unfamiliar language come to dinner, we try to invite someone who knows their language to join our company. Furthermore a gracious host will make an effort to learn at least a few words of the guests' language. We are well aware that understanding one another enhances the joy of eating together.

In the same way, when the table of worship is extended to all whom Christ calls to the table, those who lead worship will pay attention to the language used in worship. The concept of a trilingual worship leader can be useful in making these choices. To extend the table of worship, many worship leaders and preachers will need to be conversant with at least three languages: the language of scripture and Christian tradition, the language of the local congregation (including all ages and social groups), and the language of the surrounding geographic community. Sometimes these three languages will be similar to one another; at other times they will be so distinct as to create significant communication challenges. At all times, worship leaders will need to discern which languages must be included so people can encounter the living God, experience the dynamic reality of the Christian community, and be empowered by the Spirit for faithful living.

The language of scripture and Christian tradition. Our first language in church, the language of scripture and Christian tradition, is the inheritance of all Christians. Around the world, Christians pray the Psalms and the Lord's Prayer; they tell the stories of David and Goliath and Mary and Martha; they recite 1 Corinthians 11:23–26 when they gather at the Lord's Table; they repeat the Apostles' Creed; they sing early Christian hymns such as the vesper hymn "O gladsome light" (*Phos Hilaron*). Although translated into local languages, these texts emerge from a common source. Uniting the Christian church throughout history, such texts sustain the original vision of the followers of Jesus, nourish faith for daily life, and will continue to shape the body of Christ until the end of time. It would be inhospitable as well as unfaithful to deprive worshipers of resources that have so powerfully kept faith alive through the generations.

On any given Sunday, a trilingual worship leader will draw from the abundant treasury of Christian resources to enrich worship. In some cases, the ancient texts will be used simply—for example, when a Gospel story is read or the creed is recited. At other times, for the sake of creating a fresh context for what is already familiar, worship leaders will adapt or augment traditional texts. For example, some congregations have added movements to the Lord's Prayer. When the congregation stands to pray, they join hands and raise them as a way of proclaiming and affirming their desire for Christ's everlasting reign, as they speak the closing acclamation, "For thine is the kingdom and the power and the glory, forever. Amen."

Worship leaders and preachers also have access to a variety of scripture translations—from committee efforts such as the Revised Standard Version or the New International Version, to individual translations or paraphrases such as Eugene Peterson's *The Message* or Nan Merrill's *The Psalms for Praying*. For obvious reasons, it is important for congregations to use a common translation for most public reading, teaching, and preaching; other choices can also be appropriate for the sake of making ancient texts more accessible or to enhance a particular theme or focus in worship. For example, we can use a variety of versions of the Psalms: we may read them from a common translation, we may sing them set to Scottish Psalter tunes or contemporary melodies, or we may borrow a fresh translation for the sake of more inclusive language or a different language style. Psalm 140, as translated and paraphrased on page 343, offers three different voices and emphases, which allow planners to use the psalm for a variety of prayerful purposes in worship. The New Revised Standard Version offers just that—a clear, reputable, standard version. Eugene Peterson's paraphrase is realistic, hard-edged, and even humorous, while Nan Merrill uses more inward, more intimate language. A few verses illustrate the differences.

Psalm 140:1–4, 6, 8

New Revised Standard Version
Deliver me, O LORD, from evildoers;
protect me from those who are violent,
who plan evil things in their minds
and stir up wars continually.
They make their tongue sharp as a snake's,
and under their lips is the venom of vipers.

Guard me, O LORD, from the hands of the wicked;
protect me from the violent
who have planned my downfall.
I say to the LORD, "You are my God;
give ear, O LORD, to the voice of my supplications.
Do not grant, O LORD, the desires of the wicked;
do not further their evil plot.

Eugene H. Peterson, *The Message*[5]
God, get me out of here, away from this evil;
protect me from these vicious people.
All they do is think up new ways to be bad;
they spend their days plotting war games.
They practice the sharp rhetoric of hate and hurt,
speak venomous words that maim and kill.
I prayed, "God, you're my God!
Listen, God! Mercy!
God, my Lord, Strong Savior,
protect me when the fighting breaks out!
Don't let the wicked have their way, God,
don't give them an inch!"

Nan C. Merrill, *Psalms for Praying: An Invitation to Wholeness*[6]
Deliver me, O Giver of Breath and Life,
from the fears that beset me;
help me confront the inner shadows
that hold me in bondage,
like a prisoner who knows not freedom.
They distract me from all that I yearn to be,
and hinder the awakening of hidden gifts
that I long to share with others.

For I desire to be a channel of peace,
to reflect the beauty of your creation!
O, that I might manifest your love
to all whom I meet,
and mirror your mercy and justice!
Guide me, O Beloved, that I may become spiritually mature;
Love me into new life!

The language of the local congregation. Each local congregation speaks its own language. Even though English or Spanish or some other language appears to be the common language, the language spoken in worship is shaped by a variety of local factors. What varies from one congregation to another are such features as regional idioms, the level of formality or informality, theological flavor, patterns of prayer, and even specific vocabulary. Hospitable worship leaders will evaluate language choices for their appropriateness and accessibility, and for what they may open up for the congregation.

Worship language changes over time. When hymnal project personnel charged with developing *Hymnal: A Worship Book* gathered and evaluated worship resources for this 1992 hymnal, they discovered that Mennonite church language had become far more informal in the years since 1969, when the last denominational hymnal had been published. Owing no doubt to the influences of mass media, as well as other cultural shifts, speakers were using shorter sentences, simpler vocabulary, and a more direct approach. A warmer, less sober mien often characterized public speech. In addition, words that had once been spoken mainly by ordained leaders were now being spoken by the entire congregation. Thus a worship resource that had seemed fresh, appropriate, and useable in 1969 needed revision in the 1990s if it was to continue to be fitting.

Two examples illustrate this shift. When newborn infants or children are blessed in Mennonite congregations, the congregation makes a promise to join the parents in nurturing the child's faith. The differences between the 1969 and 1992 versions of the promises are minimal, with changes mainly having to do with creating a more readable page format.

Blessing of children

[1969]	You have offered your child to the strong and tender providence of God, and to the nurture of the church. We accept with humility of spirit and seriousness of purpose our responsibility for the spiritual well-being of this child. By example and our words, we will support your parental role, in disposing this child to respond to the fullness that is in Christ. We earnestly pray that the life and witness of each of us will make your task both joyful and fruitful.

[1992]
You have offered your child
to the strong and tender providence of God.
We rejoice with you and give thanks
for the gift of your child.
We promise, with humility and seriousness,
to share in your child's nurture and well-being.
We will support, by our example and words,
your efforts to provide a loving and caring home,
where trust in God grows and Christ's way is chosen.
Our prayers will be with you and for you.
May our shared life and witness
help make your task both joyful and fruitful.

When people are received as new members of a Mennonite congregation, the congregation welcomes them into the community of faith and promises to support and uphold them. The example below shows the extensive cuts and revision of the 1969 statement: the sentences were shortened and the language was made simpler, creating a friendlier response.

Receiving new members

[1969]

Minister
These persons now presented to you, have witnessed to their faith in Jesus Christ, and offer themselves as companions in our obedience to Christ. It is our privilege and joy to welcome them into our family of faith.

Congregation
Your expressed faith and Christian intention compels us to renew our own covenant with Christ. In your coming to us, we are newly summoned to become a community in which the wholeness of Christ is realized.

We freely receive you, even as Christ has received us. We open ourselves to fellowship with you in worship, study, service, and discipline. We commit ourselves to watch over you and one another with a heart of concern and caring. We pledge our willingness to offer and to receive forgiveness in the redeemed community. We joyfully accept you as partners, both in the care of our spiritual family, and in our mission to the world.

[1992]

Leader	These persons now presented to you have witnessed to their faith in Jesus Christ and offer themselves as companions in our obedience to Christ. It is our privilege and joy to welcome them into our family of faith.
People	We freely receive you, even as Christ has received us. We open ourselves to fellowship with you in worship, study, service, and discipline. We pledge our willingness to give and receive counsel, to offer and accept forgiveness in the redeemed community. We joyfully accept you as partners, both in the care of our spiritual family, and in our mission to the world.

Although the 1992 versions use simpler language and sentence structures than the 1969 versions, they have not lost their theological focus. They still communicate a dignity worthy of the occasions. In fact, the level of language remains fairly formal. In some informal worship styles, these resources might feel too formal. In those situations, worship leaders need to consider how to communicate the same ideas in even simpler ways, probably in an oral format. In receiving new members, a minister might speak extemporaneously on behalf of the congregation or might ask the congregation to repeat several affirmations, such as these:

> We receive you as Christ receives us.
> We want to worship and fellowship with you.
> We promise to care for you and to give and receive counsel.
> We welcome you as partners in our mission in the world.

As worship leaders, we need to have a good ear for the natural register of language spoken in worship. Especially when the congregation is asked to speak words together, the language should feel clear, comfortable, and inviting. At the same time, we should not dumb down the language we use. Nor should we avoid the richness of traditional language or the vivid images and satisfying rhythms of poetic language.[7] More art than science, the choice of appropriate language for worship is part of the call of the church to incarnate the gospel.

What follows are several key principles for selecting and adapting language for worship.

Principles for selecting language for worship

1. Keep it oral, not written.
   Test everything in advance by reading the material aloud.
   Ask someone else to read it aloud.
2. Keep it short and simple.
   Avoid lengthy sentences and unfamiliar vocabulary.
   Make page arrangement clear and easy on the eyes.
3. Keep it biblical.
   Make allusions or references to biblical stories.
   Use biblical images and phrases.
4. Keep it concrete.
   Choose vivid, earthy language rather than abstract or ethereal language.
   Avoid clichés.
5. Keep it poetic, rhythmic.
   Choose interesting images; don't mix metaphors.
   Pay attention to the flow of language; include parallel expressions.
6. Keep it inclusive
   Make it corporate, yet personal.
   Consider whether the language is appropriate for women and men, old and young, rich and poor, people with disabilities, married and single, a variety or racial-ethnic groups.

Following these principles will mean making different choices in different times and places. In ordinary Sunday worship, people rightly expect a certain amount of familiarity; although they are open to being stretched and challenged, they are also looking for stability. In some other settings, such as a weekend retreat or conference, more permission to experiment is usually the norm. On such occasions, a worship leader may take more risks. Recently I used the poem-prayers of Hafiz, a fifteenth-century Sufi poet,[8] as part of worship at an annual weekend worship conference. Because this conference is a setting where many risks have been taken over the years, I felt reasonably sure that the poem-prayers, although not explicitly Christian, would be appreciated by worshipers and would open up pathways into God's presence. One woman came to me after a service and said, "I've loved these poems for years and have wanted to use them in worship but have hesitated for fear of offending someone." Acknowledging the risks involved, I encouraged her to discern whether these poem-prayers would be appropriate in her context. It is not an act of compassion or faithful leadership to create unnecessary barriers for worshipers; neither, however, is it an act of compassion or faithful leadership to resist taking risks when the Spirit nudges us to do so.

How can worship leaders keep language fresh? How can we continue to make effective, satisfying choices? Perhaps the best resource is the Psalms. If those of us who lead worship steep ourselves in biblical poetry and narratives, making use of many translations, we will absorb the best possible models for language in worship. Reading and listening to good poetry, fiction, and nonfiction can inspire a wider array of colorful language choices. In addition, we derive inspiration from gathering many worship resources for browsing, borrowing, and adapting.

Perhaps most important, worship leaders will remember that we make appropriate language choices for the sake of Christ, who came in human form so we may know God. The task of leaders is not to get in the way of worshipers but to help open a way to God. When language becomes a barrier or is unworthy of its task, then the people's offering of worship cannot be free and joyful. When language is inviting and clear, and when it gently stretches people beyond their comfort zone, then the Spirit has space to work to call people to a larger vision of God's reign. God's table is expanded.

The language of the surrounding geographic community. Even though worship is primarily an action of the community of faith, this action takes place within the context of a geographic community. It may appear that English or Spanish or French or some other language is being spoken by everyone in the town or neighborhood, but that assumption may not be entirely accurate. What typically varies from one locality to another are vocabulary, idioms, dialects, registers of language, and a variety of language taboos. In addition, the language of worship is influenced by local theological language, streams of spirituality, patterns of prayer, degrees of emotionality, and styles of public discourse, such as in preaching. Because Christians are called to a ministry of reconciliation, we must understand the geographic community's language and make deliberate choices to include rather than exclude.

In a simple gesture of reconciliation, leaders can regularly include other languages spoken in the immediate neighborhood of the church. For an English-speaking Mennonite church in Montreal, this commitment means including at least one French item each Sunday—a scripture reading or song or testimony or translated sermon—whether or not French speakers are present. Such gestures of reconciliation extend to music as well. In a racially integrated Mennonite congregation in Pennsylvania, choir and congregation have been trained to sing and appreciate four-part a cappella hymns, African-American spirituals, and Latino rhythms and melodies.

Thomas Troeger, former professor of preaching at Iliff School of Theology in Denver, Colorado, notes that it is a moral imperative for the Christian church, which is a worldwide church, to borrow worship resources from around the globe: "I believe part of our spiritual maturing as the church depends upon our singing the songs of Christians from other places and times."[9]

Going further, those who lead worship and preach need to represent the racial, ethnic, and economic diversity of the larger community surrounding the church, through such means as organizing pulpit exchanges, training new worship leaders, or hiring additional staff. Although the demands for flexibility and communication will increase dramatically, such actions also invigorate a congregation. An expanded table makes worship more engaging, more transforming for all.

Inside-out worship: Preaching that extends the table

If worship is both the source of mission and active participation in mission, how does preaching connect with the mission of the church? Does this paradoxical view of worship suggest that all preaching should be evangelistic preaching?

At the outset, we acknowledge that in some circles people carry scars from wounds inflicted by sermons designed to manipulate them into "accepting Jesus." Frightened by the prospect of going to hell were they to die that very night, they desperately sought relief. When other people think of evangelistic sermons, the image that comes to mind is the crusades of Billy Graham, whose preaching has persuaded many to commit their lives to Jesus.

Evangelism can be defined in at least three ways. *Presence evangelism* is the social action and clear presence of Christians. Whether or not words about Jesus are spoken or an invitation is given to embrace the Christian faith, the presence and actions of believers make the interaction evangelistic. *Proclaimed evangelism* happens through the preached Word in the context of worship, as people are invited to accept and follow Jesus as their Savior and Lord. *Persuasion evangelism* is the one-on-one invitation designed to convince someone who does not yet believe to listen and respond to the gospel of Jesus.

Although it may appear that the only way to preach evangelistically entails using the proclamation model as defined above, at least two other ways to preach may also be considered evangelistic. The first way is *to preach to prepare the whole congregation to be able witnesses to the saving love of Jesus.* The most effective pattern for evangelism is still person-to-person sharing of the gospel. Effective evangelistic preaching of this kind will create a climate for evangelistic activity on the part of all believers. Many believers are not particularly generous in sharing the gospel, because they think they need to be perfect before they can represent Jesus to someone else. If they are not walking the Christian walk, they are usually reluctant or afraid to talk the Christian talk.

A second group of believers is simply afraid of rejection. They need to be reminded that the Holy Spirit empowered believers of the early church to give courageous witness to their faith, even under the threat of death, and the same Spirit will give them boldness as well.

Some in our congregations simply lack the understanding that to evangelize is their work. In fact, mission is the work of all of us. Others may lack an understanding of how to invite and lead someone to faith. Still others feel unable to answer the faith questions that a new believer might ask. So evangelistic preaching can energize and equip the congregation to become knowledgeable and motivated witnesses who invite others to follow Jesus.

The second kind of evangelistic preaching is *the ordinary, ongoing pulpit ministry that reaches listeners' hearts and minds, inviting them to commit themselves to the Jesus way* by turning their lives God-ward. This preaching provides clear and simple guidance.[10]

The Monroe Motivated Sequence offers several important elements for consideration here.[11] People are seldom motivated to change unless they become aware of a significant need to do so. Preachers must present the need step in terms urgent enough that listeners develop a desire for change. Further, the solution must be within reach. Some successful advertising campaigns are founded on the premise that people cannot swallow the whole elephant at once, so they must be offered bite-size solutions: the action step in the motivated sequence must be clear and relatively simple. It need not be easy, but people who desire to respond must be able to do so without confusion.

This review of motivational strategies points to the source of much injury in evangelistic preaching of the past. Persuasion has acquired a bad reputation because it is often misunderstood. Paul W. Egertson's research on sacramental rhetoric clarifies the role of persuasion by giving it the central location of the influence spectrum, among a range of possible positions listeners may occupy:[12]

> *Apathy.* At this end of the spectrum, listeners have nearly no influence, because they have nothing to respond to. They have been given no options to choose from.

> *Interest.* The speaker has greater influence, because listeners have been given greater information. With more information, listeners have greater freedom to make choices. Much of Protestant preaching is positioned here: listeners are given plenty of information but rarely an invitation to action.

> *Persuasion.* Placed in the center of the spectrum, persuasion offers listeners everything they need to make a free decision in light of the choice at hand. If people are given freedom to make a choice, they must also be given freedom to reject or accept.

> *Manipulation.* As the speaker's influence increases, the listener's freedom of choice decreases. Manipulation usually

involves psychological strong-arm tactics, playing on emotions such as fear or guilt, but the listener can still resist.

Coercion. In the final stage on the influence spectrum, the speaker has total control, and the listener has no choice. Coercion involves lack of freedom on physical as well as psychological levels. One seldom sees this extreme in the church, just as one seldom sees total apathy.

To be effective, evangelistic preaching must speak to listeners' actual needs. But listeners must also have authentic freedom to make a choice to believe in and follow Jesus. In Acts 26, King Agrippa said he was almost persuaded by the Apostle Paul's powerful testimony, yet he chose not to become a follower. Although we may regret his choice, we respect his God-given freedom to choose or reject the call of Christ.

Not a sacred form, the motivated sequence simply describes how people think through and solve problems when they face an issue that needs to be addressed. In such situations, we try to consider the problem with great care, giving attention to all the possible angles. Then we examine the variety of possible solutions that could possibly be applied to this problem. We select the one we are convinced will best solve the problem as we understand it, and finally we take action to begin to achieve the desired outcome. Whether one is in sales or attempting to win listeners to a life with Jesus, the motivational sequence is the same.

What makes evangelistic preaching different from motivational speeches is that the Holy Spirit is also wooing listeners to follow Christ. With evangelistic preaching, the preacher joins with God's Spirit to proclaim the invitation to follow Christ and to persuade in the most vigorous and engaging way possible. And when people respond to the Spirit's loving invitation, God's reign of peace and righteousness expands now and for all time.

Inside-out worship: A foretaste of the feast to come

In chapter one, we noted that what Christians do now in worship is a rehearsal for eternity. Because we live in hope that all God has promised will come to pass, our ordinary Sunday morning worship ought to reflect and anticipate that wider horizon of God's ultimate purposes. How does our worship do so? How does the table around which we gather in worship become a foretaste of the feast to come? In the earlier part of this chapter, we focused on how hospitable language and preaching are essential for the church's life of both worship and mission. Now we turn to see how the table extended in worship points far beyond the here-and-now. The actions of worship are not only a significant dimension of the church's life of mission today; they also participate in a revelation of God's ultimate mission to heal and redeem the entire cosmos.

The following discussion identifies typical actions in worship that could expand or be reshaped to function as colorful appetizers of the feast to come, signifying the dynamic connection between worship and mission.

Gathering around the Word and Table. If our worship is an appetizer for God's feast, it will be centered on Christ, the one who hosts the meal to come. We will proclaim the story of Jesus in compelling, imaginative, transforming ways, and we will gather often at the Lord's Table.[13] Early Christians understood the story of Jesus's resurrection from the dead as the center of Christian faith. Each Sunday was a little Easter, in which they proclaimed the good news that life comes out of death. What we see in the life, death, and resurrection of Jesus is a preview of God's ultimate purposes.

Practically speaking, this means that the gospel occupies a central place in worship. Although a faithful Christian community hears a wide variety of scriptures in worship, the core message is always the good news of salvation. Such practices as standing for the reading of the gospel and surrounding the reading with a sung Alleluia help focus attention on the presence of the risen Christ.

Celebrating the Lord's Supper becomes another proclamation of the gospel. As host at the table, Christ welcomes all who are hungry and offers for our journey the sustaining grace of the bread and cup. By gathering only infrequently at the Lord's Table, we deprive ourselves of much-needed sustenance and also of the joy of anticipating the eternal banquet.

Expressing abundant praise. If our worship is an appetizer for God's feast, it will be filled with abundant praise. Whether sung or spoken, our acts of praise will rehearse God's wondrous deeds and affirm our trust in a faithful God. And just as a good appetizer partakes of the richness of the feast to come, so our praise already participates in the eternal praise of God.

Because of the time constraints we typically experience in Sunday morning worship, leaders can be tempted to shortchange this element of worship. We may feel there is something almost wasteful in spending half an hour or more reveling in God's goodness. Our North American cultural preference for efficiency and productivity can get in the way of such a lavish offering. Fortunately, one of the legacies of the charismatic renewal of the 1960s and 1970s has been a greater appreciation for the role of praise, a worship pattern that continues today in the praise-and-worship tradition.

When it comes to praise in worship, a useful guiding image for leaders might be Mary's generous gift of costly perfume with which she anointed Jesus's feet before his death. When one of the disciples protested her extravagant gesture, Jesus replied, "You always have the poor with you, but you do not always have me" (John 12:8). In the same way, our first priority in worship needs to be the praise of God, not teaching or preaching or congregational business or some other worthwhile agenda. A spacious amount of time spent with well-chosen sung and spoken acts of praise is not a luxury; rather it is an investment in the transformation of God's people.

Because praise invites us to proclaim and affirm God's presence in our midst, as well as the coming fulfillment of God's reign, it is an essential act of worship that offers us a foretaste of the eternal feast.

Including confession. If our worship is an appetizer for God's feast, it will not neglect confession. We will courageously name the truth about ourselves and our world—all the brokenness and all that falls short of God's vision—for only what is named and brought to the light can be cleansed and healed. The oppressive consequences of sin lose their power when we experience forgiveness and restoration.

Although confession may not at first seem connected with a joyful feast, it is a necessary act of preparation. Confession, which literally means "to say with," invites worshipers to say with God what is true about themselves and their world. As worshipers speak the truth about their humanity and acknowledge their desire for wholeness, God's mercy and grace flow freely in the congregation.

In some cultures, between the main course and dessert, something is provided to diners that serves to cleanse their palates of earlier flavors. In order to fully appreciate dessert, the taste buds need to be prepared to receive the sweet or refreshing flavors of the final course. Sometimes a light salad with lemon- or vinegar-laced dressing serves the purpose; other times a fresh fruit sorbet is the choice. What has come before is set aside, and this interlude prepares us to fully enjoy what comes next. In the same way, the act of confession creates a fresh opening for freedom and joy—requisite preparation for receiving the sweetness of God's feast.

Extending generous hospitality. If our worship is an appetizer for God's feast, we will extend generous hospitality. Because in eternity every tribe and nation will gather in worship, we begin now to welcome strangers and friends to God's feast. We envision gatherings for worship as having porous boundaries, always open to whomever God invites.

Perhaps nothing is as destructive of the joy of a feast as conflict—under the surface or out in the open—or the knowledge that some were not invited because of neglect or ill will. A feast demands generosity and a celebrative spirit. Where conflict among members has marred the feast, we diminish the capacity of worship to serve as an eschatological sign.

A more common failure may be inattention to hospitality or unwitting neglect. Although worshipers may not intend to ignore another's need, such lapses do occur. If a visitor is not greeted with warmth and care, God's invitation in worship is obscured. If a regular worshiper seems burdened or discouraged and no one shows concern, the practice of hospitality is compromised. Hospitality requires that the act of gathering the congregation—with a call to worship, an opening prayer, or a procession—be planned with special care. An invocation that expresses an unusually generous welcome is the following.

> Source of all hope and holiness,
> we gather this morning to be church.
> Bless those who are absent, but not from our hearts.
> Bless those who are distant, but not from your love.
> Bless each of us here that we may
>   choose justice by your Spirit,
>   draw kindness from the well of your mercy,
>   and walk humbly in your path, O God. Amen.[14]

Another kind of inhospitality can occur on occasions such as Mother's Day or Father's Day. Those struggling with painful memories of parental mistreatment or recent loss of a parent may find it difficult to rejoice on such a day. Couples dealing with infertility or the death of a child will also feel deep pain. When these losses are ignored and the horizontal focus dominates, worship becomes inhospitable and thus fails to reflect God's vision. Although there is certainly a place to honor parents, the primary focus of worship is the God who mothers and fathers us all. In other words, the vertical focus of worship should remain strong.

Worship creates a space for people loved by God but neglected by society to take their place in God's reign. Those who are poor, physically or emotionally abused, disabled, unemployed, or elderly receive God's promise of justice in words, music, and gestures that respect the reality of their circumstances. We mourn and lament their difficulties and celebrate their contributions. Here they may stand among the rich and powerful as equals in integrity and righteousness. Their praise honors God in the midst of hardship and despair.

Just as the giver of the banquet in the gospel parable invited and made welcome everyone who could be found, so the worshipping church in mission opens its arms wide to embrace people as they are. The good news of God's reign is that a table has already been set for us, and we are honored guests.

Singing and praying with many nations. In worship we experience a powerful indicator of the feast to come when the congregation borrows the prayers or songs of other cultures or nations. Singing worship songs created by Christians in other parts of the world cultivates an international awareness of the global church. Even when the performance falls short, the act of reaching across boundaries is a sign that we affirm and join with God's loving intentions. The circle of God's family expands when sisters and brothers in Christ take time to understand and experience one another's worship music.

Songs with strong melodies that often sound minor to Western ears—such as those from Japan, China, Korea, or Philippines—reach deep places in the soul and stir reflection. Or the breathtaking leaps these melodies contain create a sense of dramatic tension—like a vocal free-fall—that requires careful attuning. These melodies are beautiful in their reserve and vigor. Many Native American songs and

African-American spirituals have similar dramatic tension created by covering a wide range of tones in the melody, which is neither major nor minor. Such songs have an alluring, haunting quality.

Rhythms from Africa, Latin America, and the deep south of the United States stir the body to move—to dance—with freedom, carried by the repeating patterns that give shape to melody. Whether tempos are fast or slow, the rhythms work their way to our muscles and bones, so that feet, hands, and torsos cannot remain still. We must clap, sway, or stomp to the beat.

Harmony enriches melodies by giving them texture and depth. Whether harmonies are improvised or carefully planned, they require a community of singers. Their voices create tension as chords seek resolution. To the ears of worshipers accustomed to Western harmonies, such tensions and resolutions provide deep satisfaction and security, a sense of being at home. Many contemporary North American hymn tune writers who practice the craft of harmony know how to use vocal and instrumental textures to interpret the words worshipers sing. Black gospel music freely uses the flatted harmonies of jazz and blues to build interesting chords around melodies. These chords bend the ear to a mellow or bittersweet mood that touches the deeper reaches of the soul and gives voice to truthful lament. Contemporary worship music drawn from Latin American, African, or Celtic roots may have harmonies that move in parallel with the melody, creating a satisfying sense of vocal texture without concern for building tensions and resolutions.

When Christians sing the songs of brothers and sisters from around the world, they expand their abilities to respond to God through new melodies, rhythms, and harmonies. Culture-bound assumptions about what makes music good are challenged as we experience the power of songs created by the world's Christians to express praise, confession, thanksgiving, and offering.

While each congregation stands in solidarity with all other Christian congregations, it also stands in relationship with other religious traditions. Through worship, we affirm the unique character of Christian faith while praying in ways that respect people of other religious traditions. Some congregations fear direct engagement with people of other faiths or are simply indifferent to the religious pluralism of North American culture. Other congregations actively seek discussion and partnership with adherents of Judaism, Islam, Hinduism, or Buddhism, trusting in the presence of God's Spirit for discernment. As Christians pray for God's reign to be fulfilled, they pray for the restoration and redemption for all peoples—as in the following prayer.

Leader	God of all nations,
	your love is without limit and without end.
	Enlarge our vision of your redeeming purpose for
	   all people.
	By the example of your Son,
	make us ready to serve the needs of the whole
	   world.

All	*May neither pride of race nor hardness of heart* *make us despise any for whom Christ died* *or injure any in whom Christ lives;* *through the same Jesus Christ our Lord. Amen.*[15]

Offering our gifts with open hands. The offerings we bring to worship extend the table as they provide financial support for the church's ministries in the world. And they serve as appetizers of an even more generous feast to come. Practiced nearly universally, the offering introduces a moment when doors open wide into the world and worshipers joyfully share with whoever has need. If, however, the offering becomes perfunctory, is overly sober, or is not carefully integrated into the service, it loses its capacity to participate in and point to God's reign of justice and love.

Offering prayers that make a direct connection between our giving and our hope for the expansion of God's reign help us grasp the significance of this action. The following two examples illuminate that connection.

Offering prayer
Great God *[lifting the offering plates toward heaven],*
these gifts represent the first and best of the resources we have from you.
We want you to have them.
[Name of particular recipient or group] will get some of the money.
So will *[another name].*
We ask you to follow the flow of this money,
and to use it to speed the coming of your kingdom. Amen.[16]

Offering prayer for Advent Sunday
(when gifts of money and food are being given to a local charity)
We have proclaimed your greatness, God;
we have honored you with our lips.
Now we honor you with the work of our hands.
Let the gifts we bring magnify your name.

Bless these offerings of money
so your love may be made known in all the earth.

Bless too the offerings of food
that will be distributed to those in need.
May each one who receives food also know your love and care.
We pray in the name of Jesus our Savior. Amen.[17]

One approach that allows the offering to partake of a more generous sense of hospitality invites people to move, to bring their offerings forward, while joyful music is played or sung. Still another approach invites worshipers themselves to become the recipients of the offering, as the following example illustrates:

Once there was a church where the people took the offering back
home with them.
First it was collected and brought to the altar.
After they asked God to bless it, they put it back into their pockets.
They mixed it up with all their other money, so that they couldn't
tell which was blessed and which was not.
Then they left.
All week they spent as though each piece was blessed.
And was to be used lovingly.[18]

When worship leaders and preachers begin to understand the critical role of hospitality in proclaiming God's reign, they will discover many ways to enhance the spirit of generosity and hospitality in worship, thus shaping a people capable of openhanded living.

Praying fervently. If our worship is an appetizer for God's feast, our prayers will be fervent. Abraham Joshua Heschel says, "To pray is to dream in league with God, to envision God's holy visions."[19] As we express our deepest longings to God, we persist in praying that God's kingdom will come on earth as in heaven. Nor do we pray alone. Joining us are all the saints of heaven, whose prayers rise with incense before God's throne (Rev 8:3–4).

Sometimes our prayers in worship fall short of such a vision. We may pray too little. We may pray without conviction. We may expect only the leaders to pray and not the entire congregation. If prayer in worship is to connect us with God's transforming vision, then praying must have a substantial place in worship, it must engage all the people of God, and it must expand to include the concerns of those near and far.

How can prayer become more fervent? Those of us who stand before the congregation on Sunday morning—preachers, music leaders, and worship leaders—all need to understand our pivotal role as guides of communal prayer. Shaped by our own life of prayer, we will prepare for leading the congregation in a prayerful spirit. In addition, we will choose words and phrases carefully. We may not write prayers in advance, but we will thoughtfully consider the purpose of each prayer and the language, whether spoken or sung, that will best express to God the desires of the people.

To experience more significant prayer in worship takes time. An unhurried, leisurely atmosphere invites people to become more aware of God's presence and open themselves to an encounter with God. Moments of silence or interspersing a sung refrain (such as "Lord, listen to your children praying") between sections of a spoken prayer also creates more space for prayer to deepen.

Prayer becomes more meaningful when all the people participate. Even young children can join the congregation at prayer. In one congregation, when a worship leader suggested a variety of themes for a silent prayer of intercession, she began by addressing the grown-ups and then rephrased each intercession for the children and invited them to join the prayer:

> *[spoken to all:]*   Let us pray for the people of
>   *[a country in crisis]*.
>
> *[spoken to children:]* Boys and girls, you can pray for
>   children who might not have blankets
>   or food or who might be afraid.

As prayer deepens and becomes more participatory, the people of God begin to see more of God's wider horizon. Prayers of intercession for the world's peoples, neighbors, the local community, civic and national leaders, or mission and service workers extend the congregation's consciousness of God's work in and through the world. By commissioning workers and blessing projects that serve the community, the congregation reaches beyond the needs of its own members in caring service. Worship expands the congregation's heart for other citizens of God's reign and for those seeking the shalom of God's saving grace. Thus prayer becomes an act of engagement in God's mission.

Trusting the arts in worship. If our worship is an appetizer for God's feast, we will trust the arts to help us touch the hem of mystery. Open to mystery, we will sometimes catch sight of a veil drawn aside and be illumined by the splendor of God's glory.

Although some radical reformers were iconoclasts who were suspicious of the role of art in worship, that resistance is rapidly diminishing today. In our time, we are newly awakened to the reality that a song, a poem, a story, flowing cloth, or a cluster of lit candles can open spaces in our imagination through which the Spirit can move.

Sometimes a few lines of poetry printed in a church bulletin become a prayer for those waiting for the service to begin. A well-chosen prelude creates a similar space. A tablescape fashioned to evoke the theme of worship draws us into God's presence. When we include such elements in our planning, we take care not to be overly literal. We seek instead to trust these arts as expressions of God-given creativity, letting a song or symbol speak its own truth without needing to explain or justify—and perhaps get in the way of the Spirit.[20]

When we have allowed the arts to do their work of opening people to the wider realm of God's presence and activity, they proceed to call worshipers to faithful response to the gospel. Singing "I bind my heart this tide" or "You are salt for the earth" (*HWB* 411 and 226) confronts each worshiper with a moment of decision and action: Will I give—or continue to give—my heart, time, and energy to the neighbor near at hand and the stranger far away? Thus God's reign expands.

Making space for prophets. If our worship is an appetizer for God's feast, we will make space for prophets to speak and act in worship. Although they are not always comfortable company, we will respond to the truth they bring, even when that message is judgment.

Keenly aware of the intimate connection between the worship of

God's people and living justly in the world, the Old Testament prophets spoke boldly, as in Micah's classic declaration:

> "With what shall I come before the LORD,
> and bow myself before God on high?
> Shall I come before him with burnt offerings,
> with calves a year old?
> Will the LORD be pleased with thousands of rams,
> with ten thousands of rivers of oil?
> Shall I give my firstborn for my transgressions,
> the fruit of my body for the sin of my soul?"
> He has told you, O mortal, what is good;
> and what does the LORD require of you
> but to do justice, and to love kindness,
> and to walk humbly with your God? (Mic 6:6–8)

Yet the temptation is strong to mute the voice or the vision of prophets. In middle class and upper class congregations, where prophetic words can threaten the status quo, preachers and worship leaders often need to plan and work quite intentionally to give such words and images a prominent place in worship. Although lower class and poor congregations may be more willing to hear the prophet's critique, they sometimes struggle to find appropriate ways to act for justice. And if a congregation includes a variety of ethnic groups, they can get distracted from prophetic speech or action by the internal challenges of living and working together in harmony. Few churches find it easy to respond to prophets.

When we encourage prophetic voices, worship can inadvertently become captive to specific political interests. Preachers, worship leaders, and music leaders can take advantage of their leadership role to promote a partisan political agenda. Such actions are, of course, distracting to the central purpose of worship, which is to glorify God. They may also incite unrest in the congregation, because those who hold other political views will likely chafe under such practices or rebel outright and demand equal time!

Although the purpose of the church remains distinct from the purpose of the state or nation, worship can become an arena where these purposes become confused. While Christians are called to respect the role of governmental institutions, our primary allegiance is to God's justice and righteousness. The proclamation, offering, prayer, and witness of worship keep God's purposes for the entire world in focus. When governmental leaders implement policies or pursue practices that work against the ethics of God's reign, then congregations are obliged to pray and testify against such actions. When good government aligns with God's purposes of reconciliation, justice, and peace, and not with agendas that advance the power of the nation at the expense of others, then Christians rejoice.

One way to keep a healthy balance on these issues is to make liberal use of the words of scripture in worship rather than using so many of our own words. A congregation found a powerful way to do this during Advent, when many of the prophetic texts spoke vividly to current situations of injustice. Instead of making political statements, the worship leaders integrated the lighting of Advent candles into the act of confession each week. As candles were lit, a promise or word of hope was read from the Prophets. The scripture reading was followed immediately with a brief story or comment from the newspapers of the past week. Sometimes the newspaper story illuminated God's vision; more often, worshipers saw how far their world fell short of God's intentions. The readings concluded with a prayer confessing the brokenness of the world, asking God to bring light, and giving thanks for places where God's light already shines. In this way, the focus remained on the ways God longs to transform the world, not on our limited human efforts or on particular political programs.

Connecting worship and work. If our worship is an appetizer for God's feast, a lively traffic will flow back and forth between worship and work. Because this is the world God loves and labors to redeem, our work will participate in that redemption. Thus we cannot ignore the world around us as we worship, but neither can we allow the world's agenda to dominate worship. Instead, faithful worship requires an attentiveness to God's vision that continually transforms our vision and behavior in everyday life.

One way congregations make explicit connections between worship and work is to pray regularly for members in their workplaces. From time to time, individuals can share in worship about the way they live their faith in the marketplace. Stories from the world of work can also be woven into sermons. Other connections can be made through rituals for blessing young adults who are entering the world of work or for retirees departing from the workforce to live out their faith in new arenas.[21]

Prophetic texts, in particular, speak of God's concern for just and ethical practices in the workplace. The prophet Isaiah rebukes the people of Israel who follow their religious traditions but do not act justly: "Look, you serve your own interest on your fast day, and oppress all your workers" (Isa 58:3). The worship God desires looses the bonds of injustice, lets the oppressed go free, breaks every yoke, and shares bread with the hungry (Isa 58:6–7). Through these life-giving actions, God's reign becomes visible in the world.

Joyfully celebrating baptisms. If our worship is an appetizer for God's feast, baptisms will be joyful celebrations. As new believers commit themselves to Christ and the church, we will rejoice to catch a glimpse of the expansion of God's reign.

Perhaps nowhere is God's vision clearer than in our baptismal ceremonies. The classic baptismal formulas handed down through the centuries emphasize that the new Christian has died to the power of sin and death, including all that impedes God's reign in our world, and has come alive to the power of the resurrection, entering into the freedom and joy of God's new age. In the baptismal ritual itself, water flows freely—cleansing from sin, birthing a new Christian, and offering a preview of the abundant river of life flowing for all nations.

Several things may keep baptismal ceremonies from manifesting their full potential as signs of God's reign already breaking into our reality. One is a lack of joy; we forget that the angels of heaven are jubilant on such a day! Another is a too narrow, overly horizontal focus on the individual at the expense of the church and God's reign. A third is an overemphasis on sin, in the absence of a vision for redemption and freedom in Christ.

Baptismal ceremonies that joyfully announce God's reign are occasions for inviting friends, neighbors, and relatives. Young children may be invited to sit on the floor in front where they can watch the ritual closely, anticipating the time when they will be baptized. And certainly a welcoming party should take place afterward in the fellowship hall.

The following call to worship invites the whole community to joyfully celebrate new life:

Leader	Come, family of God, come join the celebration of new life!
Left	Come, mothers and fathers,
Right	come, sisters and brothers,
Left	come, grandparents, friends, and neighbors,
Right	come, family of God!
Leader	God is about to do a new thing. Be glad and rejoice in what God creates!

All	*We have come to witness a birth;*
	we have come to welcome new members to
	   the body of Christ;
	we have come to see God's reign expand in
	   the earth.
	Praise God, the giver of new life! [22]

A service of baptism also provides opportunity for proclaiming the good news in powerful, compelling ways. In clear and simple terms, preachers can present the call of Jesus Christ to repent, believe, and become a new creation. The testimony of new Christians, an act that initiates them into their life of witness, gives opportunity to tell the good news of what Christ has done for them. The following prayer speaks such a testimony with eloquence:

Refreshing God,
for every stream and spring
that wells up grace from deep within your love,
I give my free and heartfelt thanks.
The day has come
when I draw forth rejoicing the water of trust and comfort
from deep within your wells.
May all people hear my thanks to you resound in song.
May I hear my own voice glad with laughter
praise you for this amazing day of days—
for I who would be so lost, so lost,
am saved. Amen.[23]

Holding fast to hope. If our worship is an appetizer for God's feast, we will hold fast to hope in the midst of grief and pain. When we lay to rest our beloved sisters and brothers in Christ, commending them to God's eternal care and keeping, we will surely grieve. Yet through our tears we will also claim the hope of new life in God's eternal future.

Bursting forth from the tomb on Easter morning, Jesus entered God's ultimate horizon. In that stunning defeat of sin and death, we too are assured of the victory of love and life. And with the unleashing of the Spirit's power at Pentecost, we too are set free from the curse of sin and death and enter God's spacious realm of life and peace. Thus the appetizers we sample now in worship are not just a promise of a feast to come, they signify that the banquet has already begun.

Conclusion

Worship always looks far ahead toward the broad, beckoning horizon. Although it is intimately connected with the here-and-now, it never loses sight of our ultimate allegiance. Whether we bow down to the triune God or to lesser gods such as money, fame, and power, we humans worship what we love most deeply. God, who is sovereign over all creation, claims loyalty over all that competes for our love, service, and praise. Worship names God as Creator, Redeemer, and Sustainer of all life. God's story of salvation, not the stories of family or nation, is the primary story we should be telling. God's story will be fulfilled when the kingdom of heaven is a reality on earth and creation's original blessing is restored. Christian worship is a threat to national governments not because it incites anarchy or revolution but because worship names God as the only ruler worthy of our complete surrender and commitment. Such a universal vision is the vision toward which Christian worship points.

The book of Revelation creates a picture of that universal vision when it describes all peoples, tribes, and nations—regardless of race, gender, education, economic class, profession, or age—coming together to worship the Lamb. When local congregations extend their table in worship, they not only point toward the Lamb's feast, they offer a foretaste of that wondrous celebration that will mark the fulfillment of all God's dreams for this world.

13

NEGOTIATING THE POLITICS OF SUNDAY DINNER

> When you come together as a church, I hear that there are divisions
> among you. . . . For when the time comes to eat, each of you goes
> ahead with your own supper, and one goes hungry and another becomes
> drunk. (1 Cor 11:18, 21)

To ruin a perfectly fine dinner, just bring up the topic of politics.
Along with the other taboo subjects—religion, money, and sex—politics is just not discussed in polite company. Political matters provoke
our deepest loyalties, most fervent passions, and strongest opinions.
We argue. We cajole. We vigorously try to persuade our dinner partners to our point of view. We may grudgingly concede the credibility
of someone else's position. But often the conversation ends in disap-
pointing stalemate. No doubt—debates about politics overheat the
body, rile the system, and disrupt the digestion.

Whenever two or three people are gathered together, there are
politics, broadly understood as the art of negotiating conflicting values, beliefs, or principles so that some action can get done.
Relationships are inherently political, because our values, beliefs,
principles, needs, and desires rarely mesh neatly, and we must negotiate in order to live and work together.

My spouse and I have vastly different perspectives on time. I see
time as a quantity parceled out as a series of deadlines: things happen
on time, in time, or past time. Joe, on the other hand, works with time
as a quality, a space in which things happen—or don't happen. If
something doesn't happen today, perhaps it will happen tomorrow.
Needless to say, our different understandings do not always make living together easy. The maddening thing is that we are both right and
neither of us is right, so we have to negotiate about whose under-

standing of time we are using when. Sometimes my deadline approach is necessary; in other instances his open-ended process approach serves best. Our love for each other does not eliminate our differences. The art of negotiation is always part of our relationship.

Collaboration, one of the central values of this book, requires skills in negotiation. This type of teamwork draws on the knowledge and wisdom of various people, some of it conflicting. Collaboration necessitates that each team member holds clear values, beliefs, and principles, which they can explain. It also requires that they be open to the views of others. Capacities to give, take, and hold firm when necessary are essential in political negotiations.

In writing this book, we three authors negotiated a variety of decisions: the sequence of the later chapters, the chapter titles, whether there would be an appendix and a bibliography, the order in which our names would appear, how much weight to give to the critiques of our individuals chapters. After discussions, we have agreed unanimously on nearly all decisions. But there are a couple final decisions that at least one of us has a qualm about. These few points have been thoroughly discussed, the pros and cons evaluated. We all have been heard; our individual views have been treated with respect. No decision for this book was forced on a dissenting sister. We can all honestly live with the decisions we have made, though on a couple of points one of us might have felt more enthusiasm for another option.

Many of us shy away from facing the political nature of our relationships, because we have trouble acknowledging the ways we inevitably use power in our interactions with one another. Individual power, which every person possesses, can control or manipulate negotiations. We can come to fear the power exercised by other people or the power we ourselves exercise. Power itself is neither positive nor negative; it is the capacity to get things done. People with forceful personalities can exercise significant power in a group. People with skills or knowledge that a group needs possess power. People who speak persuasively have power. Those with significant economic resources are powerful. People with appointed roles in an organization, such as the pastor and other leaders, are granted power to carry out our responsibilities. The ways we use our power in negotiation can benefit others. If we abuse power and skew the process of negotiation, we can get ourselves into trouble and hurt many people.

Pastors and other leaders exercise power in their negotiations to influence hearts and minds. When we exercise this power justly and wisely, everyone benefits. But those of us who are not identified as leaders also have power—to discern what is true, to speak the truth of our lives and our communities, to voice affirmation or dissent, to support our leaders, to do our part in church and world. We have the power to support what is good in our communities or to obstruct what is fair and just. We have the power to make scapegoats of officials when conflicts seem irresolvable.

Negotiations, and the power dynamics that are always at play in them, can be tense. Conflicts that result take time to resolve. Negotiating vision and procedures for a group sharing a common life can be difficult. It is a process that is inefficient by every conceivable measure valued by North Americans, who cherish the freedom of individual choice, getting their own way or going it alone. For these reasons, most of us prefer to ignore the power issues in our congregations rather than address the challenges and opportunities they present.

We would like to think that congregational issues, especially worship, are above politics. But since congregations are all about relationships, this wish is obviously naïve. Worship always has political dimensions, because it brings to life relationships among God, God's people, and the world. How the congregation worships—its leadership, its styles, its ways of addressing God and one another—represents a variety of explicit and implicit negotiations. Worship expresses our deepest beliefs, central values, and primary allegiance to God and the reign of Christ. Worship is the place where we "go public" with our commitments to be Christ's body, which may create stresses and strains in our relationships as members of his body, even as it may put us in conflict with the societal beliefs and values. Worship demonstrates a stance from which we negotiate the primary allegiances of our lives with the societies and nations in which we live.

In this chapter, we examine several arenas in which the political negotiations of worship are most obvious and most often fraught with conflict. The first section explores political issues related to worship that have tested the negotiating skills of pastoral and congregational leaders. The second section looks at the issues related to collaboration of a smaller group of leaders charged with responsibility for planning worship and preaching.

Politics of the congregation

Worship leadership, including preaching, is political. Worship leaders and preachers hold the formational aspects of worship in our care. We have power and authority to influence the views and practices of our congregation.

Solo and shared leadership. Some congregations give their pastors authority to plan and lead the entire service, as well as to preach. Music may be led by a musician, but in some congregations the pastor selects the songs for congregational singing. This arrangement provides consistency and stylistic coherence. Week after week, the congregational ethos is shaped by the spirituality and expressiveness of the pastor. If the pastor's style is formal, with a liturgical bent, the congregation is trained in this style. If the pastor's approach is casual, folksy, and unstructured, the congregation reflects these qualities. What the congregation is—or wishes to become—through worship is reflected in the pastor's manner, at least when all is well. But if the pastor's style is always formal, worship can begin to feel stifling. And a warm folksiness may eventually feel phony if it exudes an intimacy that is lacking in the congregation.

In other congregations, worship is led by several people, including the worship leader, music leader, preacher, and/or scripture reader(s). Sharing leadership demonstrates the ministry gifts present in the congregation. All leaders are empowered by the Holy Spirit to guide God's people in praise, prayer, and witness. The Spirit must also instill and strengthen trust among the leaders. At its best, the flow of leadership is seamless—the music leader giving way to the primary worship leader, who eventually yields to the preacher. These leaders embody the functions of hosts, prophets, or priests. Competitive personalities, who need to be the center of attention, rarely share leadership roles well. A song leader who talks too much before or between songs may be vying for attention. A scripture reader who provides a lengthy introduction to the reading may be upstaging the preacher. Preachers who read the scripture text a second time when they get up to preach undermine the ministry of the designated scripture reader. Worship leaders whose long prayers tend toward a preaching mode have lost track of their first responsibility.

Women in leadership. For generations, men provided the preaching and worship leadership in congregations. But women increasingly serve as worship and preachers. Some congregations find this change hard to navigate, because it strikes at the heart of how they interpret scriptures. Scripture provides a variety of images of women in leadership, as well as injunctions against women's participation in certain worship activities. Given a chance, women often fulfill the functions of host and priest in particularly gracious ways. And men and women in worship leadership display publicly the complementarity of male and female in Christ's body. But some people are not ready to see women in active leadership, and others resist the dominance of men in the public ministry of the church. These deep-seated beliefs—often rooted as much in our psychology as in our theology—are difficult to negotiate. In most congregational settings, it is male leaders who must open the way for women to serve in leadership.

Misuses of leadership. Worship leaders and preachers can misuse their authority and power in various ways. The following are among the most obvious.[1]

> *Emotional manipulation.* Sometimes worship leaders and preachers try to pump up the congregation by being overly dramatic and emotionally excessive, acting coy, or joking and teasing. No leader can control how worshipers will feel at a particular moment, and we should not try to drive the congregation toward some desired level of enthusiasm, receptivity, or vulnerability.
>
> *Pursuit of creativity.* Pursuit of novelty for its own sake is a misuse of power, particularly when the quest to be creative displaces what has been authentic to a congregation's expression. The presence of Christ in the midst of the body and the movement of the Holy Spirit make things new.
>
> *Pursuit of specific desired outcomes.* Worship leaders and preachers misuse our power when we predetermine what we want the congregation to get out of a service or how we want the congregation to respond. We set up circumstances to yield the ends we desire. Abuses around the practice of the altar call illustrate this temptation.

Tight control of all worship elements. Worship leaders who cannot graciously respond to the unplanned and spontaneous place limits on the range of acceptable congregational response. Leaders who are overly invested in how things ought to go mishandle their power. The desire to control worship—or, more precisely, to control the worshipers—is a primary power issue that we must continually confront.

Amplifications. Sound projection, a legitimate need in many worship spaces, holds significant potential for misuse. The amplification of the worship leader's and preacher's voices over those of the congregation opens the way for power imbalance and distortion. Hearing our voices amplified can be a head-swelling experience.

When sound engineers, who are extremely important members of the worship leadership team, can simply turn down the volume of a singer or speaker at will, power issues are also present.

Lighting that focuses attention on the worship leader or preacher, dramatizing the difference between the enlightened and the unenlightened, can be misused. Larger-than-life projections of worship leaders and preachers can create a distorted sense of authority. The impact of celebrity worship leaders and singers is heightened by the large projections of their soulful singing. The power issues may seem insignificant to those in leadership, who see the congregation in its actual size, but the superhuman images the congregation views can magnify the power they attribute to the leaders.

Spiritual massage. Worship leaders singing into a microphone with eyes closed, as if the congregation did not exist, may be engaged in ego-massage and thus lose sight of our true leadership responsibility, which is leading the congregation in song.

Abdicating responsibility. If we fail to prepare adequately to lead worship or to preach, we may believe we are acting humbly, but our behavior reflects arrogance. Lack of preparation draws attention to itself. To disregard our priestly responsibilities is a misuse of the authority that the congregation has entrusted to us.

First and foremost, worship leaders and preachers serve God by serving the congregation. The authority given to us is not based on our personalities, pieties, or desires. Our power does not arise principally from our well-honed words, decisive actions, keen insights, or vast knowledge. The power of this leadership comes from the Holy Spirit, who gives the spiritual gifts required for the congregation's worship.

Using the Bible

Biblical interpretation. Issues surrounding how the Bible is interpreted carry a multitude of political implications. In any congregation, some people read the Bible in literal and piecemeal ways. Often selecting a number of specific verses, these people read texts at a surface level, not necessarily allowing other scriptures to interpret their favorite texts. The interpretation process is easy; the text says exactly what it means. These people tend to favor scriptures that proscribe, prescribe, and describe appropriate behavior. The texts they desire for preaching are often short, with one specific point. For people preferring this approach to interpretation, worship is regulated exactly by what the Bible prescribes and allows. The literal approach to biblical texts has much to commend it, because it takes the details of individual texts with utmost seriousness.[2]

Many people following this interpretive approach believe the Bible says clearly that women should not engage in the public ministry of the congregation, especially not in preaching. Paul writes that women should be silent in the churches (1 Cor 14:34–35) and that they should not have authority over men (1 Tim 2:12). A literal reading of these two passages makes moot any question of women leading worship or preaching.

At the other end of the interpretation continuum are worshipers who use the Bible as a repository of interesting stories, sayings, and moral wisdom. They read a passage as a springboard into their own thoughts and analogies. The details of a text may be lost to the interesting image or idea ("the nugget") that sparks their imaginations. These people take the Bible seriously, but as a source for their own musings. Much is possible. This approach stimulates creativity and openness to consider a wide variety of meanings.[3]

For people espousing this interpretive mode, the question of women preaching or leading worship is also moot, but for a different reason than for the more literal minded. These people may look to Peter's Pentecost sermon in Acts 2, in which he quotes from the prophet Joel: "In the last days it will be, God declares, that I will pour out my Spirit upon all flesh, and your sons *and your daughters* shall prophesy, and your young men shall see visions, and your old men shall dream dreams. Even upon my slaves, both men *and women*, in those days I will pour out my Spirit; and they shall prophesy."

Or they may look to Paul's description in 1 Corinthians 12 of the varieties of spiritual gifts given by the Holy Spirit, none of which is designated specifically for men or for women. They would read further and claim the image of the body with many members who are all given the same Spirit. These people would point to Galatians 3:28— "There is no longer Jew or Greek, there is no longer slave or free, there is no longer male and female; for all of you are one in Christ Jesus"—and claim an egalitarian relationship of men and women in Christ. If men can lead, preach, and prophesy, so can women.

Between these two interpretive poles is one that takes the literal sense of scriptures seriously but interprets the texts within a variety of contexts: the larger context of the biblical story; the social context in which it was written; the context of the church's understanding of the text throughout history; and the contemporary context in which its meaning is discerned. This approach tends toward identifying significant biblical themes that recur in God's story. It also holds interpretive tension as various passages are used to interpret one another. People committed to this way of working with scripture embrace the demanding discipline of discernment.

When they consider whether women should serve as worship leaders or preachers, people of this third way are not compelled to dismiss either the injunctions against women speaking in church or to disregard the imagery of a body united by Christ, in which God's Spirit empowers all who believe for ministry. They would likely look throughout the Bible for other examples of women who were called to serve God's people in leadership roles. With a more comprehensive view of God's empowering Spirit, the limitations placed on women, and the freedoms women have exercised for the sake of God's work, they would be ready to discern what these examples from scripture mean for women in their congregation and for their gifts for ministry.

Variations on all three of these approaches are used in most congregations for different purposes. A well-rounded use of scripture in congregational life should include a variety of practices:

1. Hearing large sections of scripture read aloud nearly every time people meet—for worship, Sunday school, Bible study, small group—and simply letting the words soak into our awareness

2. Telling over and over again as many stories from the Bible as possible, even the difficult ones, in worship, Sunday school, Bible study, small groups

3. Using the words of scripture to form prayers for public and private use

4. Quoting or adapting scripture texts for the various actions of public worship

5. Memorizing scripture as a regular congregational discipline

6. Studying scripture (not just reading and answering set questions) in small groups

7. Making studies of significant and recurring words in the Old and New Testament, noting how meanings change within the biblical tradition

8. Exploring imaginatively the myriad of biblical images and metaphors used to understand God's ways

9. Hearing sermons rooted in careful exegesis that make persuasive connections with contemporary life

10. Using musical resources and visual art based on specific scriptures to experience a different point of view in the text

These and other practices of scripture build a deep foundation for interpreting scriptures and discerning their meaning for congregational life. Worship leaders and preachers let the literary genre of specific scripture passages guide the interpretation of texts for worship. We will approach the poetry of the Psalms differently than the histories of kings, the parables of the Gospels, or the Pauline exhortations.

No single interpretive method will work for the variety of biblical literature available for worship. Whenever necessary, preachers and worship leaders should inform the congregation of our interpretive approach to the Bible as we prepare sermons and services. No doubt, negotiating across the spectrum of approaches to biblical interpretation within a congregation can test the Christian character and patience of any preacher or worship leader.

Inclusive language. The issue of inclusive language has created much conflict and frustration in recent decades. Tension arises as people with different interpretive approaches try to address the issue of numerous masculine references to God and people in congregational worship.

People at one end of the interpretive continuum reject any names for God not found in scripture. For them, the constant use of *Father* and *he* poses no critical problem. Even masculine human language is unproblematic, because Paul endorsed the belief that the man is the head of the woman, or because English speakers traditionally have understood "man" to refer to humankind. Those on the other end of the spectrum applaud changing biblical texts and using names for God that reflect our personal experience with God. People following a third way may try to remain faithful to scripture but limit the number of *he* references in prayers and songs when they can do so in aesthetically unobtrusive ways. These people also dig deeper in scripture, discovering images, metaphors, and themes that identify God with "feminine" attributes such as tenderness and nurture, or address God using gender-free terms such as Rock, Light, Stronghold, or Creator.

Many congregations are still negotiating issues of inclusive language. Congregational hymns and songs become a battleground for contending interpretive approaches. The change in the second verse of Isaac Watts's "Joy to the World" is slight—*men* to *all*—three letters for three letters. Yet the alteration signals a shift in who is invited to sing for joy: "Joy to the earth the Savior reigns! Let *all* their songs employ while fields and floods, rocks, hills, and plains repeat the sounding joy." In the original text, only men are invited join creation in announcing Christ's messianic reign. The omission of women in this verse would not be so troubling if Watts had written a verse for them. He didn't. So this awkward situation arises yet again in the church's story: women, although present, are treated as if they were absent. The contribution of women's voices to the heralding of the world's Savior apparently counts for nothing.

Some people say, "You're making a big deal about nothing. Just sing the words and forget it. You're taking the whole thing too personally. Besides, it is unethical to change the original work of a dead poet. And to make alterations is to tamper with the memories of people who learned the hymn in its original form."

Compared to *men,* the word *all* does lack specificity, which is the more noticeable because Watts's language is so concrete. On the other hand, the change does open the possibility for women's songs to join those of men and of the earth—which women also inhabit—in heralding the Savior.

The political issue that remains for hymn revision committees and worship committees is whether the benefits of the change (opening women, girls, and boys to the awareness that they are part of the earthly choir) outweigh the losses (making men the only model of faithfulness and altering the original text). Different people in a congregation will answer this question differently. Of course, solutions will also vary from congregation to congregation.

Commitment to worship patterns. Contrasting views on the nature of corporate worship also arise from different interpretive approaches to the Bible and different commitments regarding how the Bible should be used in worship.

The Bible sets out no single image or prescription for worship. Congregations and theologians tend to build their case for particular worship practices using a few key biblical passages. Many congregations that follow a contemporary worship structure use the image of the Old Testament temple for organizing the opening song service. The *outer courts* portion gathers the congregation in song. Songs of praise and adoration then characterize movement into the *inner courts.* In the *Holy of Holies,* worshipers sing songs of intimate prayer and offering. This image is indeed biblical. But confession of sin and a call to service, which were Isaiah's responses to the encounter with the living God in the temple (Isa 6:1–8), are rarely included in the song service. Why not? In light of Hebrews 9, which describes Jesus as the fulfillment of temple worship, we may wonder whether this progression is the best image for Christian worship.

Much of the new music for congregational singing that spawned so-called contemporary worship accommodates well the *outer courts—inner courts—Holy of Holies* structure. Heavily influenced by Pentecostal piety, these songs usually express a deep personal spirituality, whether the worship action is praise, offering, or personal petitions. With the help of soft rock styles, worshipers move in a reassuring flow of sound. Many people, younger and older, like the emotional intensity these songs can evoke. The majority are written with the idea that they will not last; their usefulness for worship is fleeting. The Holy Spirit is always inspiring the creation of new songs to replace the ones that are discarded when they have served their purpose.

Congregations that follow liturgies set out by their denominations benefit from a theologically balanced worship pattern. Such liturgies draw together a range of worship actions found repeatedly in the Bible. The particular arrangement of the actions favored by a denomination is documented by historical sources but not by scripture. A lectionary provides the basic guide for biblical texts that shape preaching or seasonal thematic focus. The congregation hears scripture interpreting scripture through the use of Old Testament, Gospel, and Epistle readings. The big themes of salvation history dominate these worship patterns. Although no two congregations do the liturgy in exactly the same way, the basic formative pattern remains constant.

In contrast to the contemporary worship music that uses rock idioms, other contemporary hymns and the tunes created for them borrow from the long tradition of strong, durable melodies with secure downbeats. Tuneful melodies with regular rhythms have helped congregations sing for generations. Some new tunes use the old practice of tone painting, employing melody and harmonies to interpret the words the congregation sings. These songs tend to evoke thought first, and then feeling. The ones that endure gain their vitality as the congregation sings them over time. These songs accommodate themselves easily to the liturgical structure, and they are often written expressly for that type of worship.

Clearly, these two approaches to contemporary music for congregational singing do not always mesh well each other. Each of these musical styles suggests a particular worship pattern (so-called contemporary, traditional, or liturgical). Hymnody in a traditional style may not easily fit into a contemporary worship service. New worship music in a rock idiom can seem out of place in a traditional service.

Many congregations include people who appreciate both types of music. A mismatch between music style and worship pattern has caused stress and strain in many congregations. Finding a pattern of worship that can accommodate both styles poses creative challenges for a congregation and its leaders. Negotiating a way through them requires insight, skill, care, and respect for the contributions of a wide range of worship patterns and musical styles.

In congregations led by a single pastor or staff of pastors, decisions about what the congregation will sing are often made by these leaders. They may elect to sing music of a wide variety of types, using many different instruments, or they may make a commitment to use only contemporary worship music (of one kind or another) or only traditional hymns. These leaders set the congregation's musical course and make whatever changes are necessary to adapt its current practices to it. In newly formed congregations, leaders often have more freedom to define a musical style for the worshipping group, because there are no shared traditions that have defined another character or identity.

In other congregations, a decision by the pastor would not carry the day. Perhaps the pastor or pastoral staff is not sufficiently trained in music to make an informed decision about what the congregation should sing. Perhaps the pastor would like to use a style that no one in the congregation appreciates, or one that people cannot sing because it is too difficult or too unfamiliar. Perhaps the congregation is deeply divided on questions of musical style, and any decision about what the congregation should sing would result in conflict. Perhaps two services, each with a distinct musical style, might seem to offer a solution. But this solution will prove unworkable unless the congregation has enough musicians to cover the needs of both services.

Conflict around such emotionally charged issues is extremely difficult to negotiate. Pastors and congregational leaders must be willing to use our authority to help the congregation refocus on its life as a body and seek deeper unity. When conflict about musical styles threatened, leaders in one congregation held a series of meetings to which people across the age spectrum brought their favorite hymn or worship song. Each person talked about why the song was important to him or her. The group sang each song that was presented or listened to a recording of it. The conversation generated a deep respect for how many kinds of music open the way of worship. The process instilled appreciation and care for the experience and insights of other brothers and sisters in the congregation. Worship leaders and musicians were no longer immobilized by tensions surrounding what the congregation should sing, and they began working with greater confidence and creativity.

In recent decades, the issue of musical styles for congregational singing has been perhaps the most explosive political issue worship leaders and preachers have encountered. This discussion demonstrates how scripture has been used to form and validate positions. These are political choices that express deeply held understandings about scriptural authority and the place of tradition in shaping congregational practice.

Dominant spiritualities

Many worship disputes center around tensions among dominant spiritualities found in North American Protestantism. Chapter two introduced the broad categories of mindful and heartfelt spirituality. Here we will expand the description of these spiritualities, and add two more types.

Corinne Ware identifies four spiritual types: head spirituality, heart spirituality, mystic spirituality, and kingdom spirituality.[4] The table below draws on her work, to outline characteristics of each spiritual type.

Head spirituality
Thinking spirituality
Values what can be seen and touched
Imaginative
Choices based on activity
Values congregational gathering
Seeks theological renewal
Primary goal to fulfill vocation
Creates works of theological reflection
Values education and publications

Heart spirituality
Feeling spirituality
Values the concrete, real-life stuff
Enjoys freedom of expression

Energy, warmth are valued
Holiness of life driving purpose
Seeks transformation, conversion
Primary goal to witness, emphasis on evangelism
Enjoys testimonials
Values shared personal experience

Mystical spirituality
Active visionary
Witness to God's reign here and now
Primary goal is transformation of society
Obedience to God is driving purpose
Focused outward, crusading
Sacrifices personal life for hope in God's fulfilled kingdom

Kingdom spirituality
Knowing spirituality
Hearing from God more important than speaking
Primary goal is union with the Holy
Focused on inner world
Mystery of God compels them—God is unnamable I AM
    WHO I AM
Seeks contemplation/introspection
Values simplicity

Head and kingdom spiritualities share a strong rational foundation. Heart and mystic spiritualities have in common a strong emotional foundation. Head and heart spiritualities are both oriented toward the concrete realities of God's presence. Those who embrace kingdom and mystical spiritualities give themselves to what they cannot yet see, touch, taste, or smell; they trust the mystery of God as much as what God has revealed.

Ware has discovered that most North American Christians are drawn to head and heart spiritualities. A cursory look at the more detailed descriptions of these spiritual types readily shows why people who adopt head spirituality might clash with those of heart spirituality. What counts as authentic religious experience for each is quite different. The head spirituality values words and metaphors, images and ideas that stimulate thinking, while the heart spirituality values words, sounds, and drama that stir the emotions. The differences between these two spiritual types account for much of the tension between people who desire traditional hymns (proponents of head spirituality), and those who want scripture songs, choruses, and praise songs (proponents of heart spirituality).

People whose bent is toward kingdom or mystical spiritualities have their own convictions about what constitutes authentic religious experience, but these folks have little impact on worship-related conflict, because most Protestant congregations do not include many of their persuasions. People of a mystical spirituality frequently attend prayer retreats or participate in small groups with likeminded contemplative seekers. Many find that the repetitive music of the Taizé community aids their prayer. Those with a kingdom spirituality are usually active in their local community, seeing social ministry as their primary form of worship. Their presence in our congregations often takes the form of prophetic witness. They appreciate any music that inspires them and their congregations to continue working for the kingdom of God.

Most of the recent worship controversies have demonstrated a profound failure on the part of congregations to live as the body of Christ comprised of members who need each other. Christians within the same congregation have demonstrated amazing antagonism. Of course, the controversies have been especially intense around issues of music for congregational singing, but biblical interpretation and inclusive language issues have also been rancorous.

Ultimately, worship leaders, preachers, and church elders bear responsibility for negotiating the political implications of leadership, biblical interpretation, and dominant spiritualities in the congregation. This essential ministry is rarely taken seriously enough. Spiritual discernment lies at the heart of negotiating on behalf of the congregation—the kind of discernment that steps back from the relentless hurly-burly of the Sunday schedule to notice how God's Spirit is or is not moving in the congregation.

When controversies arise around worship practices, preachers, worship planners, and other leaders need to make several commitments with one another and with the congregation, as they discern what changes, if any, are necessary.

Commitment 1: As preachers, worship leaders, and planners, we commit ourselves to treat the congregation as a body united in Christ. It is not united by a particular musical style, worship order, or biblical interpretation. The congregation is more than a collection of individuals. It has a larger purpose in God's mission in the world. We who serve as leaders of the congregation's worship need to keep our own stylistic preferences in check as we attempt to discern what is best for the entire body.

Commitment 2: We commit ourselves to value all the spiritual types present in the congregation. Life would be simpler if we all had the same kind of spirituality. But the fact is, head people desperately need heart people to balance their intellectualism. Heart people need kingdom people to draw them out of the cocoon of good feeling. Mystics need head people to help them articulate what they know but cannot find words for. People who prefer a more literal approach to biblical interpretation need the imagination of people who are drawn to metaphor and analogy. Those who love to spin out varieties of meaning in a scripture text need the gifts of the literal minded to keep them focused on down-to-earth readings of the text. In short, all members of the congregation need one another to keep distortions in check. When discerning future directions for congregational worship, all the spiritual gifts of the congregation must be valued. The challenge is to negotiate the styles preferred by these various spiritual types in ways that authentically deepen the congregation's responsiveness to God. The leadership group must continually remind the congregation that no worship style is preeminent; no single style is biblically mandated.

Commitment 3: We as preachers, worship leaders, and planners commit ourselves to keep learning about the people in the congregation. We will return often to the questions suggested in chapter two. And we will remember that if the face of the congregation is changing in discernible ways, changes in worship practices are probably warranted.

Commitment 4: We commit ourselves to deal with conflict or political issues using a larger frame of reference than personal preferences. The congregation as a sign of God's reign cannot afford to get bent out of shape by personal conflicts fueled by impatience or arrogance. Helpful questions for setting a larger frame around conflict will focus on the purpose of worship, the congregation's part in God's mission in the world, the well-being of the congregation, and how the Spirit of God is working in the body.

Commitment 5: We commit ourselves to bring in those who teach about worship or preaching, consultants, mediators, or judicatory officials, if tensions grow to such an intensity that people in the congregation can no longer work together or speak to one another in love.

As preachers, worship leaders, and planners, we must regularly go public with these commitments, so the congregation can trust that we are caring for the body as whole. Particular individuals may need to be reminded that their opinions and preferences do not carry more weight than those of other members. The discernment process may move more slowly than some people would wish. Overall, everyone providing oversight and leadership for the congregation's worship should speak openly about the political aspects of the way decisions are made that shape practice.

The politics of planning and leading in collaboration

Within the worship leadership group, the political process of negotiating is constant and should happen within the context of the leadership group rather than in a public forum or with those outside the group. Many congregations include planners, preachers, worship leaders, musicians, and other artists in the planning and leading process. Naturally, more opinions, values, and commitments are at play.

Everyone engaged in leading worship must work toward developing common understandings of the biblical and theological purposes of worship and of the people who make up the congregation. Each leader must be willing to support and nurture these understandings. Serving as a worship leader does not give one license to push a particular agenda, draw attention to one's pet concerns, or arbitrarily make changes. Leaders and planners must consent to work as a team for the sake of the congregation.

Frequently people are asked to serve in worship leadership because of gifts and skills in a particular field, such as public speaking, music, visual imagination, or spiritual counsel. But these people may not be knowledgeable about the purposes of corporate worship. They will need education and a commitment to develop skills for planning worship.

All group members who are given authority to plan worship must be ready to interpret to the congregation how choices for services are made and to explain those choices to those who offer criticism, as inevitably happens. Regardless of leaders' personal preferences and agreements or disagreements with specific decisions, they represent the leadership group to the congregation. They must faithfully and accurately report criticism and praise from congregational members back to the leadership group.[5]

As worship planners and leaders, we need to develop agreements for how we will work together. Among other things, we will agree to the following:

Commitments for worship planners
- Faithfully attend meetings
- Prepare for meetings, doing advanced reading, research, brainstorming, or communication with other people as needed
- Demonstrate willingness to follow the identified leader of the meetings
- Complete assigned tasks
- Speak our opinions and perspectives openly and appropriately
- Listen respectfully with openness to all opinions
- Participate responsibly in discernment about choices before the group
- Support reasonable worship choices that may challenge personal tastes or preferences
- Support the work of all members of the leadership group
- Pray regularly for the Holy Spirit's empowerment, for those who lead specific services, for the congregation's spiritual growth and its wholehearted worship

Often these commitments are taken for granted but not explicitly affirmed. But we work together more effectively when we have clarified our expectations of one another and of our way of working together.

Each leader of the group will have particular style preferences for worship. Some are committed to particular aesthetic expressions—beautiful visual environments, appropriate decorum, tasteful and well-executed music. These people find that aesthetic expressions open their minds and hearts to the glory of God. Other leaders value a particular style of worship—an upbeat and exuberantly expressive style; an intensely quiet, fervent, and contemplative one; or perhaps a blend of exuberance and contemplation. Some find most meaningful a style that is free, spontaneous, and improvisational. Others like set orders and predictable patterns. Congregations need all of these possibilities. Worship leaders understandably will lean toward the style most conducive to their own spiritual expressiveness and giftedness. But we need to recognize and value the benefits of other worship styles if we and our congregations are to grow. The congregation's growth in spiritual gifts (such as humility, love, and gratitude) is the standard for evaluating the effectiveness of our worship patterns and styles.

Timely, accurate, and direct communication aids the negotiation required of worship leaders. If the planning group is coordinated by a designated leader, this person sets an example for how information is shared, how issues will be discussed, and how assignments are carried out. Political wrangling happens in groups if communication is inconsistent, information is shared unevenly, and if the flow of information is controlled by a few people. Good communication builds trust among leaders and increases the possibility of careful discernment and appropriate decision making.

Communication between worship leaders and the congregation is vital. Information about upcoming celebrations, seasonal themes, and special preaching series helps worshipers prepare for what is to come. Leaders also teach the congregation about worship in a wide variety of ways. Inviting evaluation of the congregation's worship practices opens avenues of communication that help leaders assess their work.

Criticism is inevitable and we should generally welcome it. Asking people to communicate their concerns fully and directly invites them to be accountable for their complaints. Of course, some criticism is merely a form of nay saying. But much thoughtful criticism relates to significant issues worthy of leaders' attention.

How assigned tasks are completed causes anxiety in many groups. Some efficient and orderly people get anxious when they work with people who get things done just as the deadline falls. Others who focus their time and energy best when the need is right in front of them feel hounded by those who complete assignments a week ahead of time. Neither approach is wrong, but people operating with differing work styles often cause one another grief. Again, communication is essential, particularly in stating clearly what is needed and when it must be completed.

Leaders sometimes fail to treat their tasks with the care and attention they deserve. They wait too long to contact people, to choose scripture texts or songs, or to order the service details. When they need assistance from others, their desperate calls for help may yield no response, and their ambitious plans must be radically revised on short notice. They may proceed in Lone Ranger style to do everything themselves, often with inadequate preparation and perhaps with ill grace. Or they may lean on others to lead or help out but give them insufficient time to prepare.

None of these alternatives fosters good relationships or breeds goodwill. Sometimes people are willing to help in a pinch, but rarely will they say yes more than a time or two. The task of worship planners is to establish conditions under which leaders of a service can feel mentally, spiritually, and emotionally prepared to move freely with the congregation through the worship time. This work is thwarted by poor, last-minute planning.

Failure to follow through on tasks contributes to failure in the most essential aspect of shared leadership—trust. As planners, worship leaders, preachers, and musicians, we must trust all who are providing leadership during the service. We must trust that everyone understands their purpose as a leader: to help the congregation connect with God through the Spirit's gracious help. We trust that all the leaders know the basic service outline and will step into leadership at the appropriate time with appropriate energy and grace. We trust that other leaders are opening themselves to God's Spirit for the congregation's sake and not to grab attention or glory. We trust that our leadership partners will communicate respect for our ministry, as we extend appreciation to them. The work of the worship planning group serves the trust, support, and freedom of all worship leaders.

The politics of worship are never ending. But these negotiations need not sour our stomachs or disrupt our digestion. The negotiations of worship are often challenging because they can stir our deepest passions. They can be time consuming, because the careful listening of discernment cannot be short-circuited. And they can be deeply rewarding, when the congregation is united to praise, pray, and hear God's Word. Rather than run from the negotiations and the exercise of power and authority that worship requires, we need to embrace these dimensions as a vital part of the Spirit's work.

14

CARING FOR THE COOKS AND THE KITCHEN

And all ate and were filled; and they took up what was left over of the broken pieces, twelve baskets full. (Matt 14:20)

Years ago, I lived with two friends who are good cooks. I envied their skill in creating tasty meals and their knack for transforming leftovers into imaginative casseroles, sandwich fillings, and soups. Both had a flair for sensing what new ingredient in just the right amount would make a dish especially pleasing to the taste. Because of their ingenuity, we ate well *and* economically.

Cleaning up the kitchen, dealing with leftovers, replenishing the pantry, and preparing for the next meal are vital household tasks that contribute to the economy of a well-managed kitchen. Preparation for the next meal begins with cleaning up the last one. Nothing saps inspiration for cooking more than dirty dishes cluttering the countertops, burners sticky with what boiled over last night, leftovers moldering in the far reaches of the refrigerator, and a cupboard depleted of basic ingredients.

Like cooks whose work is enhanced by their care for the kitchen, worship leaders and planners must attend to the many tasks that follow the end of a worship service. Disciplined follow-through aids leaders in moving on to the next round of preparations. This chapter explores the activities of preachers, worship planners, and leaders after a service has ended and the preparation for future services begins.

Cleaning up
Effective preachers, worship leaders, and church musicians expend vast amounts of energy in preparing and leading worship. The afterglow and emotional release of a service may carry us in the minutes and hours that follow, but fatigue eventually sets in. The need to clean

up looms before us, and the pressure of the next service slowly begin to build.

Cleaning up after worship is every bit as important as worship planning. For those who led the service, these tasks often bring a satisfying conclusion to the work of planning. Few of us want to do this work immediately after worship has ended, but some things need attention. Cleaning up well assures us a fresh start for the work of the next service.

The worship space

No space remains orderly during a congregation's worship. When the last chords have died away and the faithful have departed, chairs are askew, bulletins and papers forgotten. Songbooks and Bibles lean every which way on racks and benches; music stands are abandoned. Microphone cords snake across the floor. Screens are left down. Children's toys and crayons remain, and Cheerios crunch underfoot. Whether it is worship leaders, volunteers, or staff who restore order to the worship area, cleanup needs to happen early in the week. Then the space is ready for planned events and for unanticipated gatherings—such as funerals—which may happen on short notice. A tidy room expresses hospitality and a sense of anticipation for whatever might happen.

One Saturday two weeks after Easter, I visited with a pastor at his church building. All the lilies on the platform of the worship space and at the entrance of the building were dead. My friend said they had been dying for well over a week, but no one had taken responsibility for removing them. Not only did they communicate a general sense of neglect, but they were a visible contradiction of the new life of Easter which they had been brought into the worship space to celebrate!

No worship service is over until the cleanup is done. Delaying these tasks slows preparation for the next service. They nag at the back of our minds, diverting energy that could be better channeled toward sermon preparation, communicating with worship leaders, and rehearsing new music and scripture presentations.

Saying thank you

The worship leaders and the preacher should take responsibility to personally thank all who helped to lead the service. Musicians, scripture readers, people leading the time with children, the sound technicians—any one with a specific leadership role—deserves words of gratitude, whether or not their contributions went well. The time for critique and evaluation comes later. Leaders and preachers feel vulnerable before the congregation, whatever their level of experience. Hearing words of appreciation immediately after a service helps one feel valued and supported. One preacher asks someone—her spouse, a good friend, the worship leader—to tell her immediately after the service about something he heard in the sermon. Compliments are fine, but she especially wants to know that something she said connected with someone. Comments from a trusted person help her feel grounded.

Other worship leaders, the planning team, and pastoral staff should care for the worship leaders themselves. They also feel vulnerable, even as they extend gratitude to others. Many leaders, musicians, and preachers engage in the wise practice of gathering before worship for last-minute instructions and prayer. Rarely do they gather after worship to thank God and one another for their valuable service.

Receiving comments

Worshipers often offer comments to preachers and other leaders after a service. Beyond "nice service," "good sermon," or "I didn't like . . .," astute observations and questions from people in the congregation can help leaders know whether people understood what we intended to convey. If we are able to probe with additional questions, helpful information can emerge.

Unhelpful criticism and lukewarm affirmation should be received without defensiveness and probed further as appropriate, but worship leaders and preachers should not dwell on these comments at that moment. None of us should be obliged to confront criticism immediately after a service. We are likely to be too tired to respond well to criticism or faint praise. It's enough to make a note of the comment for future conversation and reflection. Simple comments such as "Thanks for telling me what you thought" or "I'll need to think about that" acknowledge the concern without engaging it in the moment. Worshipers may need to learn how and when to give counsel about something that happened during a particular service.

Regaining energy

Preaching and leading worship and music are joyous but demanding endeavors. Most people in the congregation do not realize how much physical, emotional, and mental energy these ministries require. For many leaders and preachers, especially those who are introverts, the effort required to plan a service and muster the concentration to lead it are exhausting. Leaders must take this expenditure of energy seriously and plan to rest afterward. It may not be possible to leave the building or go into hiding immediately after a service; perhaps there is a noon potluck or a Sunday school class gathering. But leaders must steward their energies to manage all the obligations of the day. This kind of cleanup often stretches into the afternoon. A congregation may extend care to preachers and worship leaders by inviting their children to spend the afternoon with friends so leaders can relax. Sunday afternoon naps and early bedtimes help restore depleted energy.

Dealing with the leftovers

Leftovers from one meal often form the base for lunches or snacks in the following days. Sermon and worship planning leftovers can be significant resources for planning future services. To make effective use of these leftovers requires creating a simple system for filing such ideas. Preachers and worship planners might organize files by scripture texts (for example, John 20:1–19 or Ps 23), by theme (for example, prayer, baptism, gratitude, or atonement), or by season or celebration (for example, Lent, Christmas, or Worldwide Communion Sunday). A system may combine categories. Whether we use electronic files or manila folders, or both, these files become the storage place for themes, ideas, and topics to be developed.

Nearly all biblical texts offer several themes or images that could be developed in a sermon. As preachers determine their sermon purpose, they must decide what in the text to focus on. Many good ideas must be set aside. These leftovers go into the folder for future sermons. Any notes from personal study of the passage or from commentary reading are filed away. Research on theological themes, doctrine, and church practices are stored for future reference. Preachers who use visual images in their sermons can keep these graphic elements on file. Any illustrations that were considered but not used are stored. The next time that biblical text, that season, or that theme comes around, the preacher need not start from scratch.

Worship planners and leaders will include unused ideas, themes, or images in their files. Notes from their scripture study; hymns, songs, and other musical resources; visual art ideas; dramatic readings, prayers, and other written materials for congregational use can all be stashed away. Cumulative files of leftover ideas are especially helpful for future worship committees or planning groups.

Record keeping

For congregations that use a printed bulletin, order of worship, or worship folder, keeping records of past worship services is a wise practice. Worship planners and preachers can track the frequency of sermons on specific biblical texts or assess how often the congregation sings particular songs. Seeing what has been planned for worship over time is valuable. The church secretary, pastor, or worship committee chair should make sure that a copy for each service is routinely filed.

Musicians who care about nurturing congregational singing keep records of songs and hymns sung each Sunday. Some music and worship leaders write the date when a song is led on the page of the hymnal or song collection the congregation uses. Others create a small database, either electronic or paper, with song title, source, and date used. Over time, this simple record-keeping method tells musicians and worship planners what music the congregation sings regularly. If musicians are leading many songs or hymns of the same type, they might consider whether some change in the congregation's musical diet will enhance balance. Another benefit of such records is that they make regular reports to licensing agents easy to generate.

Follow-up

Midweek is a good time to look more critically at the previous Sunday's worship service. Examining what worked and what didn't work helps worship leaders understand how verbal, nonverbal, and implied communication happens for the congregation. Did the service feel coherent? Did the actions flow? Were worshipers able to anticipate what would happen next, so they could move together? Or did the service feel like one darn thing after another?

Checking in with worship planners, leaders, musicians, and preachers in the days immediately following the service provides opportunity to reflect on what communicated well, what was confusing, and what modifications should be made for future services. Any

issues that arose in the planning process, including last-minute communications, can be addressed. This kind of reflection is especially
important when a theme or an order of worship will be followed over
several weeks. If anything failed to draw people into worship because
of confused instructions, inadequate preparation, or any other short-
coming, the problem must be addressed.

A congregation's introduction to a new song may be disappoint-
ing, if not downright discouraging. After a service, musicians need to
review their approach to introducing the song. Perhaps the leaders
did not sing or play the piece in a way that demonstrated to the congregation how it should sound. Maybe the music and words were too
hard for the congregation to manage all at once; perhaps hearing a
small group sing the song would have been more successful. Perhaps
the congregation's sense of the melody needs to be more solid before
they are asked to add harmony. Or the congregation's first exposure
may proceed better if a small group or choir sings verses and the
whole body sings the refrain. Or perhaps the congregation joins in
singing the last verse. Whatever went wrong the first time should not
be repeated. Careful analysis helps musicians create a more successful plan for reintroducing the song.

Another leftover that may need attention is response to comments
made by worshipers after the service. Not everything offered to the
preacher or worship leader at the close of a service is worthy of more
attention. A designated member of the worship planning group,
preferably not a person who led the most recent service, should
receive worshipers' responses. Several days after a service, this person
can check in with people who offered comments; after this interval,
responses are more likely to be seasoned and thoughtful. A troubling
question or insightful comment deserves more conversation.
Listening to worshipers who were disturbed or distracted by something in the past service can clear the air and allow them to reenter
worship with less anxiety and frustration. And their perspectives may
yield helpful information about how people in the congregation perceived aspects of the service.

The leftover blahs

Few people relish leftovers. We generally feel more excitement
about putting the past behind us and moving on to the next new
thing. But careful attention to the leftover "to do" list frees energy for

preparing the next service and is an investment in future services. Storing good but undeveloped ideas, maintaining records of what we have done, and learning from what happened during specific services helps everyone move toward the next service with greater confidence.

This cycle of action and reflection should be an unending process for worship planners, leaders, and preachers.[1] Anyone who expects to grow in the ministry of leading worship and preaching will find that the interplay between leading worship or preaching (action) and dealing with the leftovers (reflection) is a life-giving discipline. Through this process, week to week, service to service, we develop skills for leadership.

The next two sections describe shorter and longer action-reflection cycles for evaluating the congregation's worship practices over time.

Evaluating the fare in the short term

The primary reason to evaluate worship patterns and innovations is *not* so leaders can satisfy the individual tastes of worshipers. Congregational worship gains vitality and integrity as worship leaders systematically ask what helped people worship. Responses to the questions What did you like? and What didn't you like? are of little help in critical discernment. The number of worshipers who like the same thing is painfully small. Most can say clearly what they don't like, but they often cannot say why something annoyed them.

The other reason not to pursue questions about worshipers' tastes is that worship is not grounded in our personal preferences. Few people have a preference for confessing sin. Others would not choose disquieting sermons, silence, or pastoral prayers. Still others see no good reason to include hymns or contemporary worship songs. To ask what people like in worship leads them to believe that their tastes should shape worship. To pander to personal preferences—however insistently these are impressed upon worship leaders—is a misuse of the authority given to leaders. It is best to drop the "like" questions all together.

Evaluating the service

Worship leaders and preachers must take initiative here, as in other ministries, to seek specific and focused response from the congregation. And intentionally eliciting this response may help protect worship leaders and preacher who are in recovery or clean-up modes.

After worship each Sunday, selected members of the worship-planning group may engage in informal conversation with several worshipers who reflect the congregation's diversity. One leader might chat with a teenager and an older adult. Another might choose to talk with a single and a married person, or with an old-timer in the congregation and a newcomer. The point is to survey a range of people who reflect the variety of worshipers in the congregation, in terms of age, gender, marital status, level of formal education, class, ethnicity, and other pertinent factors.

Opening questions for this conversation might include the following:

Initial questions for short-term evaluation

What in this service helped you worship God?

What hindered your worship?

What affirmations do you have for worship planners?

What suggestions for strengthening our congregation's worship would you offer?

If time and the openness of the person permit, some of the following questions might be explored for deeper reflection:

Further questions for short-term evaluation

In what ways did you sense God's Spirit moving in the congregation today?

In what ways did you experience the presence of Christ?

In what ways did you sense the majesty (glory? grandeur? awesomeness? power? love? grace? etc.) of God?

Did anything distract your worship?

When in the service did your mind wander?

What helped you refocus your attention?

Did you feel connected or in unity with other worshipers?

How would you describe the character of the congregation's unity (intense, eager, still, passionate, attentive, etc.)?

Did you experience any moment(s) when you knew you were part of something bigger than yourself?

What words describe what you take away from the service? (inspiration, boredom, motivation, peacefulness, assurance, blessing, anger, trust, doubt, anxiety, empowerment, etc.)

Did you sense that the Lord was present in this place?

These questions move the conversation toward the scope of the worshipers' experiences rather than focusing on irritants and trivialities. They draw worshipers back into their experiences, to feel again and reflect on the service as a whole.

Worship leaders who seek this type of response should probe with follow-up questions to help people speak as clearly and as forthrightly as possible about their experience of worship. Answers to these questions often reveal deeply held values and assumptions about worship that leaders and planners benefit from knowing. Then leaders can address inaccurate assumptions and articulate their intentions and approach. One gratifying result of eliciting this kind of response is that it often yields far more positive feedback than negative—a wonderfully affirming outcome for planners and leaders!

On occasion, someone questions me about the way I led a particular song. Perhaps he found the tempo too fast. In my best moments, I ask how it was troublesome. If I observe an opening to explain my decision, he has an opportunity to consider my approach. He may see something in the words or music he had not noticed before, and I have a chance to learn something about another person's way of appropriating the song. Rarely does the conversation change anyone's mind, but it may expand our understanding of the way the piece can function in worship. In the future, if I choose the same tempo, I do so respectfully and with an awareness that some worshipers will be stretched by it.

The comments gathered in these informal conversations are reported to the worship planning group. Along with the evaluations provided by individual leaders, they provide a good foundation for improving what we plan for worship. Over time, these conversations build the congregation's trust in and respect for leaders by including more voices in the collaborative planning process.

Evaluating preaching and worship leadership

Periodic evaluations, lasting three to five weeks, can greatly improve a preacher's sermon preparation and delivery. Such evaluations are most effective when preachers themselves initiate the process. A preacher selects a listening group of four to seven worshipers—of varying ages, both genders, and a range of life experiences—to listen for specific things in the sermon structure and content as well as to observe aspects of the sermon delivery. She identifies several questions that focus on the issues she wishes to learn about and gives these to her small group. For example, she might ask four or five of the following questions.

Sermon evaluation questions

What was the main theme of this week's sermon?
What were the sermon's main points?
Did the presentation of the points make sense to you?
Did the illustrations or stories I used serve the sermon's main points?
What would you say was the purpose of this sermon?
Did this sermon connect with your life? If so, how?
Was there anything about the sermon that distracted you?
Did I speak clearly enough for you to understand what I was saying?
Did my gestures help or hinder the sermon's delivery?
Did the outline of my main points or the images I chose to project during the sermon help you understand what I was saying?
What can you affirm?
What suggestions do you have for improving the sermon or my delivery?

The preacher might ask her small listening group to write responses to her questions after each sermon. Or she might use her questions in an interview with individual members of the group. Alternatively she could meet with the group after each sermon to discuss their responses. Ideally her group will meet together at least once during the evaluation period to discuss their reactions in depth. When the listeners have expressed contradictory responses, a group discussion often helps clarify the real issues.

This kind of short-term evaluation can move preachers toward greater competence and confidence in preaching. Preachers who feel uninspired or who often receive critical feedback should consider using short-term evaluations to refocus their preaching ministry. When preachers are experimenting with something new—for example, using PowerPoint outlines or projecting images during their sermons—several weeks of evaluation by a listening group are valuable for assessing whether the purposes that led to instituting the change are being achieved. Short-term evaluations serve an educational purpose for the group of evaluators as well, by sharpening their listening skills.

Responses to focused questions provided by a group of careful observers will also help worship leaders and musicians improve their ministry skills. Comments on how leaders are communicating with the congregation can guide them in determining which leadership skills to develop next.

Without question, the Holy Spirit works to draw the congregation into the worship of God. In a basic sense, the Spirit's movement is independent of worship leaders and their plans. But the Spirit moves through leaders to give human form to its guidance. Worship leaders can get in the way of the Spirit's work by talking too much and by giving confusing instructions. Discovering how communication between leaders and worshipers is working establishes one safeguard in aiding the movement of the Spirit.

Evaluation in the long term

Another type of worship evaluation occurs over a longer period of time—weeks, months, and even years. This longer view is concerned with how worship forms the congregation as a body responding to God. Because worship is an activity involving the entire congregation—young children through elder sages—the patterns and practices employed shape its character and the discipleship of its members. Worship leaders and preachers, in consultation with other members of the pastoral staff and congregational leaders, should routinely—at least once a year—review the health of the congregation and its worship. Here again, leaders seek out and welcome responses from worshipers across the congregational age and social/cultural spectrum.

Some congregations have initiated a yearly worship forum. This public meeting, on Sunday afternoon or another suitable time in the congregational schedule, is hosted by the worship planning group to discuss worship issues. Everyone in the congregation is invited to attend.

In preparation for the conversation, the committee may compile a handout that briefly lists the previous year's services, by theme or central text, for example—whatever will help people remember individual services and seasonal emphases. This tool can contribute significantly to making the conversation more substantive. People can identify with greater specificity what they had found meaningful. These summary sheets are also helpful records for getting a big picture of the congregation's worship.

When the group gathers, the discussion leader opens the meeting with a brief worship period. A member of the worship committee reviews the congregation's vision for worship and its mandate and goals. The discussion focuses on questions such as the following.

> **Questions for long-term evaluation by the congregation**
> What helps you worship God on Sunday mornings?
> What hinders your worship? What obstacles or barriers do you encounter in our worship?
> What affirmations or suggestions for strengthening worship can you offer the planning group? What are we doing well? Where are our opportunities for improvement?
> In whom do you see gifts for worship leadership that could be called forth and developed?
> What response can you offer to our yearly goals?
> Are we listening well to the congregation?

The discussion leader makes sure that each voice is heard. Members of the planning group respond to the discussion with information or clarifying comments. To the best of their abilities, they try not to be defensive about their work. Instead they listen for what is constructive in the criticism and discard the chaff. Notes from this discussion inform the planning group's future work. The discussion may also open broader issues that require further conversation among other congregational leaders or in other congregational committees.

Once every year or two, pastors, worship planners, and congregational leaders need time to review and evaluate the congregation's worship life. Many pastoral teams and worship planning groups have yearly worship retreats to plan for the coming year. But this planning needs to be rooted in a discerning evaluation of what has happened in the recent past and how the congregation is growing in faith formation and spiritual maturity through its worship.

Questions for a long-term evaluation, which focuses on the inner dynamics of the congregation's life within God's story, may include the following.

Questions for long-term evaluation by leaders

Is the congregation hearing and living the breadth of the biblical story through preaching and worship? What stories are receiving undue attention? What biblical texts and stories are being neglected?

Is the congregation developing a shared biblical and congregational memory, common theological understandings, and expressions of faith that are wise and just?

Is the congregation growing in spiritual maturity? What is the evidence of this growth: Greater outreach? Deeper prayer life? Greater honesty in personal confession? More graciousness? Deeper gratitude? Wiser discernment of congregational issues? Freedom in witnessing? Deeper personal commitment?

Are the rituals of worship (baptism, communion, anointing, etc.) shaping congregational attitudes and defining Christian character?

Are spiritual gifts emerging in the congregation? Are they being used to build up the congregation? Are they helping members develop in faithful use of their gifts?

Is the congregation calling out new worship leaders, including musicians and preachers?

Is the congregation growing in its capacity for discernment? Stillness? Silence? Gratitude? Conversion?

Is there a deepening sense of unity rooted in graciousness, love, compassion, and accountability, and not limited to doctrine or articles of faith?

Are the fruits of the Spirit—love, joy, peace, patience, kindness, generosity, faithfulness, gentleness, and self-control (Gal 5:22-23) —increasingly evident in the lives of worshipers and in their work in the world?

Are worshipers growing in their capacities to follow Jesus, to trust his saving work in their lives, and to witness to his reign on earth?

These questions are not easy to ask, and they are rarely easy to answer. Yet if God's presence in the temple changed Isaiah, and Jesus's presence transformed those who met and followed him, then worship leaders should expect to see evidence of transformation in the lives of worshipers as a result of their encounter with the living God in worship.

In many cases, preachers address these questions in their sermons over time, and their teachings and exhortations focus the ideals to which these questions point. Careful attention to using a balanced range of scripture texts for sermons is essential. Preaching primarily from Paul, or Revelation, or the Gospels, or the Pentateuch will not adequately ground worshipers in the breadth and richness of the biblical story. Using a lectionary does not ensure complete coverage of essential biblical texts. Pastoral teams and worship planners must still do the work of analyzing what texts are absent from the established cycle of readings.[2]

The pattern of worship actions also shapes attitudes that deepen the congregation's response to God. A congregation with a well-ordered and theologically balanced worship pattern identified two places for extended pastoral prayers. The first, early in the service, routinely offered petitions for the worship gathering and moved into praise and thanksgiving for God's saving blessings. The second, near the end of the service, interceded for congregational members who were ill, recovering, or grieving the loss of loved ones. As things were structured, the congregation offered no prayers of intercession for the world's people, for those suffering as a result of violence or natural disaster, or for political leaders. The omission of such prayer was painfully obvious the Sunday after a second hurricane devastated the Florida coast, rebels took schoolchildren and teachers hostage in Russia, and violence in the Iraq war escalated again. Many in the congregation ached to speak this great sadness to God, but the usual places for pastoral prayer were not appropriate. Some members brought this omission to the attention of a member of the pastoral team immediately after the service, and by the next week, leaders had instituted an emotionally and theologically sound place for intercessory prayers.

Not to pray for the local community, for the world, for other Christians, and for elected leaders is a problem. But this omission was the more ironic because this congregation was giving increased attention to community outreach. Worshipers were working with people who perform public service; who administer government programs; who face unemployment, ill health, homelessness, or unrelenting violence. Members of the congregation participated in Christian Peacemaker Teams[3] and went on study tours to Central and South America. But praying for the people they ministered to and learned with was not a consistent part of their public worship.

When some Roman Catholic congregations in Latin American rediscovered the power of the Christian community gathered for Eucharist, they began to notice the contradictions between their Eucharistic practice, their theology, and their daily life. The poor and the wealthy shared the same blessed bread and cup from the same table. The presence of the whole community brought oppressed and oppressors face-to-face as members of Christ's body. The community of faith also became an expression of Christ's sacramental love. The Eucharist was no longer a private transaction between Christ and the individual believer. Slowly the way toward social and economic justice began to open.

Beliefs and values espoused by the congregation may routinely be contradicted by specific actions of worship. Without doubt, it is difficult to achieve complete consistency between the words of our worship and the actions we practice. But when the gap between what we proclaim and what we practice remains wide, then the rituals of our worship lie.[4] The damage caused by the lies may seem negligible at first glance, but the distortions go deep. It may take years to alter the beliefs and values that bad practice has instilled.

In neither example above did anyone take offense at how the services were actually performed; the aesthetic experience of worship was not disturbed. The problem lay in the theological contradictions, in the rift between worship and practice. Evaluation of worship practices over time, in light of the congregation's life of faith, is an exceedingly important discipline for worship leaders and preachers. Questions and observations that probe beneath the surface of our preferences are the ones that matter. This kind of worship evaluation moves congregations from milk to meat.

Stocking the pantry

Worship leaders and preachers need to collaborate with people beyond their own congregation who are involved with worship planning. Left to our own small pool of knowledge and resources, we will deplete our fund of ideas. We will tend to get stuck in the same patterns, when we could be drawing on the creativity of other Christians who provide tangible evidence of the inexhaustible riches of God. By garnering new ideas about using the arts and various worship patterns, information about the church's worship, and deeper understandings of God's unfolding story of redemption, preachers and leaders build a storehouse of resources which they can adapt for appropriate use in their congregation.

Worship-planning groups should have available for consultation and inspiration a variety of resources, perhaps gathered in the congregation's library or in another readily accessible spot. A good basic collection would include the following:

Two reliable translations of the Bible for comparing specific texts
>Sometimes the wording of one translation can be adapted more easily for prayers or other spoken parts of worship. An inclusive language version can expand our sensitivities to gender language concerns.

A Bible paraphrase
>This resource can often stir the imagination with fresh images or turns of phrase. However, a paraphrase should be used for scripture reading in worship only rarely; reading from a reliable translation should be the norm.

A good Bible commentary
>This resource may be a one-volume general overview of each book of the Bible, with a brief analysis of individual texts, or it may be a multivolume series that treats each book of the Bible in depth.

Several books of sample worship resources
>Many good collections of prayers, calls to worship, and blessings are published by denominations and independent publishers. These collections stimulate our imagination for using words creatively and extending the congregation's horizons.

Aids in creating worship materials
>Several fine books are available that foster our abilities to craft prayers and other spoken pieces for worship. *Let the Whole Church Say Amen! A Guide for Those Who Pray in Public*, by Laurence Hull Stookey (Nashville, TN: Abingdon Press, 2001); *Finding Words for Worship: A Guide for Leaders*, by Ruth Duck (Louisville: Westminster John Knox Press, 1995); and *Worship in the Shape of Scripture*, by F. Russell Mitman (Cleveland: Pilgrim Press, 2001), provide excellent guidance for learning the art of writing for congregational worship. Whether we write congregational prayers and responses or speak them extemporaneously, these resources train our minds and hearts to work with structure and evocative words for better communication.

Several copies of the current hymnal or song collection used by the congregation
>Worship planning groups must be familiar with the variety of hymns and songs available for the congregation to sing. Ideally each member of the planning group will own a copy of the song collection regularly used by the congregation, but this may not be

possible. Making multiple copies available for planning may give
members incentive to get to know the contents of the collection(s).
Having on hand copies of hymnals or songbooks the congregation
has used in the past is also a good idea; sometimes a congregational favorite is not found in the hymnal currently in use.

Several books or collections of visual art
Because of increased interest in the visual aspects of faith, many
publishers are producing collections of religious art. Images of
Jesus throughout the ages is a popular theme. The biblical works
of Rembrandt are an excellent resource. Many of Van Gogh's
paintings play with biblical and theological ideas. Such collections
can enrich the ways worship planners "see" biblical stories and
themes. Whether the images are ever used in Sunday worship is
secondary to the value for planners of looking together at a visual interpretation of a religious theme.

The number of worship resources available now is almost endless. The above list may be seen as a minimum requirement, a starting place for worship planners. A variety of Internet sites, which
cover the gamut of expressive worship styles, also expand the
resources available to preachers and worship planners. On-line commentaries help preachers with scripture studies for sermon preparation. Sermons published on-line stimulate the preacher's imagination;
banks of illustrations help out in a pinch. Books and periodicals provide practical suggestions for enlivening worship. Seminars and
workshops give leaders resources for and experience with particular
worship styles.[3] (See Appendix 8 for suggested resources.)

How do worship leaders and preachers use these resources effectively and judiciously? Too often we turn to such resources and use
them willy-nilly, to save us from the hard work of thinking, imaging,
listening, writing, and planning in behalf of the congregation. Few
ideas pulled from the Internet, books, periodicals, and seminars
should be imported directly into the worship of a particular congregation without modification. Adaptations are often necessary to
make a resource fitting for our context.

Before getting deeply invested in any particular resource, leaders
and preachers must do some detective work. The following questions
guide our investigation.

Questions for evaluating worship resources

Who produced the resource: A denominational office? A publishing enterprise? A well-informed individual? A knowledgeable group sharing its experience?

Are the people who produced the resource credible? Are they aware of the Christian church's worship practices? Is their counsel wise? Are their suggestions sound, in terms of human and religious experience? What is their polity? What type of leadership do they value? What are the theological and biblical commitments or beliefs presented in the source? Orthodox? Heterodox? Roman Catholic? Protestant?

Where is this resource on the theological spectrum: Fundamentalist? Pentecostal/Charismatic? Evangelical? Conservative? Mainline? Liberal? Eclectic? Beyond the pale?

Is the resource best used in congregations with fixed liturgies and worship patterns or in congregations with flexible worship patterns?

Anyone can find interesting sermon bits or clever turns of phrase for prayers by surfing the Internet or buying a worship resource book. But planning worship is more than stringing together sound bytes. Knowing where words and ideas for worship come from is a significant step toward ensuring integrity in our worship practices. Publishing a book or a web page does not make a source credible or infallible. Everything related to worship needs to be scrutinized with a hint of suspicion.

Evaluating specific resources also requires critical awareness. Another set of questions comes into play as we assess a reading, song, drama, illustration, or prayer.

No matter how inspiring a song from the Internet sounds, if it does not fit seamlessly into the flow of worship, it is a clanging cymbal. If a terrific sermon illustration does not match the spirit of the message, it is a sounding gong. If the words of a reading or drama are too formal or filled with too much slang for the congregation's shared speech, they are silly caricatures. Things borrowed from external sources must be evaluated and often adapted to fit the shared experience of the congregation and the smooth flow of communication in worship.

Questions for evaluating a reading, song, drama, etc.

How does this resource connect with the scripture text for the day?

What worship action does it accomplish?

Where would it fit best in the service? Why?

Does the resource speak to the spiritual and social needs of the congregation and its individual members?

Is it consistent with the shared experience of the congregation? Does it extend that shared experience in ways that are respectful and hospitable?

Can the resource be adapted so that the words, gestures, stories, and rhythms are authentic for the congregation?

Does the resource build a sense of coherence within the service? Does it strengthen biblical, theological, spiritual, or aesthetic coherence?

If worship leaders or preachers use ideas, images, sermons, or material created by other people, they should acknowledge their sources publicly. Credit can be given in the worship bulletin or folder or on projected slides. An announcement about the original author, preacher, or artist can be made in the service prior to using the resource. Leaders or preachers who claim the work of others as their own deceive their congregations and damage their personal integrity.

Blessed is the congregation with worship leaders and preachers who are able to write, craft, and compose fresh material. Original prayers, songs, and readings will extend and enrich the congregation's expressiveness in ways that are compatible with their shared experience. These leaders will know from experience what communicates deeply to the congregation and what gently pushes the group to expand its horizons. Creative leaders consult trusted resources. They read widely—in newspapers, magazines, novels, poetry. They watch challenging television programs and films. In the quietness of their thoughtful listening, the Holy Spirit forges the words, songs, and gestures needed for leading worship. Published worship resources stoke their imaginative fires. Ultimately, the best resources arise out of the life of the congregation, not from the Internet or the latest seminar. Understandably, less experienced worship leaders and preachers rely more heavily on the words and ideas of others. And as they listen deeply to the congregation's life and to the community that surrounds them, they begin to sense what fits and what needs to nudge at the edges of comfort. As their experience grows, their direct dependence on other resources will diminish, but it will never disappear.

Attending worship conferences and retreats gives preachers and worship leaders face-to-face contact with other people who also carry responsibility for worship oversight and planning. In these wonderful environments, we learn more about what is happening in worship in other parts of the church, see how new worship practices are introduced, and discuss common problems. Sharing experiences and wrestling with new possibilities for expressing the primary worship actions can be invigorating. In large part, worship conferences nourish simply because we are able to participate in services that others have planned and carry primary responsibility for leading. Many times, we return to our congregations with new energy, with a renewed sense of purpose, and with souls restored. Slowly we begin the process of translating and adapting our new ideas to the worship of our congregation.

Preachers benefit from periodic refresher courses in preaching, no matter how many sermons we have delivered in our years of ministry. We may have settled into ruts or simply have lost our zest for preaching. Preaching seminars provide useful information that we can readily apply. And having sermons and delivery evaluated by a preaching professional outside our congregations can help us isolate communication problems. Good coaching on specific preaching issues encourages us to improve our patterns of communication and to curtail our bad preaching or preparation habits.

Congregations should ask their preachers and worship planners to attend conferences or retreats focused on worship and should provide financial support for attendance. Doing so is an excellent way to show appreciation for the demanding work that worship leadership entails, and leaders will also bring back ideas and information that will deepen the congregation's expressiveness in worship. Too often, congregations take their worship leaders and preachers for granted. Making attendance at worship conferences possible demonstrates the congregation's commitment to expanding the skills of members who have gifts in preaching and leading worship. Such recognition shows special care for the people who plan, lead, and clean up after the congregation's worship week after week after week.

Caring for the cooks

The relentless weekly cycle of Sunday worship—complicated by weekday services, funerals, weddings, and other impromptu devotional needs—can exhaust the most experienced ministers. Who cares for them? We usually have to care for ourselves and for one another.

At a basic physical level, leaders and preachers need to eat properly and get enough sleep, especially the day before we lead worship. Regular exercise raises heart rates, strengthens breathing, and builds endurance. Physical activities increase our capacity to focus and concentrate. We should do our part to minimize stress in relationships with other worship leaders, family members, friends, and co-workers. No worship leader or preacher who is sleep deprived, fighting low blood sugar, or stressed about personal relationships can be fully present to the congregation. The night before Sunday services, worship leaders and preachers do best to spend evenings quietly at home or with restful friends. Seeing violent films, overeating, or dancing into the wee hours increases distractibility and decreases our ability to be attentive to the ministry at hand.

Many people's bodies react to the demands of worship leadership or preaching. Some people sweat profusely or develop a dry mouth. They need to be sure that water is available before and after the service. Nausea or a fluttery stomach affects some leaders. They should be careful about what they eat the day before and determine how much to eat prior to preaching or singing. Worship leaders and preachers must care for their bodies' reactions discreetly, for sure, but lovingly. New leaders and preachers may panic when nervous reactions show up. They may see sweating, cottonmouth, or diarrhea as signs that they are not really cut out for leadership. Candid conversations about how bodies respond to stress can alleviate many misplaced fears.[5]

Most worship teams meet just before the service for prayer. Often the time is hurried and perfunctory, because there are many demands on our attention. This exercise is probably one of our most underutilized resources. To sense the emotional, spiritual, and physical bond that unites us takes more time than we usually set aside. Singing, praying, breathing, and listening together begins the process of sensing the Spirit's presence drawing us and eventually the congregation together. Ideally someone with no responsibility for the service itself should lead this time of preparation, so those responsible for leading worship today can receive the ministry of another trusted person.

Worship leaders and preachers hold clearly in mind the worship order of that particular day. They know the agreed-on direction of the service, but they will gracefully adapt elements as circumstances require. Leaders who take care of themselves and one another let go of their expectations about how things should go and are present to what is happening before their eyes and ears. More importantly, they easily let go of mistakes they make in leading; they do not dwell on the errors of others either. They strive to enjoy the surprises of life each day and especially take pleasure in those that arise serendipitously in worship, seeing them as manifestations of the presence of the Spirit who makes all things new. They live in wonder and cultivate gratitude.

A group to support worship leaders and preachers builds solidarity in this central ministry of the congregation. Affirming demonstrations of strong leadership, validating growth in leadership skills, and examining contributions to specific services are primary forms of pastoral care and spiritual discipline for worship leaders and preachers. These disciplines say, "What you do is important—we value your gifts and want to help you develop your skills." Nurturing leaders instills a sense of service and discipleship.

Evaluating, supporting, and caring for one another builds friendship among leaders. Within this circle, trust and respect flourish. These are primary fruits of collaboration. Friends can speak truth to each other, however delicate or difficult that process may be, and they encourage each other's growth. They rejoice in each other's gifts without fear of diminishing their own. They share ideas freely and thank each other often. Worshipers can easily tell whether the worship leaders and preachers care for one another. They also know when mistrust infects relationships. This circle of friends is not a closed or cliquish group, but one that seeks to expand and include others. Strong leadership displays a generosity of spirit that nurtures and cares compassionately for all who lead the congregation's worship.

Summary

Cultivating the art of worship requires commitment, discipline, collaboration, but above all a deep love for God and for the people God's Spirit has drawn into Christ's body. The responsibilities of worship leadership, including planning and preaching, can be overwhelming. No one can provide for the congregation's nourishment alone. We learn skills for communicating with God and the congregation week by week. We also refine practices of discernment over time. The disciplines of listening, looking, sensing, asking, and leading are never ending.

Listening for God
   Looking for Jesus in the midst of his body
      Listening for the deepest needs and longings of the congregation
         Sensing the Spirit of God moving through it
            Listening for the congregation's part in God's mission in the world
               Asking what would help the congregation go deeper into God's story
               Listening for the openings where that story could enter
                  Leading the congregation into deeper relationship with God
                  Listening
                    Looking, sensing, asking, leading
                    Listening

EPILOGUE

For the kingdom of God is not food and drink but righteousness and peace and joy in the Holy Spirit. (Rom 14:17)

Day in and day out, ordinary cooks put food on the table with monotonous regularity. And sooner or later, they confront the inevitable truth that not every culinary effort is appreciated. Morning after morning, breakfast must be served again. Although for a while pancakes seem like a perfect offering, the family eventually tires of them and longs for a change of menu. Some may not show up when called. Teenagers decide they'd prefer to sleep in rather than eat breakfast. Does the cook quit when discouragement sets in? Probably not—because life itself depends on eating.

As important as eating is, we often cannot remember exactly what we ate as recently as two or three meals ago. What did we eat for lunch yesterday? What did we have for breakfast last Saturday morning? What was it we served at our family gathering last Christmas? Even though we appreciate the tastes and textures of food, the specific memory of most meals fades quickly. Yet the nourishment of each meal sustains our life. Our bodies are renewed, and we are strengthened to live another day.

Our life together as communities of faith is also sustained by the nourishment of worship. Every Sunday morning, we gather for worship, to "taste and see that the LORD is good" (Ps 34:8). Sometimes we can remember a sermon or a song a month later; at other times, we struggle to recall exactly what happened the week before. But just as a nourishing meal does not have to be remembered to do its work, so Sunday worship continues to strengthen and renew God's people if it contains the nutrients necessary for spiritual health.

Of course, the goal of worship planners and preachers is not to plan and lead forgettable worship. Rather our goal is to provide attractive, nourishing spiritual food that forms the faith of God's people and empowers them to live and witness with power and joy. But the deepest truth about worship is that it is as necessary as daily

413

bread. We cannot thrive without regular worship. Whether or not we are fully aware of its effect, our worship of God is what keeps us alive. So we, too, keep cooking.

And despite all we've said in this book about carefully planned, well-balanced worship, even meals that are inadequately planned or poorly executed may serve a good purpose. Thomas Long describes one such meal from his childhood:

> When my brother and I were children, we once planned a special observance for Mother's Day. We knocked on our parents' bedroom door at first light and, when admitted, entered with the Sunday paper and the announcement that, today being a special day, breakfast would be served to them in bed. As our surprised, but pleased, parents leafed through the newspaper, they were serenaded by the homey kitchen sounds of their breakfast being prepared: glass shattering, grease fires being extinguished, reams of paper towels being spun off the roll. At long last we returned to their room with a steaming breakfast of defiant coffee, molten eggs, carbonized bacon, and biscuits which would have rivaled an apprentice stonemason. If that meal had been served at San Quentin, it would have precipitated a riot. But our parents savored every morsel, seasoning their food with the spice of long-suffering love. Inept as we were at cooking, we had so obviously prepared that meal with respect and devotion that, even though they surely found it virtually indigestible, they still counted it among their most beloved dining experiences. Somehow I believe that worship is just this way: Often half-baked or over-done, but when entered into with care and devotion, graciously received and even savored by our long-suffering God.[1]

A great danger for worship planners and worship leaders is to so focus on the preparation of the service that we are not present for the meal. These worship planners are in danger of over-owning the worship event. As writers, we pray that our readers will have great expectations for worship, but that these expectations will focus on the grace that God's Spirit brings to our worship.

Most of all, when we are overburdened with our responsibility to prepare the worship meal, let us not forget the meal that God prepares for us, for indeed it is God who can be trusted to feed the congregation. As Barbara Brown Taylor writes, "We are not invited to understand; we are simply invited to be fed, holding out our hands to receive what it has pleased God to put into them. Like holy manna, it is not the meal that we had planned [or] even the meal that we had thought to want, but it is the meal God has given us, the very bread of heaven."[2]

It is our sincere desire that this book will provide insights that will stick to the ribs of worshipping souls; that it will aid the creation of sermons so crisply delivered that they leave us hungry for more; that our services will be inspired by the freshest of ingredients; and that all of the above will be served with joy and beauty to the loving Parent for whom they are intended.

APPENDIX 1

QUESTIONS FOR STUDY OF A BIBLICAL TEXT

An initial literary reading of a biblical text

Focus	Questions
1. character	Who are the main characters? What are they like? How can they be described?
2. plot	What happens in this text? Why does it happen? What is the sequence of events?
3. context	What happened before this section? After? How does context affect the meaning here?
4. conflict	What is the main conflict here? What caused it?
5. resolution	What is needed for resolution? Who must do it? Or, if conflict is resolved, will resolution last?
6. author	What can be said about the human author or writer? Why was it written?
7. audience	For whom is it written? What effect was intended?
8. reader identification	With whom in the text do I identify? Why have I made that choice?
9. form	What is the form (or genre) of this passage? Is it a song? Letter? Law? Epic? Parable? Saying?
10. function	What is the function of this passage in terms of the entire work?
11. structure	How could the structure be sketched? Does it build to a climax? Does it have separate parts?
12. style	What is distinctive about the author's style? Are there distinctive phrases or key words?
13. power	Who has money? Power? Who is poor? Powerless?

14. patterns	Are there unusual patterns? (e.g., three times of questioning? Two acts that fail? Four journeys)?
15. connections	Do any of the above connect with similar things elsewhere in the Bible?
16. translations	How do several English versions compare? What does the original Greek or Hebrew say?
17. parallels	Do parallel accounts differ (e.g., between the Gospels, or Samuel, Kings, and Chronicles)?
18. puzzles	What is surprising or does not fit? What questions do I take to the commentaries?
19. emotions	Do I like this text? Do I dislike it? Why? With what feelings am I left?

An initial theological reading of a biblical text

Focus	Questions
1. God in the text	What is God doing in the text itself?
2. God behind the text	What is God doing behind the text, in the larger events?
3. judgment	What is God's judgment (i.e., law, condemnation, identification of human failing)?
4. change	What change is demanded of humanity?
5. hope	What is the hope (i.e., grace, good news, empowerment)?
6. empowerment in the text	How does the text itself indicate what God does to enable change?
7. empowerment beyond the text	What is God doing in the larger story to which this text belongs?
8. identity	What does this tell us about who we are? Who God is?
9. belief	What are we asked to believe?
10. action	What is God instructing and therefore enabling us to do?
11. Christology	What does the cross and the resurrection say to Christians concerning themes raised in this text?

From Paul Scott Wilson, *The Practice of Preaching* (Nashville, TN: Abingdon Press, 1996), 133–34; 138–39. Used by permission.

APPENDIX 2

SEQUENCE FOR PREPARING A TOPICAL SERMON

1. Determine the topic is of sufficient size for the pulpit.
2. Identify pre-associations with the topic.
3. List everything you need to know about the topic.
4. Search for biblical perspectives.
5. Trace how the topic has been interpreted in the history of the church.
6. Focus on two theologians on the topic.
7. Bring out the denomination's position on the topic.
8. Investigate relevant dimensions of the topic.
9. Inventory the congregation's experience with the topic.
10. Imagine what it is like to be different persons in different situations relevant to the topic.
11. Evaluate the topic theologically.
12. State your own position on the topic.
13. Articulate viewpoints different from your own.
14. Consider the mindset and situation of the listeners in relation to the topic.
15. Locate the listeners in relationship to your position on the topic.
16. State what you want to say in the sermon.
17. Decide what you hope will be the result of the listeners' hearing of the sermon.
18. Design the sermon so it will have a good chance of accomplishing its purposes.

Reproduced from *Preaching the Topical Sermon* Copyright ©1995 Ronald J. Allen. Used by permission of Westminster John Knox Press.

APPENDIX 3

QUESTIONS FOR SELECTING MUSIC FOR WORSHIP

A good melody will enrich the meaning of words. Tensions and releases, calmness and drama matched with the carefully chosen words of hymns and songs deepen a congregation's expressive response. Music leaders, in particular, should pay attention to the connection between melody and words, so the possibilities for emphasis and color they offer can be used to fullest advantage.

Effective and satisfying music selections will fit naturally into a service where there is a clear plan and sense of movement. They connect with the energy and purpose of what has happened immediately before the song is sung, and they prepare the congregation for what will follow. *Flow* describes the way music contributes to the movement of worship, providing easy access for worshipers to enter the actions. No matter what type of service is planned, music—particularly congregational singing—should help move the action of worship along in ways that sustain the congregation's flow of energy, thought, emotion, and will.

Selecting hymns and songs that fit into a service requires careful analysis. Music and worship leaders must ask important questions, whether they are deciding on songs for the opening praise service, hymns for the offering, a musical opening for a time of prayer, songs for the Lord's Supper celebration, or another worship action. The words of songs, the character of the music, and combinations of worship actions all require consideration. Choosing fitting music for congregational singing is an art that is cultivated through curiosity, study, practice, and imagination.

Preliminary steps
Sing through the song completely, simply noticing what it feels like. Play around with the tempo until the song has settled into the one that seems appropriate for the words and feels comfortable to sing.

Word analysis

1. What are worshipers doing as they sing the words? Are they praying? Inviting? Declaring? Telling a story? Confessing faith? Naming sin? Exhorting? Making a response? Thanking? Offering? Praising? Adoring? Committing themselves to action? Through some songs, the congregation prays. In others, it will name sin and pray for forgiveness. Others will commit worshipers to service or bring them to exhort one another to deeper faith. In many songs, the congregation is doing several things as music unfolds: praising, confessing faith, and offering themselves.

2. What are the primary images or metaphors found in the song's words? Images and metaphors make abstract concepts concrete and real for worshipers. They demonstrate important relationships between the worshipers and their world and their God. Experiences in other aspects of life can help singers understand the mysteries of faith. The interplay of images and metaphors must make sense to worshipers. Too many images or unrelated metaphors will leave them confused.

3. What is the theme the congregation will sing about? The actions the congregation does through the words, along with the images and metaphors, reveal a theme. This theme often provokes deeper thought and moves worshipers emotionally. Often worship leaders and musicians begin and end their analysis by identifying a theme (often superficially). Failing to notice what the congregation is doing through the words, planners have lost an opportunity to connect the song with the deeper movements of the worship service.

4. How are the words structured? Are the verses continuous and develop a train of thought. Are there verses with a refrain? Short verses to be repeated? Short verses with bridge(s)? Short verses and refrains intermixed? The structure of the words frequently demonstrates the primary action the congregation is doing. Refrains often encapsulate the central action or commitment of the song. "I will arise and go to Jesus"[1] is a commitment to repent and return in confidence to Jesus. "This is my story, this is my song"[2] is an affirmation of faith and a testimony to the singer's blessed relationship to Jesus. Knowing the structure of the words can give music and worship leaders clues for ways the congregation can enter a new song (for example, joining on the refrain, hearing a short verse as

a solo and then repeating it), or how parts of songs can be used as congregational responses.

5. What descriptions summarize the character of the words? Adjectives and verbs that distill your analysis into three to five key words are helpful for remembering aspects of the song's character for future reference. These key words may include specific words from the song, the mood of the words, the worship actions the song accomplishes, or words that describe its theme. NOTE: Keep your records of these descriptions to save future analysis work!

Music analysis

1. What is the shape of the melody? How many phrases does it have? Any repeating phrases? Does the melody move stepwise? Are there any large leaps upward or downward? Where are its dramatic high and low points? Is the rhythm even or syncopated? Does it have beat groups of two (which feels like walking or marching) or beat groups of three (which feels like a waltz or a jig)? Working through these questions opens the character of the music, revealing the ingenious ways that melody and words strengthen each other's meaning. Ideas for accompaniment, improvisation, or different ways of using voices develop from this careful analysis. Knowing the structure of the melody (for example, the number of repeating phrases, the different sections or musical themes, the dramatic high points and resolutions) can be very helpful when teaching a new song to the congregation.

2. What feeling or mood does the melody evoke? Is the melody in a major or minor key? Singers quickly respond to the difference between major and minor keys. In Western music, major keys tend to sound happy, hopeful, or restful to singers. Minor keys tend to sound sad, unresolved, or unsettled to the ear. Some major keys have bright sounds; some minor keys sound dark and foreboding. Westerners are deeply affected psychologically by the brightness and key of the music they sing, even if they cannot describe why this is so. Key and tempo are musical elements that most often set mood.

3. What are the best tempos for the melody and words? Most songs have a range of tempos from which an appropriate one can be selected for a specific moment in worship, a particular style of performance, or a combination of accompanying instruments. Tempos

that are too fast make it difficult for singers to breathe properly or to sing the words. They will become frustrated and stop singing. Tempos that are too slow for the melody make it difficult for singers to sing entire phrases easily in one breath. Often slow tempos cause the song to feel heavy, as if it were an incredible load to bear. When they have to work too hard, singers get frustrated. Knowing the range of appropriate tempos at which a song can be sung helps match the pace of our singing with the flow of a service.

4. What kind of harmony or instrumental accompaniment is appropriate? Can the melody be sung with harmonizing voices (two parts? three parts? four parts? more?)? Does the melody require instrumental accompaniment? The harmony (either vocal or instrumental) creates additional layers of sound that add richness, texture, and excitement that supports the melody. Sometimes good melodies need no harmony at all and are in fact stifled by it. Other melodies depend heavily on vocal harmony or instrumental accompaniment to expand their expressive possibilities. Music leaders must make sound judgments about how to use harmony effectively to enhance the congregation's singing of specific songs.

5. What musical and/or impressionistic descriptions summarize the way the music sounds? Exercise the discipline of distilling your analysis of the music into three to five key words. They will helpful for remembering aspects of the music's character for future reference. They will likely be what you think of first when searching for melodies with a particular character at critical points in a worship service. NOTE: Keep your records of these descriptions to save future analysis work!

Service analysis

Using the analysis of words and music, worship leaders and musicians can think about how particular songs and hymns will fit in specific places of a service. The following questions are essential for making informed decisions that can sustain the worship flow.

1. Where in the service could the song be used?
2. What is the purpose of the congregational song at particular points in the service?

3. What is happening immediately prior to the hymn/song? What kind of energy is anticipated? What volume? What intensity? What tempo?
4. What is happening immediately after the hymn/song? What kind of energy is anticipated? What volume? What intensity? What tempo?
5. How will the hymn/song be best led at this point in the service? By an instrument or instruments? By a small vocal group? By a music leader who will voice lead or hand lead? By a leader who will line out the phrases?
6. What kind of introduction will be necessary for the hymn/song to get off to a good start and match the momentum of the previous worship action?

Cultivating the art of choosing music for worship demands discipline, along with curiosity about how hymns and songs are constructed. This knowledge will yield greater skill in selecting songs for congregational singing with sensitivity and imagination.

APPENDIX 4
QUESTIONS FOR CONSIDERING VISUAL ART

A Christmas slide show

This idea for a Christmas season slide show serves as an example for the kind of thinking required for creating visual art for use in worship.

Five to seven slides of historical and contemporary artworks of Jesus and Mary make up the show. The images should be by artists from various cultures of the world. Contemporary pictures of a mother and infant of different nationalities could be included. As the images are projected (changed every 20–30 seconds), a small music group sings a song announcing Jesus's birth in the world. The work is introduced on Christmas Eve with Alfred Burt's "Some children see Him." It is shown again the Sunday after Christmas using "O come, all ye faithful" (*HWB* 212), "Where is this stupendous Stranger?" (*HWB* 200), or "Joy to the world" (*HWB* 318). On Epiphany Sunday, "What Child is this" (*HWB* 215) or "The virgin Mary had a baby boy" (*HWB* 202) are appropriate. The key themes are Jesus's **birth**, his presence in the **world**, and his **incarnation** known in many cultures throughout time.

The questions

Artists and worship planners creating visual art for worship must continually ask the kinds of questions outlined below, as they conceive and execute their work. Using the slide show example, we'll explore the questions.

1. What is the purpose of this artwork in this particular service?

This slide show's purpose is *to proclaim* the wonder of Jesus's incarnation known throughout the world.

2. How might this work help the congregation move deeper into God's redeeming work?

By seeing images of Mary and Jesus or mother and child created by artists in different cultures, we can feel the meaning of John 3:15: God sent his into the world, "in order that that the world might be saved through him."

3. Is the artistic concept strong enough to carry the theological purpose of the work?

This slide show requires arresting, and unsentimental images showing mother and child in different cultures and times. If the images are too sweet, precious, sentimental, or represent only one culture, the theological purpose would be lost. The accompanying hymns/songs should have strong— preferably familiar or easily understood words—to help interpret the images.

4. How will the congregation engage the work?

The congregation will first take in the images and song. If a well-known song is used by the small group during the second or third showing, the congregation could sing along *from memory.*

5. What other worship actions are needed for this work to achieve its purpose?

The show cries for some type of congregational response: an affirmation of faith based on Philippians 2:5–11; a proclamation such as John 1:1–5, 14–16; the canon "Gloria" (*HWB* 204); or a prayer inviting Jesus to be born or reborn in us. (This question is seldom asked about visual art used in worship. Work appears, but is rarely integrated into the actions of worship.)

6. How long will the work be in place to accomplish its purpose? Will it change in any way? If so, why and how?

This show should be seen several times with different songs. The images will sink into our consciousness, creating deep impressions. Changing songs each time can expand our capacities to see deeper into the images.

7. Do the materials used have the physical characteristics to accomplish the work's purpose with integrity?

Here a slide show will always fall short. Original paintings, icons, and photos communicate a sense of real presence that slides can never convey. Jesus's incarnation is God's real presence in the world, not a copy. Theological integrity is compromised. These reasons could be causes to abandon the idea. However, it may be still justified as a way to stir our imaginations to wonder what Jesus's birth means for the world and for us.

8. Is the scale and proportion of the work adequate to accomplish its purpose?

To get a sense of Jesus's coming into the world, the projections must be large, so the congregation feels the immensity of his birth and its world-changing impact. If the screen, projector, or lighting is inadequate to convey this greatness, then the primary theological point is betrayed.

The slide show holds good possibilities, but has two significant limitations. If the artist(s) cannot deal adequately with these limitations, the project has to be redefined or abandoned. Poor execution closes rather than opens new dimensions of God's story.

Worship planners and artists must grapple with questions such as these; otherwise the art created will be ill-conceived, trite, or will stand in the way of the central theological theme it seeks to explore. Creativity, aesthetic pleasure, or the desire to be trendy do not justify the use of visual art in worship. What we see with our eyes must be vital enough to draw us deeper into the Word of life to which we testify.

Adapted from "What We Have Seen with Our Eyes" by Rebecca Slough in the Summer 2005 issue of *Leader: Equipping the Missional Congregation*. Used with permission.

APPENDIX 5

GATHERING, IN THE VARIOUS MODES OF KNOWING

The following examples use the action of gathering to demonstrate the modes of knowing described in chapter ten.

Literal

In the literal mode, words of gathering are concrete, factual, informational: we come, we enter.

> Come, now is the time to worship.
> Come, now is the time to give your hearts.
> Come, just as you are to worship.
> Come, just as you are before your God.
> Come.
>
> One day every tongue will confess you are God,
> one day every knee will bow.
> Still the greatest treasure remains for those who gladly choose you
> now.
>
> Come, now is the time to worship.
> Come, now is the time to give your hears.
> Come just as your are to worship.
> Come just as you are before your God.
> Come.[1]

> We gather
>   to praise
>   pray
>   sing
>   listen
>   offer
>   and give thanks.
> We serve our God, who gathers us here.

Representational

In the representational mode of gathering, literal knowledge is translated into a form of action: We welcome. This greeting invites worshipers to represent Christ to each other as they pass the peace. The greeting takes on a priestly character.

> Grace to you and peace.
> I welcome you in the name of Jesus Christ,
> who welcomed into his presence
> children, women, men,
> the sick, the sinful, and the skeptical,
> the rich and the powerful,
> Jews and Gentiles,
> Pharisees, drunkards, and tax collectors . . .,
> you and me.
>
> Welcome each other with the peace of Christ.

Narrative

In the narrative mode the stories of God gives shape to our identity: we are called as a people. Stories tell us who and where we are.

Leader	Who is so great a God?
	Our God has done awesome wonders.
	If God had only made a covenant with Abraham and Sarah
People	*It would have been enough.*
Leader	If God had only rescued us from Egypt.
People	*It would have been enough.*
Leader	If God had only given us the law.
People	*It would have been enough.*
Leader	If God had only sent us prophets.
People	*It would have been enough.*
Leader	If God had only brought us back from exile.
People	*It would have been enough.*
Leader	If God had only sent the son as Immanuel for us.
People	*It would have been enough.*
Leader	If God had only saved us through Jesus's life, death, and resurrection.
People	*It would have been enough.*
Leader	If God had only sent the Holy Spirit.
People	*It would have been enough.*
Leader	If God had only created the church.
People	*It would have been enough.*

Leader	If God had only given us the scriptures.
People	*It would have been enough.*
Leader	If God had only promised to be with us.
People	*It would have been enough.*

Leader	Let us pray:
	God of awesome power and wondrous love,
	You have called a people of faith and sustained them
	    throughout time.
	Form us into your people of praise, prayer, and purpose
	through our worship today and all days.
	We pray in the name of Jesus, which is always enough.
	                               AMEN

Metaphoric

The metaphoric mode creates a relationship between something we know a lot about and a condition, situation, or reality that is hard to explain. Paul uses our knowledge of the human body to show us something intangible about the nature of the church: we are Christ's body.

Asking people to stand, raise their hands, and then join them creates physical and visual senses of what the body of Christ might be. The congregation's response gives auditory witness to the unity of that body.

Leader	We are members of one body *[groups of people stand* *as they are named]* elders young adults children retirees youth those of the middle years
People	*Gathered into one*
Leader	males *[people raise hands]* females fathers mothers daughters sons
People	*Gathered into one*
Leader	rich and poor *[people join hands]* wise and foolish saints and sinners
People	*Gathered into one*

Leader	Gathered members of one body
	Drawn together as Christ's body
People	*Gathered into one*
Hymn	"Here in this place" (*HWB* 6)

Symbolic

In the symbolic mode, a variety of meanings are set in motion and the senses are often more fully engaged: We pray, praise, and offer ourselves as a body. Symbols, like those suggested in Huub Oosterhuis's hymn, awaken the imagination, alerting worshipers to sense the presence of Christ in the midst of his body.

| Hymn | "What is this place" (*HWB* 1) *[with procession of Bible, bread, cup, and rich instrumental accompaniment]* |

What is this place, where we are meeting?
Only a house, the earth its floor.
Walls and a roof, sheltering people,
windows for light, an open door.
Yet it becomes a body that lives when we are gathered
    here,
and know our God is near.

Word from afar, stars that are falling.
Sparks that are sown in us like seed:
names for our God, dreams, signs, and wonders
sent from the past are all we need.
We in this place remember and speak again what we
    have heard:
God's free redeeming word.

And we accept bread at his table,
broken and shared, a living sign.
Here in this world, dying and living,
we are each other's bread and wine.
This is place where we can receive what we need to
    increase:
our justice and God's peace.[2]

Universal

In the universal mode, everything converges into a sense of wholeness that transcends the immediate moment: We join with the worldwide body of Christ and worship with all of heaven's hosts. We experience

God in all dimensions of our being. Rationality, profound feeling, bodily expression, and spiritual depth are integrated. David Ruis's song—accompanied by a band with a variety of instruments, an exuberant procession or a dance, and a standing congregation—could open to an experience of the universal. Singing and dancing in the present, the congregation participates in the glorious future when we will endlessly worship the Lamb.

> Sing a song of celebration
> lift up a shout of praise,
> for the Bridegroom will come, the glorious One.
> And oh, we will look on His face.
> We'll go to a much better place.
>
> Dance with all your might,
> lift up your hands and clap for joy.
> The time's drawing near when he will appear.
> And oh, we will stand by His side,
> a strong, pure, spotless bride.
>
> We will dance on the streets that are golden,
> the glorious bride and the great Son of Man.
> From every tongue and tribe and nation
> we'll join in the song of the Lamb.[3]

APPENDIX 6

ABOUT THE LECTIONARY

Providing a rich, varied and sustaining biblical diet for a congregation is an important responsibility of pastors and worship leaders. Christians are formed and shaped by their ongoing encounter with the Word of God—the Living Word in Jesus Christ and the written Word of scripture. Although the Revised Common Lectionary is not the only suitable scripture calendar for worship and preaching, leaders should be aware of this important ecumenical calendar and also a wide variety of lectionary-related resources.

A brief but helpful explanation of the structure and purposes of the Revised Common Lectionary (used by Protestants since 1992) can be found in Gail Ramshaw, *A Three-Year Banquet: The Lectionary for the Assembly* (Augsburg Fortress, 2004) and in Frank C. Senn, *Christian Liturgy: Catholic and Evangelical* (Fortress Press, 1997). Explanatory material for other lectionaries can be found in Horace T. Allen, *A Handbook for the Lectionary* (Geneva Press, 1980) and in William Skudlarek, *The Word in Worship: Preaching in a Liturgical Context* (Abingdon, 1981).

Congregations exploring the lectionary should be aware that more than one lectionary is available to churches. For example, Roman Catholics and Anglicans use a slightly different lectionary than the Revised Common Lectionary. The Uniform Series Sunday School Lessons follow a 6-year Bible reading calendar rather than a typical 3-year calendar. Since lectionary-related sermon helps and worship resources are linked to a variety of lectionaries, it is useful to find out which lectionary is being used.

Introduction to the Lectionary Calendar

An ordered system of selected Bible readings, the lectionary provides four texts for every Sunday over a three-year period. The four readings are drawn respectively from the Old Testament and the Psalms, the Epistles (and Revelation), and the Gospels. The purpose is to provide a witness to the unity of the Old and New Testaments and to proclaim the whole story of salvation. God's plan for redemption is announced and initiated in the Old Testament and reaches its fulfillment in the death and resurrection of Jesus Christ. Through the witness of the church, the gospel is proclaimed to all generations.

Calendar of Scripture Readings

Gospel Readings. The reading of the gospel is the high point of Christian worship. Matthew is read in Year A, Mark in Year B, and Luke in Year C. But this arrangement is not rigid: John's Gospel enjoys pride of place during the seasons of Christmas, Lent and Easter. Readings from John's Gospel, Chapter 6, take up five Sundays in Year B, which gets over the problem of Mark being shorter than the other gospels.

Psalms. An appropriate psalm or canticle is chosen for each Sunday. The psalm can be used as a responsive reading and can also be sung as part of the congregation's praise and adoration of God. It can also be used as the central text for worship.

Old Testament Readings. A reading from the Old Testament is included each week. In the Revised Common Lectionary (1992), two choices are available for the Old Testament reading during the post-Pentecost season: a text which is closely linked to the gospel reading or semi-continuous reading of the Old Testament. In response to feedback from pastors and church leaders, Mennonite Publishing Network currently uses the Old Testament text more closely connected to the gospel reading in the Church Bulletin Series.

Although many preachers focus on the gospel reading in their weekly preaching, leaders may also choose to preach a series focusing on Old Testament texts or readings from the epistles, especially in the post-Pentecost season. The Old Testament cycles are as follows:

Year A: 25 Sundays of Pentateuch texts, focusing on the major narratives from Genesis, the covenant with Moses, and the establishment of Israel in the Promised Land;

Year B: 14 Sundays of the Davidic narrative (including stories of Samuel and Solomon); 11 Sundays of Wisdom literature (including Proverbs and Job) as well as stories of Ruth and Hannah;

Year C: 25 Sundays of prophetic texts, including the Elijah-Elisha narrative and readings from Isaiah, Jeremiah (6 weeks), Lamentations, Amos, Hosea, Joel, Habakkuk, and Haggai.

Epistle Readings. Because readings from the epistles are arranged in a continuous pattern, they often have little thematic connection with the other two readings. In worship, these readings can be used as part of prayer or as the benediction. They may also be used as central texts for worship planning and preaching.

Readings for Sundays of the Major Seasons

For the Sundays of the major liturgical seasons (Advent, Christmas, Lent and Easter), the readings have been chosen with reference to the biblical/theological themes of the feast or season.

Advent. Each gospel reading has a specific theme: the Lord's coming in glory at the end of time (first Sunday), John the Baptist (second and third Sundays), and the events which immediately prepared for the Lord's birth (fourth Sunday). On the third Sunday of Advent, all of the texts include references to joy or rejoicing, thus foreshadowing the good news of the incarnation in the birth of Jesus. The Old Testament readings are prophecies about the Messiah and messianic times, especially those taken from the Book of Isaiah.

Christmas. Christmas season readings are selected from Isaiah, Luke, Matthew and selected epistles. The gospel of the Sunday after Christmas tells of Jesus's childhood; the other readings concern family life. The reading for the second Sunday after Christmas refers to the mystery of incarnation.

Epiphany. The gospel reading for the Feast of Epiphany (which may not fall on Sunday) is the Matthean account of the visit of the magi. The first Sunday after Epiphany focuses on the baptism of Jesus, introducing a brief season of ordinary time in which Jesus's earthly ministry and teachings are central. The last Sunday before Lent focuses on Jesus's transfiguration.

Lent. The readings for Lent are arranged to coincide with the preparation of candidates for baptism and the renewal of baptismal vows among all the faithful. Year A focuses on new believers or conversion, Year B on the faithful, and Year C on penitents who are restored to fellowship with Christ and the community of faith. The gospel selection for the first Sunday of Lent each year recounts Jesus's temptations in the wilderness. For Year A the stories concerning Nicodemus, the Samaritan woman, the man born blind, and Lazarus are given a pivotal role because of the call to conversion and new life. Year B texts tell the story of salvation history, beginning with Noah's obedience and continuing with Abraham and Sarah's call, the wanderings of the children of Israel in the desert, and the giving of the law. The central text of Year C is the parable of the prodigal father and son, illuminating God's patient, forgiving love and desire for all to be reconciled. In general, Old Testament readings for Lent emphasize the developments of salvation history.

Holy Week texts are derived from the Passion and from Old Testament prophesies of Jesus's suffering and death.

Easter. Until the third Sunday of Easter, the gospel selections recount the appearances of the risen Christ. The readings about the Good Shepherd are assigned to the fourth Sunday of Easter. The gospels of the fifth, sixth and seventh Sundays of Easter are excerpts from the teaching and prayer of Jesus after the last supper. Instead of an Old Testament passage, readings from the Acts of the Apostles are arranged in a three-year cycle of parallel and progressive selections. Thus the life, growth, and witness of the early Church are presented every year.

Pentecost. After a focus on the story of the Holy Spirit being poured out on the church at Pentecost, the Scripture readings for the Sundays after Pentecost (ordinary time) pick up where they left off after Epiphany with continuous readings of the gospels and epistles.

Other feasts. Christ the King Sunday is the conclusion of the Christian year (the last Sunday before Advent). The last Sunday after Epiphany (and before Lent) is known as Transfiguration Sunday.

Sources:
"The Structure and Use of the Lectionary," by William Skudlarek, *The Word in Worship: Preaching in a Liturgical Context* (Abingdon, 1981); and *The Revised Common Lectionary: The Consultation on Common Texts* (Abingdon, 1992). Further information can be found on websites such as: www.textweek.com; www.lectionary.org; www.sermonwriter.com; www.esermons.com.

APPENDIX 7

RITUALS FOR ENTERING AND LEAVING THE WORLD OF WORK

Blessing for fruitfulness

Most people spend the majority of their adult years gainfully employed in the world of work. Young adults are often eager to get a job, earn a living, and make a difference in the world. Forty or forty-five years later, older adults may be just as eager to relinquish their work roles and responsibilities and look forward to the more leisurely pace of retirement.

The desire to serve or be useful does not end, however, when employment ends. Nor does the Christian call to discipleship end. Because much of our life of discipleship occurs in the work world, the church needs to be alert to recognize and bless the ministries that occur there. It also needs to highlight the potential for ongoing ministry in the post-work years and bless the energy and creativity invested there. Two pivotal events offer the church such an opportunity: one of those is our entry into the world of work; the second is our departure from gainful employment. At such times, we need a heightened sense of God's presence through the Spirit, and we also need the care and support of our sisters and brothers in the faith.

The following rituals of blessing may be incorporated into Sunday morning worship or small group settings. In larger congregations, the ritual might occur only once a year and include a variety of people. In smaller congregations, these rituals could occur each time someone experiences such a transition. Labor Day weekend, with its secular celebration of work, might offer an appropriate occasion for such recognition and blessing in the church.

The rituals include suggestions for scripture readings, songs, storytelling, prayers of blessing, and ritual actions. Anointing with oil, a sign of the Spirit's blessing and empowering, can also be included. The central symbol in each ritual is a bowl of fruit which will be given to the person being blessed at the conclusion of the ritual.

Ritual for entering work: "Go and bear fruit"
Purpose of ritual

As they conclude formal schooling or after a period of trial-and-error searching, young adults may be blessed by the congregation as they enter the work world or embark upon a career. Though this can be a very exciting time, it may also bring fears about competence or security. The purpose of this ritual is to:

- remember and celebrate God's nurturing presence in childhood and youth and the call to ministry that comes to all Christians through baptism;

- give thanks for faith nurture received from family, friends, and the community of faith and open the way for ongoing care and support;

- invoke the Spirit's guiding, protecting, creative, empowering presence as new roles and responsibilities are accepted.

Scripture focus

John 5:7–11,16a. A meditation might emphasize abiding in love as the prerequisite for fruitfulness; it might also emphasize "bearing fruit that will last." Other texts that could be considered are Isaiah 6:1–8; Matthew 10:37–39; Romans 12:1, 2; Galatians 5:22.

Song suggestions

"Lord, you have come to the lakeshore" (*HWB* 229)
"Thou true Vine, that heals the nations" (*HWB* 373)
"God, whose giving knows no ending" (*HWB* 383)
"We give thee but thine own" (*HWB* 384)
"God of the fertile fields" (*HWB* 390)
"Heart and mind, possessions, Lord" (*HWB* 392)
"I bind my heart this tide" (*HWB* 413)
"Bwana awabiriki (May God grant you a blessing)" (*HWB* 422)
"How bless'd are they" (*HWB* 525)
"Guide my feet" (*HWB* 546)

Ritual action

Young adults may be invited to tell the congregation about the new work or setting to which they have been called. People who have been closely involved in nurturing their faith and discernment (parents, pastor, mentor, spiritual friend or guide, etc.) may speak of the potential for fruitful ministry which they see. As each one concludes their brief comments, they add a few pieces of fruit to a large bowl on a table covered with a colorful cloth.

Those who have spoken (and others) are invited to form a circle of blessing around the young people, place hands on them, and join in a prayer of blessing and commissioning. If desired, the young people may also be anointed with oil to signify their desire for the Holy Spirit's presence and power.

At the conclusion of the ritual, a bowl of fruit may be offered to each young person as tangible evidence of the congregation's hopes and blessings.

Prayer of blessing and anointing

Lord Jesus Christ,
> you have called *[name]* to be your disciple in the world of work
>> as a *[role at work]*.

We give thanks for the faith you have given *[name]*
> and for all the blessings she/he has received through family,
>> friends, mentors,
> and this entire congregation.

We thank you especially for the call to ministry *[name]* received in
> her/his baptism
> and for the gifts you have poured upon her/him as your disciple.

Now *[name]* is taking an important step in entering the adult world of
> work.

She/he will have new responsibilities and new opportunities to be your
> disciple:
>> to love, serve, witness, work for justice, and care for others.

We anoint her/him with the oil of blessing:
> Guide and protect her/him on this journey.
> Grant strength, skill, and confidence for the work to which
>> she/has been called.
> Provide friends and companions who will care for her/him.
> Make her/him a strong, clear, joyful witness for your love in
>> her/his place of work.

When she/he is troubled or afraid, remind her/him that we are here
to support.
Most of all, fill her/him with your Holy Spirit who will be a
constant companion and source of creativity.

We commit our sister/brother into your hands
and give thanks for all the fruit she/he will bear for your glory.
In the name of the One who calls us to follow with joy. Amen.

Benediction
1 Corinthians 16:13–14

∾

Ritual for leaving work: "They still produce fruit"
Purpose of ritual
As they complete their days in the work world, older adults may
be blessed by the congregation as they take up the joys and responsibilities of retirement. Though they often experience a satisfying sense
of achievement, some may also face fears and uncertainties in these
years. Many will be seeking a new sense of purpose. The purpose of
this ritual is to:

- remember and celebrate God's presence in the years given to work;

- provide a context of loving care, support, and discernment as individuals withdraw from a role in which they have made a significant
  investment of time, energy, and creativity and now seek new direction;

- bless the ongoing journey of discipleship as retirees continue to follow
  Christ in the church and in the world.

Scripture focus
Psalms 92:1–4, 12–15. A meditation might emphasize the goodness of God's provisions throughout the person's lifetime, as well as
our hope in God's continuing care. The image of "remaining green
and full of sap" (v. 14) adds a delightful touch. Other texts which
might be considered are Matthew 5:1–16; Philippians 3:7–14;
1 Timothy 6:11b–16.

Song suggestions

"For the fruit of all creation" (*HWB* 90)
"Will you let me be your servant" (*HWB* 307)
"Lord, whose love in humble service" (*HWB* 369)
"What gift can we bring" (*HWB* 385)
"Grant us, Lord, the grace" (*HWB* 388)
"Bwana awabariki (May God grant you a blessing)" (*HWB* 422)
"Go now in peace" (*HWB* 429)
"O God, your constant care" (*HWB* 481)
"God of our life" (*HWB* 486)
"Gracious Spirit, dwell with me" (*HWB* 507)

Ritual action

Those who will be leaving the world of work are introduced. In brief interviews, stories may be told of how persons came to do the work of their life. Following this introduction, several storytellers share stories that illustrate the gifts offered by these persons in their place of work. At the conclusion of each story, clusters of fruit are added to the large bowl placed on a colorful cloth.

Those who have spoken (and others) form a circle of blessing around the older adults, place hands on them, and join in a prayer of blessing and commissioning. If they desire it, these people may also be anointed with oil to signify their desire for the Holy Spirit's presence and power.

At the conclusion of the ritual, a bowl of fruit is offered to each older adult as tangible evidence of the congregation's hopes and blessings.

Prayer of blessing and anointing

Lord Jesus Christ,
    you called *[name]* to be your disciple in the world of work
    as a *[role at work]*.
We give thanks for your call,
for your strengthening grace,
and for the harvest of the Spirit that has been gathered
through the faithfulness of your servant.
We are grateful that your love has been shared and your way made
    known
through her/his efforts at work.

Now *[name]* is leaving a comfortable, familiar role
    to enter a new stage of life with new opportunities to minister
        and serve.

We anoint her/him with the oil of blessing:
Guide and protect her/him on this journey.

Grant courage and hope for the unknown.
Make her/him flourish like a palm tree;
in old age let her/him still produce fruit;
keep her/him green and always full of sap.

Into your hands we commit our sister/brother;
we give thanks that you will never leave nor forsake her/him.
In the name of the One who is our faithful companion. Amen.

Benediction
1 Corinthians 15:58

Resource prepared by Marlene Kropf, June 2000.

APPENDIX 8

A WELL-STOCKED PANTRY FOR PASTORS AND WORSHIP LEADERS

In the following listing, the starred items at the beginning of each section are highly recommended selections as you begin to develop a pantry of worship resources. When the time comes to expand your pantry, the second set of titles in each section includes well recommended resources.

Planning and Leading Worship

*Doran, Carol, and Thomas H. Troeger. *Trouble at the Table: Gathering the Tribes for Worship*. Abingdon Press, 1992.

*Malefyt, Norma DeWaal, and Howard Vanderwell. *Designing Worship Together: Models and Strategies for Worship Planning*. Alban Institute, 2005.

*Rempel, John D., editor. *Minister's Manual* (Mennonite). Faith & Life Press and Herald Press, 1998.

*Yoder, June Alliman, Marlene Kropf, and Rebecca Slough. *Preparing Sunday Dinner: A Collaborative Approach to Worship and Preaching*. Herald Press, 2006.

For All Who Minister: A Worship Manual for the Church of the Brethren. Brethren Press, 1993.

Johnson, Todd E., editor. *The Conviction of Things Not Seen: Worship and Ministry in the 21st Century*. Brazos Press, 2002.

Kreider, Eleanor. *Enter His Gates: Fitting Worship Together*. Herald Press, 1990.

Mitman, F. Russell. *Worship in the Shape of Scripture*. Pilgrim Press, 2001.

Ray, David R. *Wonderful Worship in Smaller Churches*. Pilgrim Press, 2000.
White, Daniel S., et al. *Worship Feast: 50 Complete Multi-Sensory Services for Youth*. Abingdon Press, 2003.

Preaching

*Allen, Ronald J. *Preaching the Topical Sermon*. Westminster John Knox Press, 1992.
*Greiser, David B., and Michael A. King, ed. *Anabaptist Preaching: A Conversation Between Pulpit, Pew & Bible*. Cascadia Publishing House and Herald Press, 2003.
*Lowry, Eugene. *The Homiletical Plot: The Sermon as Narrative Art Form*, expanded edition. Westminster John Knox Press, 2001.

Allen, Ronald J. *The Teaching Sermon*. Abingdon Press, 1995.
Childers, Jana. *Birthing the Sermon*. Chalice Press, 2001.
_____ *Performing the Word: Preaching as Theatre*. Abingdon Press, 1998.
Greenshaw, David M., and Ronald J. Allen, editors. *Preaching in the Context of Worship*. Chalice Press, 2000.
Long, Thomas G. *The Senses of Preaching*. John Knox Press, 1988.
Lowry, Eugene. *Living with the Lectionary: Preaching through the Revised Common Lectionary*. Abingdon Press, 1992.
McClure, John S. *The Roundtable Pulpit: Where Leadership and Preaching Meet*. Abingdon Press, 1995.
Schlafer, David. *What Makes This Day Different? Preaching Grace on Special Occasions*. Cowley Publications, 1998.
Taylor, Barbara Brown. *The Preaching Life*. Cowley Publications, 1993.
Tisdale, Leonora Tubbs. *Preaching as Local Theology and Folk Art*. Fortress Press, 1997.
Webb, Stephen W. *The Divine Voice: Christian Proclamation and the Theology of Sound*. Brazos Press, 2004.
Wilson, Paul Scott. *The Practice of Preaching*. Abingdon Press, 1996.

Worship Resource Collections

*Lawrence, Kenneth T., and Susan A. Blain, editors. *Imaging the Word: An Arts and Lectionary Resource* (Volumes 1, 2, 3). United Church Press, 1994-1996.

*Mark, Arlene. *Words for Worship*. Herald Press, 1995.

*Morley, Janet. *All Desires Known: Inclusive Prayers for Worship and Meditation* (expanded edition). Morehouse Publishing, 1994.

*Wild Goose Worship Group. *A Wee Worship Book, 4ᵗʰ Incarnation*. GIA Publications, 1999.

Iona Community. *Iona Abbey Worship Book*. Wild Goose Publications, 2001.

McIlhagga, Kate. *The Green Heart of the Snowdrop*. Wild Goose Publications, 2004.

Carden, John, compiler. *A Procession of Prayer: Prayers and Meditations from Around the World*. Morehouse Publishing, 1998.

Consultation on Common Texts. *Revised Common Lectionary Prayers*. Fortress Press, 2002.

Curzon, David, editor. *The Gospels in Our Images: An Anthology of Twentieth-Century Poetry Based on Biblical Texts*. Harcourt, Brace & Co., 1995.

Drescher, John M., editor. *Invocations and Benedictions for the Revised Common Lectionary*. Abingdon Press, 1998.

Keay, Kathy. *Laughter, Silence and Shouting: An Anthology of Women's Prayers*. HarperSanFrancisco, 1994.

Panel on Worship of the Church of Scotland. *Book of Common Order of the Church of Scotland*. Saint Andrew Press, 1994.

Prayers Encircling the World: An International Anthology. Westminster John Knox Press, 1999.

Skinner, Don C. *Prayers for the Gathered Community: Resources for the Liturgical Year*. United Church Press, 1997.

The Theology and Worship Ministry Unit, Presbyterian Church (USA). *Book of Common Worship*. Westminster/John Knox Press, 1993.

Tirabassi, Maren C., and Joan Jordan Grant. *An Improbable Gift of Blessing: Prayers to Nurture the Spirit*. United Church Press, 1998.

Tirabassi, Maren C., and Kathy Wonson Eddy. *Gifts of Many Cultures: Worship Resources for the Global Community.* United Church Press, 1995.

Ward, Hannah, and Jennifer Wild, compilers. *Resources for Preaching and Worship: Years A, B, C—Quotations, Meditations, Poetry and Prayers* (3 volumes). Westminster John Knox Press, 2002-2004.

Developing and Writing Worship Resources

*Duck, Ruth C. *Finding Words for Worship: A Guide for Leaders.* Westminster John Knox Press, 1995.

*Stookey, Laurence Hull. *Let the Whole Church Say Amen! A Guide for Those Who Pray in Public.* Abingdon, 2001.

Burgess, Ruth. *A Book of Blessings: And How to Write Your Own.* Wild Goose Publications, 2001.

_____ *Friends and Enemies: A Book of Short Prayer and Some Ways to Write Your Own.* Wild Goose Publications, 2004.

Music and Worship

*Farlee, Robert Buckley, and Eric Vollen, editors. *Leading the Church's Song.* Augsburg Fortress, 1998.

*Kropf, Marlene, and Kenneth Nafziger. *Singing: A Mennonite Voice.* Herald Press, 2001.

*Neufeld, Bernie, ed. *Music in Worship: A Mennonite Perspective.* Herald Press, 1998.

*Slough, Rebecca. *A House for our Hymns.* Mennonite Publishing House, 1992.

Bell, John L. *The Singing Thing: A Case for Congregational Song.* GIA Publications, 2000.

Cherwien, David. *Let the People Sing! A Keyboardist's Creative and Practical Guide to Engaging God's People in Meaningful Song.* Concordia Publishing House, 1997.

McLean, Terri Bocklund. *New Harmonies: Choosing Contemporary Music for Worship.* Alban Institute, 1998.

Parker, Alice. *Melodious Accord: Good Singing in the Church.* Liturgy Training Publications, 1991.

Westermeyer, Paul. *The Heart of the Matter: Church Music as Praise, Prayer, Proclamation, Story and Gift.* GIA Publications, 2001.

Visual Arts in Worship

*Chinn, Nancy. *Spaces for Spirit: Adorning the Church.* Liturgy Training Publications, 1998.

*James, Leslie, and Karmen Krahn. *Proclamation by Design.* Faith & Life Resources, 2006.

*Jensen, Robin M. *The Substance of Things Seen: Art, Faith and the Christian Community.* Eerdmans, 2004.

*Liddell, Jill. *The Patchwork Pilgrimage: How to Create Vibrant Church Decorations and Vestments with Quilting Techniques.* Viking Studio Books, 1993.

Dilasser, Maurice. *The Symbols of the Church.* The Liturgical Press, 1999.

Klein, Patricia S. *Worship Without Words: The Signs and Symbols of Our Faith.* Paraclete Press, 2000.

Mazar, Peter. *To Crown the Year: Decorating the Church through the Seasons.* Liturgy Training Publications, 1995.

Schultze, Quentin J. *High-Tech Worship? Using Presentational Technologies Wisely.* Baker Books, 2004.

Stone, Karen. *Image and Spirit: Finding Meaning in Visual Art.* Augsburg, 2003.

Arts in Worship: Drama, Movement, Scripture Presentation

*Chevalier, Rebekah. *Spirit Mourn, Spirit Dance.* United Church Publications, 1998.

*Morton, Craig, and Ken Hawkley. *Word of Mouth: Creative Ways to Present Scripture.* Faith & Life Press, 2000.

*Shelley, Patricia J. *Let All Within Us Praise! Dramatic Resources for Worship.* Faith & Life Press, 1996.

DeSola, Carla. *The Spirit Moves: A Handbook of Dance and Prayer.* The Liturgical Conference, 1977.

Meyer, Susan E. *Pronunciation Guide for the Sunday Lectionary.* Liturgy Training Publications, 1998.

Rang, Jack C. *How to Read the Bible Aloud: Oral Interpretation of Scripture.* Paulist Press, 1994.

Rosser, Aelred A. *A Well-Trained Tongue: Formation in the Ministry of Reader.* Liturgy Training Publications, 1996.

_____ *A Word That Will Rouse Them: Reflections on the Ministry of Reader.* Liturgy Training Publications, 1995.

Children in Worship

*Berryman, Jerome, and Sonja Stewart. *Young Children and Worship.* Westminster/John Knox Press, 1988.

*Sandell, Elizabeth J. *Including Children in Worship: A Planning Guide for Congregations.* Augsburg, 1991.

*Snyder, Eleanor. *Including Children in the Life of the Congregation: A Contemporary Mennonite Exploration.* Unpublished manuscript, 1999 (available through Mennonite Publishing Network).

Christian Year

*Floyd, Pat, compiler. *The Special Days and Seasons of the Christian Year: How They Came About and How They Are Observed Today.* Abingdon, 1998.

*Richardson, Jan L. *In Wisdom's Path: Discovering the Sacred in Every Season.* Pilgrim Press, 2000.

*Stookey, Laurence Hull. *Calendar: Christ's Time for the Church.* Abingdon Press, 1996.

*For seasonal worship resources, see *Leader* (www.leaderonline.org), a quarterly journal publication of Mennonite Publishing Network.

Hickman, Hoyt L., Don E. Saliers, Laurence Hull Stookey, and James F. White. *The New Handbook of the Christian Year (Based on the Revised Common Lectionary).* Abingdon Press, 1992 (revised edition).

Webber, Robert E., ed. *The Services of the Christian Year, Vol. 5 (The Complete Library of Christian Worship).* Star Song Publishing Group, 1994.

Wright, Wendy M. *The Time Between: Cycles and Rhythms in Ordinary Time*. Upper Room Books, 1999.

Advent, Christmas and Epiphany

*Iona Community (Wild Goose Worship Group). *Cloth for the Cradle: Worship Resources and Readings for Advent. Christmas and Epiphany.* GIA Publications, 2000.

*O'Gormon, Thomas, ed. *An Advent Sourcebook*. Liturgy Training Publications, 1988.

*Richardson, Jan L. *Night Visions: Searching the Shadows of Advent and Christmas*. United Church Press, 1998.

*Simcoe, Mary Ann, ed. *A Christmas Sourcebook*. Liturgy Training Publications, 1984.

Duerksen, Carol. *Sacred Search: Encountering God During Advent*. Faith & Life Resources, 2005.

Hendrix, John, Susan Meadors, and David Miller. *Celebrate Advent: Worship & Learning Resources*. Smyth & Helwys, 1999.

Redding, Mary Lou. *While We Wait: Living the Questions of Advent*. Upper Room Books, 2002.

Wright, Wendy. *The Vigil: Keeping Watch in the Season of Christ's Coming*. Upper Room Books, 1996.

Lent and Holy Week

*Baker, J. Robert, Evelyn Kaehler, and Peter Mazar, ed. *A Lent Sourcebook (Volumes 1 and 2)*. Liturgy Training Publications, 1991.

*Burgess, Ruth, and Chris Polhill. *Eggs and Ashes: Practical & Liturgical Resources for Lent and Holy Week*. Wild Goose Publications, 2004.

*Huck, Gabe, and Mary Ann Simcoe, ed. *A Triduum Sourcebook*. Liturgy Training Publications, 1996 (revised edition).

*Wild Goose Worship Group. *Stages on the Way: Worship Resources for Lent, Holy Week and Easter*. Wild Goose Publications, 1998.

Hauerwas, Stanley. *Cross-Shattered Christ: Meditations on the Seven Last Words*. Brazos Press, 2004.

Marcheschi, Graziano. *The Way of the Cross*. GIA Publications, 1999.

Nouwen, Henri J. M. *The Return of the Prodigal Son: A Meditation on Fathers, Brothers and Sons*. Doubleday, 1996.

Ramshaw, Gail. *Words around the Fire*. Liturgy Training Publications, 1990.

Reed, Angela. *Sacred Search: Encountering God During Lent*. Faith & Life Resources, 2004.

Rosenthal, Peggy. *Praying the Gospels through Poetry: Lent to Easter*. St. Anthony Messenger Press, 2002.

Stowe, Robert E., Donna E. Schaper, Anne McKinstry, and Janet E. Powers. *Breathing New Life into Lent: A Collection of Creative Worship Resources*. Judson Press, 1999.

Wright, Wendy M. *The Rising: Living the Mysteries of Lent, Easter and Pentecost*. Upper Room Books, 1994.

Easter to Pentecost

*Huck, Gabe, Gail Ramshaw, and Gordon Lathrop. *An Easter Sourcebook*. Liturgy Training Publications, 1987.

*Walker, Andrew. *Journey into Joy: Stations of the Resurrection*. Paulist Press, 2001.

Allen, O. Wesley. *Preaching Resurrection*. Chalice Press, 2000.

Chapman, Raymond. *Stations of the Resurrection*. Morehouse Publishing, 1999.

Maxwell, Bernard J., Judy Foster, and Jill Shirvington. *Easter for 50 Days*. Twenty-Third Publications, 1989.

Tickle, Phyllis A. *Final Sanity: Stories of Lent, Easter, and the Great Fifty Days*. The Upper Room, 1987.

Worship and Ritual

*Anderson, Herbert and Edward Foley. *Mighty Stories, Dangerous Rituals: Weaving Together the Human and Divine*. Jossey-Bass Publishers, 1998.

*Driver, Tom F. *Liberating Rites: Understanding the Transformative Power of Ritual*. Westview Press, 1998.

*Landers, Bertha. *Through Laughter and Tears: The Church Celebrates!* Faith & Life Resources, 2001.
*Oswald, Roy M., with Jean Morris Trumbauer. *Transforming Rituals: Daily Practices for Changing Lives.* Alban Institute, 1999.

Grimes, Ronald L. *Deeply Into the Bone: Re-Inventing Rites of Passage.* University of California Press, 2000.
Harris, Chris. *Creating Relevant Rituals: Celebrations for Religious Education.* E. J. Dwyer, 1992.
Morseth, Ellen. *Ritual and the Arts in Spiritual Discernment.* Worshipful Work, 1999.

Baptism

*Baker, J. Robert, Larry J. Nyberg, and Victoria M. Tufano. *A Baptism Sourcebook.* Liturgy Training Publications, 1993.
*Yamasaki, April. *Making Disciples: Preparing People for Baptism, Christian Living, and Church Membership.* Faith & Life Resources, 2003.

Thurian, Max, and Geoffrey Wainwright, ed. *Baptism and Eucharist: Ecumenical Convergence in Celebration.* Eerdmans, 1983.

Communion and Foot Washing

*Baker, J. Robert, and Barbara Budde. *A Eucharist Sourcebook.* Liturgy Training Publications, 1999.
*Kreider, Eleanor. *Communion Shapes Character.* Herald Press, 1997.
*McAvoy, Jane. *Table Talk: Resources for the Communion Meal.* Chalice Press, 1993.

Bodey, Richard Allen, and Robert Leslie Holmes, editors. *Come to the Banquet: Meditations for the Lord's Table.* Baker Books, 1998.
Dixon, Michael E. *Bread of Blessing, Cup of Hope.* Chalice Press, 1987.
Hellwig, Monika K. *The Eucharist and the Hunger of the World.* Sheed and Ward, 1992.

Weddings

*Baker, J. Robert, Joni Reiff Gibley, and Kevin Charles Gibley, editors. *A Marriage Sourcebook*. Liturgy Training Publications, 1994.

*Batts, Sidney F. *The Protestant Wedding Sourcebook: A Complete Guide for Developing Your Own Service*. Westminster/John Knox Press, 1993.

*Marchesi, Graziano, with Nancy Seitz Marchesi. *Scripture at Weddings: Choosing and Proclaiming the Word of God*. Liturgy Training Publications, 1992.

Funerals

*Kehler, Larry, editor. *Going Gracefully: A Resource Collection on Dying, Death, Funerals and Grief*. Mennonite Church Canada, 2001 (available online at www.mennonitechurch.ca.)

*Sloyan, Virginia, ed. *A Sourcebook about Christian Death*. Liturgy Training Publications, 1990.

*Vogel, Linda J. *Rituals for Resurrection: Celebrating Life and Death*. Upper Room Books, 1996.

Bell, John L. *The Last Journey: Reflections for the Time of Grieving* (songbook, cassette, CD). GIA Publications, 1996.

Henderson, J. Frank. *Liturgies of Lament*. Liturgy Training Publications, 1994.

Lloyd, Dan S. *Leading Today's Funerals: A Pastoral Guide for Improving Bereavement Ministry*. Baker Books, 1997.

Wolfelt, Alan D. *Creating Meaningful Funeral Ceremonies: A Guide for Caregivers*. Companion Press (The Center for Loss and Life Transition), 1994.

Healing Services

*Brooke, Avery. *Healing in the Landscape of Prayer*. Cowley Publications, 1996.

*Cowie, Ian. *Prayers and Ideas for Healing Services*. Wild Goose Publications, 1995.

*Thomas, Leo, with Jan Alkire. *Healing Ministry: A Practical Guide*. Sheed and Ward, 1994.

Anderson, Vienna Cobb. *Prayers of Our Hearts in Word and Action*. Crossroad Publishing Company, 1991.

Norberg, Tilda, and Robert D. Webber. *Stretch Out Your Hand: Exploring Healing Prayer*. United Church Press, 1990.

Weems, Ann. *Psalms of Lament*. Westminster John Knox Press, 1995.

Zimmerman, Mari West. *Take and Make Holy: Honoring the Sacred in the Healing Journey of Abuse and Survivors*. Liturgy Training Publications, 1995.

Christian Worship: Theology and History

*Dawn, Marva J. *A Royal "Waste" of Time: The Splendor of Worshiping God and Being Church for the World*. Eerdmans, 1999.

*Ramshaw, Gail. *A Three-Year Banquet: The Lectionary for the Assembly*. Augsburg Fortress, 2004.

*White, James F. *Introduction to Christian Worship* (third edition). Abingdon Press, 2000.

*Witvliet, John D. *Worship Seeking Understanding: Windows into Christian Practice*. Baker Book House, 2003.

Edwards, Tilden. *Sabbath Time*. Seabury Press, 1982.

Keifert, Patrick R. *Welcoming the Stranger: A Public Theology of Worship and Evangelism*. Fortress Press, 1992.

Moeller, Pamela Ann. *Exploring Worship Anew: Dreams and Visions*. Chalice Press, 1998.

Peterson, David. *Engaging with God: A Biblical Theology of Worship*. InterVarsity Press, 2001.

Plantinga, Cornelius, Jr., and Sue A. Rozeboom. *Discerning the Spirits: A Guide to Thinking about Christian Worship Today*. Eerdmans, 2003.

Pfatteicher, Philip H. *A Dictionary of Liturgical Terms*. Trinity Press International, 1991.

_____ *The School of the Church: Worship and Christian Formation*. Trinity Press International, 1995.

Schattauer, Thomas H., editor. *Inside Out: Worship in an Age of Mission*. Fortress Press, 1999.

Schmidt, Clayton J. *Too Deep for Words: A Theology of Liturgical Expression*. Westminster John Knox Press, 2001.

Stake, Donald Wilson. *The ABC's of Worship: A Concise Dictionary.* Westminster/John Knox Press, 1992.
White, James F. *A Brief History of Christian Worship.* Abingdon Press, 1993.

Web Resources

www.leaderonline.org	Mennonite church year resources
www.reformedworship.org	Reformed tradition worship resources
www.worshiplinks.com	Launch pad to other worship sites
www.worshipleader.org	Companion site to periodical
www.worshipworks.com	Resources (prayers, music, etc.) for weekly planning
www.homileticsonline.com	Sermon resource—subscription required
www.lectionary.org	Lectionary and exegesis resources
www.textweek.com	Week-by-week text-related material
www.jameslove.com/lectors.html	Preparation for scripture readers

APPENDIX 9
MUSIC

The God of Abraham praise

LEONI 66.84D

The God of A-brah'm praise. All prais-ed be the Name,
who was, and is, and is to be, is still the same;
the one e-ter-nal God, ere all that now ap-pears,
the First, the Last, be-yond all thought through time-less years!

Text: *Yigdal prayer* (Jewish doxology), 14th c., alt.
Music: Hebrew melody transcribed by Meyer Leoni, ca. 1770

Praise the Lord

SAKURA Irregular

Praise the Lord,   praise the Lord,   for the green-ness

of the   trees,   for the beau-ty of the   flow'rs, for the blue-ness

of the   sky,   for the great-ness of the   sea.   Praise the Lord,

praise the Lord,   now and for - ev - er-more.

Text: Nobuaki Hanaoka, 1980, *Hymns from the Four Winds,* 1983. Copyright © 1980 Nobuaki Hanaoka
Music: Traditional Japanese melody. Transcription copyright © 1983 assigned to Abingdon Press

Shout to the North

Men of faith, rise up and sing of the great and glo-rious King, You are strong when you feel weak in your bro-ken-ness com-plete. Shout to the North and the South, sing to the East and the West; Je - sus is Sav-ior to all, Lord of Heaven and earth.

Text: Martin Smith

Music: Martin Smith. Text and music copyright © 1995 Curious? Music UK (PRS). Administered in the United States and Canada by EMI Christian Music Publishing, P.O. Box 5085, 101 Winners Circle, Brentwood, TN 37024-5085. All rights reserved. International copyright secured. Used by permission.

Jesus Lord, how joyful you have made us

Irregular

Je-sus Lord, how joy-ful you   have   made   us   to come to-geth -

er here with you now!   In your mer-cy you   have   called us.

You say, "I   am   the way."   We hear   you call   us.

We ask you, "Come lead us   day   by day." We fol-low your   way.

Text: John Heap of Birds, *Jesus Nehetotaetanome;* tr. David Graber and others, *Tsese-Ma'heone-Nemeototse,* 1982.
Copyright © 1982 Mennonite Indian Leaders' Council
Music: Plains Indian melody

Lord, listen to your children

CHILDREN PRAYING 98.99

Lord, list-en to your children pray - ing,

Lord, send your Spir-it in this place.

Lord, list-en to your children pray - ing, send us

love, send us pow'r, send us grace!

Text: Ken Medema, 1970
Music: Ken Medema, 1970. Text and music copyright © 1973 Hope Publishing Co.

APPENDIX 10
WORSHIP INGREDIENT TABLE

Worship action (course)	Art form (ingredient)
Gathering	Music • Congregational songs that invite people to come, gather, enter, and worship • Visual displays • Banners, streamers that progressively draw people into the worship space • Projected images or mural that focuses worshipers' attention on a central place Video • Congregationally produced video of neighborhood, people arriving at church building and entering worship space Movement • Organized procession of worshipers into worship space
Praising Adoring Thanksgiving Lament	Music • Congregational songs that are robust, vibrant, and passionate—naming God's steadfast love, God's character, God's gracious actions • Congregational songs that draw the mood inward—naming sadness, suffering, alienation, abandonment • Congregational songs of hope that demonstrate musically and with words the bittersweet tension between lament and thanksgiving

Worship action (course)	Art form (ingredient)
Praising **Adoring** **Thanksgiving** **Lament** **(continued)**	Poetry and psalms • Psalms or other poetry expressing thanksgiving Visual • Slide show on a particular theme of praise or thanksgiving (e.g., creation, blessing, reconciliation, etc.) Movement • Signing congregational songs • Improvised dance • Congregational hand dances/wave offerings
Confessing	Music • Choral anthems that open the spirit of the congregation for confession • Congregational songs that tell the truth about our sinful condition Poetry • Psalms or poems naming conditions of sin or results of sin Drama • Dramatic readings that retell the results of sin • Short play displaying the consequences of sin Visual • Images, possibly slide show, showing behavior that devalues, degrades, injures, or oppresses other people and the created world • Icon of Christ that invites confession and offers assurance of forgiveness Movement or posture • Kneeling • Arms outstretched • Turning away from other worshipers Silence

Worship action (course)	Art form (ingredient)
Proclaiming	Music • Congregational songs that recount biblical stories • Anthems that paraphrase scriptures Poetry/language • Strong images, metaphors in sermons • Rhythm, alliteration, phrasing in sermons • Economy of words, well-chosen words • Engaging storytelling • Well-crafted illustrations Drama • Enacted story or parable • Readers theater presentation of scripture text Visual • Slide show of images (with poetry or music) interpreting scripture texts or sermon Video • Visual interpretation of scripture text illustrating central points of the sermon Movement • Congregation standing for scripture reading • Blessing of scripture reader and preacher • Dancers interpreting scripture through movement
Praying	Music • Congregational songs that name needs, attitudes, and desires, formed into petitions • Repetitive congregational songs that focus the mind and quiet the spirit • Choral anthems that open the heart and mind for prayer

Worship action (course)	Art form (ingredient)
Praying (continued)	Poetry/language • Words that are expansive, evocative, and stretch the horizons of the worshipers' collective prayer Visual • Icon of Christ through whom the congregation prays • Image of people praying to focus stillness Movement • Praying "on behalf of" • Arms outstretched in prayer
Affirming	Music • Hymns confessing faith (e.g., many gospel songs) Movement or posture • Standing • Arms open
Offering	Music • Congregational songs of personal offering Visual • Video clips of organizations supported by congregational outreach • Image(s) that display openness, giving, sharing (e.g., open hands, service, shared abundance) Movement • Processing gifts to worship center • Wave offering* • Passing offering, passing peace Arms uplifted

Worship action (course)	Art form (ingredient)
Witnessing/ testifying	Music • Hymns that reflect images of God's shalom • Songs from the worldwide church • Improvisational offerings Visual • Video clips of congregational activities that extend God's reign • Images of congregational activities that serve the community • Images of congregational members engaged in daily work • Images of people living the gospel in daily life
Sending	Music • Robust congregational song that moves worshipers out • Instrumental improvisation Visual • Banners, flags leading procession out of worship space Movement • Arms raised in blessing • Processional into the world • Dancers leading worshipers out

* In Leviticus 23, God ordains the various festivals the Hebrews are to observe, along with the appropriate offerings. The wave offering (NIV), or the raised, elevated offering (NRSV) is a grain offering the priest raises before God, "so that you may find acceptance." Following this precedent, some congregations regularly practice a wave offering; worshipers hold up their hands as a sign of offering themselves, their monetary gifts, or any other material contribution they are making for God's sake and the good of their communities.

APPENDIX 11
SAMPLE CHART

Scripture Homework

Advent 1 – Year A –

The Lesson   Isaiah 2:1-5

The word that Isaiah son of Amoz saw concerning Judah and Jerusalem. In days to come the mountain of the LORD's house shall be established as the highest of the mountains, and shall be raised above the hills; all the nations shall stream to it. Many peoples shall come and say, "Come, let us go up to the mountain of the LORD, to the house of the God of Jacob; that he may teach us his ways and that we may walk in his paths." For out of Zion shall go forth instruction, and the word of the LORD from Jerusalem. He shall judge between the nations, and shall arbitrate for many peoples; they shall beat their swords into plowshares, and their spears into pruning hooks; nation shall not lift up sword against nation, neither shall they learn war any more. O house of Jacob, come, let us walk in the light of the LORD!

The Response   Psalm 122

1 I was glad when they said to me,
   "Let us go to the house of the LORD!"
2 Our feet are standing within your gates, O Jerusalem.
3 Jerusalem—built as a city that is bound firmly together.
4 To it the tribes go up, the tribes of the LORD,
   as was decreed for Israel,
   to give thanks to the name of the LORD.
5 For there the thrones for judgment were set up,
   the thrones of the house of David.
6 Pray for the peace of Jerusalem:
   "May they prosper who love you.
7 Peace be within your walls, and security within your towers."
8 For the sake of my relatives and friends I will say,
   "Peace be within you."
9 For the sake of the house of the LORD our God
   I will seek your good.

The Epistle   Romans 13:11-14

You know what time it is, how it is now the moment for you to wake from sleep. For salvation is nearer to us now than when we became believers; the night is far gone, the day is near. Let us then lay aside the works of darkness and put on the armor of light; let us live honorably as in the day, not in reveling and drunkenness, not in debauchery and licentiousness, not in quarreling and jealousy. Instead, put on the Lord Jesus Christ, and make no provision for the flesh, to gratify its desires.

The Gospel   Matthew 24:36-44

On the Mount of Olives, Jesus said to his disciples privately about his coming, "But about that day and hour no one knows, neither the angels of heaven, nor the Son, but only the Father. For as the days of Noah were, so will be the coming of the Son of Man. For as in those days before the flood they were eating and drinking, marrying and giving in marriage, until the day Noah entered the ark, and they knew nothing until the flood came and swept them all away, so too will be the coming of the Son of Man. Then two will be in the field; one will be taken and one will be left. Two women will be grinding meal together; one will be taken and one will be left. Keep awake therefore, for you do not know on what day your Lord is coming. But understand this: if the owner of the house had known in what part of the night the thief was coming, he would have stayed awake and would not have let his house be broken into. Therefore you also must be ready, for the Son of Man is coming at an unexpected hour."

Images: mountain, house, path/way

Actions: go up, walk, wake from sleep, be ready; pray for peace/not learn war;

Themes: salvation is near; be ready for the coming of the Son of Man; now is the moment; walk in the light of the Lord

471

APPENDIX 12
TASTE AND SEE MUSIC

Taste and see

Taste and see, taste and see the goodness of the Lord. O taste and see, taste and see the goodness of the Lord, of the Lord.

Text: Psalm 34; James E. Moore, Jr., b. 1951
Music: James E. Moore, Jr., b. 1951. Copyright © 1983, GIA Publications, Inc.

NOTES

Introduction

1. Worship scholars are fond of noting the specific language embedded in this story. The same verbs used to describe Jesus's action in this story—taking the bread, blessing it, breaking it, and giving it—are used elsewhere in the Gospels in connection with what we now call the Eucharist (Matt 26:26–29; Mark 14:22–25; Luke 22:15–20). According to the accounts of the Last Supper, Jesus "took a loaf of bread, and when he had given thanks, he broke it and gave it to them" (Luke 22:19). Similarly, in the Emmaus meal recorded in Luke 24:30, Jesus engages in the same series of actions. Over and over again, we see the magnificent outpouring of God's grace that continually sustains us in ministry and in daily life.

2. See chapter seven for a more detailed discussion of the roles on a collaborative worship leadership team.

3. Mary Oliver, "Logos," in *Why I Wake Early: New Poems* (Boston: Beacon Press, 2005), 40.

4. Remarks offered in a teaching and research seminar at AMBS, March 9, 2005.

Chapter 1: Why eat?

1. The phrase "the common creatures of bread and wine" is used in the Anglican-Episcopal Eucharistic liturgy. Early in the history of the church, Christians understood the liturgical act of partaking of the body of the Christ as being akin to a child receiving milk at a mother's breast. In the second century, Clement of Alexandria wrote:

> Jesus Christ,
> celestial milk out-pressed
> from a young bride's fragrant breasts
> (your Wisdom's graces),
> your little children
> with their tender mouths
> slake their thirst there,
> drink their fill
> of the Spirit flowing
> from those incorporeal nipples.

Medieval mystics such as Julian of Norwich and Mechtild of Magdeburg used similar images.

2. Although worship is the central source of nourishment for the body of Christ, many other corporate spiritual practices also contribute to the health of the body. Study of scripture, engaging in acts of service and peacemaking, spiritual friendship and spiritual direction, hospitality, Sabbath keeping, and other

disciplines strengthen our faith and shape the character of Christians. In addition, personal spiritual practices such as prayer, fasting, and meditating on scripture play their part in keeping faith vital and sound.

3. The Institute for Social Research at the University of Michigan found, in a recent survey, that 44 percent of people in the United States and 38 percent of those in Canada say they attend religious services at least once a week. But when church attendance data are checked against other data, the figures show that only about 20 percent of Americans and 10 percent of Canadians actually go to church one or more times a week.

4. "Church Going" by Philip Larkin is reprinted from *The Less Deceived* by permission of The Marvell Press, England and Australia, and excerpted from *The Norton Anthology of Modern Poetry* (New York: W. W. Norton, 1973), 1015.

5. Eugene H. Peterson, "Spirit Quest," *Christianity Today* (8 Nov. 1993), 28.

6. In Genesis 2:3, rest is identified as the first purpose of the Sabbath day: "So God blessed the seventh day and hallowed it, because on it God rested from all the work that he had done in creation." Exodus 31:12–17 reiterates the command to follow God's example and rest on the Sabbath. In addition, keeping the Sabbath is a sign of a perpetual covenant relationship with God: "You shall keep my Sabbaths, for this is a sign between me and you through your generations, given in order that you may know that I, the LORD, sanctify you." A specific activity commanded for the Sabbath is to remember and tell the stories of God's mighty acts of deliverance: "Remember that you were a slave in the land of Egypt, and the LORD your God brought you out from there with a mighty hand and an outstretched arm; therefore the LORD your God commanded you to keep the Sabbath day" (Deut 5:15).

7. Tim Stafford, "The Pentecostal Gold Standard," *Christianity Today* (July 2005), 28.

8. John H. Westerhoff III, *Living the Faith Community: The Church That Makes a Difference* (Minneapolis: Winston Press, 1985), 68. Re-released in 2004 as a Seabury Classic by Church Publishing Incorporated, New York.

9. See chapter two for helpful perspectives on this topic.

10. Some typical elements of worship mentioned in the New Testament include the following: scripture reading (1 Tim 4:13); praying (Acts 1:14); singing hymns and songs (Eph 5:19); breaking bread (Acts 20:7); preaching (Acts 4:31); the holy kiss or kiss of peace (1 Cor 16:20); ecstatic utterances and prophecies (1 Cor 14:26–33); giving of offerings (1 Cor 16:2); and teaching, admonishing, and encouraging one another (Col 3:16). Benedictions, doxologies, and creedal phrases are embedded in New Testament texts along with hymn fragments. Although not mentioned directly in the New Testament, dancing also occurred in worship: paintings on the walls of the catacombs depict Christians celebrating the joy of the resurrection in circle dances as they gathered to commemorate the death of martyrs.

11. This arrangement of the Isa 6:1-8 scripture reading is attributed to Clarence Rempel, of Newton, Kansas. Used by permission.

12. Frederick Buechner, *Telling the Truth: The Gospel as Tragedy, Comedy and Fairytale* (San Francisco: Harper & Row, 1977), 56.

13. Annie Dillard, *Teaching a Stone to Talk: Expeditions and Encounters* (New York: Harper & Row, 1982), 43–44.

14. Quoted in *A Reconciliation Sourcebook*, ed. Kathleen Hughes and Joseph A. Favazza (Chicago: Liturgy Training Publications, 1997), 52. The orig-

inal quotation is from Dag Hammarskjöld in *Markings*, translated by Leif Sjöberg and W. H. Auden (Alfred A Knopf, and Faber and Faber, 1964).

15. Reproduced from *The Senses of Preaching* © 1988 Thomas G. Long. Used by permission of Westminster John Knox Press.

16. Millard C. Lind, *Biblical Foundations for Christian Worship* (Scottdale, PA: Herald Press, 1973), 5.

17. In *Israel's Praise: Doxology against Idolatry and Ideology* (Philadelphia: Fortress Press, 1988), Walter Brueggemann writes, "For the community gathered around Jesus, it is precisely the act of worship that is the act of world-formation" (27).

18. See chapter four for a more extensive discussion of the elements of worship.

19. See chapter twelve for an extended discussion of the role of Sunday worship as appetizer for the eternal feast.

20. "The tree of life," set to a tune by Alice Parker, is printed in *Hymnal: A Worship Book* [*HWB*] (Elgin, IL: Brethren Press; Newton, KS: Faith & Life Press; Scottdale, PA: Mennonite Publishing House, 1992), 509. Where hymnal numbers are given in this book, they refer to this source.

Chapter 2: Who's coming to dinner?

1. The meaning of *culture* is frequently disputed in academic circles. In this book *culture* refers to the communication systems, patterns, and practices used by groups of people to create and sustain meaning and shared action. Anthropologist Clifford Geertz, representing a cognitive anthropological understanding of culture, writes that culture "denotes an historically transmitted pattern of meanings in symbols, a system of inherited conceptions, expressed in symbolic forms by means of which [people] communicate, perpetuate, and develop their knowledge about and attitudes toward life" ("Religion as a Cultural System," chapter 4 in *The Interpretation of Cultures* [New York: Basic Books, Inc., 1973], 89). The tendency to believe that cultures are unchanging, static, and bounded is misguided. They are dynamic—changing slowly or rapidly—adapting to changes in physical living conditions, resource allocations, demographics, new technologies, unforeseen problems, or environmental changes. For this reason, leaders must continually notice what is happening within the congregational culture.

2. See chapter ten for a more detailed analysis of various ways of knowing.

3. Ruby K. Payne and Bill Ehlig, *What Every Church Member Should Know about Poverty* (Highlands, TX: Aha! Process, Inc., 1999).

4. Ibid., 12.

5. Ibid., 24.

6. Ibid., 33.

7. Walter Ong and Jack Goody studied the effects of reading and writing on cultural communication patterns. Few, if any, living cultures are purely oral or written, but the choice to communicate in speech or print greatly affects what is communicated and the quality of relationship between the communicators. Neither oral nor written communication is superior, but rather each serves distinct functions within a culture. See Walter Ong, *Orality and Literacy: The Technologizing of the Word* (London: Metheun, 1982); and Jack Goody, *The Interface between the Written and the Oral* (Cambridge: Cambridge University Press, 1987).

8. David Keirsey and Marilyn Bates, *Please Understand Me: Character and Temperament Types,* 5th ed. (Del Mar, CA: Prometheus Nemesis Book Co., 1984), 14.

9. Ibid.

10. Ibid., 16.

11. See more about story in chapter six.

12. Here I distinguish between *ritual,* which consists of general patterns of action that can be easily adapted, extended, or improvised, and *rites,* which are tightly regulated, usually scripted, and have been reviewed by some body with authority to require their use in specific situations (for example, baptism, communion, weddings, etc.).

13. See chapters ten and eleven for more on ritual.

Chapter 3: Planning the menu

1. For more discussion of record keeping, see chapter fourteen.

2. See chapter two for more on how the congregation influences the worship event.

3. The relationship between preacher and worship planners is discussed more fully in chapter seven, on cooking collaboratively.

4. *The One Year Bible: Arranged in 365 Daily Readings* (Wheaton, IL: Tyndale House Publishers, 1986).

5. Eugene L. Lowry, *Living with the Lectionary: Preaching through the Revised Common Lectionary* (Nashville, TN: Abingdon Press, 1992).

Chapter 4: Designing the courses

1. Theodore Jennings, *Life as Worship: Praise and Prayer in Jesus' Name* (Grand Rapids: Eerdmans, 1982), 5.

2. Robert Webber, *Worship Is a Verb* (Waco: Word Books, 1985).

3. The authors worship in a Protestant tradition that celebrates communion (the Lord's Supper) several times during the year, not every Sunday. This chapter examines the basic actions that are part of a regular Sunday service when communion is not observed. Chapter eleven examines the Lord's Supper as a course in the Sunday meal.

4. "Come and rejoice" by Don Moen and Gerrit Gustafson. Copyright © 1989 Integrity's Hosanna! Music/ASCAP. c/o Integrity Media, Inc., 1000 Cody Road, Mobile, AL 36695.

5. "Gather us in," Copyright © 1983 by GIA Publications, Inc., 7404 S. Mason Ave., Chicago, IL 60638. www.giamusic.com 800.442.1358. All rights reserved. Used by permission. Marty Haugen, composer. HWB 6.

6. John Austin's description and analysis of the nature of speech acts in *How to Do Things with Words* (New York: Oxford University Press, 1965) remains useful. Speech acts involve a person in engaging speech that has moral, and therefore relational, qualities.

7. Claude Frayssé, 1976; trans. Ken Morse, 1988, *Hymnal Sampler,* 1989. Translation copyright © The Hymnal Project; *HWB* 76.

8. "Your love is never ending," Copyright © 1983 by GIA Publications, Inc., 7404 S. Mason Ave., Chicago, IL 60638. www.giamusic.com 800.442.1358. All rights reserved. Used by permission. Marty Haugen, composer. *HWB* 161.

9. The Sanctus.

10. "Lord have mercy" by Steve Merkel ©2000 Integrity's Hosanna! Music/ASCAP. c/o Integrity Media, Inc., 1000 Cody Road, Mobile, AL 36695.

11. Charles Wesley, "Open Lord, my inward ear," in *Hymns and Spiritual Songs*, 1742; *HWB* 140.

12. Don C. Skinner, *Prayers for the Gathered Community: Resources for the Liturgical Year* (Cleveland: United Church Press, 1997), 154. Used by permission.

13. Jeffrey N. Stinehelfer, "Rich Enough to Be Generous," *Church Worship* (July 1997): 13.

14. Frances R. Havergal, *Songs of Grace and Glory, Appendix,* 1874; *HWB* 389.

15. Words: Robert L. Edwards, Copyright © 1961 Renewal 1989 The Hymn Society. Admin. by Hope Publishing Co., Carol Stream, IL 60188. All rights reserved. Used by permission. *HWB* 383.

16. See chapter two for an extended treatment of this process. Chapter five describes the importance of collaboration with worship leaders in preparing the sermon.

17. "Tow Fisherman," Copyright © 1986 by GIA Publications, Inc., 7404 S. Mason Ave., Chicago, IL 60638. www.giamusic.com 800.442.1358. All rights reserved. Used by permission. Suzanne Toolan, composer. *HWB* 227.

18. Based on Isaiah 6, Daniel Schutte, 1980, *Lord of Light.* Copyright © 1981 Daniel L. Schutte and New Dawn Music. TEXT AND MUSIC ©1981, OCP Publications, 5536 NE HASSALO, PORTLAND, OR 97213. All rights reserved. Used with permission. Daniel Schutte, composer. *HWB* 395.

19. Based on Nicene creed, 4ᵗʰ c.; translation composite. Copyright © S. C. Ochieng Okeyo; *HWB* 330.

20. *HWB* 165, 329.

21. "Shout to the North" by Martin Smith. Copyright © 1995 Curious? Music UK. Administered by EMI Christian Music Publishing. Used by Permission.

22. "What wondrous love is this," in *Cluster of Spiritual Songs,* 3ʳᵈ ed., 1823; *HWB* 530.

23. Horatio Spafford, "When peace, like a river," in *Gospel Hymns, No. 2,* 1876; *HWB* 336.

24. Copyright © 1999 Vineyard Songs (UK/EIRE) ADMIN. IN NORTH AMERICA BY MUSIC SERVICES o/b/o VINEYARD MUSIC GLOBAL INC. (PRS). All Rights Reserved. Used By Permission. Kathryn Scott, composer.

25. Ernest Y. L. Yang, 1934, *Hymns of Universal Praise,* 1977; trans. Frank W. Price. Copyright © 1977 The Chinese Christian Literature Council, Ltd.; *HWB* 354.

26. Skinner, *Prayers for the Gathered Community,* xix–xx.

27. "Lord, whose love in humble service," Text: Albert Bayly (1901-1984), in *Seven New Social Welfare Hymns,* 1961. Copyright © 1961 Oxford University Press, London; Used by Permission. All rights reserved. *HWB* 369.

28. "O Lord hear my prayer" Copyright ©1982, 1983 and 1984 by Ateliers et Presses de Taizé, Taizé Community, France. GIA Publications, Inc., exclusive North American agent, 7404 S. Mason Ave., Chicago, IL 60638 www.giamusic.com 800.442.1358. All rights reserved. Used by permission. Jacques Berthier, composer. *HWB* 348.

29. Copyright © 1988, Bob Hurd. Published by OCP Publications, 5536 NE HASSALO, PORTLAND, OR 97213. All rights reserved. Used with permission. Owen Alstott, author; Mary F. Reza, Spanish translation. *HWB* 358.

30. "Through our fragmentary prayers" Text: Thomas H. Troeger (born

1945) from *New Hymns for the Life of the Church*, © 1992 Oxford University Press, Inc. Used by permission. All rights reserved. *HWB* 347.

31. Skinner, *Prayers for the Gathered Community*, 221. Used by permission.

32. Text by Jaroslav J. Vajda. Copyright © 1983 Concordia Publishing House. Used by permission. *HWB* 433.

33. Patricia Shelly, "Benediction." Copyright © 1983 by Patricia J. Shelly.

34. Robert Webber, *Planning Blended Worship: The Creative Mixture of Old and New* (Nashville, TN: Abingdon Press, 1998). Used by permission.

35. See chapter seven for explanation of this action.

36. The free-flowing praise model consists of five movements: Invitation, Engagement, Exaltation, Adoration, and Intimacy. Each movement is accomplished through songs that reach the highest intensity in the exaltation phase, and then move to adoration and intimacy. A final song provides a transition into the remainder of the service. In *Let Us Worship* ([South Plainfield, NJ: Bridge Publishing, 1983], 153–58), Judson Cornwall shows an adaptation of Old Testament temple worship. Barry Wayne Liesch (*The New Worship: Straight Talk on Music and the Church* [Grand Rapids: Baker Books, 1996], 64–67) cites Cornwall's work, noting similarities in movement and mood with the Wimber/Espinosa model.

37. *The United Methodist Hymnal: Book of United Methodist Worship* (Nashville, TN: The United Methodist Publishing House, 1989), 3. Used by permission.

38. The collect is an ancient Christian prayer form. This prayer addresses God, names a divine attribute or deed, asks for a particular need, and requests a desired outcome. It is offered in Jesus's name, with congregational Amen. The example below (*HWB* 746) illustrates this pattern.

Tender and compassionate God,	addresses God
you long to gather us in your arms as a hen gathers her chicks.	names a divine attribute or deed
Draw us to yourself in love, surround us with your grace, and keep us in the shelter of your wings	asks for a particular need
so that in our time of testing we may not fall away.	requests a desired outcome
In Jesus's name. Amen.	is offered in Jesus's name, with Amen.

Chapter 5: Preparing the entrée

1. Those who read scripture for public worship will be aided by having on hand a pronunciation guide, such as Susan E. Meyer's *Pronunciation Guide for the Sunday Lectionary* (Chicago: Liturgy Training Publications, 1998). Jack C. Rang, *How to Read the Bible Aloud: Oral Interpretation of Scripture* (New York: Paulist Press, 1994), is a complete guide that helps readers understand their role as interpreters of scripture; this resource will be particularly useful to readers who find it difficult to see themselves as interpreters of the Word. Another fine resource is Craig Morton and Ken Hawkley, *Word of Mouth: Creative Ways to Present Scripture* (Newton, KS: Faith & Life Press; Waterloo, ON, and Scottdale, PA: Herald Press, 2000). A small book that aids understanding the

ministry of the reader is Aelard R. Rosser's *A Word That Will Rouse Them: Reflections on the Ministry of the Reader* (Chicago: Liturgy Training Publications, 1995); it is not a "how-to" but a "why" book. If your congregation uses the lectionary, your scripture readers may profitably consult the Liturgy Training Publications resources for Years A, B, and C, *Workbook for Lectors and Gospel Readers*. The Canadian edition uses more inclusive human language than does the U.S. edition. See also chapter six of this book, on drama in worship.

2. Deane A. Kemper, *Effective Preaching: A Manual for Students and Pastors* (Philadelphia: Westminster Press, 1985), 17.

3. Stephen H. Webb, *The Divine Voice: Christian Proclamation and the Theology of Sound* (Grand Rapids: Brazos Press, 2004), 25.

4. Ibid. See Karl Barth, *Church Dogmatics* 1:2, trans. G. T. Thomson and Harold Knight (Edinburgh: T. & T. Clark, 1938), 803, 813.

5. Carol Lakey Hess, "Educating in the Spirit," in *Theological Perspectives on Christian Education,* ed. Jeff Astley, Leslie J. Francis, and Colin Crowder (Leominster, U.K.: Gracewing, 1996).

6. For more on this subject, see chapter three, on menu planning.

7. Paul Scott Wilson, *The Practice of Preaching* (Nashville, TN: Abingdon Press, 1996), 133–39. See Appendix 1 for a list of Wilson's study questions.

8. The congregational analysis tools discussed in chapter two are an important resource in the process of knowing our congregations.

9. Lucy Atkinson Rose, *Sharing the Word: Preaching in the Roundtable Church* (Louisville: Westminster John Knox Press, 1997).

10. John S. McClure, *The Roundtable Pulpit: Where Leadership and Preaching Meet* (Nashville, TN: Abingdon Press, 1995).

11. Another dimension of collaboration is the conversation between the preacher and worship planners, addressed in chapter seven. For worship to come together as a unified whole, the preacher, worship planners and worship leaders, including music leaders, all need to participate in listening conversations with one another.

12. Ronald J. Allen, *Patterns of Preaching: A Sermon Sampler* (St. Louis: Chalice Press, 1998).

13. Ronald J. Allen, *Preaching Verse by Verse* (Louisville: Westminster John Knox Press, 2000).

14. Henry H. Mitchell, *Celebration and Experience in Preaching* (Nashville, TN: Abingdon Press, 1990).

15. Eugene L. Lowry, *The Homiletical Plot: The Sermon as Narrative Art Form,* expanded ed. (Louisville: Westminster John Knox Press, 2001).

16. Douglas Ehninger, Bruce E. Gronbeck, and Alan H. Monroe, *Principles of Speech Communication,* 9th ed. (Glenview, IL: Scott Foresman, 1984).

17. See chapter twelve, "Extending the Table," for a fuller explanation of the role of persuasion in preaching.

18. Some of these presentation issues are discussed in chapter nine.

19. Chapter nine also focuses on presentation in the worship service, including presentation of the sermon.

20. Ronald J. Allen, *Preaching the Topical Sermon* (Louisville: Westminster John Knox Press, 1992), 4. Those who frequently preach topical sermons will benefit from reading Allen's thorough treatment of topical preaching.

21. See Appendix 2 for Allen's sequence for preparing the topical sermon.

Chapter 6: Choosing ingredients

1. William Bausch, *Storytelling: Imagination and Faith* (Mystic, CT: Twenty-Third Publications, 1984), 29–63. Other characteristics include the following: (1) stories unite us in a holistic way to nature, our common stuff of existence; (2) stories use a special language; (3) stories provide escape; (4) stories evoke in us right-brain imagination, tenderness, and therefore wholeness; (5) stories promote healing; (6) every story is our story.

2. A true story may be fictional, mythic, imaginative, but it will examine something true about the human condition.

3. *The Little Engine That Could,* by Watty Piper (pseudonym of Mabel Caroline Bragg), was first published in 1930. Publisher Platt and Munk continues to issue reprint editions.

4. Jean-François Lyotard first wrote about the distrust postmodern men and women have of "metanarratives" in *The Postmodern Condition: A Report on Knowledge* (Manchester, U.K.: Manchester University Press, 1984). Metanarratives present unifying principles or stories that explain "how these are," at least for people with social or political power. Henry Giroux, also writing about the postmodern condition, called the universal categories or assumptions of culturally shared stories *master narratives.* Uncritical acceptance of master narratives has tended to privilege the experience, knowledge, and authority of some groups over others. See Henry Giroux, "Postmodernism as Border Pedagogy: Redefining the Boundaries of Race and Ethnicity," in *Postmodernism, Feminism, and Cultural Politics: Rethinking Educational Boundaries,* ed. Henry A. Giroux (Albany, NY: SUNY Press, 1991), 217–56; reprinted in *A Postmodern Reader,* ed. Joseph Natoli and Linda Hutcheon (Albany, NY: SUNY Press, 1993), 463. For a short summary of Postmodernism and metanarrative, see Critical Pedagogy on the Web: Postmodernism, at mingo.infoscience.uiowa.edu/~stevens/critped/post.htm Gregory Wolfe's provocative editorial on master narrative and Christianity appears in the fall 1997 issue of *Image: Art, Faith, Mystery,* available on-line at www.imagejournal.org/back/017/editorial.asp

5. Anne Lamott, *Traveling Mercies* (New York: Pantheon Books, 1999), 65.

6. Yigdal prayer (Jewish doxology), 14th century; translated and paraphrased by Max Landsberg and Newton Mann, ca. 1885, alt.; Hebrew melody transcribed by Meyer Leoni, ca. 1770; *HWB* 162.

7. Nobuaki Hanaoka, Copyright © 1980 Nobuaki Hanaoka; traditional Japanese melody, transcription copyright © 1983 assigned to Abingdon Press; *HWB* 52.

8. "Shout to the North" by Martin Smith. Copyright © 1995 Curious? Music UK. Administered by EMI Christian Music Publishing. Used by permission.

9. John Heap of Birds, translated from the Cheyenne by David Graber and others, *Tsese-Ma'heone-Nemeótse* copyright © 1982 Mennonite Indian Leaders' Council. Plains Indian melody. *HWB* 9.

10. "Lord, listen to your children praying" © 1973 Hope Publishing Co., Carol Stream, IL 60188. All rights reserved. Used by permission. Ken Medema, composer. *HWB* 353.

11. Appendix 3 offers essential questions for selecting music for congregational singing.

12. Robert Jourdain, *Music, the Brain, and Ecstasy: How Music Captures Our Imagination* (New York: W. Morrow, 1997), 301, 329.

13. Ibid., 190.

14. For more information on differences between oral and written language, see chapter two.

15. For more information, visit the Ted & Lee TheaterWorks web-site at www.tedandlee.com.

16. A tablescape is an arrangement using fabric, candles, pictures, and other items to create a visual center of focus in a worship space.

17. Margaret Miles, *Image as Insight: Visual Understanding in Western Christianity and Secular Culture* (Boston: Beacon Press, 1985), 32.

18. Miles draws a connection between the iconoclasm of sixteenth-century Protestant reformers and the reordering of society the Protestant Reformation unleashed. She contends that when artwork that pictured a hierarchical religious and social order was removed from churches, people began to imagine other configurations of social and religious relationships (ibid., 106–07).

19. David Morgan, *Visual Piety: A History and Theory of Popular Religious Images* (Berkeley: University of California Press, 1998), 32.

20. Miles, *Image as Insight*, 150. Miles insists on the importance of balancing the formative characteristics of visual art with the analytic and descriptive powers of language to correct our misunderstandings and misperceptions of the world (145).

21. Ibid., 34.

22. Miles's categories here overlap with categories used in chapter ten to describe ways of knowing in the context of worship. Miles's iconic type overlaps most with our representational category. Her representational type also overlaps with our representational categories, but it might also have narrative qualities. Visually, both of Miles's types require viewers to recognize the religious significance of images and be able to associate traditional religious meanings with them. Both types denote a particular range of meanings that are generally recognized and widely accepted. The impressionistic and abstract types may be experienced through several of our categories, but they do not overlap with these categories as completely.

23. Ibid., 35.

24. Elaine Klassen, "The Godliness of Beauty," *The Mennonite* (9 May 2000), 6. Klassen writes that the process of creating the banners became a metaphor for knowing God. "The contrast between the original design and the tangible reality is the same contrast we see between our idea of God and the reality of God in our lives through making many tiny decisions based on our idea" (7).

25. Appendix 4 offers questions for considering the use of visual art in worship.

26. For more information about InterPlay®, visit www.bodywisdom.org.

27. Presentation at Art of Worship weekend on worship and evangelism, Amigo Centre (Sturgis, MI), 25-27 April 2003.

28. The sense of taste is discussed in chapter ten.

Chapter 7: Cooking collaboratively

1. Ken Nafziger, "Hymn Performance," *The Hymn*, vol. 55, no. 1 [January 2004]: 36.

2. See the discussion of ways of knowing in chapter ten.

3. See chapter thirteen for more discussion of the politics of taste.

4. Ken Nafziger, professor of music at Eastern Mennonite University (Harrisonburg, VA), is the source of this idea that music leaders are pastors or shepherds of sound in worship.

5. See related discussion on stocking the pantry in chapter fourteen.

6. For a related discussion of the weekly planning process, see "Weekly Worship Planning," chapter 5 in *Designing Worship Together: Models and Strategies for Worship Planning*, by Norma deWaal Malefyt and Howard Vanderwell (Herdon, VA: Alban Institute, 2005).

7. See chapter two for fuller discussion about understanding the composition of the congregation.

8. See chapter fourteen for a variety of strategies for effectively eliciting helpful congregational response.

Chapter 8: Hosting the guests

1. From a personal conversation with John Bell (Glasgow, Scotland).

2. Contemporary writers such as Anne Lamott, Nora Gallagher, Diana Butler Bass, and Tony Hendra give insight into language as a window into God's presence.

3. From *Awed to Heaven, Rooted in Earth: Prayers of Walter Brueggemann* copyright © 2002 Augsburg Fortress. Used by permission. Edwin Searcy, ed., (Minneapolis: Fortress Press, 2003), xvi.

4. See chapter two for a much more extended discussion of issues related to who is present for worship.

5. Marlene Kropf.

6. See chapter six for more discussion about choosing ingredients for worship.

7. A number of worship resources are especially good for foraging. *Imaging the Word*, edited by Kenneth Lawrence et al. (Cleveland: United Church Press, 1994-96), is a stimulating three-volume series that includes visual images, poetry, music, bits of story and other quotations related to each Sunday of the three-year lectionary cycle. Another three-volume series, *Resources for Preaching and Worship: Quotations, Meditations, Poetry and Prayers*, compiled by Hannah Ward and Jennifer Wild (Louisville: Westminster John Knox Press, 2002-2004), is also linked to the three-year lectionary cycle.

8. See chapter four for more discussion of issues related to the order and flow of worship.

9. Suzanne Toolan, *Music for the Requiem Mass*, copyright 1970 GIA Publications; *HWB* 472.

10. For a more extensive discussion of the balancing and interweaving of both old and new elements in worship, see chapter eleven, especially the section on structure and anti-structure.

11. In *Too Deep for Words: A Theology of Liturgical Expression* ([Louisville: Westminster John Knox Press, 2002], 68), Clayton J. Schmit describes four traits of "hiddenness," which are the hallmarks of excellent worship leading: servanthood, diligence, authenticity, and humility. All these traits emphasize that worship leading is not a matter of self-expression; rather, it is an act of hospitality on behalf of the gathered congregation.

12. From *Liberating Rites: Understanding the Transformative Power of Ritual*, by Tom Driver (Boulder, CO: Westview Press, 1998), 63. Copyright © 1998 by Tom Driver. Reprinted by permission of Westview Press, a member of Perseus Books, L.L.C.

13. Janet Morley, *All Desires Known: Inclusive Prayers for Worship and Meditation*, expanded ed. (Harrisburg, PA: Morehouse Publishing, 1994), 81. *All Desires Known* © Janet Morley 1988, 1992 Used by Permission of Morehouse Publishing.

14. Annie Dillard, *Holy the Firm* (New York: Perennial Library, 1998), 59.

15. John D. Rempel, ed. *Minister's Manual* (Newton, KS: Faith & Life Press; Scottdale, PA: Herald Press, 1998), 49.

16. Ibid., 194.

17. Reproduced from *Psalms of Lament* © 1995 Ann Barr Weems. Used by permission of Westminster John Knox Press. 43-44.

18. From *Awed to Heaven, Rooted in Earth: Prayers of Walter Brueggemann* copyright © 2002 Augsburg Fortress. Used by permission. 88.

19. "In you, gracious God" from *A Wee Worship Book*, Copyright © 1999 by Wild Goose Resource Group, Iona Community, Scotland. GIA Publications, Inc., exclusive North American agent, 7404 S. Mason Ave., Chicago, IL 60638 www.giamusic.com 800.442.1358 All rights reserved. Used by permission. 14-15.

20. For "All that God can do within us" from *A Wee Worship Book*, Copyright © 1999 by Wild Goose Resource Group, Iona Community, Scotland. GIA Publications, Inc., exclusive North American agent, 7404 S. Mason Ave., Chicago, IL 60638 www.giamusic.com 800.442.1358 All rights reserved. Used by permission. 17–18.

21. See chapter 14 fourteen for more extensive discussion of evaulation of worship.

Chapter 9: Presenting the meal

1. Quentin J. Schultze, "The 'God-Problem' in Communication Study," *The Journal of Communication and Religion* 28 (March 2005): 1–22.

2. See the discussion of this subject in chapter eight.

3. Albert Mehrabian, *Silent Messages: Implicit Communication of Emotions and Attitudes* (Belmont, CA: Wadsworth Publishing, 1971), 43–44.

4. In *Performing the Word: Preaching as Theatre* (Nashville, TN: Abingdon Press, 1998), Jana Childers gives great care to the concerns of the vocal presentation and the physical presentation. Those with interest in the role of the voice in public worship should read this book carefully. The voice is the medium of creation and revelation, beginning and end. Stephen H. Webb's book, *The Divine Voice: Christian Proclamation and the Theology of Sound* (Grand Rapids: Brazos Press, 2004), explores the theology of sound with a seriousness that it seldom receives.

Chapter 10: Enriching the fare

1. Yvonne Young Tarr, *The New York Times Bread and Soup Cookbook* (New York: Quadrangle, 1972); quoted in *An Easter Sourcebook,* ed. Gabe Huck, Gail Ramshaw, and Gordon Lathrop (Chicago: Liturgy Training Publications, 1988).

2. The table was inspired by the work of Karmen Krahn, a liturgical artist and former student at Associated Mennonite Biblical Seminary. We have reworked her categories and are grateful for the inspiration she provided in her original work.

3. David Morgan, *Visual Piety: A History and Theory of Popular Religious Images* (Berkeley: University of California Press, 1998), 59-96.

4. Chapter six describes in greater detail the biblical story as the main ingredient of Christian worship.

5. Sam Keen, *To a Dancing God: Notes of a Spiritual Traveler* (San Francisco: Harper & Row, 1990), 8–9.

6. See Appendix 5 for examples of how the action of gathering may incorporate a variety of modes of knowing.

7. *Minister's Manual* (Newton, KS: Faith & Life Press; Scottdale, PA: Herald Press, 1998), 75–78.

8. *Hymnal: A Worship Book* (*HWB*) (Elgin, IL: Brethren Press; Newton, KS: Faith & Life Press; Scottdale, PA: Mennonite Publishing House, 1992), 784.

9. Monika H. Hellwig, *The Eucharist and the Hunger of the World,* rev. ed. (Kansas City, MO: Sheed & Ward, 1992), 3–4.

10. *HWB* 474.

11. "Let the Hungry Come to Me" Copyright © 1985, The Sisters of Saint Benedict. Published by World Library Publications. www.wlpmusic.com Delores Dufner, author. *HWB* 464.

12. "Taste and See" Copyright © 1983 by GIA Publications, Inc., 7404 S. Mason Ave., Chicago, IL 60638 www.giamusic.com 800.442.1358 All rights reserved. Used by permission. In Robert J. Batastini and Michael A. Cymbala, ed., *Gather Comprehensive* (Chicago: GIA Publications, 1994), 814.

13. "Discordants," in *The Oxford Book of American Verse,* ed. F. O. Matthiessen (Oxford: Oxford University Press, 1950).

14. Hope Douglas J. Harle-Mould, pastor and teacher at St. Peter's UCC, West Seneca, NY. Printed in Hymnal Subscription Service 2002:2. Available from Faith & Life Resources, Scottdale, PA.

15. "Eat This Bread" Copyright © 1982, 1983 and 1984 by Ateliers et Presses de Taizé, Taizé Community, France. GIA Publications, Inc., exclusive North American agent, 7404 S. Mason Ave., Chicago, IL 60638 www.giamusic.com 800.442.1358 All rights reserved. Used by permission. Jacques Berthier, composer. In Robert Batastini and the Taizé community, 1983, *Music from Taizé,* Vol. 2, 1982, 1983, 1984; Based on John 6:35. *HWB* 471.

16. Evelyn Underhill, *Worship* (New York: Crossroad, 1984), 152; quoted in *A Eucharist Sourcebook,* ed. J. Robert Baker and Barbara Budde (Chicago: Liturgy Training Publications, 1999), 53.

17. "I Come With Joy" © 1971 Hope Publishing Co., Carol Stream, IL 60188. All rights reserved. Used by permission. Brian Wren, author. In *The Hymnbook* [Canada], 1971; copyright 1971 Hope Publishing Co.; *HWB* 459.

18. Adapted from *We Gather Together,* Alvin Franz Brightbill, copyright 1979 Brethren Press; *HWB* 717.

19. John S. B. Monsell, *Hymns of Love and Praise,* 2nd ed., 1866, alt.; *HWB* 474.

20. Nathan Mitchell, "Symbols Are Actions, Not Objects," *Living Worship,* 13, no. 2 (1997); quoted in *A Sourcebook about Liturgy,* ed. Gabe Huck (Chicago, IL: Liturgy Training Publications, 1994), 140.

21. Flannery O'Connor's aphorism, "If it were only a symbol, I'd say to hell with it," is a testimony of the power of symbols to endure and prevail, despite such dismissals.

22. Workers in community soup kitchens in Lima, Peru; quoted in *Psalms for Life and Peace* (Lima, Peru: Latinamerica Press, 1987).

23. "I Am the Bread of Life" Copyright © 1966 by GIA Publications, Inc., 7404 S. Mason Ave., Chicago, IL 60638 www.giamusic.com 800.442.1358 All rights reserved. Used by permission. Suzanne Toolan, composer. In *Music for the Requiem Mass,* copyright 1970 GIA Publications. *HWB* 472.

24. Jane Walker, O.P. "Sketch of Our Congregation's Charism" (New Orleans: Eucharistic Missionaries of St. Dominic, 1975); quoted in *A Eucharist Sourcebook*, 71.

25. *Hymns of Faith and Hope,* 1857; *HWB* 465.

26. Karl Rahner, *Meditations on the Sacraments* (New York: Seabury Press, 1977), 35; quoted in *A Eucharist Sourcebook, 82.*
27. Leslie James, "June 6," *Bridgefolk* (Fall 2004), 9.
28. Rubem A. Alves (Brazil). Reproduced from *Prayers Encircling the World* © 1998 SPCK, Great Britain. Used by permission of Westminster John Knox Press. 30.
29. John W. Arthur, *Lutheran Book of Worship,* 1978, used by permission; *HWB* 476.

Chapter 11: Making occasions special

1. Isak Dinesen, *Anecdotes of Destiny; and, Ehrengard* (New York: Vintage, 1993).
2. An excellent example of a funeral homily that struck an appropriate balance between the vertical and horizontal was Joseph Cardinal Ratzinger's homily at the 2005 funeral of Pope John Paul II. Preaching from the Gospel text of Peter's encounter with Jesus in John 21, Ratzinger wove together the story of Peter's response to Jesus's call to "Feed my sheep" with Pope John Paul's response as he became a priest and then a pope—all the while emphasizing Christ as the Good Shepherd who loves his sheep and gives his life for them.
3. For more information on the history of ritual in Christian worship, see James F. White, *Introduction to Christian Worship,* 3rd ed. (Nashville, TN: Abingdon Press, 2000).
4. Some traditions prefer to use the language of *sign* rather than *symbol* or *sacrament.* For example, *Confession of Faith in a Mennonite Perspective* (Scottdale, PA, and Waterloo, ON: Herald Press, 1995) says: "In this confession of faith, these ceremonies [baptisms, Lord's Supper, etc.] are called *signs,* a biblical term rich in meanings." When the document goes on to define *sign* as both an act of God and a human response, it is describing what most modern Christians understand by sacramental action.
Discussing the difference between symbols and signs, liturgical theologian Aidan Kavanagh notes in *Elements of Rite: A Handbook of Liturgical Style* (New York: Pueblo Publishing Co., 1982), 5. "Ritual is a system of symbols rather than of mere signs. Symbols, being roomy, allow many different people to put them on, so to speak, in different ways. Signs do not. Signs are unambiguous because they exist to give precise information. Symbols coax one into a swamp of meaning and require one to frolic in it."
5. "We are each other's bread and wine" (*HWB* 1), an affirmation of faith in the much-loved hymn "What is this place," expresses the consequences of the incarnation.
6. Barbara Brown Taylor, *The Living Pulpit* (July/September 2003), 13.
7. Tom F. Driver, *Liberating Rites: Understanding the Transformative Power of Ritual* (Boulder, CO: Westview Press, 1998). See especially Part 3, "Ritual's Social Gifts," 131–91.
8. Driver, *Liberating Rites,* 156.
9. In *Ritual Criticism: Case Studies in Its Practice, Essays on Its Theory* (Columbia, SC: University of South Carolina Press, 1990), Ronald L. Grimes describes a variety of types of infelicitous performance of ritual, including nonplays, misapplication, flaws, hitches, insincerity, breaches, glosses, flops, violations, contagion, conflict, opacity, omission, misframes, and defeat. See pages 199–205 for more discussion of ritual failures.

10. For further development of these ideas, see Carol Doran and Thomas H. Troeger, *Trouble at the Table: Gathering the Tribes for Worship* (Nashville, TN: Abingdon Press, 1992), 93–100.

11. If a ritual is repeated *exactly* as it has been done before, then the local context and the particulars of the occasion have not been adequately taken into account in the planning. Because the community never gathers in exactly the same way twice, our rituals cannot be exact replicas of the past—even though the words or actions may be the same.

12. The idea for the chart was inspired by James F. White, *Introduction to Christian Worship*, 217–20; 248–51.

13. Nancy Chinn, *Spaces for Spirit: Adorning the Church* (Chicago: Liturgy Training Publications, 1998), 35.

14. Adapted from Susan J. White, "Shaping the Vocabulary of Christian Ritual," *Reformed Liturgy & Music*, (Winter 1987): 5–8. *Reformed Liturgy & Music* is now published as *Call to Worship*.

15. Andre Dubus, *The Times Are Never So Bad: A Novella and Eight Short Stories* (Boston: David R. Godine, 1983); quoted in *A Sourcebook about Liturgy*, ed. Gabe Huck (Chicago: Liturgy Training Publications, 1994), 1.

16. *Hymns to an Unknown God: Awakening the Spirit in Everyday Life* by Sam Keen. Copyright © 1994 by Sam Keen. Used by permission of Bantam Books, a division of Random House, Inc. 5–6.

17. Malidoma Patrice Somé, *Ritual: Power, Healing and Community* (New York: Arkana, 1997), 25.

18. Herb Gardner, *A Thousand Clowns: A New Comedy* (New York: Random House, 1962). This quotation comes from the film based on this book.

19. A brief but helpful explanation of the structure and purposes of the Revised Common Lectionary (used by Protestants since 1992) can be found in Gail Ramshaw, *A Three-Year Banquet: The Lectionary for the Assembly* (Minneapolis: Augsburg Fortress, 2004) and in Frank C. Senn, *Christian Liturgy: Catholic and Evangelical* (Minneapolis: Fortress Press, 1997). Explanations of earlier versions of the common lectionary can be found in Horace T. Allen, *A Handbook for the Lectionary* (Philadelphia: Geneva Press, 1980); and in William Skudlarek, *The Word in Worship: Preaching in a Liturgical Context* (Nashville, TN: Abingdon, 1981).

20. For more detailed information on the purposes and structure of the lectionary, see Appendix 6: About the Lectionary. See also chapter three, "Planning the Menu."

21. Taken from "How Shallow Former Shadows Seem" by Carl P. Daw, Jr. Copyright © 1990 Hope Publishing Co., Carol Stream, IL 60188. All rights reserved. Used by permission. In *A Year of Grace: Hymns for the Church Year* (Carol Stream, IL: Hope Publishing Co., 1990); *HWB* 251.

22. *Leader,* a monthly magazine published by Mennonites in North America, regularly includes original worship resources for the Christian year www.leaderonline.org. *Reformed Worship,* published by the Reformed Church in America is also a source for church year material www.reformedworship.org. See Appendix 8, "A Well-Stocked Pantry for Pastors and Worship Leaders" for additional resources related to the Christian year and to the rituals of the church.

Chapter 12: Extending the table

1. Doris Janzen Longacre, *More-with-Less Cookbook* (Scottdale, PA, and Waterloo, ON: Herald Press, 1976); and Joetta Handrich Schlabach, *Extending*

the Table: A World Community Cookbook (Scottdale, PA, and Waterloo, ON: Herald Press, 1991).

2. See chapter two for a comprehensive discussion of issues of hospitality related to worship.

3. Patrick Keifert, workshop at Eastern Mennonite Seminary School for Leaders, Harrisonburg, VA, January 18, 2005.

4. Thomas H. Schattauer, ed., *Inside Out: Worship in an Age of Mission* (Minneapolis: Fortress Press, 1999), 5.

5. *The Message* by Eugene H. Peterson, copyright © 1993, 1994, 1995, 1996, 2000, 2001, 2002. Used by permission of NavPress Publishing Group. All rights reserved.

6. PSALM 140 from *PSALMS FOR PRAYING: An Invitation to Wholeness* by Nan C. Merrill. Copyright © 1996 by the author. Reprinted by permission of THE CONTINUUM INTERNATIONAL PUBLISHING GROUP.

7. Explaining the importance of rhythm and poetic speech in worship, liturgical scholar Aidan Kavanagh says: "Rhythm . . . makes things memorable, as in music, poetry, rhetoric, architecture, and the plastic arts no less than in liturgical worship. Rhythm constantly insinuates, as propagandists know. It constantly reasserts, as good teachers know. It constantly forms individuals into units, as demagogues and cheerleaders know. It both shrouds and bares meaning which escapes mere words, as poets know. It fuses people to their values and forges them to a common purpose, as orators such as Cato, Churchill, and Martin Luther King know. It frees from sound and offers vision for those who yearn for it, as the preacher of the Sermon on the Mount knew. Liturgical ministers who are irreparably arrhythmic should be restrained from ministering in the liturgy" (*Elements of the Rite* [New York: Pueblo Publishing Co., 1982], 28).

8, Hafiz, *The Gift: Poems by the Great Sufi Master,* trans. Daniel James Ladinsky (New York: Penguin Compass, 1999).

9. From a presentation at Music and Worship Leaders Weekend, Laurelville Mennonite Church Center, Mount Pleasant, Pennsylvania, January 13–15, 1995.

10. See chapter five, stage ten, option seven: persuasion organization.

11. Douglas Ehninger, Bruce E. Gronbeck, Alan H. Monroe, *Principles of Speech Communication,* 9th ed. (Glenview, IL: Scott Foresman, 1984).

12. Paul W. Egertson, *Sacramental Rhetoric: The Relation of Preaching to Persuasion in American Lutheran Homiletics* (Ann Arbor: University Microfilms, Inc., 1976).

13. Although many Protestants, including Mennonites, have tended to celebrate communion infrequently, the most recent Mennonite confession of faith, *Confession of Faith in a Mennonite Perspective* (Scottdale, PA, and Waterloo, ON: Herald Press, 1995), reminds us of the practice of frequent observance of the Lord's Supper among the first Anabaptists and concludes, "Our churches are encouraged to celebrate the Lord's Supper frequently, so that they may participate in the rich meanings of this event for the worship and life of the church" (52).

14. Maren C. Tirabassi and Joan Jordan Grant, *An Improbable Gift of Blessing: Prayers to Nurture the Spirit* (Cleveland: United Church Press, 1998), 38 (altered). Used by permission.

15. *Book of Common Order of the Church of Scotland* (Edinburgh: Saint Andrew Press, 1994), 478 (altered).

16. Mark Vincent, *Teaching a Christian View of Money: Celebrating God's Generosity* (Scottdale, PA, and Waterloo, ON: Herald Press, 1997), 41.

17. Marlene Kropf.

18. Herbert F. Brokering, *"I" Opener: 80 Parables* (St. Louis: Concordia Publishing House, 1974), 31.

19. Abraham Joshua Heschel, *Man's Quest for God: Studies in Prayer and Symbolism* (New York: Charles Scribner's Sons, 1954), 19.

20. See chapter ten for an expanded discussion of the many levels of meaning found in symbols.

21. See Appendix 7: Rituals for Entering and Leaving the World of Work.

22. Marlene Kropf.

23. Tirabassi and Grant, *An Improbable Gift of Blessings*, 32. Used by permission.

Chapter 13: Negotiating the politics of Sunday dinner

1. These examples first appeared in my article, "Power, authority, and worship leadership," in *Vision: A Journal for Church and Theology* 5 (Fall 2004): 52–54.

2. For more on the literal mode of knowing, see chapter ten.

3. For more on the metaphoric mode of knowing, see chapter ten.

4. Corinne Ware, *Discover Your Spiritual Type: A Guide to Individual and Congregational Growth* (Bethesda, MD: Alban Institute, 1995).

5. See chapter fourteen for suggestions on how to deal with criticism and gather helpful feedback.

Chapter 14: Caring for the cooks and the kitchen

1. Donald Schön, *The Reflective Practitioner: How Professionals Think in Action* (New York: Basic Books, 1983).

2. The book of Job, for example, is not adequately used, and psalms of lament are underrepresented. See chapter three for information about assessing the theological balance of worship and preaching practices.

3. Christian Peacemaker Teams (CPT) offers an organized, nonviolent alternative to war and other forms of lethal inter-group conflict. CPT provides organizational support to persons committed to faith-based nonviolent alternatives in situations where lethal conflict is an immediate reality or is supported by public policy. Their website is www.cpt.org.

4. Ronald Grimes lists fourteen ways in which ritual practices may not achieve their intended purpose. Borrowing John L. Austin's term, he labels such practices *infelicitous*. Our practice may belie our beliefs in any of the following ways: (1) *Insincerities*. Beliefs are professed but without the requisite thoughts, feelings, or intentions; beliefs are spoken and acted on but they seem hollow. (2) *Glosses*. The procedures ignore or contradict major problems; for example, the procedures fail to take into account conflict or dissent. (3) *Flops*. The procedures are done correctly, but the ritual fails to resonate; it does not generate the proper tone, ethos, and atmosphere. (4) *Ineffectualities*. Rituals fail to bring about intended change. See *Ritual Criticism: Case Studies in Its Practice, Essays on Its Theory* (Columbia, SC: University of South Carolina Press, 1990), 200–02.

5. See chapter nine for more discussion of performance anxiety.

Epilogue

1. Reproduced from *The Senses of Preaching* © 1988 Thomas G. Long. Used by permission of Westminster John Knox Press. 92–93.

2. Barbara Brown Taylor, *The Preaching Life* (Boston: Cowley Publication, 1993), 74.

Appendix 3

1. Refrain of "Far, far away from my living Father"; *HWB* 139.

2. Refrain of "Blessed assurance, Jesus is mine"; *HWB* 332.

Appendix 5

1 "Come, Now is the Time to Worship" Copyright ©1998 VINEYARD SONGS (UK/EIRE) ADMIN. IN NORTH AMERICA BY MUSIC SERVICES o/b/o VINEYARD MUSIC GLOBAL INC. (PRS). All Rights Reserved. Used By Permission. Brian Doerksen, composer.

2. Huub Oosterhuis, Zomaar een dak boven wat hoofden, 1968; trans. David Smith. © 1967, Gooi en Sticht, BV., Baarn, The Netherlands. All rights reserved. Exclusive agent for English language countries: OCP Publications, 5536 NE Hassalo, Portland OR 97213. All rights reserved. Used with permission.

3 "We Will Dance" Copyright © 1993 MERCY/VINEYARD PUBLISHING. ADMIN. IN NORTH AMERICA BY MUSIC SERVICES o/b/o VINEYARD MUSIC GLOBAL INC. (ASCAP). All Rights Reserved. Used By Permission. David Ruis, composer.

INDEX

ABOUT THE AUTHORS

Dr. June Alliman Yoder is Professor of Communication and Preaching at Associated Mennonite Biblical Seminary. Her articles are published in *Vision*, *Anabaptist Preaching*, *The Heart of the Matter*, *Biblical Preaching Journal*, and *The Word* (a Korean preaching journal). June is an ordained Minister of the Word in Mennonite Church USA and is a member of College Mennonite Church, Goshen, Indiana.

Dr. Marlene Kropf serves as Denominational Minister of Worship for Mennonite Church USA. For more than twenty years she has taught at Associated Mennonite Biblical Seminary. She served on the Worship Committee and Hymnal Council for *Hymnal: A Worship Book* and is coauthor of *Singing: A Mennonite Voice*. Marlene is an ordained minister in Mennonite Church USA. She is a member of Belmont Mennonite Church, Elkhart, Indiana.

Dr. Rebecca Slough is Associate Professor of Worship and the Arts at Associated Mennonite Biblical Seminary. Rebecca was managing editor of *Hymnal: A Worship Book*. She reviews books on music, ritual, and liturgy for *Religious Studies Review*. Rebecca is an ordained minister in Mennonite Church USA and is a member of College Mennonite Church, Goshen, Indiana.